PR
3458
.D7 Hume, Robert D.
H8
1988 HENRY FIELDING AND THE
LONDON THEATRE, 1728-1737
16831540

HENRY FIELDING AND THE LONDON THEATRE

HENRY FIELDING AND THE LONDON THEATRE

1728–1737

ROBERT D. HUME

CLARENDON PRESS · OXFORD
1988

Oxford University Press, Walton Street, Oxford OX2 6DP

Oxford New York Toronto
Delhi Bombay Calcutta Madras Karachi
Petaling Jaya Singapore Hong Kong Tokyo
Nairobi Dar es Salaam Cape Town
Melbourne Auckland

and associated companies in
Beirut Berlin Ibadan Nicosia

Oxford is a trade mark of Oxford University Press

Published in the United States
by Oxford University Press, New York

British Library Cataloguing in Publication Data
Hume, Robert D.
Henry Fielding and the London theatre:
1728–1737.
1. Fielding, Henry—Dramatic works
I. Title
822'.5 PR3458.D7
ISBN 0–19–812864–9

Library of Congress Cataloging in Publication Data
Hume, Robert D.
Henry Fielding and the London theatre. 1728–1737
Robert D. Hume. p. cm. Includes index.
1. Fielding, Henry, 1707–1754—Dramatic works.
2. Fielding, Henry, 1707–1754—Stage history.
3. Theater—England—London—History—18th century.
4. Dramatists, English—18th century—Biography.
5. Theatrical managers—Great Britain—Biography. I. Title.
PR3458.D7H8 1987 823'.5—dc 19
ISBN 0–19–812864–9

Typeset by Joshua Associates Limited, Oxford
Printed in Great Britain by
Biddles Ltd.
Guildford and King's Lynn

For Jean H. Hagstrum

PREFACE

FIELDING has been much studied, but most critics have been interested primarily in Fielding the novelist. Attention to Fielding's ten years as England's premier dramatist has been scanty and often dismissive: the plays of the 1730s have usually been seen as an awkward apprenticeship for the novels of the 1740s. Such an estimate seems to me very wide of the mark. In this book I argue that appraisals of Fielding's plays have been based on misleading criteria and inadequate knowledge of the London theatres in the 1730s, and that what Fielding accomplished as a dramatist was by no means a false start in a genre with which he was uncomfortable.

I have approached Fielding's plays as a theatre historian, not as a specialist in fiction. My object has been to study Fielding's theatrical career in context. I have tried to provide a fresh critical assessment of the plays based on knowledge of the theatres in which he worked; the writers with whom he competed; and the theatrical, economic, and political conditions that affected him. This book is, in short, a contextual history of Fielding as dramatist and theatre manager, neither a biography nor a critical analysis of texts taken in isolation.

Most accounts of Fielding's plays have been distorted by the assumption that by 1730 he was already a vehement opponent of Walpole. Wilbur Cross established this view as orthodoxy in 1918; John Loftis modified it in 1963; not until 1976 was it demolished by Bertrand Goldgar in his account of *Walpole and the Wits.* The abrupt collapse of the political reading, however, has left critics floundering. If the young Fielding was not a fiery political satirist, what was he? The answer is 'an aspirant playwright, intent on making a career in the theatre'. And that is what this book is about.

Only fairly recently have full performance records for the period been available, and no full history of the London theatre in the 1730s has yet been written. Many misunderstandings about Fielding's early career have resulted from lack of relevant contextual information. The stormy history of the various theatre companies in this decade is complex, but it is vital to any understanding of what Fielding wrote and why. The 'company at the Little Haymarket' was in fact not a company at all, and we can only delude ourselves about Fielding's relations with it between 1730 and 1736 if we imagine that it had a manager, a repertory policy, and a stable roster of actors. Fielding's 'moves' from theatre to theatre have been treated as an index to changing political allegiances—but what they actually reflect is managerial upheaval and the exigencies of peddling playscripts on the open market. Scholars concentrating on the texts of the plays, or on politics, have not sufficiently understood the practical implications of major events in the London theatre—such as the dissolution of the triumvirate management in 1732 and the actor rebellion in 1733 that brought Fielding's Drury Lane phase to an untimely end.

To comprehend Fielding's early career, we must start by recognizing that he quickly made himself a highly professional man of the theatre, and that what he wrote is intimately connected with theatrical competition, theatre company politics and personnel, and the frenetic experimentation characteristic of English drama in the 1730s. No proper study of this drama has ever been written, but, for generic innovation, the 1730s are comparable to the 1660s—a time in which young playwrights learnt their trade and opened up new possibilities in both subject and form. The boom triggered by the unprecedented success of *The Beggar's Opera* in 1728 (just at the start of Fielding's theatrical career) gave rise to heated competition, with up to six companies operating simultaneously, conditions unprecedented since before 1642. If many of the new plays seem disappointing, we must remember that so do those of the 1660s. Had there been no Licensing Act of 1737, the developments of the 1740s might have equalled those of the 1670s. But the imposition of censorship and the suppression of all theatres except Drury Lane and Covent Garden abruptly terminated the lively experimentation of the thirties—and ended Fielding's promising career as playwright and manager. The effects of the Licensing Act on English drama can scarcely be overstated: secure in their possession of a monopoly, the patent theatres chose to stage few new plays, and almost never any that were innovative or controversial. Fielding left the theatre not because he wanted to, or because he was ready to move on into the novel, but because he had been put out of a lucrative business and needed to make a living.

Fielding's theatrical career is, at bottom, a simple story, however complex its contextual details. He started out as a young hopeful, peddling plays where he could (1729–31). His success earned him an entrée at Drury Lane, where for a brief period he enjoyed privileged status in a glamorous patent theatre (1732–33). The breakup of the old Drury Lane company and the unsatisfactoriness of the new managements that fought to control the theatre left Fielding in search of an alternate venue (1734–35). Not getting on well with management at either Drury Lane or Covent Garden, Fielding assembled a scratch company of his own and rented the Little Haymarket (1736–37), a successful experiment squelched by the Licensing Act.

While the primary object of this book is to supply an account of the theatrical and generic contexts in which Fielding worked, I hope that my discussion of his plays will contribute to bestowing upon them a higher critical reputation than they currently enjoy. While most of them are interpretively simple—which helps to explain their low standing with critics—Fielding's plays are certainly variegated: he was ready to try all sorts of experiments. Inevitably, some of them flopped. But I do not see that the inclination to experiment makes him an 'uncertain' writer in search of values and commitments, as Brian McCrea suggests. To say that Fielding suffered from a damaging inability 'to choose between . . . two different concepts of the nature of man' exemplified in the work of Cibber and Gay seems to me to misrepresent all three writers. What McCrea sees as tortured insecurity I see as breadth, complexity, and surprising maturity for a playwright in his twenties. I find no more evidence of 'mercurial' shifts 'between opposing literary camps' than I do of rapid shifts in Fielding's political allegiances. Fielding was a professional dramatist ready to employ successful formulas, and he took them where he found them. His greatest fault lay in his ambition to write 'serious' social satire, a form for which he had little aptitude. We should remember, however, that Fielding wrote only one original five-act play after 1730, and none after 1733 save *The Good-Natur'd Man*, which was not performed in his lifetime. However reluctantly, he learned from his failures.

Fielding's commitment to the theatre as a career has been underestimated by almost every scholar since Cross, and the real possibility that he would build a theatre and establish a permanent company under his own direction has been almost ignored. Far from having an 'unsuccessful' or 'undistinguished' career as a playwright (as is often said), Fielding quickly made himself the most dominant professional playwright in London since Dryden. He had his share of failures (what professional dramatist does not?), but in the spring of 1737 any theatrical insider would have assumed that Fielding would soon control a major company of his own, and that he would go on to write a long string of hits.

Wilbur Cross is one of the few scholars to have treated Fielding's theatrical career with any real attempt at understanding what it meant to him, and Cross's summation remains well worth quoting:

> He had hardly more than discovered where his talent lay before his dramatic career was ended. As he used to say, 'he left off writing for the stage when he ought to have begun'. But for the Licensing Act he would have rebuilt or enlarged his theatre and continued to delight London audiences for another decade or more. On Fielding's stage rather than Giffard's Garrick would have won his spurs. . . . The drama, I have tried to make clear, was to Fielding much more than a means of support; it was his soul; it was his life. Underlying all his plays—farce as well as comedy—was a serious intent. (I, 235–6)

Cross had only a sketchy grasp of the theatre world in which Fielding worked, and he greatly distorted our picture of Fielding's politics, but he did understand Fielding's passionate commitment to the theatre and the seriousness with which he wrote even some of his most farcical plays. Cross's successors have paid him great, even excessive, deference in many realms, but in this one his views have been oddly uninfluential.

To dismiss the plays with impatience or contempt is to treat Fielding with less respect than he deserves. We need to recognize that Fielding's plays have a strong moral bent, despite their tearing high spirits and exuberant jokiness. Tone and genre notwithstanding, they seem to me much more of a piece with his later writing than most commentators have found them. If we look anew at Fielding's highly successful decade writing plays and managing theatres we do not find 'uncertainty', or a 'search for political identity'. Rather, we will find that Fielding was a brash young man who made a good living with his pen in a field where few others had been doing so; who developed some highly successful new forms of drama; and who was able to sustain genuine ethical commitments while aggressively pursuing a career in the commercial theatre.

ACKNOWLEDGEMENTS

For advice, assistance, and criticism of various sorts, I wish to express my particular thanks to William J. Burling, John T. Harwood, Kit Hume, Thomas Lockwood, and Judith Milhous. I owe a special debt of gratitude to Martin Battestin, who generously shared his unique knowledge of Fielding with me—saving me from some embarrassing errors and solving some problems that had sorely puzzled me. For help with the index I want to thank Aparna Dharwadker and C. A. Prettiman.

I am grateful to Philip H. Highfill, jun., Kalman A. Burnim, and Edward A. Langhans for their gracious assistance in allowing me access to their files on performers in not-yet-published volumes of their *Biographical Dictionary* of theatrical personnel in London.

For permission to use in altered form material published in two earlier essays, I wish to thank Southern Illinois University Press ('The London Theatre from *The Beggar's Opera* to the Licensing Act', Chapter 9 of *The Rakish Stage*, by Robert D. Hume, copyright © 1983 by the Board of Trustees, Southern Illinois University) and the University of California Press ('Henry Fielding and Politics at the Little Haymarket, 1728–1737', Chapter 4 of *The Golden and the Brazen World: Papers in Literature and History, 1650–1800*, ed. John M. Wallace (1985)).

Much of the basic work on this book was carried out during a year spent in London as a Guggenheim Fellow. To the Guggenheim Foundation I am deeply grateful, both for the chance to work in peace and for the opportunity to attend 171 plays and operas in the course of the year. I can imagine more efficient working circumstances, but none better or more rewarding.

CONTENTS

A NOTE ON TEXTS, DATES, AND DOCUMENTATION

ALL quotations from eighteenth-century plays are from the first London edition unless otherwise indicated. Dates are Old Style unless 'NS' is specified or both are given with a slash. The new year is treated as beginning 1 January; those sources (mostly newspapers) for which change of year can be a matter of confusion are cited with a slash date or a bracketed slash date as appropriate.

In writing this book I have attempted to return to primary sources and consider them afresh. Consequently, I have cited Cross and Dudden to agree or disagree with an interpretation, or to borrow a felicitous phrasing, but almost never as authority for facts. I have not hesitated to offer some speculations, clearly labelled as such. But in a large number of instances we lack needed facts; and while I hate to keep saying 'we do not know' and 'we can only guess', and so forth, I prefer to issue these monotonous disclaimers rather than to feign a certainty that present evidence does not warrant.

LIST OF TABLES

WORKS FREQUENTLY CITED

An Apology For . . . T . . . C . . ., Comedian	Anon., *An Apology For the Life of Mr. T . . . C . . ., Comedian* (London, 1740).
Arnott and Robinson	James Fullarton Arnott and John William Robinson, *English Theatrical Literature 1559–1900: A Bibliography* (London, 1970).
Biographical Dictionary	Philip H. Highfill, jun., Kalman A. Burnim, and Edward A. Langhans, *A Biographical Dictionary of Actors, Actresses, Musicians, Dancers, Managers and Other Stage Personnel in London, 1660–1800*, 16 vols. (in progress) (Carbondale, 1973–).
Cibber, *Apology*	*An Apology for the Life of Mr. Colley Cibber*, ed. Robert W. Lowe, 2 vols. (London, 1889; repr. New York, 1966).
Cleary	Thomas R. Cleary, *Henry Fielding: Political Writer* (Waterloo, Ont., 1984).
Cross	Wilbur L. Cross, *The History of Henry Fielding*, 3 vols. (New Haven, Conn., 1918).
Ducrocq	Jean Ducrocq, *Le Théatre de Fielding: 1728–1737* (Dijon, 1975).
Dudden	F. Homes Dudden, *Henry Fielding: His Life, Works, and Times*, 2 vols. (Oxford, 1952).
Goldgar	Bertrand A. Goldgar, *Walpole and the Wits: The Relation of Politics to Literature, 1722–1742* (Lincoln, Nebr., 1976).
HMC	Reports of the Historical Manuscripts Commission.
Hunter	J. Paul Hunter, *Occasional Form: Henry Fielding and the Chains of Circumstance* (Baltimore, 1975).
Kern	Jean B. Kern, *Dramatic Satire in the Age of Walpole 1720–1750* (Ames, Ia., 1976).
Liesenfeld	Vincent J. Liesenfeld, *The Licensing Act of 1737* (Madison, 1984).
Loftis, *Comedy and Society*	John Loftis, *Comedy and Society from Congreve to Fielding* (Stanford, 1959).
Loftis, *Politics of Drama*	John Loftis, *The Politics of Drama in Augustan England* (Oxford, 1963).
The London Stage	*The London Stage, 1660–1800*, Part 2: 1700–1729, ed. Emmett L. Avery, 2 vols. (Carbondale, 1960); Part 3:

	1729–1747, ed. Arthur H. Scouten, 2 vols. (Carbondale, 1961).
The London Theatre World	*The London Theatre World, 1660–1800*, ed. Robert D. Hume (Carbondale, 1980).
McCrea	Brian McCrea, *Henry Fielding and the Politics of Mid-Eighteenth-Century England* (Athens, Ga., 1981).
PRO LC	Lord Chamberlain's records in the Public Record Office, London.
PRO SP	State Papers (Domestic) in the Public Record Office, London.
Rogers	Pat Rogers, *Henry Fielding: A Biography* (New York, 1979).
Victor	Benjamin Victor, *The History of the Theatres of London and Dublin*, 3 vols. (London, 1761–71).

1

The London Theatre World of the 1720s

To understand Fielding's ten years as playwright and aspirant manager, we must know something of the world in which he earned his living. As Samuel Johnson was to discover a decade later, supporting oneself with the pen was no easy business in early eighteenth-century London. Poetry did not pay (unless one were an Alexander Pope); the novel as we conceive it was practically undreamt of; journalism and hack writing were barely past their infancy, and decidedly ill-paid. The young writer's best hope had traditionally been the theatre, but by the 1720s those prospects were far from bright. That Fielding was quickly to become a celebrated playwright—and one both prolific and prosperous—could hardly have been predicted in 1728. Few writers had been making a living out of the theatre.

The dominant fact about the London theatre in 1728 is simple: it was a patent monopoly. And the managers of the two theatres holding that monopoly took a very dim view of new plays. The stunning and unprecedented success of *The Provok'd Husband* and *The Beggar's Opera* in 1728 was to trigger rapid changes in the theatrical situation. But though the stodgy world of cartels and non-competition was transformed almost beyond recognition in less than two years, the competition and experimentation thus unleashed remained profoundly unwelcome to the patentees—and in due course the Licensing Act of 1737 enabled them to re-establish their stultifying but profitable monopoly. To understand the events and infighting of the 1728–1737 period one must begin by learning something of the patent monopoly, the ways in which Drury Lane and Lincoln's Inn Fields carried on their business, and the state of the theatre before 1728. Fielding's entry into the theatre world with his first play coincides precisely with the events that were to set off the theatre boom of the 1730s. But, for the moment, my concern is to see what the situation looked like before that event—both to established managers and to an impecunious young would-be writer who was trying to peddle a play in the autumn of 1727.

I. THE HISTORY OF THE PATENT MONOPOLY

In 1727 the patent monopoly must have seemed an immutable fact. The London theatre world consisted of Drury Lane, Lincoln's Inn Fields, and the Royal Academy of Music, an opera company granted a patent in 1719 and occupying the King's Theatre, Haymarket. The tortuous history of theatre companies after 1660 notwithstanding—they had competed, combined, and redivided in bewildering ways—the net result was what Charles II had originally envisaged: a monopoly confined to two acting companies. The only other theatre in London was the 'Little Haymarket', a road-house built by John Potter in 1720 to accommodate visiting French troupes, jugglers, rope-dancers, and other 'illegitimate' entertainments. An attempt to start a third repertory company there in 1721–22 never got off the ground. A playwright could carry a script to either Drury Lane or Lincoln's Inn Fields, but to persuade one of them to take any interest in his work was no easy matter. The background to this discouraging state of affairs is both complicated and crucially relevant to Fielding's life in the theatre. If some of the technicalities that follow seem remote from the yet-unborn Henry Fielding, the reader must have patience. The legal complexities that the government skirted for more than six decades were finally to be confronted in the 1730s.

Origins and Early History

In the summer of 1660 Charles II agreed to grant a theatrical monopoly to two favoured courtiers, Thomas Killigrew (to run the 'King's Company') and Sir William Davenant (to run the 'Duke's Company').[1] Charles being Charles, the matter was not quite so simple. Killigrew did not actually receive his patent until 25 April 1662, and Davenant not until 15 January 1662/3. In the interval Charles confused the situation by granting two other patents: not until 1667 did Davenant and Killigrew finally stamp out all vestiges of competition.[2]

[1] A copy of the King's warrant for the proposed grant is preserved in BL Add. MS 19,256, fol. 47 (dated 21 Aug. 1660).

[2] The Killigrew patent is PRO C66/3013, no. 20; the Davenant patent is C66/3009, no. 3. Charles granted an opera patent to Giulio Gentileschi on 22 Oct. 1660 (SP 29/19, no. 16), though nothing came of this project. George Jolly received authorization to operate a theatre ('notwithstanding any former grant') on 24 Dec. 1660 (SP 29/44, no. 37). For the complex tale of how Davenant and Killigrew combined to cheat Jolly out of his rights, see Leslie Hotson, *The Commonwealth and Restoration Stage* (Cambridge, Mass., 1928), ch. 4.

For our purposes, two of the clauses in the Davenant and Killigrew patents are particularly important. (1) The grants were perpetual: not only the recipients but their 'heires & assignes' were to have the right to present 'Tragedyes Comedyes Playes Operas Musick Scenes & all other enterteinments of the Stage Whatsoever'. (2) Charles declared that *only* the Davenant and Killigrew companies were to be tolerated, and that 'all other ... Companyes' were to be 'silenced & suppressed'.[3] To the lay mind, this might seem to imply not only a grant in perpetuity, but also a guarantee of joint monopoly in perpetuity. The former proved true, the latter did not—and this loophole was to be the source of much infighting over the next seventy-five years.

In 1682 the collapse of the King's Company led to a 'union' of both patents and companies. In the articles of union, the proprietors agreed 'That all the powers and Authorityes put in the 1st Letters Pattents should be joyned and united with the powers in the 2d Letters Pattents and from thenceforth the same should be as one and soe for ever continued'.[4] (Whether the two patents so combined could subsequently be disunited—thereby authorizing an additional company—was to become a hot legal issue in the 1790s.) Against all expectation, however, the single-company monopoly lasted only a dozen seasons. The rock on which the United Company split was rights of ownership, an issue to be central to the actor rebellion of 1733. Both of the original companies of 1660 had divided ownership among the patentee, 'sharers' (senior actors), and 'adventurers' (outside investors). When the company was profitable, the actors were usually left to manage their own affairs, though quarrels between Thomas Killigrew and his actors did much to undermine the King's Company in the mid-1670s. Ownership of the original Davenant and Killigrew shares passed in due course to their sons in the 1670s, but the United Company was actually managed by a pair of senior actors, Thomas Betterton and William Smith, and generally the company ran very well. But in 1687 Alexander Davenant bought out his brother Charles, using money secretly borrowed from Christopher Rich and Sir Thomas Skipwith (junior?). When the bankrupt Alexander decamped to the Canary

[3] For a helpful analysis of the original patent grants, see Judith Milhous, *Thomas Betterton and the Management of Lincoln's Inn Fields, 1695–1708* (Carbondale, 1979), pp. 4–7.

[4] A copy of the articles of union is in BL Add. MS 20,726, fols. 10–13^v, pub. verbatim in Judith Milhous and Robert D. Hume, 'Charles Killigrew's "Abstract of Title to the Playhouse": British Library Add. MS 20,726, fols. 1–14', *Theatre History Studies*, 6 (1986), 57–71. Contemporary accounts of the union are to be found in PRO C6/316/21 and C24/1144/55.

Islands in December 1693, Rich came forward as principal owner and took managerial power into his own hands. Believing himself secure in an absolute monopoly, Rich could see no reason to pay big salaries to star actors or to continue their customary perquisites. Within a year the actors were in open rebellion. The old prompter John Downes offers a terse summation of what happened:

> . . . a difference happening between the United Patentees, and the chief *Actors*: As Mr. *Betterton*; Mrs. *Barry* and Mrs. *Bracegirdle*; the latter complaining of Oppression from the former; they for Redress, Appeal'd to my Lord of *Dorset*, then Lord Chamberlain, for Justice; who Espousing the Cause of the Actors, with the assistance of Sir *Robert Howard*, finding their Complaints just, procur'd from King *William*, a Seperate License for Mr. *Congreve*, Mr. *Betterton*, Mrs. *Bracegirdle* and Mrs. *Barry*, and others, to set up a new Company, calling it the New Theatre in *Lincolns-Inn-Fields*; and the House being fitted up from a Tennis-Court, they Open'd it the last Day of *April*, 1695.[5]

This precedent for a 'Seperate License' is crucial. Its legal basis is correctly explained by Cibber: '. . . their Grievances were laid before the Earl of *Dorset* . . . who took the most effectual Method for their Relief. The Learned of the Law were advised with, and they gave their Opinion that no Patent for acting Plays, *&c.* could tie up the Hands of a succeeding Prince from granting the like Authority where it might be thought proper to trust it.'[6] What one king could grant, so could another. In this instance, however, what was granted was not a *patent* (perpetual or otherwise) but a *licence*. The exact terms are sufficiently important to warrant quoting them.

> Charles Earle of Dorsett . . . Lord Chamberlaine . . . In pursuance of His Majesties Pleasure & Command given unto mee herein, I doe hereby give and grant full Power Lycence and Authority unto Thomas Betterton, Elizabeth Barry, Anne Bracegirdle [*and eight other actors and actresses, named*], His Majesties Sworne Servants & Comoedians, in Ordinary . . . from time to time, in any convenient place or Places, to Act and represent, all and all manner of Comedyes, & Tragedyes, Playes Enterludes, & Opera's, and to performe all other Theatricall & Musicall Enterteynments, of what kind soever, But so as

[5] John Downes, *Roscius Anglicanus* (London, 1708), p. 43. Downes is in error in stating that Congreve was among the recipients of the licence. For details of the disputes, see 'The Petition of the Players' and 'The Reply of the Patentees' in PRO LC 7/3. Both documents are printed in full and analysed in Milhous, *Thomas Betterton*, ch. 3 and Appendices A and B.

[6] *Apology*, I, 192–3.

to bee allwayes under my government & Regulation, from time to times as hath been Exercised by my predecessors.[7]

The crux is that this is a licence to perform *at pleasure*. It destroyed the monopoly but could be withdrawn at any time. For the moment it solved the rebel actors' problem, but it created others. Who would invest heavily in a theatre and a stock of scenery and costumes if the venture might be shut down at any time? The rebels set up shop as a co-operative (specifically excluding outside investors), but their theatre was small and ill-equipped, they lacked capital, and they quickly discovered the difficulties of government by committee.[8]

No one ever faced the questions implicit in the confrontation of 1694–95. What protection should actors have against tyranny exercised by outside investors who had purchased the patent under which the company was allowed to perform? Should actors be allowed self-government? Was the King damaging the property rights of investors by issuing new licences or patents? Since actors in the patent company had been sworn as household servants of the King (a move designed in 1660 to free them from harassment), the Lord Chamberlain exercised control over them as head of the royal household. But licences for previous troupes and for all 'strolling' companies had always been issued by the Master of the Revels, and Dorset's solution to the crisis of 1694–95 blurred the lines of authority between the two offices. Rich and his fellow investor-patentees were outraged by the licence; at the same time it left the actors in an insecure and unsatisfactory position.

The next fifteen years were to see the waters muddied considerably more. The Lincoln's Inn Fields' licence was rewritten and issued to Vanbrugh and Congreve in 1704 when Vanbrugh took over management of the company and prepared to move it into the fancy new theatre he had built.[9] Vanbrugh's plan, we should note, was to engineer a new union and give himself a monopoly—but the wily Rich refused to co-operate. In December 1707 Vanbrugh more or less got his way by persuading the Lord Chamberlain to issue an order

[7] PRO LC 7/1, p. 38 (also in LC 7/3, fol. 7), printed in Allardyce Nicoll, *A History of English Drama, 1660–1900*, rev. edn., 6 vols. (Cambridge, 1952–59), I, 361. The licence is dated 25 March 1695.

[8] For a detailed account of the co-operative company, see Milhous, *Thomas Betterton*, *passim*.

[9] PRO LC 5/154, p. 35 (14 Dec. 1704). Printed in *William Congreve: Letters and Documents*, ed. John C. Hodges (New York, 1964), no. 70. Vanbrugh had friends in high places, and he probably had private assurances of permission to perform, or he would hardly have risked building the Haymarket theatre.

separating plays and operas.[10] This gave Vanbrugh the opera monopoly he craved (and with which he went bankrupt in four months) while serving as a *de facto* 'order of union' for the two acting companies thus reunited at Drury Lane under Rich. The results were predictably explosive: within little more than a year Rich was again mistreating his actors, and they persuaded the Lord Chamberlain to enter into a conspiracy to put Rich out of business, patent or no patent.

The Lord Chamberlain's order of 6 June 1709 was a seemingly innocent document.[11] It ordered the Drury Lane theatre closed for defiance of an order of 30 April about the patentees detaining excessive 'house charges' from actors' benefits. There was ample precedent. The Lord Chamberlain had occasionally 'silenced' theatres for various misdemeanours; such stoppages normally lasted less than a week. But this time the Lord Chamberlain had no intention of lifting his interdict, and great was the consternation of actors, patentees, and owners of the theatre building when this became clear to them at the end of the summer. Without clear legal authority, Lord Chamberlain Kent simply shut down the patent company, and then proceeded to issue a licence for acting to a Tory MP named William Collier.[12] The actors were ready to work for anyone who could get authority to perform; most of the sharers in the theatre building were equally pragmatic; and possession was obtained by the simple expedient of breaking in and seizing the theatre, an event described in mock-heroic terms in *Tatler*, no. 99 (24–26 November 1709). The investors in the acting company (as distinct from investors in the theatre building) were naturally furious and promptly presented a petition to the Queen in Council, asking for investigation and redress.[13] But the wheels of bureaucracy ground slowly indeed, and not until 8 October 1711 was the Northey–Lechmere report completed, by which time so much else had happened that the situation

[10] PRO LC 5/154, pp. 299–300 (31 Dec. 1707). For discussion, see Milhous, *Thomas Betterton*, ch. 7. For the text of the order, see *Vice Chamberlain Coke's Theatrical Papers, 1706–1715*, ed. Milhous and Hume (Carbondale, 1982), pp. 49–50.

[11] PRO LC 5/154, p. 437. For analysis of this episode, see Milhous and Hume, 'The Silencing of Drury Lane in 1709', *Theatre Journal*, 32 (1980), 427–47. A good deal of relevant documentation is printed in the *Coke Papers*.

[12] The text of the licence itself apparently does not survive, but a letter about it from the Lord Chamberlain's secretary to Collier, dated 19 Nov. 1709, is preserved in PRO LC 7/3, fol. 33 (and is printed in the *Coke Papers*, p. 136).

[13] The petition is described in an account of the Council meeting of 18 Feb. 1709[/10] in the report of the investigation ordered at that time. See BL Add. MS 20,726, fol. 24.

was virtually impossible to disentangle.[14] Why Rich did not take his case to Chancery is a good question. That the Lord Chamberlain had acted arbitrarily and illegally to abrogate a perpetual grant from the crown seems quite clear. For whatever reasons, Rich decided to bide his time, perhaps concluding that he would be subject to merciless government harassment even if he won his case, and that he was better off waiting for more favourable conditions.

Thus in 1709–10 both acting companies in London were operating under 'at pleasure' licences. At the Haymarket, Owen Swiney (who took over Vanbrugh's opera company in 1708) was allowed to hire the actors he wanted in order to stage plays and went into partnership with Robert Wilks, Colley Cibber, and Thomas Doggett—the first 'triumvirate'. Meanwhile at Drury Lane in 1709–10 Collier had delegated management to young Aaron Hill, who proved incapable of maintaining order and was deposed in the famous riot of June 1710.[15] In the shake-up that followed in the autumn of 1710, the two acting companies were reunited at Drury Lane (with Wilks, Cibber, and Doggett gradually taking full control) while the opera limped on alone at the Haymarket. By April 1712 the three actors had managed to force Swiney out, and in a complex trade-off they took in William Collier as a silent partner.

No one reflecting on this tangled history in the summer of 1714 could have been certain of the basis on which a theatre might legally operate, or of the extent of the Lord Chamberlain's regulatory authority. The united patents had been indefinitely silenced; other companies had run on a bewildering succession of *ad hoc* licences. In November 1713 the Lord Chamberlain had arbitrarily ordered the triumvirate to take in Barton Booth as a partner, and Doggett had promptly walked out and sued his partners—who protested that they had merely obeyed the Lord Chamberlain. The powers of the Lord Chamberlain were great but ill-defined.

Regulatory Power and the Beginnings of the Cartel

At the accession of George I in August 1714, the triumvirate realized that their Tory partner William Collier was no further use to them, and with superb effrontery they simply dropped him and invited Richard Steele (a stalwart Whig) to join them. Steele had no trouble

[14] A copy of the report is preserved in BL Add. MS 20,726, fols. 24–32.

[15] For Hill's vivid account of the riot, see the *Coke Papers*, no. 86.

getting a new licence for himself and his partners.[16] Meanwhile Rich requested and received permission to reopen at Lincoln's Inn Fields, which he had bought and rebuilt. (He died in November, but his son John carried on.) The renewal of competition—and the desertion of a flock of their actors—infuriated the Drury Lane managers. Steele protested against the theft of personnel and then petitioned for replacement of the licence with a patent valid 'during your Petitioner's natural Life and for three years after his Death'.[17] In just two days the Attorney General and Solicitor General had recommended favourably; the warrant was drawn up on 14 January 1715, and the patent passed the Great Seal on the 19th.[18]

Steele's patent introduced new complexities. Since he might die at any time, it offered only marginally more security than a licence. More important, however, is the vagueness of the document itself. Most of the grant is formulaic and essentially similar to the original Killigrew and Davenant grants, but one clause was to lead to a major dispute: 'the said Company shall be under the Sole Government and Authority of the said Richard Steele.'[19] Did this mean that the Lord Chamberlain and the Master of the Revels held no regulatory powers over a company operated under this patent? So Steele and the triumvirs believed, or affected to believe. Cibber explains with glee that in 1715 they refused to submit scripts to the Master of the Revels for censorship, or to pay his fees.

The Patent . . . made us sole Judges of what Plays might be proper for the Stage, without submitting them to the Approbation or License of any other particular Person. Notwithstanding which, the Master of the Revels demanded his Fee of Forty Shillings upon our acting a new One, tho' we had spared him the Trouble of perusing it. This occasion'd my being deputed to him to enquire into the Right of his Demand, and to make an Amicable End of our Dispute. I . . . told him . . . That I came not to defend even our own Right in prejudice to his; that if our Patent had inadvertently superseded the Grant of any former Power or Warrant whereon he might ground his Pretensions, we would not insist upon our Broad Seal, but would readily answer his Demands upon sight of such his Warrant, any thing in our Patent to the contrary

[16] PRO LC 5/156, p. 31 (18 Oct. 1714).

[17] PRO SP 44/246, p. 386, and LC 7/3, fols. 38–9 (referred to the Attorney or Solicitor General on 10 Jan. 1714[/5]).

[18] PRO LC 7/3, fols. 42–3; LC 7/3, fols. 35–7; C66/3501, no. 13. The order to draw up a patent is printed from the LC 7/3 version by John Loftis, *Steele at Drury Lane* (Berkeley, 1952; repr. Westport, Conn., 1973), pp. 244–5.

[19] PRO C66/3501, no. 13.

notwithstanding. This I had reason to think he could not do. . . . I was forc'd in the end to conclude with telling him, That as his Pretensions were not back'd with any visible Instrument of Right, and as his strongest Plea was Custom, we could not so far extend our Complaisance as to continue his Fees upon so slender a Claim to them: And from that Time neither our Plays or his Fees gave either of us any farther trouble.[20]

Charles Killigrew was too indolent to fight for the rights of the office Sir Henry Herbert had defended with such tenacity fifty years earlier. Killigrew presented a petition of protest to the King, but it seems to have generated no response and Killigrew apparently just dropped the matter.[21] The Lord Chamberlain's office was not so spineless. In March 1716[/17]—just before leaving office—the Duke of Bolton had his secretary send a query to the Attorney and Solicitor General: 'Q Whether his Majesty may not by his Lord Chamberlain give orders from time to time for ye better regulation & government of ye Playhouse as formerly notwithstanding ye present grant to Sir Richard Steel ye Patentee & ye players under him. Q In case of refusal to obey or comply with such orders of ye Lord Chamberlain what may be done to compell them.'[22] In October 1718 Lord Chamberlain Newcastle formally asked Attorney General Nicholas Lechmere to define the exact scope of the powers conferred by Steele's patent.[23] A set of queries submitted to serjeant-at-law Thomas Pengelly (around January 1720?) asks:

Whether a patent granted for Erecting & forming a Company of Comedians or stage players to Act in any part of the Kingdom be not against Law.

Whether the Patent granted to Sir Richard Steele . . . be not against Law & consequently void.

Whether his Majesty may not by the Chamberlain of his Household make Orders . . . for the good Government and Regulation of the Players under Sir Richard Steele, any words or Clauses in his patent to the contrary notwithstanding.

[20] *Apology*, I, 276–8. In the 1660s Sir Henry Herbert had with great difficulty reimposed the Master of the Revels' traditional powers of censorship. See *The Dramatic Records of Sir Henry Herbert*, ed. Joseph Quincy Adams (New Haven, 1917). Charles Killigrew had been collecting the fees (£2 per new play, £1 per revival) since 1677, but rarely bothered to look at the scripts submitted to him.

[21] The petition (in French) is preserved in BL Add. MS 61,615, fols. 149–50. For text, translation, and discussion, see Milhous and Hume, 'Charles Killigrew's Petition about the Master of the Revels' Power as Censor (1715)', in *Theatre Notebook* 41 (1987), 74–9.

[22] Draft in PRO LC 7/3, fol. 41.

[23] PRO LC 5/157, pp. 142–4; copy in LC 7/3, fol. 40.

> In case of Disobedience to such Orders, whether the Lord Chamberlain may not . . . silence the company and whether Sir Richard Steeles patent will not thereby be forfeited.[24]

The replies to these inquiries are lost; they were probably less than clear-cut.

The violent dispute between Lord Chamberlain Newcastle and Steele between December 1719 and May 1721 has been analysed in detail elsewhere, and is in any case largely irrelevant to my purposes here.[25] Advised by Pengelly, Newcastle silenced the theatre; cancelled the licence of October 1714; and issued a new licence to Wilks, Cibber, and Booth.[26] Steele held that the patent entirely superseded the licence; Newcastle simply ignored the patent, in essence maintaining that a licence was necessary in order to exercise a patent. Vanbrugh's terse summation is interesting: '[Steele] has a month ago work'd a Quarrell So high with my Lord Chamberlain, That a New Licence has been granted to Wilks, Cibber & Booth which they accepting of, and acting under; have Left him with his Patent, but not one Player, and so the Lord Chamberlains Authority over the Playhouse is restor'd, and the Patent ends in a joke.'[27] Newcastle won his battle in the spring of 1720, but a year later, when Steele's friends regained the upper hand in the government, Steele was reinstated and granted past profits due to him.[28] This ended the battle, but without any legal clarification of the issues involved.

Newcastle had briefly succeeded in silencing the theatre. But he apparently did not issue a licence to Lincoln's Inn Fields (as logically he ought to have done). And the tenuous nature of his authority over the actors is indicated by Pengelly's advice that the actors be 'sworn'—a custom in desuetude since 1710.[29] If the actors were members of the royal household, then of course they were subject to the Lord Chamberlain's authority. Wilks expressed the actors' uneasiness with

[24] Bodleian MS Eng. lett. c.17, fol. 16; calendared in HMC VII (1879), p. 684b (tentatively dated Oct. 1718).

[25] For a very thorough account, see Loftis, *Steele at Drury Lane*, pp. 121–80.

[26] The order of silence is PRO LC 5/157, pp. 280–1 (25 Jan. 1719[/20]); the new licence, which explicitly revokes all previous licences, is LC 5/157, p. 282 (27 Jan. 1719[/20]).

[27] *The Complete Works of Sir John Vanbrugh*, ed. Bonamy Dobrée and Geoffrey Webb, 4 vols. (Bloomsbury, 1927–28), IV, 125 (letter of 18 Feb. 1719/20).

[28] Newcastle's order for this, dated 2 May 1721, is in PRO LC 5/157, pp. 415–16 (printed by Loftis, *Steele at Drury Lane*, p. 158).

[29] For Pengelly's advice, see PRO SP 35/74, fol. 160 (24 January 1719/20). The oaths were duly administered on 4 March (*London Journal*, 5 March 1720).

this arrangement in a letter to Newcastle of 29 February.[30] But George I clearly had no desire to make actors part of his household. And if a group of actors declined the honour (supposing it were offered), then on what basis could the Lord Chamberlain claim to regulate them? Neither the patents of 1662 and 1663 nor that of 1715 mentioned the Lord Chamberlain or his powers. Attacking Steele's position, the anonymous author of *The State of the Case . . . Restated* argued that Steele's patent must be subject to the same regulation that had long been imposed by the Lord Chamberlain on other patent theatre companies.[31] This is a potent argument—but what of non-patent companies choosing to operate without a licence? The Master of the Revels had always granted licences for companies outside the precincts of London and Westminster but held no apparent jurisdiction within those bounds. The Lord Chamberlain's right to issue licences—for whatever they might be worth—was undisputed, but whether actors in London and Westminster needed such licences was legally far from clear.

In the midst of all this controversy, a non-patent theatre was built and opened—the Little Haymarket, which was to be the scene of Fielding's greatest successes. We know practically nothing about the theatre. It was built by John Potter (a carpenter who did scene construction for the Haymarket opera); in 1735 he testified that it cost £1,000 to build.[32] His plans for it may be deduced in part from a slightly sour report in the *Weekly Journal, or British Gazeteer* (3 December 1720): 'The new French Theatre in the Hay-Market is just finished; and the Actors are soon expected from Paris to open there, at the same time that One of our own, for want of due Encouragement, is ready to be pull'd down.'[33] The scanty evidence suggests that the Little Haymarket was built as a venue for foreign companies,

[30] BL Add. MS 32,685, fols. 51–2.

[31] *The State of the Case, between The Lord Chamberlain of his Majesty's Houshold, and Sir Richard Steele, as Represented by that Knight. Restated, In Vindication of King George, and the Most Noble the Duke of Newcastle* (London, 1720), pp. 19–20. Arnott and Robinson, no. 156.

[32] *Journal of the House of Commons*, 22 (1735), 456.

[33] An exaggeration, but Lincoln's Inn Fields had been no better than a marginal operation since it reopened in December 1714. On 6 August 1720 *Applebee's Weekly Journal* reported that 'Two Executions having seiz'd the New Play-House in Lincolns Inn Fields on violent Presumptions of Debt, the Company is dissolv'd, and the Playing suspended till they have compos'd the Matter.' On the sorry state of Rich's company, see Denise Elliott Shane, 'John Rich and the Reopening of Lincoln's Inn Fields', forthcoming in *Theatre Notebook*, and PRO C11/1411/37 (Rich *v*. Bullock).

amateurs, and quasi-theatrical entertainments, not as the home for a permanent repertory company.

The authority on which Potter built and operated the Little Haymarket is extremely cloudy. A notice in the *London Journal* (23 December 1721) claims that a patent was 'obtain'd in the late Reign for twenty Years, nine of which are already elapsed'—but no record of a patent or licence issued around 1711–13 has survived. No harassment of the theatre is known, possibly because it was owned or protected by the Duke of Montagu. This is known from the one attempt to use the house for English plays with a resident company in the early 1720s. This scheme was the brain-child of Aaron Hill. He had investigated the matter of authority to act, as we learn from his letter to John Rich of 9 September 1721. Hill denies that he lacks 'authority for the company' he is establishing, and sends Rich 'judge *Pemberton*'s opinion, on some queries, of your *father's* own stating'. And Hill reports an agreement that he would have the theatre half of each week and a company of '*french vermin*, the other half', but suggests that he would rather use Lincoln's Inn Fields if Rich will let him have it 'for *two* nights a week, in *Lent*, and *three* a week, after', offering to pay 'the full actual charge' of Rich's company as well as his own on those nights.[34] Hill's venture was puffed in the *Daily Journal* (11 December 1721):

A new Theatre will in a few Days time be open'd in the Hay-Market, where the French Comedians now play, of which *Aaron Hill*, Esq; will be sole Manager and Director: The Scenes are contriv'd after a Fashion entirely new, the Habits all new; the principal Characters of the Men, and all the Womens Characters will be play'd by Persons who never appear'd upon the Stage before. The chief End and Design of this Theatre is the Regulation of the Stage, and the Benefit and Encouragement of Authors, whose Works very often, tho' good, are despis'd and set aside.

This slightly implausible venture came to naught. Three letters from Hill to the Duke of Montagu between 20 and 24 January 1722 show that Montagu blocked the venture and resisted all pleas for compromise.[35] Hill's woes are not our concern here, but his letters show that he had 'made an absolute agreement with Mr. Potter for the House, and

[34] Hill, *Works* (London, 1753), II, 46–8. I deduce that Christopher Rich had sought expensive legal advice (probably after the silencing of 1709). How the results came into Hill's hands we can only guess.

[35] MSS now in the Northampton Record Office, Montagu (Boughton) Correspondence, vol. VII, 139–43.

undertook to pay him £540 for two seasons' (a figure of some importance when we come to consider Fielding's tenancy in the theatre). Hill also says that Montagu was the patron of the visiting French comedians, and that he had not known 'that the House itself was your Grace's'. This may mean that Potter was serving as a front for the Duke; that Montagu had taken a lease on the premises and refused to allow Potter to sublet on his behalf; or that Montagu held a mortgage on the place. In any case, Hill's plans and investment in 'very expensive' scenery went by the board, and the patent houses retained their monopoly unchallenged. But the construction of a fourth theatre building suggests a growing market for entertainment in London. And the optimistic Hill, at any rate, had believed that he could operate a theatre company without either a patent or a licence.

Relations between the two patent houses were naturally strained for several years after 1714. Steele was quite bitter about competition and theft of personnel and kept hoping that Lincoln's Inn Fields would collapse or that Rich could be bribed to shut it down, perhaps with 'a Sallary while there is but one House'.[36] As Lincoln's Inn Fields' dire financial problems in August 1720 show, this was not just an idle hope. But when tempers cooled, collusion seemed attractive. In October 1720 the two managements engaged in abortive negotiations to enter into a five-year pact not to steal each other's personnel under penalty of £500.[37] A year and a half later, Steele, Wilks, Cibber, and Booth (for Drury Lane) and John and Christopher Mosyer Rich (for Lincoln's Inn Fields) concluded a formal legal contract not to hire any person who had worked at the other theatre without the prior agreement of the other management.[38]

This 'cartel agreement', as it became known, was used ruthlessly to block actor transfers and keep salaries down. A decade later the actors' resentment over it, and their fear of its reimposition, were significant factors in the rebellion of 1733. In theory, actor transfers since 1660 had always required the Lord Chamberlain's permission. In practice, the rules had rarely been enforced. In 1722, for the first time, we see two managements (one of them consisting principally of actors) making an agreement to exploit actors for the advantage of

[36] Letter of 11 June 1717, *The Correspondence of Richard Steele*, ed. Rae Blanchard (Oxford, 1941), p. 353.

[37] See BL Add. Charter 9306 (unexecuted), 1 Nov. 1720.

[38] BL Add. Charter 9308 (12 April 1722). For transcription and analysis, see Milhous and Hume, 'The London Theatre Cartel of the 1720s: British Library Additional Charters 9306 and 9308', *Theatre Survey*, 26 (1985), 21–37.

'proprietors'.[39] This was not an isolated event. Christopher Rich had tried it in 1694 and again in 1709—to be foiled each time by a Lord Chamberlain sympathetic to the actors. The actor rebellion of 1733 was to succeed because the Lord Chamberlain was powerless and the courts upheld the actors. The rebellion of 1743 led by Garrick and Macklin was to fail because the Licensing Act had changed the law, and the Lord Chamberlain had refused to issue a licence to the rebels. What we see in the 1720s is a clear move by the patent theatre managements towards the monopolistic collusion that—enforced by the Licensing Act—was to stifle the London theatre for more than a century.

The vagueness of the government's actual regulatory powers in the 1720s seems to have been obscured by the contradictory results of earlier disputes. From the perspective of 1728, we must deduce a great sense of permanence and solidity in London's theatrical arrangements. Despite the complicated history, London had two patent theatres and one patent opera company (the opera sliding towards bankruptcy, but extravagantly supported by the King and the nobility). For fourteen years the managements of the two theatre companies had remained unchanged—the longest period of such stability since the original patent companies were founded in 1660. John Rich was still a young man (and he was in fact to rule his company until his death in 1761). The triumvirs ranged in age from 49 to 63, but they showed not the slightest sign of relaxing the iron grip they had maintained over their company since 1709—the longest tenure of any management since 1660. Impregnable as the patent monopoly must have seemed, it was soon to be challenged and destroyed. For the moment, however, our concern is with the operation of the monopoly before 1728 and with the state of the drama brought about by the patentees' methods of operation.

II. REPERTORY PATTERNS AND NEW PLAYS

Neither Drury Lane nor Lincoln's Inn Fields had been particularly receptive to new plays after 1714, despite the re-establishment of

[39] Between the demise of the United Company in 1695 and the mid-1720s, actors became increasingly subordinate to proprietors, a development partially camouflaged by the fact that at Drury Lane the triumvirs were actors. Their outlook, however, was closer to Rich's than to Betterton's.

competition, which historically had encouraged the staging of fresh fare. Lincoln's Inn Fields had barely survived its first half-dozen seasons—and had done so, and prospered, mostly as a result of John Rich's introduction of pantomime afterpieces. The managers at Drury Lane had been content with proven favourites and a minimum of experimentation and risk-taking. The *modus vivendi* signalled in the cartel of 1722 simply reinforced the set pattern of each house.

A brief survey of the two theatres' repertory in 1726–27 (believed by Cross to have been Fielding's first season in London)[40] will illustrate just how conservative, even stagnant, these theatres had become. They opened the season by politely playing on alternate nights from the beginning of September to the last Saturday in October. During this season Drury Lane performed a total of sixty-five plays (only one of them new) on a total of 178 nights.[41] The one new play, James Moore Smythe's *The Rival Modes*, a derivative and old-fashioned love-chase comedy, lasted six nights and was never revived. Lincoln's Inn Fields countered with fifty plays on a total of 169 nights. Four of these plays were new, but two of them lasted only two nights each, and another managed five.[42] Philip Frowde's *The Fall of Saguntum* had a good initial run (eleven nights), but was mounted only once more this season and never revived. The conservatism in the theatres' repertory policy is made even clearer if we break their plays down into period of origin. (See Table 1.) Thus at Drury Lane only 8 per cent of the plays staged had been written within the previous twenty years, and thirty-seven of them (57 per cent) were more than thirty years old. Even that figure does not tell the whole story, since most of the plays from the

TABLE 1: Mainpieces Performed in the Season of 1726–27

	DL	%	LIF	%
Pre-1660	11	(17)	9	(18)
1660–94	26	(40)	16	(32)
1695–1707	23	(35)	16	(32)
1708–20	3	(5)	4	(8)
Post-1720	2 (1 new)	(3)	5 (4 new)	(10)
	65		50	

[40] Cross, I, 55–6.

[41] In these figures I am counting only mainpieces.

[42] Anon., *The Savage* (unpublished and lost); David Lewis, *Philip of Macedon*; Leonard Welsted, *The Dissembled Wanton*. None was revived.

1660–1694 period pre-date the union of 1682. We should remember that Wilks, Cibber, and Booth favoured plays written in the decade after 1695, having created roles in many of them. Rich's company had no such direct tie to turn-of-the-century repertory. None the less, the figures at Lincoln's Inn Fields are only slightly less discouraging to the prospective dramatist. Both theatres had a set of Shakespeare-era war-horses, and both relied heavily on stock plays of the Carolean period. Likewise, both relied almost equally on the flock of 'perennial favorites' written around the turn of the century at the height of the competition between Drury Lane and the rebel actors at Lincoln's Inn Fields under Betterton.[43] We should note also that sixteen plays were in both theatres' repertories in 1726–27,[44] occupying a total of eighty nights at the two theatres.

One of the most striking facts about both repertories is the small number of performances of any single play. Drury Lane performed no old play more than five times; six plays enjoyed five performances each (*The Albion Queens*, *Cato*, *The Careless Husband*, *The Committee*, *The Relapse*, *Tamerlane*). Seven plays managed four performances each (*The Amorous Widow*, *2 Henry IV*, *Love for Love*, *The Provok'd Wife*, *Rule a Wife*, *Sir Courtly Nice*, *The Way of the World*). Twenty-three were given three performances each; all others one or two. At Lincoln's Inn Fields (which kept a smaller active repertory) the picture is only slightly different. Two plays enjoyed seven performances (*The Confederacy* and *The Country-Wife*) and one had six (*The Prophetess*). Three plays managed five nights (*The Beaux Stratagem*, *Merry Wives*, *The Mistake*), and eight had four nights. Only seven more achieved three nights; the rest one or two. The situation at Lincoln's Inn Fields this season differed principally in that the theatre enjoyed a striking success with a revival of *Camilla* (1706), a translated Italian opera that had been off the stage for seven years. *Camilla* received a startling twenty-five performances.

Of the stock plays performed more than three times, only three had been written since the union of 1708—Centlivre's *The Busie Body* (1709), Addison's *Cato* (1713), and Bullock's *Woman's Revenge* (1715–

[43] See Shirley Strum Kenny, 'Perennial Favorites: Congreve, Vanbrugh, Cibber, Farquhar, and Steele', *Modern Philology*, 73, no. 4, Part 2 [Friedman *Festschrift*] (1976), S4–S11.

[44] *Aesop*, *The Beaux Stratagem*, *The Country-Wife*, *Hamlet*, *Julius Caesar*, *King Lear* (Tate), *Macbeth*, *The Old Batchelour*, *The Orphan*, *Oroonoko*, *The Provok'd Wife*, *The Recruiting Officer*, *Richard III*, *The Rover*, *The Spanish Fryar*, and *Tamerlane*.

an adaptation of a 1680 Behn adaptation). The other post-1708 plays in the repertory were Philips's *The Distrest Mother* (1712), Rowe's *Jane Shore* (1714), and Addison's *The Drummer* (1716). The one post-1720 play in the repertory was *The Conscious Lovers* (1722), whose author was, of course, the patentee at Drury Lane.

Looking at total nights of performance during this quite typical season, we find that at Drury Lane 6 per cent of the performances (eleven of 172) of revived plays featured post-1708 plays (only one of them less than ten years old). At Lincoln's Inn Fields—which staged more new plays this year—the corresponding figures are 5 per cent (eight of 149), with *no* revivals of any play fewer than ten years old. Such variety as the theatres offered came in their selection of old plays, not in their choice of new ones. Given this repertory pattern, we can scarcely be surprised that the prospects for aspiring playwrights were bleak. To realize just how bleak, we must remember that Centlivre and Rowe were established professional playwrights by 1708; Christopher Bullock had been an actor at Lincoln's Inn Fields; Addison was one of the great names in early eighteenth-century letters.

Thus far our consideration has excluded afterpieces, but they do not much change the picture. In the first quarter of the eighteenth century, afterpieces usually reflect the vigour of competition.[45] Neither company offered an afterpiece at even half its performances this season. (In many cases entr'acte singing and dancing were offered instead.) Drury Lane mounted seventy-four afterpiece performances in 178 nights. Five old stand-bys occupied a total of eight nights, all in the benefit season.[46] Thurmond's long-popular *Harlequin Dr. Faustus* ran throughout the season, and the house got good runs from Thurmond's *Apollo and Daphne; or, Harlequin's Metamorphosis*, *The Miser*, and *Harlequin's Triumph*. Drury Lane's new afterpieces were all written by an insider, its dancing master. At Lincoln's Inn Fields seventy-six nights of afterpieces were split among twelve plays, but thirty-two were devoted to Theobald's new *The Rape of Proserpine*. The afterpiece had not really become an established tradition until 1715: hence, most afterpieces were relatively recent. The boom in

[45] See Kevin Pry, 'Theatrical Competition and the Rise of the Afterpiece Tradition 1700–24', *Theatre Notebook*, 36 (1982), 21–7.

[46] *The Strollers* (3), *The Stage-Coach* (2), *The School-Boy*, *Hob*, *The What d'ye Call It*.

pantomime started by John Rich, however, meant that the theatres were far from anxious to secure legitimate two-act comedies.[47]

Commenting long afterwards on the triumvirate management, Thomas Davies explained the managers' dilemma:

> The most difficult and irksome task which a manager of a theatre can, perhaps, undergo, arises from his connexion with authors. . . . The time bestowed in rehearsing the piece, and the expense of new scenes, dresses, music, and other decorations, make it often very ineligible to a director of a theatre to accept a new play; especially when it is considered that the reviving of a good old play will answer his end of profit, and reputation too, perhaps, as well. Booth often declared in public company, that he and his partners lost money by new plays; and that, if he were not obliged to it, he would seldom give his consent to perform one of them.[48]

Fear of recrimination and satire aside, what 'obliged' the managers to mount new plays? Clearly one factor was publicity. The newspapers were increasingly full of theatrical gossip in the 1720s, and new plays had news value. Second, the public evidently wanted *some* variety. Third, the importunities of writers were hard to resist all the time, and the theatres could not have lost much on most new plays.[49] And fourth, the managers could always hope for a hit. We have no box-office reports for Drury Lane in 1726–27, but those for Lincoln's Inn Fields show an enormous fluctuation in the take—from £12 (*Julius Caesar*, 11 November) to £216 (*The Cheats of Scapin*, 13 February). In the latter case the theatre was benefitting from the phenomenal popularity of an afterpiece, *The Rape of Proserpine*. Expenses ran about £50 a night at this time, and many days the theatre took in less or very little more. A success with a new play, or a lucky revival like *Camilla*, was eagerly sought.

Unless a theatre chose to offer a new play 'New Dress'd', or it required special new scenery, investment in a new play was more a matter of time and trouble than money. The author received profits only during the first run. The nuisance, however, was considerable.

[47] The early history of pantomime in London remains practically unstudied. For the most helpful account to date, see Viola Papetti, *Arlecchino a Londra: La Pantomima Inglese 1700–1728*, Aion Quaderni Degli Annali Sezione Germanica, 13 (Napoli: Istituto Universitario Orientale, 1977).

[48] Thomas Davies, *Memoirs of the Life of David Garrick* (1808; repr. New York, 1969), I, 244–5.

[49] Extant figures from Rich's company suggest that curiosity often gave the theatre a decent house the first night, and the author's friends generally made the third night productive of house charges or better. Second nights were often quite unprofitable.

Typically, each theatre mounted six different mainpieces every week. As a rule plays were not repeated within two weeks except during first runs of new plays or major revivals. Learning the lines and rehearsing a new script likely to survive all of three nights (on the average) was not, therefore, a welcome proposition on top of the usual demands of the repertory system.

Another reason that managers may have been chary of new plays—especially after 1728—was the vague legal status of such plays. If a successful new play could be pirated by the opposition, it was less valuable than if it remained the exclusive property of the company that first mounted it. Rights to plays had been a sore subject back in 1660,[50] and the matter had never really been settled. The Carolean arrangement had been that pre-1660 plays were divided (very unequally) by the Lord Chamberlain; new plays belonged exclusively to the company that first performed them. The union of 1682 gave the United Company rights to all plays. After the rebellion of 1695, both companies performed the old plays and had exclusive right to new ones, but this distinction collapsed with the actor transfers of 1706 and the new union of 1708. Between 1714 and 1728 Drury Lane and Lincoln's Inn Fields refrained from poaching each other's new plays, but this appears to have been a matter of private co-operation. There seems to have been no legal barrier to a competitor's buying a copy of a play and producing it—as a non-patent company was to do at the Little Haymarket in 1728 with *The Beggar's Opera*.

The dismal prospects for new plays were perfectly obvious, and commentary on the managers' stodgy repertory policies in newspapers and pamphlets was frequently acerbic.[51] But hope has always sprung

[50] See Robert D. Hume, 'Securing a Repertory: Plays on the London Stage 1660–5', *Poetry and Drama, 1570–1700: Essays in Honour of Harold F. Brooks*, ed. Antony Coleman and Antony Hammond (London, 1981), pp. 156–72.

[51] See, for example, the *Weekly Journal or Saturday's-Post* of 9 and 16 March 1723: 'The Occasion of the miserable Decay of Dramatick Poetry within this last eight Years, has been intirely owing to the Management of Drury-Lane Theatre.' The author calls it 'a wrong to *Posterity*, that the Management of a Theatre should be committed to such ignorant and mercenary *Creatures*'. Rich is attacked just as ferociously, especially for his emphasis on pantomime, in the *Weekly Journal or British Gazetteer* of 11 March 1727. For sour but slightly less polemical views of repertory policy, see anon., *A Letter to My Lord ******* on The Present Diversions of the Town* (London, 1725); Gabriel Rennel, *Reflections, of a Moral and Political Tendency, occasioned By the Present State of the two Rival-Theatres in Drury-Lane and Lincoln's-Inn-Fields* (London, [1725?]); and the introduction to 'Thomas D'Urfey's' *The English Stage Italianiz'd* (London, 1727). Every theatre manager from Betterton to Garrick drew his share of fire from disappointed authors and disgruntled outsiders, but the contempt heaped upon Cibber and John Rich is extraordinarily bitter.

eternal in playwrights' breasts, and bad as the prospects of performance (let alone success) clearly were, the managers always had plenty of scripts to consider. Writing a gossipy letter to Jacob Tonson, Vanbrugh mentions that 'Cibber tells me, 'tis not to be conceiv'd, how many and how bad Plays, are brought to them.'[52]

Studying the market, such as it was, how would an intelligent young man like Fielding have regarded the prospects for new plays? Were there bandwagons on which to leap, or camps to join? Unfortunately, the situation was not so tidy. One certainly cannot legitimately distinguish 'laughing' and 'sentimental' camps associated with Gay and Cibber respectively, as Brian McCrea would like to do.[53] John Loftis has seen in the comedies of the twenties the gradual modification and displacement of 'Restoration stereotypes', and though he is thinking as much of ideology as genre, his view seems basically correct.[54] The new plays of the early and mid-1720s largely continue the modes established around the turn of the century. A Rip Van Winkle who saw *The Beaux Stratagem* and fell asleep in 1707 would not have found great changes had he awakened in 1727. The standard types were (1) farce—*A Fond Husband*, *The London Cuckolds*; (2) satiric comedy—*The Provok'd Wife*, *The Man of Mode*; (3) humane comedy—*The Funeral*, *The Beaux Stratagem*; and (4) reform comedy—*The Careless Husband*, Centlivre's *The Gamester*. All of them had been stock plays around 1707 and remained so around 1727. All of these types had been tried after 1714. Examples are Benjamin Griffin's *Love in a Sack* (farce), William Taverner's *The Artful Wife* (satiric), Addison's *The Drummer* (humane), and Charles Johnson's *The Masquerade* (reform). Ideologically, the view of merchants and commerce had become more favourable (hardly surprising under a mercantile-minded Whig government), and the appearance of Steele's *The Conscious Lovers* in 1722 had extended the possibilities of exemplary comedy. But we may fairly say that a wide range of generic possibilities was open to a writer of mainpiece comedies. The problem was not with the sort of play acceptable to the audience, but with the managers' reluctance to stage new plays at all.

[52] *Works*, IV, 146 (18 June 1722).
[53] McCrea, ch. 3, esp. p. 53.
[54] *Comedy and Society*, ch. 5.

III. THE PROFESSION OF PLAYWRIGHT

How did a play get accepted and staged? What could the playwright hope to earn from a play? We know less than we would like about such matters, but quite enough to see how precarious the life of a playwright must have been; why Fielding rapidly grew so disenchanted with the patent-theatre managers; and why he ultimately turned to management himself. But for the moment, our concern is with the state of affairs when Fielding first came to London.

The proud parent of a new script had first to persuade a manager to look at it—seldom an easy business. John Rich read the submissions to Lincoln's Inn Fields (or judged them, at any rate), and quickly became notorious for his curt refusals: 'It will not do.'[55] At Drury Lane Cibber seems to have dealt summarily with most of the new offerings, though Booth read tragedies and even Wilks sometimes yielded to the importunities of a friend like Aaron Hill. Davies vividly reports Cibber's lack of 'that delicacy and politeness which is so necessary upon an unwelcome repulse. . . . His practice of giving back their plays he wantonly called *the choaking of singing birds*.'[56] Small wonder that authors cadged introductions and recommendations from actors, friends of the managers, and persons of social distinction—though whether such recommendations really helped is doubtful.

In the 1720s, unlike the late seventeenth century, there were no 'attached' playwrights—authors receiving a retainer in return for the first rights to their new scripts. The theatres were not that anxious for new plays, and consequently the long-standard practice of writing for particular actors was in decline. An author might hope that Wilks and Oldfield would grace his lead roles, but he could not count on it, and so had to write parts suitable for different performers.

Supposing that the managers had somehow been induced to accept a new play and schedule its production, the first step was the author's 'reading' to the assembled company, an event which usually seems to have taken place five to eight weeks before the anticipated première. Author and managers consulted about casting. Try-outs were virtually unknown: the author was allowed to pick the cast, subject to managerial veto. Except for the most senior people, actors were not allowed to refuse parts, or were fined for doing so. As a rule, actors did

[55] *The Life of Mr. James Quin, Comedian* (London, 1766), p. 54.
[56] Davies, *Memoirs of Garrick*, I, 246–8.

not especially welcome learning parts in new plays. They were paid nothing extra, and few new plays lasted more than a week. Even fewer were revived after their initial season. Only in an extraordinary case did performers feud over a new part—as in the celebrated fracas between Anne Oldfield and Jane Rogers about Andromache in *The Distrest Mother* (1712).[57]

Since there was no 'director' as such in the eighteenth-century theatre, scholars have sometimes assumed that the actors made shift for themselves as best they could—a very implausible idea. As far as I can determine, from the mid-seventeenth century on, new plays were directed by the author if he were able and willing. In other cases, as with revivals, one of the managers exercised directorial functions.[58] Benjamin Victor describes the production process as the triumvirate handled it:

> If a new Play was coming on, the first three Readings fell to the Share of the Author. If a revived Play, it fell to the Share of that Manager who was the principal Performer in it. The Readings over, there followed a limited Number of Rehearsals, with their Parts in their Hands; after which, a distant Morning was appointed for every Person in the Play to appear perfect, because the Rehearsals only then begin to be of Use to the Actor. . . . Thus the Rehearsals went on, under the Eye of a Person who had Ability to instruct, and Power to encourage and advance those of Industry and Merit; and to forfeit and discharge the negligent and worthless.[59]

An Aaron Hill or a Charles Johnson doubtless had very definite ideas of how his piece should be performed. A novice writer must have relied much more heavily on the assistance of the manager or a senior actor. We can presume, however, that the author was involved in blocking, choice of scenery, explanation of characters to actors, gestures, and instruction in delivery of lines. The actual conduct of the public performances was, of course, the responsibility of the prompter, who handled matters that would today be the province of a stage manager.

[57] See Milhous and Hume, 'Theatrical Politics at Drury Lane: New Light on Letitia Cross, Jane Rogers, and Anne Oldfield', *Bulletin of Research in the Humanities*, 85 (1982), 412–29.

[58] For a detailed discussion relevant to the late seventeenth-century period, see Milhous and Hume, *Producible Interpretation: Eight English Plays, 1675–1707* (Carbondale, 1985), ch. 2. For a mid-18th-cent. perspective, see Kalman A. Burnim, *David Garrick, Director* (Pittsburgh, 1961; repr. Carbondale, 1973).

[59] Victor, II, 4–5. 'Reading' I take to mean a seated run-through with the author or one of the managers coaching the actors.

I deduce that on the great night of the première the author normally sat out front with his friends, hoping to bask in applause. If things went badly, this was no doubt embarrassing. Following a rocky reception for Aaron Hill's *King Henry the Fifth*, we find Barton Booth assuring Hill that the performance improved the second night, and suggesting that Hill come again, offering to let him sit 'behind the Scenes . . . where you shall be invisible to the Audience'.[60] Eighteenth-century audiences had little charity towards new plays that displeased them.[61]

Remuneration for playwrights came principally from one or more author's benefit nights during the first run. Traditionally, the playwright received the profits of the third night (i.e. gross receipts minus 'house charges'). Around 1690 writers started to bargain for the 'sixth' night as well, supposing the play lasted that long. By the beginning of the eighteenth century, writers were usually allowed the profits from every third night throughout the first unbroken run. After that, the play could be staged for decades by every company in town with no further payment to the writer. This system often over-rewarded writers whose plays survived only three nights, if their friends turned out *en masse* for the all-important benefit. But it clearly under-rewarded a writer whose play survived and entered the repertory. And it tended to discourage managers from mounting new plays, as we will see.

A look at the specifics of the author benefits at Lincoln's Inn Fields in 1726–27 will illustrate possibilities, pitfalls, and complexities.[62] Leonard Welsted's *The Dissembled Wanton* opened 14 December and survived a total of five nights. It grossed £63 12*s.* at the première; £38 5*s.* the second night; and £138 7*s.* at the author's benefit. The figure for house charges at this date was about £50, and that was what was actually charged at author's benefits. Thus the company made £13 the first night; lost £12 the second; and made its expenses while paying the

[60] *A Collection of Letters . . . To the Late Aaron Hill, Esq;* (London, 1751), pp. 78–81 ('Sunday Morning' [8 Dec. 1723]). Addison, although 'a very sober man', is said to have required considerable alcoholic sustenance at the première of *Cato*, and even so he insisted on sitting inconspicuously in a side-box. See Peter Smithers, *The Life of Joseph Addison*, 2nd edn. (Oxford, 1968), p. 263.

[61] For the best general account of the audience in this period, see Leo Hughes, *The Drama's Patrons* (Austin, 1971).

[62] I select Lincoln's Inn Fields because account books preserved in the BL (Egerton MS 2266) and the Harvard Theatre Collection give us exact daily receipts (summarized day by day in *The London Stage*). No daily receipts for Drury Lane are known before the 1740s.

fortunate author £88 the third. These figures do not, of course, take into account any money the theatre spent on scenery and costumes. Most new plays, to be sure, used scenery and costumes pulled from stock. In this case, the theatre might have made £1, assuming no ancillary expenses, as its reward for its trouble in getting up the production.[63] The second night total is usually an indication of appeal. Curiosity usually brought some people out the first night, and the author solicited his friends for the third.

Philip Frowde's *The Fall of Saguntum* opened 16 January and managed eleven nights. Gross receipts were as follows: 1st night = £148; 2nd = £56; 3rd = £164; 4th = £46; 5th = £50; 6th = £113; 7th = £50; 8th = £42; 9th = £72; 10th = £45; 11th = £70 (with a popular pantomime added). Frowde's net was £114, £63, and £22. Had he been given (or chosen to take?) a fourth benefit, he would presumably have had to guarantee house charges, so he might even have wound up out of pocket. From 'Rich's Register' we discover that Frowde had to make up the difference to £50 on the fourth and eighth nights—Rich had no intention of absorbing losses to extend the run.[64]

David Lewis's *Philip of Macedon* received its première on 2 May. The weather was hot and Rich plainly had little faith in the piece, since he made the première the author's benefit. The total take was £145, giving Lewis a very respectable £95. But we may note that only £18 came in at the door, the rest from tickets, which the author had evidently peddled with vigour (standard practice for the time). Rich probably saved himself two nights of dismally low receipts by going straight to the benefit. The only other performance was a second author's benefit on 11 May, which grossed a surprisingly good £85 16*s.* 6*d.* Despite these figures, Rich chose not to perform the play again; obviously he did not think it would pay.

These three examples make very clear the financial basis of the managers' qualms about mounting new plays. Even *The Fall of Saguntum*, with an exceptionally good initial run, did not in fact make any money for the company after the first night. The company's profit was £124 (disregarding production costs), or about £11 per night over the whole run. Maximum gross was rarely above £200 at Lincoln's Inn

[63] The company used the play twice more, but relatively good receipts must be ascribed to the appeal of *Harlequin a Sorcerer*, which served as afterpiece on those occasions.

[64] For discussion, see *The London Stage*, Part 2, Introduction, I, p. ci.

Fields, even at advanced prices,[65] but the potentiality for a net of £150 or better existed, as every author with a benefit must have been well aware.

At this point we must consider some complexities. How long would the run go on? If a play did not make its charges the fourth or fifth night, could the managers call a halt, even if the author believed his friends would turn out in force again for the sixth? Were they obliged to continue the run if the author made up the deficiency, as Frowde did? In the dedication to *The Invader of His Country* (Drury Lane, 1719), John Dennis complained bitterly that the triumvirs had halted the initial run after three nights, 'contrary to an Ancient Rule, which has been always observ'd till now . . . never to give over a new Play . . . as long as it brings Charges'.[66] The possible ramifications are illustrated in Cibber's contract with Christopher Rich for *Woman's Wit* in 1696.[67] Cibber was to pay house charges for the third night, but they would be returned if the fourth night receipts were £55 or more. The play would be acted a fifth night if fourth night receipts were £40 or better (house charges were £30–£35 at this time). Cibber would receive net profits of a sixth night, if any, but would pay the difference if the receipts fell below charges. A seventh night would be given if sixth night receipts amounted to £40 or more. And so forth.

This discussion has concerned payment for mainpieces. What of afterpieces? Here we find ourselves on uncertain ground. We simply do not know what financial arrangements were made for new afterpieces. Author benefits were sometimes advertised—and often not. We have no way to tell in most cases what charges were deducted for the benefits; nor do we know what flat fees were paid in lieu of a benefit. We may wonder what *The Rape of Proserpine* (13 February 1727) brought Lewis Theobald for the words and Galliard for the music. The work was a smashing success: the theatre grossed above £200 its first eight nights, and £198 the ninth. But the two benefits advertised were for John Rich, who choreographed it and starred in it. My best guess is that authors usually got a flat fee (£25–£50?) for an afterpiece, but this is simply speculation.

[65] Boxes were usually raised from 4*s.* to 5*s.* during first runs; the pit from 2*s.* 6*d.* to 3*s.*; the first gallery from 1*s.* 6*d.* to 2*s.*

[66] *The Invader of His Country* (London, 1720), sig. A4^{v}.

[67] PRO LC 7/3, fols. 76–7 (29 Oct. 1696). This contract is almost unique. That playwrights normally signed such agreements seems very unlikely. In this instance Cibber had scored a major hit with *Love's Last Shift* and then had been wooed away to the Lincoln's Inn Fields company; Rich was stealing him back.

Beyond author benefits in the first run of a mainpiece, the author had only two sources of supplementary income—publication and gifts from the dedicatee. Since the 1690s, normal procedure for the publication of a play seems to have been for the author to strike an agreement with a publisher before the première. In virtually every instance, this was for outright sale of copyright; the royalty system was unknown. Prices varied wildly, but from the figures that have come down to us we may deduce that anything over £30–£40 was exceptional. Mrs Centlivre got £10 for *The Busie Body*; Farquhar £16 2*s.* 6*d.* for *The Recruiting Officer*; £30 for *The Beaux Stratagem*.[68] Cibber—a big name and a hard bargainer—got a surprising £36 11*s.* for *Perolla and Izadora* (1706), and £105 for *The Non-Juror* (1718), but Steele only £40 and 'other good Causes and Consideration' for *The Conscious Lovers*.[69] The usual price for a mainpiece was 1*s.* 6*d.*, meaning that the play would have to sell 400 copies just to pay off an author's fee of £30—not a bad fee, under the circumstances.

A single play rarely made the publisher a significant profit at this rate, but one *Cato* could underwrite a lot of damp squibs. Publishers were also conscious that for an author who attained sufficient standing there would be a demand for the collected plays, which might ultimately make even a failure in the theatre valuable. Shirley Strum Kenny points out that Steele's *The Lying Lover*, a dismal flop in 1703, was regularly reprinted for decades because of demand for complete sets of Steele's plays. But the author would not benefit at all from later editions, which helps explain authors' disinclination to correct such editions as they went through the press. A writer of distinction could revise old plays and issue a *Works* (as Congreve did in 1710), but this was profitable only because a new agreement could be struck with the publisher.

The final source of income from a play was the dedication to the printed edition. We do not know the cash value of dedications. George I gave Cibber £200 for *The Non-Juror* and Steele £500 for *The Conscious Lovers*, but these were extraordinary cases involving royal bounty for celebrated plays. My impression is that many dedications

[68] These figures are drawn from John Nichols, *Literary Anecdotes of the Eighteenth Century* (London, 1812–15), VIII, 293–303, and are discussed in Shirley Strum Kenny, 'The Publication of Plays', *The London Theatre World*, ch. 11.

[69] I would guess that Steele had Tonson pay off a small but pressing debt, though £40 was by no means unreasonable. On this transaction, see Rodney M. Baine, 'The Publication of Steele's *Conscious Lovers*', *Studies in Bibliography*, 2 (1949–50), 169–73.

to friends produced no cash at all, while those addressed to gentry or noted patrons might generate ten to twenty-five guineas. This is not a negligible sum: £20 was an annual salary for a novice actor at the patent theatres. By the mid-1720s government place-hunting was a big business, and some writers sought salaries for political hack-writing. I am not aware, however, of evidence that dedications of plays were an effective way to get such employment.

An author might make little or nothing from his third night. The maximum take from a single benefit was somewhat in excess of £150, and was very rarely achieved.[70] Studying the figures available from Lincoln's Inn Fields in the 1720s, we may deduce that an author's total net from a play was likely to be between £50 and £250, with £100 a reasonable expectation. This is not bad pay: a gentleman could live decently in London for a year on £100, if he avoided luxuries.[71] (A seat at the opera was half a guinea; a ticket to a masquerade a guinea and a half.) One hundred pounds was an annual income for a third-rank actor, and theatre staff were probably lucky to make more than half that, even with a share in a benefit.

The problem with writing plays as a way of earning a living was that the hundred pounds one might plausibly hope to make from a play was in no sense a certainty—and one had first to get the play accepted. Between 1714 and 1728 no writer had a new play staged annually, or even close to annually. I know of no writer after 1720 who had a play staged three years running, not even established figures or actor-playwrights.[72] The blunt truth is that, as far as we can tell, no one was making a living by writing plays in the mid-1720s. How apparent this was to ambitious tiros we cannot be sure, but someone like Fielding, who had in Lady Mary Wortley Montagu a relative well-connected in literary circles, must certainly have known the harsh facts. And, once Fielding was in touch with the Drury Lane management, Cibber would not have failed to enlighten him as to his future as a singing

[70] More money was possible if the author could persuade friends and patrons to pay more than list price for tickets. But few authors had the persuasive powers of favourite actresses and glamorous opera stars. Nicolini and Senesino could clear 800 guineas on a benefit, but this was largely on the basis of huge gifts from a few wealthy admirers.

[71] Spending more was easy, as the young Boswell was to find a generation later. In 1762 Boswell's father allowed him £200 for the year. For the budget he devised, see *Boswell's London Journal*, ed. Frederick A. Pottle (New York, 1950), pp. 335–7.

[72] Compare the 1670s, when Dryden had 10 plays staged, Shadwell 10, Behn 11, Lee 7 in 6 years, Otway 6 in 5 years. Or take the period around 1700, when Mrs Pix had 12 plays performed in 11 years, Mrs Centlivre 12 in 11 years, Cibber 14 in 14 years, Vanbrugh 9 in 10 years.

bird. In short, at the time Fielding got *Love in Several Masques* accepted for production at Drury Lane, he could not have supposed that he would be able to make his living in the theatre. The prospects were not so much precarious as non-existent.

IV. *LOVE IN SEVERAL MASQUES*

Given the difficulties under which any would-be playwright laboured in 1727, we must feel some surprise that Fielding managed to get his first play produced. About Fielding himself at this time we know precious little.[73] We can, however, enquire how he got his play staged, what sort of work it is, and what promise it offered.

We know virtually nothing of Fielding's life between November 1725 (when he attempted to elope with Sarah Andrew from Lyme Regis) and 29 January 1728 (when his satiric poem *The Masquerade* was published).[74] Cross speculates that Fielding came to London at some time during 1726 (at the age of 19), and that he spent the theatre season of 1726–27 'nibbling, as his grandmother would wish, at the law'.[75] This is as plausible as it is unprovable. We have no reason to believe that Fielding felt any urgent need to earn his living. At the time of the Lyme Regis episode he had been able to employ a valet. We may suppose that he was receiving an allowance, either from his father or from his grandmother.

Knowing something of the theatre, and lacking biographical evidence, we must presume that like other authors of the 1720s Fielding wrote his first play as a gentleman amateur. We know that it received its première on 16 February 1728 at Drury Lane (sixteen

[73] As this study makes no pretensions to being a biography, I feel no obligation to review the scanty but familiar facts of Fielding's early life. Martin Battestin's long-awaited biography will unquestionably be definitive for our time, and I am indebted to Professor Battestin for advice and assistance on various matters of biographical fact and interpretation. For standard information and speculation, I have drawn principally on Cross, Dudden, and Rogers.

[74] Publication was advertised for this date in the *Craftsman* of 27 Jan. 1728. We do know that Fielding apparently published a pair of poems in honour of George II's coronation and birthday: they were advertised in the *Daily Post* and *Daily Journal* on 10 Nov. 1727. This fact was first reported by Martin Battestin in 'Four New Fielding Attributions: His Earliest Satires of Walpole', *Studies in Bibliography*, 36 (1983), 70. No copy is known.

[75] Cross, I, 53, 55. Fielding's presence in London in Nov. 1726 is confirmed by evidence in PRO KB 10/19, Part I (Michaelmas 13 George I), recently discovered by Martin Battestin ('Four New Fielding Attributions', p. 74 n.). Fielding was accused of assault.

nights into the spectacular first run of *The Beggar's Opera* at Lincoln's Inn Fields), and that it survived only four nights.[76] Beyond this, almost all our information comes from the author's dedication and preface to the printed edition. The dedication is addressed 'To the Right Honourable the Lady Mary Wortley Mountague' (Fielding's second cousin, though he does not say so). In the midst of the usual panegyrical rhetoric, two passages seem significant. Fielding says, 'I wou'd not insinuate to the World that this Play past free from your Censure; since I know it not free from Faults, not one of which escaped your immediate Penetration.'[77] And Fielding begs leave 'to give a Sanction to this Comedy, by informing the World that its Representation was twice honoured with your Ladyship's Presence'. From these innocuous passages Wilbur Cross draws some rather excessive conclusions about Lady Mary's part in the venture. 'She read the sketch of his comedy in manuscript, suggested changes, and encouraged him to complete it. Largely if not entirely through her influence it reached the stage.'[78] Fielding does say that the play 'arose from a Vanity, to which your Indulgence, on the first Perusal of it, gave Birth', which implies that Lady Mary read a rough draft for her young cousin.[79] That Lady Mary exercised significant influence in getting the piece staged is quite unlikely. She was not a professional playwright; nothing in her letters suggests theatrical involvements; and Drury Lane did not work that way. If gentry could get a work staged by dropping hints to management, many more new plays would have been on the boards. Lady Mary might have introduced Fielding

[76] The play was accepted for production at Drury Lane at least 5 months earlier. See the *British Journal* of 23 Sept. 1727, where it is included in a list of new works to be produced at Drury Lane during the next season. (For this reference I am indebted to the kindness of Martin Battestin.)

[77] Citations are to the Watts edn. of 1728.

[78] Cross, I, 58. Both Dudden ('It was doubtless owing to a strong hint from this great lady that Cibber and Wilks, patentees of Drury Lane, consented to accept the piece' (I, 22)) and Rogers (p. 27) paraphrase this account. So does Robert Halsband, *The Life of Lady Mary Wortley Montagu* (Oxford, 1956), pp. 128–9, who cites Dudden, but adds no fresh evidence. The notion that Lady Mary 'corrected' the play may be based on confusion with Fielding's thanks to Anne Oldfield for corrections (noted below). The notion of Lady Mary's intercession with the managers seems to be founded on no definite evidence whatsoever.

[79] One possibly relevant piece of evidence is Fielding's letter to Lady Mary (dated only 'Wednesday Evening') referring to her having read 3 acts of one of his plays the previous spring. This letter has usually been associated—wrongly, in my opinion—with *The Modern Husband*. For discussion, see ch. 3, p. 121 n. 30, below. This letter could, however, refer to any of several plays, including *Love in Several Masques*.

to one of the managers (if she knew any of them), or to someone who could do so, but we must assume that Fielding's script was produced because the managers liked it well enough to accept it.

The play is not, in truth, very good, and if it had been written by James Moore Smythe or Leonard Welsted (who were writing comedies of similar merit at about this time), it would have had short shrift from modern commentators. The eye of hindsight can detect promise, but not much of it. What Fielding wrote was a rather overstuffed and very lightweight intrigue comedy. The design is clumsy. Fielding offers three minimally intertwined love plots: (1) Wisemore, a serious-minded lover, finally wins Lady Matchless, a beautiful and wealthy widow; (2) Merital, a dashing and virtuous but impecunious young lover, successfully woos Helena, ward to the foolish Sir Positive Trap; (3) Malvil, a passionate but overly jealous young lover, is united to Vermilia. Three 'rivals' are provided: Lord Formal, the fop Rattle, and Sir Apish Simple. The only blocking figure is Sir Positive Trap, a comic booby, though Lady Trap (an amorous older woman) and the maid Catchit supply complications. All of these characters are comedy stereotypes, and thin ones at that. The principal shortcoming, however, lies in Fielding's failure to create sufficient obstacles for his young lovers to overcome. Sir Positive takes precious little outwitting; Lady Matchless is free to marry whom she pleases; and Vermilia could choose to accept Malvil at any time. A more skilful writer would have created at least pro forma tensions in each plot line. Helena could be much more beleaguered; the rivals could be made more formidable; Malvil might have been subjected to a serious 'test'. Fielding brings good humour to his confection, but displays little aptitude for the taut construction and suspense necessary for effective intrigue comedy, which was not to be his comic *métier*.

Granting the mediocrity of the play, we may enquire where Fielding took his models and ask what he had in mind. Here the biographers have been misleading or worse. Cross informs us that *Love in Several Masques* 'is a comedy of intrigue' (which is accurate), but then adds 'built on the lines of Congreve' (which is not). Dudden, paraphrasing Cross for the worse as he so often does, calls it 'a comedy of manners, tempered with an infusion of "humours" . . . obviously an imitation of the work of Congreve'.[80] Not so: though Fielding dabbles inexpertly in

[80] Cross, I, 62–3; Dudden, I, 22.

repartee, his play is humane comedy, not satire, and his generic affinities are closer to Centlivre and Cibber than to Congreve.

If we scan the repertory of 1726–27 and the early autumn of 1727 to see where Fielding might have been getting ideas, the obvious plays are Centlivre's *The Busie Body* (1709), Cibber's *The Double Gallant* (1707), Vanbrugh's *The Confederacy* and *The Mistake* (both 1705), Farquhar's *The Constant Couple* (1699), Steele's *The Funeral* (1701), Welsted's *The Dissembled Wanton* (1726), and Christopher Bullock's *Woman is a Riddle* (1716). Fielding's play is less rakish than Farquhar's, and far less biting than Vanbrugh's *Confederacy*. Fielding did not risk anything as touchy as Bullock's debauched gentlewoman. But in type and tone he is working in an established tradition. Bullock's play, revived occasionally in the 1720s but virtually unknown to modern scholars, makes a particularly good comparison. *Woman is a Riddle* is a talky intrigue comedy with a social flavour appropriate to its London setting. Like Fielding's first effort, it makes clumsy use of misdirected letters. As an actor, Bullock had the sense not to overstuff his plot, but several of the main characters could practically step from one play into the other. Following the 'double gallant' convention, Bullock gives us a gentleman of fortune and a younger brother 'of a small Fortune' (the romantic leads), Sir Amorous Vainwit (a wealthy fop), a rich young widow, a young lady of beauty and fortune, and the inevitable scheming maid—in this case, two of them. Mr Vulture is 'an Old Rich Litigious Stock-Jobber' (in place of Fielding's fatuous country squire), but the plot function thus filled is much the same.

My point is not that *Love in Several Masques* is specifically indebted to Bullock's play, or to any of the others, but that Fielding was working in a standard generic mode. His first play is an imitative exercise in a popular form, not an attempt to write a Congrevean throw-back. Fielding's prologue ('Occasioned by this Comedy's succeeding . . . the *Provok'd Husband*') displays his awareness of how far short he fell of Vanbrugh and Cibber as a writer of comedy, let alone social comedy. Cross suggests, misleadingly, that 'In giving final form to his comedy, Fielding was . . . considerably influenced by "The Provoked Husband".' But given the lead time required by the theatre, this is virtually impossible. The parallels in 'the town lady, the country gentleman, and ladies in masque' that Cross points out are evidence of reliance on comic formula, not of specific indebtedness.

Fielding's claim in the prologue to present 'Light, Airy Scenes . . . free from an indecent Flame' is fair enough. Merital's encounter with

Lady Trap in the dark (43 ff.) is as close as Fielding comes to using the devices of sex comedy, and he makes plain from the outset of that scene that Merital recognizes the aunt and has not the slightest interest in taking advantage of the opportunity she offers him. *Love in Several Masques* is indeed a chaste entertainment. The degree to which all of Fielding's lovers are men of sense is apparent in their rhetoric. We cannot be surprised to find Wisemore spouting pieties ('Fortune . . . can never raise my Love' (50)), but even Merital proceeds to do so ('I am guilty of undeserved Reproaches, . . . Yet, impute what I have said to the Sincerity of my Love' (68)). In the tradition of the 'double gallant' design, Merital should be the wild young man who talks like a libertine and reforms when he wins his heiress. In this instance he is depressingly blameless from the outset and apparently has always been so.

Fielding claims satiric intention in his prologue, but Lord Formal, Rattle, Sir Apish, Sir Positive, and Lady Trap are all comic grotesques of a completely standard kind, and are presented without real bite. Fielding's idea of dramatic satire is entirely conventional. Thus Sir Positive reflects of his ward: 'I must sell her soon, or she will go off but as a piece of Second-hand Goods' (26). A wiser writer would have realized that this hoary crack comes better from the mouth of a city merchant than from a country squire. Fielding's picture of Lord Formal is mildly amusing but hardly satire. When Dudden informs us that Lord Formal is 'plagiarized from Vanbrugh's Lord Foppington' (in *The Relapse*), he is wildly off the mark. Foppington is monstrously affected, but he is also smart, tough, and dangerous—a genuinely unpleasant and threatening character who is quite willing to let his younger brother starve. Lord Formal is a stock butt, and a rather pallid one at that.

Comparison with something like Vanbrugh's *The Confederacy* instantly makes plain the degree to which Fielding's first effort is infused with a genial tolerance for its characters. Vanbrugh's harsh view of his money-lenders Gripe and Moneytrap and their pretentious wives, and his tough-minded realism about human nature, give *The Confederacy* an edge that *Love in Several Masques* simply does not have. The plays are alike in the farcicality of their intrigues, but one cannot imagine Vanbrugh concluding with Fielding's tag moral:

> . . . when the Men of Sense their Passions prove,
> You seldom fail rewarding 'em with Love:

Justly on them, the Fair their Hearts bestow,
Since they, alone, the Worth of virtue know.

Fielding always sympathized with young prodigals, but from the start his commitment is to the 'man of sense', not to the rake. In this respect, Fielding is part of the 'humane comedy' tradition, and to see him as the direct inheritor of Congreve and Vanbrugh is to ignore twenty-five years of change in English comedy.

The greatest virtue of Fielding's play is the vehicles it offers the principal actors. Because Fielding is working in clichés, he contrives parts squarely in the 'lines' favoured by Drury Lane's most prominent performers. Merital is the sort of dashing young man that Robert Wilks played many times over each season. Wisemore is the more serious-minded hero in which Wilks's good friend John Mills had long specialized. Rattle is a fop perfectly fitted to Colley Cibber's talents. Lady Matchless is a good display piece for Anne Oldfield, a specialist in captivating beauties. These were, of course, four of the most celebrated living actors. The rest of the cast was also exceptionally strong. Mrs Porter as Vermilia and Mrs Booth as Helena were front-line performers. John Harper—whom we will encounter in 1733 as a conspicuous figure in the actor rebellion—was a distinguished Falstaff and a splendid enactor of country squires like Sir Positive Trap. Bridgwater as Malvil and Josias Miller as Sir Apish were the very best of the company's secondary actors.

Love in Several Masques appears to have been neither a success nor a fiasco. Fielding says cheerfully in his preface that 'the Play was received with greater Satisfaction than I should have promised myself from its Merit', but its demise after four nights is a clear sign that no profit could be expected the sixth night. Fielding was politic enough to thank his principals graciously in the preface. He praises Wilks and Cibber for their performances, and specifically acknowledges 'their civil and kind Behaviour' as managers. Mrs Oldfield he commends even more effusively, both for her portrayal of Lady Matchless and for 'her excellent Judgment, shewn in some Corrections, which I shall, for my own Sake, conceal'.

Love in Several Masques is interesting because it is Fielding's, but it was essentially an imitative venture taking him in the wrong direction. He was spectacularly lucky to have it performed at Drury Lane, but that production no more implied that he could support himself in the theatre than the publication of a first novel by a major publishing house would augur subsistence for life today—in fact, rather less so. All of Fielding's biographers to date have commented on his 'sudden shift' from playwright to student of letters at the University of Leyden, where he enrolled on 16 March 1728.[81] But here again we have dubious supposition built upon particular fact.

We do not know when Fielding decided to go to Leyden. If Cross is correct that the academic year there commenced on 8 February ('the birthday of the university'), then we might guess that Fielding had intended to matriculate rather earlier than he actually arrived, but was delayed by his desire to see his play performed. If so, the unexpectedly long run of *The Provok'd Husband* significantly retarded his arrival. Whether Fielding grew tired of his life in town (or of studying law?), or was leading too riotous a life for the liking of his family, or recognized that he should take some step towards a career, we do not know. Whatever the reason for his enrolling at Leyden, one can readily imagine his father or his grandmother yielding to his entreaties to be allowed to remain in London until his play had been performed. We must regard that play, however, as the diversion of a gentleman amateur. Certainly, Fielding could have had no realistic hope of ever supporting himself as a playwright when he left London in March 1728.

[81] Cross, I, 65–6; Dudden, I, 24–5; Rogers, pp. 28–9.

2

The Young Playwright, 1729–1731

WHY Fielding returned to London to try to earn his living as a writer, we do not know. Arthur Murphy claims that the cause was the discontinuance of a £200 per annum allowance from Fielding's father.[1] All biographers quote Lady Mary Wortley Montagu's comment that Fielding 'was to be pity'd at his first entrance into the World, having no choice (as he said himselfe) but to be a Hackney Writer or a Hackney Coachman'.[2] This is a fine witticism but biographically suspect. That Edmund Fielding left the allowance for anybody to pay who would—as his son is said to have joked—is not hard to believe,[3] and Martin Battestin's forthcoming biography presents proof that Fielding was sued for debt while he was at Leyden. But whether his departure from the university was an instance of Johnsonian poverty is to be doubted.

The facts are sparse. Fielding re-registered at Leyden on 22 February 1729 (late again—perhaps reluctant?), after which there is no further record of him. Dudden says that he left at the end of a term in August 1729, but this is mere conjecture.[4] *The Temple Beau* was produced at Goodman's Fields on 26 January 1730, apparently after a refusal at Drury Lane, which implies that Fielding was in town no later than the beginning of November. We have to wonder if Fielding deliberately abandoned Leyden and other sober prospects in order to go his own way. He was too well connected to become a hackney coachman except by choice. But between February 1728 and the autumn of 1729, the prospects of making one's way as a hackney playwright had improved considerably. Whether Fielding recognized the change and coolly calculated the risks, or simply abandoned

1 Arthur Murphy, 'An Essay on the Life and Genius of Henry Fielding, Esq;', prefixed to his edn. of Fielding's *Works* (London, 1762), I, 8, 10. Fielding's father married his third wife early in 1729 (see the *Daily Post* for 13 January), an event that may have affected his son's finances.

2 *The Complete Letters of Lady Mary Wortley Montagu*, ed. Robert Halsband, 3 vols. (Oxford, 1965–67), III, 66 (23 July 1754).

3 Murphy, I, 10.

4 Dudden, I, 27.

Leyden in disgust and took his chances, we cannot determine on the present evidence. In either case, he returned to a London where radically altered theatrical circumstances presented an opportunity he could exploit to the utmost.

I. THEATRICAL CONDITIONS IN LONDON, 1728–1730

The season of 1727–28 had opened without any sign that it would differ notably from the dozen that preceded it. The two companies alternated politely until the coronation of George II (11 October), an event that brought the *beau monde* to town earlier than usual and made daily performances worth while. The overall repertory patterns continued what we saw in 1726–27. Drury Lane mounted sixty-three plays (three of them new) in 188 nights. Of the sixty revived plays, only six had not been performed there in 1726–27—that is, fifty-four were carried over. At Lincoln's Inn Fields, fifty-nine plays (two of them new) were mounted in 194 nights, but eighteen of the revivals (totalling thirty-five nights) were not in the 1726–27 repertory.[5] Sixteen plays (totalling sixty-five nights) appeared in both companies' repertories. As in the previous season, the offerings were heavily weighted towards older plays.

These figures effectively mask the startling developments of the season. On 10 January Drury Lane opened the Vanbrugh–Cibber *Provok'd Husband*, which ran an astonishing twenty-eight times in succession, and another nine times later during the season. Seventeen days into the initial run, Lincoln's Inn Fields opened *The Beggar's Opera*, which ran thirty-two times without interruption and might have gone longer had it not extended into the benefit season. The total of sixty-two performances at Lincoln's Inn Fields this season was unprecedented in the history of the London theatre.

The success of *The Beggar's Opera* demonstrated conclusively that London had a large, hitherto almost untapped audience. The play pulled into the theatre not only a multitude of repeat attenders but also a large group of potential and occasional theatre-goers who could perhaps be induced to attend regularly. But how? Neither management had ever been disposed to engage in aggressive promotion. Each had been content to make moderate profits with an ultra-conservative repertory policy that attracted a solid cadre of regular theatre-goers.

[5] Many of these revivals were for benefit performances.

The key question in the spring of 1728 was whether Drury Lane and Lincoln's Inn Fields would change their stodgy ways. Neither company moved vigorously. Drury Lane seems initially to have viewed *The Beggar's Opera* as a kind of freak misfortune that would run its course. At Lincoln's Inn Fields, John Rich simply settled down to enjoy his golden goose without much thought for the morrow.

The Challenge of the Little Haymarket

The first sign that someone was prepared to capitalize aggressively on the situation created by the triumph of *The Beggar's Opera* is a pirate production at the Little Haymarket. During the season of 1727–28 the theatre was occupied by Signora Violante, whose troupe offered everything from acrobatics and rope-dancing to a pantomime called *The Rivals*. A hint of a more direct kind of competition for the patent theatres was the première of John Mottley and Thomas Cooke's *Penelope* on 8 May. This is the first of many imitations of *The Beggar's Opera*, a comic ballad opera of London low life. It survived only three nights. Starting in late May, a 'New Company of English Comedians' began to offer occasional performances of standard repertory pieces—*The Orphan*, *The Drummer*, *Tamerlane*, *The Spanish Fryar*, and *Richard III*. Summer performances of this sort were by no means unknown at the Little Haymarket, but late in June an extraordinary event occurred. For Monday 24 June 'a New Company who never appear'd on that Stage before' advertised *The Beggar's Opera* with 'All the Songs and Dances set to Musick, as it is perform'd at the Theatre in Lincoln's-Inn-Fields'. We have, unfortunately, no idea who managed this company or who its performers were. Lincoln's Inn Fields had given 'positively' its last performance of Gay's piece the previous Wednesday, and it offered only a very sketchy summer season. (Drury Lane offered none at all.) We do not know, for example, whether some of the summer performers at the Little Haymarket were moonlighting from Lincoln's Inn Fields. That Rich acquiesced in this transfer seems highly improbable: he had refused to let his performers use *The Beggar's Opera* for their benefits that spring, and the fifteen performances given this summer at the Little Haymarket suggest a distinctly profitable venture. Unless Rich was somehow getting a cut, this production represents the first major break in the *de facto* agreement to let each company retain exclusive rights to successful new plays.

The season of 1728–29 saw the two patent theatres operate pretty much as before in most respects, but it is remarkable for the appearance of full-fledged competition. For the first time since 1642, London had a third company of import. The Little Haymarket apparently operated only 115 nights (plus concerts) versus 195 for Drury Lane and 156 for Lincoln's Inn Fields. And it ran only twenty-three plays (versus sixty-eight and forty-nine respectively). But nobody could doubt that the Little Haymarket provided direct competition. Its first performance was *The Beggar's Opera* (8 October), a work already staged six times that autumn at its original Lincoln's Inn Fields venue, most recently only four days earlier. Rich would surely not have allowed this if he could have found any way to prevent it.

The repertory at the Little Haymarket for 1728–29 is an odd amalgam. The theatre offered single performances of such standard pieces as *The Recruiting Officer*, *Oroonoko*, *The Beaux Stratagem*, and *Tamerlane*, and offered two and three performances of others (*The Spanish Fryar*, *The Orphan*, *Venice Preserv'd*). It revived three pieces that had been out of the repertory ten to twenty years—*Don Carlos* (one night), *The Lunatick* (three), and *The Metamorphosis* (five). Some twenty-eight nights were occupied by old plays, and fifteen more by *The Beggar's Opera*. The rest of the season (more than 60 per cent of the nights) was devoted to new plays, singly and in combination. Ten new pieces (including afterpieces) were staged there, three of them major successes. *The Humours of Harlequin* (twenty-six performances) was merely the sort of thing that John Rich prospered on. But Coffey's *The Beggar's Wedding* (thirty-four performances) was a successful follow-up on Gay's ballad opera form, and Samuel Johnson of Cheshire's *Hurlothrumbo* (thirty-three performances) was a wonderful piece of satiric nonsense.[6]

Against this innovative fare, Drury Lane and Lincoln's Inn Fields ran pretty much their usual mixture. Drury Lane tried only two new mainpieces; Lincoln's Inn Fields, three. Drury Lane had, however, clearly been traumatized by *The Beggar's Opera*. Both of its new mainpieces were ambitious ballad operas, and their failure must have been a decided disappointment. Cibber's *Love in a Riddle* was damned by faction in two nights (though cut down as *Damon and Phillida*, it was to enjoy a long stage history); Charles Johnson's *The Village Opera*

[6] The other new plays were Mottley's *The Craftsman* (6 performances), *The Quaker's Opera* (4), *The Lottery* (6), *The Royal Captives* (1; lost), Odell's *The Smugglers* and *The Patron* (1), and Cibber's *Damon and Phillida* (2—but later a successful afterpiece for many seasons). *Damon* was an afterpiece adaptation of a Drury Lane mainpiece.

lasted only four. A ballad-opera afterpiece, *The Lover's Opera*, had a slow start but did enter the repertory. Drury Lane's one major success this season was *Perseus and Andromeda*, a fancy pantomime performed more than forty times. By way of competition Lincoln's Inn Fields proved remarkably conservative. Its three new mainpieces were all tragedies: Richard Barford's *The Virgin Queen* and Eliza Haywood's *Frederick, Duke of Brunswick-Lunenburgh* are heroic-conspiracy pieces that lasted only three nights apiece; Samuel Madden's *Themistocles*, a rather turgid patriot drama, managed nine. A ballad-opera afterpiece, *Hob's Opera*, usually known as *Flora*, became a great favourite—a musical version of Doggett's long-popular *Hob*. But the successful experimentation in 1728–29 was carried out at the Little Haymarket.

The Little Haymarket is, of course, of particular interest to us because Fielding staged so many of his plays there. For new and experimental work, it offered a venue that had been lacking in London for many years. In times of hot competition (1695–1700, for example), Drury Lane and Lincoln's Inn Fields had staged many new plays, but never before had a London theatre made new plays so important a part of its offerings. The exact nature of the Little Haymarket's management and *modus operandi* present some questions and puzzles (to be taken up in section III below), but its offerings in 1728–29 were an extremely encouraging signal to aspiring playwrights.

The Advent of Goodman's Fields

In October 1729 Thomas Odell opened yet another theatre in a converted workshop in Ayliffe Street, Goodman's Fields.[7] Many of the performers were drawn from personnel who had worked at the Little Haymarket in 1728–29. But whereas the Little Haymarket competed with the patent companies by presenting a significantly different repertory, Goodman's Fields competed by means of a different location, aiming to draw a 'city' audience for whom the West End theatres were relatively remote. As we will see, Goodman's Fields had only a tepid interest in mounting new plays, and after February 1730 Fielding apparently had no dealings with its management. None the less, it has special relevance for us because it represented a stable, profitable, non-patent venture that started from scratch and competed

[7] Scholarship on Goodman's Fields remains scanty. The study most often cited, Frederick T. Wood's 'Goodman's Fields Theatre', *Modern Language Review*, 25 (1930), 443–56, is marred by some serious errors and has been entirely superseded by the introduction and calendar in Part 3 of *The London Stage*.

successfully with the giants. When Fielding conceived his plans for his own theatre company, he must inevitably have looked to Goodman's Fields for proof that his scheme was practicable. If Odell could fit out a theatre, and Henry Giffard could run it so successfully that he was able to get financing for a new and better building (as he did in 1732), then Fielding could hope to do the same.

Goodman's Fields did not open without opposition. Odell had no patent or licence; he simply readied his premises, hired a company, and began to give performances.[8] Even before the theatre opened, its city neighbours were protesting vigorously at the intrusion of such an enticement to vice and debauchery into a sober business district. The *London Gazette* of 11–14 October 1729 printed a formal notice (dated from 'Whitechappel Court-House', 7 October) that 'great Numbers of Gentlemen and substantial Merchants and Tradesmen residing in and near' Ayliffe Street, Goodman's Fields, 'have applied to His Majesty's Justices of the Peace . . . and set forth to them the evil Consequences' of permitting the erection of such a playhouse. The justices reportedly agreed to take all possible measures 'to prevent so great a Mischief'. Despite such opposition, Goodman's Fields duly opened on 31 October 1729. That Odell could defy the local authorities is interesting; that the Lord Chamberlain and the Master of the Revels took no action is even more so. This was by no means the end of the matter, but we may deduce that the regulatory powers applicable to an unlicensed non-patent theatre were either non-existent or legally so unclear as to be ineffective.

On 30 November the Reverend Arthur Bedford—long a fiery opponent of the London theatre—preached at St Butolph's, Aldgate, against the incursion of this evil.[9] Bedford's sermon was merely a predictable moral diatribe. A more serious effort to rouse opposition appears in an anonymous pamphlet, *A Letter to the Right Honourable Sir Richard Brocas, Lord Mayor of London*, probably the work of Bishop Francis Hare.[10] The author denies that he considers all plays 'criminal', but indulges in a good deal of fulmination against 'modern

[8] *The London Stage* suggests that Odell 'obtained Letters Patent' (Part 3, I, xxi), but this assertion is founded on Watson Nicholson's extrapolation from a puff in *The Coffee-House Morning Post* of 24 Sept. 1729. I can find no evidence that Odell actually had any sort of operating authority, or that Giffard ever obtained any.

[9] Printed as *A Sermon preached . . . on Sunday the thirtieth day of November . . . Occasioned by the erecting of a play-house in the neighbourhood* (London, 1730). Arnott and Robinson, no. 377.

[10] (London, 1730), pp. 3, 5, 6, 8, 11, 21, 30. Arnott and Robinson, no. 158.

Plays' and particularly their contemptuous treatment of marriage and religion. The basic argument, however, is economic and social. The author undertakes to prove that a playhouse catering to the lower-class workers in a manufacturing and commercial district is a significant financial drain on the health of the kingdom—causing, he claims, a minimum loss of £300,000 per annum. His method of calculation will not bear serious scrutiny, but the tactic is interesting: an appeal to men of the city in economic rather than moral terms. Unlike Bedford, the author had the sense to direct his fire solely against Goodman's Fields. He admits that the legal issues are 'doubtful', but argues that the Lord Mayor and other city authorities should not allow the establishment of so great an evil to 'be past over in Silence'. Goodman's Fields is, he grants, 'not in your *immediate Jurisdiction*, but lies a little (and a very little it is) beyond the Liberties'. But, he asks, 'if Goods infected with the *Plague* had been lodged at a much *greater Distance* . . . would the Magistrates of the City have been unconcerned . . . ?'

This appeal had no immediately visible public effect, but by April 1730 the city authorities had mounted a concerted effort to get Goodman's Fields suppressed. On 7 April the Court of Aldermen dispatched Sir Gilbert Heathcote to ask the assistance of Lord Townshend, and a week later he reported that both Townshend and Walpole had promised to help.[11] On 28 April a printed petition was presented to the King on behalf of the Lord Mayor and Aldermen,[12] and the *Weekly Journal or British Gazetteer* of 2 May (which printed the petition) reported 'His Majesty's most Gracious Answer' that 'you may depend upon my complying with what you, with so much Reason and Justice, desire of me upon this Occasion.' On the same day the petition was presented, the Lord Chamberlain issued a peremptory order silencing Goodman's Fields.[13]

Why this did not put an end to the theatre we do not know. The *Grub-street Journal* of 7 May summarized the petition and the King's reply, and reported that 'Yesterday Mr. Odell, Master of the new Play-house in Goodman's-fields, waited on his Majesty at Court, begging

[11] Corporation of London Record Office, Repertories, Court of Aldermen, vol. 134 (1729–30), pp. 216, 232, 250, 262, 263–5. Discussed by Liesenfeld, pp. 16, 198, n. 29.

[12] PRO LC 7/3, fol. 28 (undated; misdated '1729' in MS on the verso). A draft dated 21 April in the Corporation of London Record Office, Misc. MSS 7.5, contains a cancelled phrase: 'to Cause an Inquiry to be made concerning such Licence'. The Court of Aldermen had evidently discovered that there was no licence to investigate.

[13] PRO LC 5/160, p. 130.

his Majesty's royal leave for continuing plays to be acted as usual; but we hear his Majesty was not pleased to grant his request.' The King's apparent refusal notwithstanding, Goodman's Fields was back in business on 11 May after being dark less than two weeks. The newspapers are frustratingly silent about this surprising reversal. The only explanation is Henry Giffard's, who says in 1735 that 'Mr. *Odell* took the Opinions of several of the most eminent Lawyers, concerning the said Order, and the Legality of the said Theatre; who having advised, that the said Mr. *Odell* had *a Right by the Law of the Land*, to proceed in his said Undertaking, he continued to carry on the Business.'[14] My best guess is that the Crown's legal advisers could find no sufficient ground or precedent for royal intervention. Odell was evidently worried enough to seek a less controversial venue. The *Grub-street Journal* of 6 August 1730 reports that 'Mr. Odell, Master of Goodman's-fields play-house, hath took a lease for 14 years of a piece of ground near Tottenham-court turnpike; upon which he has begun to build a play-house 70 foot in length.' This venture must have been quickly dropped, since Goodman's Fields reopened on 16 September. Perhaps Odell—who had friends in the government, and was subsequently to become Deputy Examiner of Plays—managed to pull some strings.[15] The whole episode of the failed suppression of Goodman's Fields is curious. But whatever the means by which Odell survived this threat to the theatre's existence, his success was a sign that others might hope to follow in his footsteps.

Of the first Goodman's Fields theatre itself, we know practically nothing, and certainly not size or capacity. If we hypothesize that Odell would not have set out to build a smaller theatre in Tottenham-Court Fields, then we may suppose its total length was no more than 70 feet, which might imply a capacity of around 500 spectators. What we know of the venture's finances is, ironically, almost entirely derived from *A Letter to . . . Sir Richard Brocas*. 'And as this new House has *succeeded* so well, if that should continue unmolested, we shall in all likelihood, soon see it followed by *many more*. The Success of this promises a large Increase; for if I am rightly informed, tho' their

[14] *The Case of Henry Giffard* (1735), a protest against the Barnard Playhouse Bill. BL 11795.k.31(9). Printed by Liesenfeld, pp. 168–9.

[15] Less than a month after his rebuff by the King, the *Universal Spectator* of 27 June reported that 'Thomas Odell, Esq; Master of the New Theatre in Goodman's-Fields, hath been at Windsor to obtain Leave to bring his Company of Comedians down thither to perform Plays during the Court's Stay at Windsor; and we hear he hath succeeded therein.'

Expences don't exceed Sixteen Pounds, yet they have never acted one Night under Fifty Pounds, usually above Sixty.'[16] Although *The London Stage* cites this passage without any caveat as evidence of the expenses and profits of Goodman's Fields, we must beware of uncritical acceptance of these figures. Goodman's Fields had probably been in operation less than two months when the *Letter* was written, and audiences that flock to see a novelty may fall off quickly. Far more worrisome is the figure of £16 for 'Expences', which is hardly credible when the constant charge at the patent theatres was approximately three times this sum. We may be sure that at Goodman's Fields the building cost, actor salaries, and incidental expenses were all lower—but hardly that much lower. The figure £16 per day might plausibly cover salaries to actors and support personnel. If we look at figures from other theatres in the mid-eighteenth century, we find that the percentage of total budget devoted to actors' and musicians' salaries ran anything from 45 to 68 per cent.[17] Without any way of judging 'incident charge' and the cost of new productions, we cannot estimate total expenses with any assurance, but £25–£30 is a reasonable estimate for constant charge. As to receipts: Goodman's Fields advertised prices of 3*s*. for boxes, 2*s*. for the pit, and 1*s*. for gallery seats (versus 4*s*., 2*s*. 6*d*., 1*s*. 6*d*., and 1*s*. at the patent theatres, which had two galleries). If we assume a capacity of 500 (250 in the boxes, 150 in the pit, 100 in the gallery), the maximum gross would be £57 10*s*. Allowing for a few more seats, the revenues reported in the *Letter* are possible. And if average attendance were 75 per cent of capacity (higher than the patent theatres achieved), we might hypothesize a typical gross of £45. If the constant charge were £30, incident charge £5, and new productions budgeted at £750 for a season, then in 140 nights (disregarding forty benefits) the proprietor might gross £6,300, spend £5,650, and come out with a very tidy £650 profit. Obviously these figures are both hypothetical and arbitrary. If we assumed attendance at 65 per cent of capacity (£39 per night), and a constant charge of only £25, the net profit would still be £510. Even if this were a shade optimistic, we can easily see why such figures would seem attractive to a playwright uncomfortably dependent on the vagaries of managers and benefit nights.

To rely uncritically on the figures given in *A Letter to . . . Sir Richard*

[16] *A Letter to . . . Sir Richard Brocas*, pp. 28–9.

[17] See Judith Milhous, 'Company Management', *The London Theatre World*, p. 23 (Table 2).

Brocas would be foolish. But extrapolating and cross-checking as I have done here, we certainly get a sense of a potentially profitable venture. The best proof that Goodman's Fields was indeed profitable is that after just two seasons Henry Giffard was able to raise the capital to erect a new and better theatre for the venture, and to do so from hard-headed city merchants expecting to make a profit on their money. But this is getting ahead of our story.

II. FIELDING'S APPRENTICESHIP

When Fielding returned to London in the summer or autumn of 1729 he evidently brought with him three plays or drafts of plays. These were *Don Quixote in England* (refused at Drury Lane, and not staged until 1734), *The Wedding-Day* (refused by John Rich, and not staged until Garrick mounted it in 1743), and *The Temple Beau* (produced at Goodman's Fields in January 1730). Practically everything we know of the early history of these three plays must be deduced from Fielding's prefaces concerning the first two (written and published years later) and James Ralph's prologue for the third. These sources leave some blanks, but the general picture is clear enough.

Fielding's second attempt at writing for the stage was evidently *Don Quixote in England*. His preface to the 1734 edition includes a full and circumstantial account of its early history.

> This Comedy was begun at *Leyden* in the Year 1728, and after it had been sketched out into a few loose Scenes, was thrown by, and for a long while no more thought of. It was originally writ for my private Amusement; as it would indeed have been little less than Quixotism itself to hope any other Fruits from attempting Characters wherein the inimitable *Cervantes* so far excelled. The Impossibility of going beyond, and the extreme Difficulty of keeping pace with him, were sufficient to infuse Despair into a very adventurous Author.
>
> I soon discovered too, that my too small Experience in, and little Knowledge of the World, had led me into an Error. I soon found it infinitely more difficult than I imagined, to vary the Scene, and give my Knight an Opportunity of displaying himself in a different manner from that wherein he appears in the Romance. Human Nature is every where the same. And the Modes and Habits of particular Nations do not change it enough, sufficiently to distinguish a *Quixote* in *England* from a *Quixote* in *Spain*.
>
> In these Sentiments Mr. *Booth* and Mr. *Cibber* concurred with me, who, upon seeing the aforesaid Sketch, both dissuaded me from suffering it to be represented on the Stage; and accordingly it was remanded back to my Shelf, where, probably, it would have perished in Oblivion, had not the Solicitations

of the distrest Actors in *Drury-Lane* prevail'd on me to revise it, at the same time that it came into my Head to add those Scenes concerning our Elections.[18]

I see no reason to doubt that the play was begun in 1728 for Fielding's 'private Amusement'; that Wilks and Cibber rejected it politely; or that Fielding revised it and added the election material when Highmore's actors begged him for a new play in 1733–34. If Fielding was honest about his own doubt of the play's merits, he may well not have offered it to any other manager in 1729.

Of the early history of *The Wedding-Day* we know no more than Fielding tells us in his preface to the *Miscellanies* in 1743.

It was the third Dramatic Performance I ever attempted; the Parts of *Millamour* and *Charlotte* being originally intended for Mr. *Wilks* and Mrs. *Oldfield*; but the latter died before it was finished; and a slight Pique which happened between me and the former, prevented him from ever seeing it. The Play was read to Mr. *Rich* upwards of twelve Years since, in the Presence of a very eminent Physician of this Age, who will bear me Testimony, that I did not recommend my Performance with the usual Warmth of an Author. Indeed I never thought, 'till this Season, that there existed on any one Stage, since the Death of that great Actor and Actress abovementioned, any two Persons capable of supplying their Loss in those Parts: for Characters of this Kind do, of all others, require most Support from the Actor, and lend the least Assistance to him.

From the Time of its being read to Mr. *Rich*, it lay by me neglected and unthought of, 'till this Winter. . . .[19]

This account makes *The Wedding-Day* Fielding's 'third Dramatic Performance' but implies that it was incomplete (or unpolished?) at the time of Anne Oldfield's death, 23 October 1730. Fielding's 'Pique' with Wilks was evidently the result of Drury Lane's refusal of *Don Quixote in England* and *The Temple Beau* in autumn 1729; and the performance of his *The Author's Farce* in the spring of 1730 certainly might have produced some coolness. Fielding's assertion that he then withheld the play until he had suitable performers for Millamour and Charlotte must be taken largely as a compliment to Garrick and Peg Woffington. Had Fielding believed in the piece, he would probably have tried it at Drury Lane in 1732 when Wilks and Jane Cibber were

[18] Quotations from *Don Quixote in England* are from the Watts edition of 1734.

[19] *Miscellanies*, vol. I, ed. Henry Knight Miller (Oxford, 1972), pp. 4–5.

available for the principal roles. Fielding's comment that he read the play to John Rich 'upwards of twelve Years since' fits well with his known flirtation with Rich in December 1730.

If *The Wedding-Day* was indeed Fielding's 'third' play, then his fourth, *The Temple Beau*, was brought to completion first. Fielding is silent about its fortunes, but James Ralph's prologue is suggestive. After expressing the wish that players might starve 'as *Authors* do', it continues

> But, if the gay, the courtly World disdain
> To hear the *Muses* and their Sons complain;
> Each injur'd Bard shall to this Refuge fly,
> And find that Comfort, which the Great deny:
> Shall frequently employ this Infant Stage,
> And boldly aim to wake a dreaming Age.

Complaining that 'Merit . . . is rarely found . . . But when it blazes in the World's broad Eye', and asking the city audience to recognize it here, Ralph concludes:

> Convince that Town, which boasts its better Breeding,
> That Riches—are not all that you exceed in.
> Merit, where-ever found, is still the same,
> And this our Stage may be the Road to Fame.

This pretty clearly implies that the play had been refused elsewhere, presumably at Drury Lane, where Fielding had suffered a 'slight Pique' with the managers. Whether he then offered it to Lincoln's Inn Fields, we do not know, but he would have been foolish not to try, and Ralph's sour comment that '*Harlequin*'s the Darling of the Town' cannot be construed as a friendly reference to Rich.

Don Quixote in England and *The Wedding-Day*

Surveying the three plays, we are at some disadvantage in trying to see what sort of work Fielding was doing in 1729 because we cannot be certain how closely the texts we possess of *Don Quixote in England* and *The Wedding-Day* approximate to what Fielding originally wrote. Fielding admits to revisions and additions in the first case, and denies them in the second, though we know that the Licenser raised numerous objections to the manuscript submitted in 1743.[20]

[20] Comparison of the Larpent MS preserved in the Huntington Library (LA 39) with the text printed in 1743 shows that a substantial number of verbal changes were made

How close that manuscript was to the 1729 original, we cannot be certain.

Why Fielding set his hand to *Don Quixote in England* is hard to guess. The lack of a genuine plot structure got him in trouble right away—these are indeed 'loose Scenes'. Most of the fifteen songs are poorly integrated: they may represent either a youthful inclination to ride the coat-tails of *The Beggar's Opera* or a 1734 afterthought, but they do not work well in either case.[21] Fielding's plan seems to have been to combine Don Quixote as humours character with the sort of love-intrigue-in-an-inn plot used to such good effect in a work like Farquhar's *The Stage-Coach*. But the Don has no necessary function in the rest of the events, and the love intrigue is so slapdash as to be uninteresting. In theory, Dorothea is eloping with Fairlove so that her father, Sir Thomas Loveland, cannot force her to marry the egregious Squire Badger. But Sir Thomas is a good fellow, easily persuaded to accept his daughter's choice after he meets the drunken and ignorant Badger ('your Daughter, Sir, is a Son of a Whore' (59)). Don Quixote's presence is never explained. He says at the end that he has come to England in 'Search of Adventures . . . I was told there was a plenteous Stock of Monsters' (61). Despite his serious moral lecture on marriage (58), he is basically a clown. Sancho is the most effective and interesting character, though unfortunately his sarcastic remarks about his master are so effective that they undercut the Don's dignity:

My Master, the Knight of the Woful Figure (and a woful Figure he makes, sure enough) sends your Ladyship his humble Service, and hopes you will not take it amiss that he has not been able to knock all the People in the House on the Head; however, he has made it pretty well up in breaking the Windows; your Ladyship will lie pure and cool, for the Devil a whole Pane is there in all your Apartment; if the Glazier had hir'd him, he cou'd not have done better. (13)

If Fielding studied Thomas Durfey's *Don Quixote* plays (3 parts, 1694–95), he did not learn much from them. Durfey's first two parts are quite

for the sake of decorum, but that the basic structure of the play was allowed to stand. For a brief discussion of the changes imposed, see L. W. Conolly, *The Censorship of English Drama 1737–1824* (San Marino, 1976), pp. 140–4. The most significant alterations concern Millamour's 'reform' in Act V, which is significantly undercut in the Larpent MS version.

[21] Given the expert integration of songs and text Fielding achieved in *The Grub-Street Opera* in 1731 (and thereafter), I am inclined to think that the many inorganic songs in *Don Quixote in England* are evidence of early and inept imitation of Gay.

good, if one can accept the handling of the Don, and Parts 1 and 2 stayed in the repertory into the 1730s. Durfey's plays may have encouraged Fielding in his extensive use of songs, for Durfey makes marvellously effective use of music.[22] But Durfey handles his plot structures with the assurance of the veteran playwright, concocting a narrative interest the young Fielding simply could not achieve.

In *The Wedding-Day* Fielding evidently decided to return to the intrigue comedy mode and to tighten up his plot. He again employs the 'double gallant', using Millamour as pseudo-rake and Heartfort as sober gentleman. The beautiful Clarinda marries old Stedfast, but is found to be his daughter before they can consummate the marriage, and so she is freed to be awarded to the penitent Millamour. Heartfort gets his Charlotte. Much of the play concerns Stedfast and Mutable, opposing father-humours of an exaggerated sort. Stedfast never alters any decision and would rather have his dinner raw than later than he ordered it (50).[23] Old Mutable's mental gymnastics regarding which lady his son should marry are so extreme as to become silly rather than comic. The discovery that Clarinda is really Stedfast's daughter by Mrs Plotwell (80–1) seems an implausibly contrived way out of an artificial tangle. The play has an attractive energy, but again the characters are underdeveloped, the events awkwardly contrived, and the humours unreal.

Millamour is given lots of feminine entanglements and the sentiments of a rake. 'Women would be charming Things . . . if, like Cloathes, we could lay them by when we are weary of them; since, like Cloathes, we are often weary of them before they are worn out' (10). But when in Act V Heartfort reproaches him ('what Privilege dost thou perceive in thyself, to invade and destroy the Happiness of another?' (66)), Millamour repents spectacularly: 'now you begin to pierce to the Quick. . . . I have been in the wrong . . . how was it possible for me to be guilty of so much Barbarity?' (67). His unrepentance two pages later, and re-repentance four pages after that ('My Dear! my only Love! Too late I see the Follies of my Life. I see the fatal Consequence of my ungovern'd, lawless Passion' (73)) are, at best, implausible.

I cannot see that Fielding meant to burlesque reform comedy, but

[22] See Curtis Alexander Price, *Henry Purcell and the London Stage* (Cambridge, 1984), pp. 205–22.

[23] References are to Millar's separate edition of 1743, which does not differ substantively from vol. II of the 1743 *Miscellanies*.

neither was he writing it effectively. The tag-moral is totally unconvincing ('From my Example let all Rakes be taught, / To shun loose Pleasure's sweet, but pois'nous Draught . . .'). One can readily see why Fielding had no luck peddling this play in 1729 and 1730. A comment about his third night in 1743 is telling: 'Benefit the author of this bad new play, which would have sunk the 1st night but for Garrick's acting'.[24] About all we can say in the play's favour in the context of 1729 is that Fielding was obviously working to improve his plot cohesion.

The Temple Beau

By the time he wrote his second staged play, Fielding had begun to master the mechanics of intrigue comedy. The results are not wonderful, but they show distinctly more technical competence. Fielding still employs more characters than he can comfortably control (two father figures, four gallants, two older women, two younger women), but at least he involves them in related complications.

Wilding, the title character played by Henry Giffard, pretends to be a serious law student while actually living a riotous life. His doting father, Sir Harry, proud of his son's bills for 'Law-Books' and related expenses (£275 in the last quarter (9)),[25] walks into his chambers and finds only plays and Rochester's poems, whereupon he breaks into a locked box and finds a compromising love letter. The son glibly explains that he has moved, and that his father is guilty of breaking and entering—a capital offence. Poor Sir Harry is tricked out of a £500 annuity before he discovers the truth. This is a pleasant enough farce line. Most of the action, however, concerns the beautiful Bellaria. Sir Harry wants his scapegrace son to marry her; Sir Avarice Pedant orders his son, young Pedant, to do so under threat of disinheritance; Valentine falls for her and tries to engineer a breach with his betrothed, Clarissa, in order to woo her. She, however, loves the sober and virtuous Veromil (who has temporarily been cheated out of most of his fortune), and eventually he regains his money and his true love.

Fielding indulges his fondness for matched pairs of characters—a predilection that reappears in Thwackum and Square twenty years later. Sir Avarice contrasts with Sir Harry; rakish Wilding with sober

[24] Winston MS from Dyer's MS; reported in *The London Stage*, Part 3, II, 1036.
[25] Citations are to the Watts edition of 1730.

Veromil (the double gallant again, with Valentine an additional and rather unsatisfactory complexity). The most extended contrast, however, is between Lady Lucy Pedant (Sir Avarice's wife, but also a coquette) and her sister Lady Gravely (a pseudo-prude). Like Stedfast and Mutable in *The Wedding-Day*, they are mildly amusing but so overdrawn that they are completely unconvincing.

The play suffers from Fielding's over-elaboration of multiple intrigues and his difficulty in integrating his Temple beau with the romantic plot. Wilding's attempt to avert discovery by his father would have made a good two-act afterpiece, but since Fielding wisely chose not to try another reform *à la* Millamour, his title device remains obstinately irrelevant to his romantic structure. In these early plays Fielding's temperamental commitment to his 'sober' lover is obvious. The Veromil–Bellaria story is conceptually central to the play, but neither psychology nor plot is sufficiently developed to make the comedy a serious romance, despite the lovers' rhetoric ('Witness Heav'n I do pity you; and while I am rack'd with Torments of my own, I feel yours too. . . . Oh! thou art all Angel' (45)). Genuine blocking forces are entirely absent. Sir Avarice is merely a dogmatic figure of fun, and Sir Harry's good nature is so obvious that Fielding omits the obligatory reconciliation scene: 'Sir *Harry* is too good-humour'd a Man to be an Exception to the universal Satisfaction of a Company' (79).

Fielding had, however, learned some things by the time he wrote *The Temple Beau*. However awkwardly, he does connect the characters better than he had before, and his exposition is far more competent. Instead of using dialogue between characters who already know everything that must be communicated to the audience, Fielding creates a quarrel between Lady Lucy and Lady Gravely to give occasion for reproaches and references to previous events.[26] Compared with *Love in Several Masques*, there is much less straining after witty passages unconnected with the events in train. But to see more than a journeyman exercise in the piece would be a mistake. Winfield Rogers has argued that Fielding intended a serious ethical statement about pedantry of various sorts, adducing *Spectator* 105 as a source and claiming that in the figure of the pedant Fielding presents 'a symbol which has the power to express his attitude toward life'.[27]

[26] Pointed out by L. P. Goggin, 'Development of Techniques in Fielding's Comedies', *PMLA* 67 (1952), 769–81.

[27] Winfield H. Rogers, 'The Significance of Fielding's *Temple Beau*', *PMLA* 55 (1940), 440–4.

This claim cannot be taken very seriously. That the play is consonant with Fielding's later ethical outlook we may agree, but pedants had been stock butts in drama for many decades. Sir Avarice and young Pedant are less symbols than commonplaces, and to insist upon their thematic significance is to read literary seriousness into a formulaic romp.

How Fielding got *The Temple Beau* accepted at Goodman's Fields, or by whom, we do not know. It was the first new play staged there and it achieved a very respectable first run of nine nights (plus four more performances later in the season). The cast was quite solid. Henry Giffard, a newcomer to London, was a competent journeyman actor well equipped to take the title character. William Penkethman, jun. (Sir Harry Wilding) and William Bullock, jun. (Young Pedant) were good actors who had been lured away from Lincoln's Inn Fields. Fielding received benefits the third, sixth, and ninth nights—no doubt very welcome indeed if he had become entirely dependent on the theatre for his livelihood. But given the smallness of the theatre, his total earnings are unlikely to have amounted to more than about £100, even with a fairly full house at all three benefits. (A £55 house less £25 expenses would yield only £30.) Goodman's Fields apparently did not raise prices for a first run, and Fielding can hardly have had either the friends or the connections to peddle many tickets above face value. He must, nevertheless, have been well pleased. Despite rejection at Drury Lane (and very likely at Lincoln's Inn Fields), he had had another play produced, and the nine-night run implies a fair success.

In all four of his apprentice efforts, Fielding makes plain his devotion to 'the Success of Virtue, Constancy and Love', to quote Veromil's concluding speech in *The Temple Beau*. Fielding may have believed that this credo was what the audience really wanted, but the feebleness of his rakes suggests that it was his own preference. But he had not found a form to suit his talents. Intrigue comedy needs a plot tension Fielding was never to achieve. Even twenty years later in the well-plotted *Tom Jones*, there is never much concern about the outcome: the interest lies in the way the story is told. Fielding's humour characters are competent, but very formulaic and overdrawn. He had no special bent for romantic dialogue of the sort that might have let him write virtue-rewarded romance comedy. By the time of *The Temple Beau* he had learned the rudiments of intrigue-comedy technique, but no more than that. Fortunately for Fielding, he was about to venture into experiments that were to take him in more fruitful directions.[28]

III. THE NATURE OF THE LITTLE HAYMARKET THEATRE

Our next record of Fielding is the première of *The Author's Farce* at the Little Haymarket on 30 March 1730. Two questions must be confronted: How and why did Fielding's work suddenly appear there? And what sort of theatre was it? Scholars have almost unanimously assumed that Fielding's changes of theatrical venue signal political shifts on his part. His 'move' to the Little Haymarket in 1730 has seemed appropriate to all those who see *Tom Thumb* and *The Grub-Street Opera* as part of a systematic campaign against Walpole by a suddenly politicized young author. Even Bertrand Goldgar tells us that 'Fielding's shift to Drury Lane [in 1732] . . . represented a sincere bid for [Walpole's] patronage', and that 'his return to the Haymarket with *Don Quixote in England* [in 1734] signaled a move toward the opposition'.[29] Brian McCrea in particular has relied heavily on such assumptions, filling his narrative with terms indicative of vacillation—'shifts', 'returned to', 'rejoined', 'left', 'moved to', 'shifting between'.[30] Unfortunately, this whole theory is unsound, and the modern critics who have taken it over from Cross have been seriously misled by it. In large part, it follows from a fundamental misunderstanding of the Little Haymarket theatre and its operations.

The plain dull truth is that Fielding was a freelance writer who peddled his plays where he could get them accepted. I am not aware of evidence that Fielding ever signed a contract with a particular theatre, even in 1732 when he 'moved' to Drury Lane. Fielding's work had been rejected at Drury Lane and very probably at Lincoln's Inn Fields in 1729. Why he wound up taking his work to the Little Haymarket in the spring of 1730 has gone almost unconsidered. Most scholars seem to have ignored the issue, presumed a political motivation, or accepted Cross's muddled guess. Cross assumes that Fielding would have stayed with Goodman's Fields, but that neighbourhood opposi-

[28] For discussion of Fielding's 'impatience with the restrictions of comedy and his consequent developing of farce as a satiric and moral medium', see Winfield H. Rogers, 'Fielding's Early Aesthetic and Technique', *Studies in Philology*, 40 (1943), 529–51.

[29] Goldgar, pp. 112, 114–15.

[30] 'As Fielding's political views changed, so did the plays he wrote, as well as the companies that performed them.' McCrea, p. 51.

tion to the playhouse made it a bad bet. 'Anticipating this result of the controversy [*the 28 April order of silence*], Fielding had already thrown in his fortunes with the Little Theatre in the Haymarket, where, on February 12, 1730, a ballad-opera entitled "Love and Revenge, or the Vintner Tricked" was performed for his benefit.'[31] But Goodman's Fields performed daily until 29 April, and Fielding is unlikely to have been so prescient as to foresee its silencing. Nor did he throw in his lot with the Little Haymarket just a week after his third benefit at Goodman's Fields: the 12 February benefit for 'Mr. Fielding' was almost unquestionably for the actor Timothy Fielding, who had been performing there regularly that winter.

Henry Fielding may well have offered *The Author's Farce* to Goodman's Fields and had it refused because the politic Odell and Giffard were chary of stepping on toes at Drury Lane. Goodman's Fields was not, in any case, to prove a promising venue for an ambitious writer. The theatre was evidently making good profits with a repertory of eighteenth-century classics, and at no time did its management plunge heavily into new mainpieces. In short, there is a high probability that Fielding took his next plays to the Little Haymarket because he had no choice.

This explanation tentatively answers our first question—Fielding went to the Little Haymarket because he had to—but the second is rather more complicated. What we actually know of the Little Haymarket and what has been assumed about it are very different, and we need to confront some considerable misapprehensions and blanks in our knowledge before we proceed with the tale of Fielding's next plays.

J. Paul Hunter's capsule description represents standard scholarly opinion:

> The Little Theatre at the Haymarket . . . was small and less elaborately equipped than the more prominent and prestigious houses at Drury Lane and Covent Garden. It specialized in topical satire, and its audiences expected an anti-Establishment theater of ideas rather than the revivals and conventional five-act plays presented at the other houses. Its actors, although usually younger and less experienced than those elsewhere, thus became practiced and adept at a certain kind of satirical performance. The Haymarket was Fielding's theatrical home for five of the next eight seasons [*following 1728–29*], and it asserted a significant control over both the frequency and the kind of writing he undertook.[32]

[31] Cross, I, 78. [32] Hunter, p. 51.

While I too have said similar things in print, this view of the Little Haymarket is neither complete nor entirely accurate.

We have, unfortunately, little evidence about the theatre's dimensions, audience capacity, or box-office maximum.[33] From John Potter's petition against the 1735 playhouse bill, we learn that he claimed to have spent 'at least' £1,000 building the theatre, as well as £200 for rights to the ground (plus, presumably, annual ground rent), and another £500 for his stock of 'Scenes, Machines, Cloaths, and other Decorations'.[34] These are startlingly low figures. Giffard's Goodman's Fields—a nice house, but done with an eye to economy—cost £2,300 in 1732; Rich's Covent Garden cost £6,000 the same year. Given the sums regularly spent by the major theatres on costumes and scenery (£100 for a single production was not unusual), £500 for the entire stock is a pittance.

We would certainly like to know how many people could be seated in the theatre. Five hundred is probably a rock-bottom minimum; 600–700 is perhaps a plausible maximum. The Haymarket Opera House is said to have been larger: its normal capacity was about 760.[35] We know that in 1721–22 Aaron Hill offered a rent of £270 per season for the theatre. Emmett Avery calls this 'a rather large figure for a small theatre'. But in fact we do not know how small it was, or how many nights Hill thought he could operate. The Drury Lane managers seem to have paid at least £3 12*s*. per day (guaranteeing 200 nights' use each season), or some £720 per annum.[36] Drury Lane probably held about a thousand at this time, and was rarely close to full. If the Little Haymarket held only 500, and Hill had been able to operate 150 nights, a rent under £2 per night would have been a bargain, even considering that like Goodman's Fields the Little Haymarket generally charged about a shilling less per seat than the patent houses.[37]

[33] We do know that the site size was approximately 48 ft. by 136 ft. See Edward A. Langhans, 'The Theatres', *The London Theatre World*, p. 63. And see n. 37, below.

[34] *Journal of the House of Commons*, 22 (1735), 456.

[35] See Judith Milhous, 'The Capacity of Vanbrugh's Theatre in the Haymarket', *Theatre History Studies*, 4 (1984), 38–46.

[36] PRO C11/1175/59. I owe this reference to the kindness of Judith Milhous.

[37] Since first writing this passage, I have stumbled across fresh evidence in Francis Gentleman's *Proposals for Printing by Subscription, a new Tragedy, called Osman*, appended to *The Dramatic Censor*, no. 1 (London, 1752). Gentleman proposes to give a gratis ticket for a single performance at the Little Haymarket to all subscribers. 5*s*. subscribers will be admitted to the boxes; 3*s*. subscribers to the pit; 2*s*. subscribers to the gallery. 'To prevent any inconvenience from a croud, no more than One hundred and fifty 5*s*.

We should neither ignore nor underestimate the significance of the Little Haymarket as a competitive spur to the patent theatres.[38] We should, however, note three significant facts. (1) We do not know who was the manager at the Little Haymarket—if, indeed, it had a 'manager'. (2) At no time between 1728 and 1737 was there a 'Little Haymarket Company' in the sense that there were regular acting companies under contract at Drury Lane, Lincoln's Inn Fields, and Goodman's Fields. (3) We cannot be certain that our performance records for the Little Haymarket are complete, or even close to complete. These are disconcerting admissions, and they are quite important to our understanding of Fielding's relationship with the theatre.

Almost all scholars have assumed that there was a permanent acting company at the Little Haymarket, a company run by *someone*. John Loftis's statement that in 1731–32 'the management of the Little Theatre grew more cautious' is typical.[39] Likewise, Pat Rogers says that 'the managers put up the price of tickets . . . when Fielding had his benefit night' for *The Welsh Opera*.[40] Plainly, John Potter retained ultimate control of what was performed at (or excluded from) his theatre, and Loftis, for example, calls him 'the theatre's manager'. But though Potter was the proprietor, there is no evidence that he functioned as manager in the sense that Wilks, Cibber, and Booth did at Drury Lane, or John Rich at Lincoln's Inn Fields (and later at Covent Garden), or Henry Giffard at Goodman's Fields after 1731.

References to management (both complimentary and apoplectic) are frequent in authors' prefaces in these years, but in editions of plays first staged at the Little Haymarket there is a singular silence about management—no thanks and no complaints. One of the few exceptions has some interesting and unexplored implications. In the preface to *The Restauration of King Charles II* (banned before performance in early 1732), Walter Aston tells a strange tale. 'Mr. *Potter*, (Master of

subscriptions will be taken in, Two hundred 3*s*. and Three hundred 2*s*.' This implies a total capacity of 650 with comfort. The proportions seem surprising, but I am not aware of basic alterations carried out in the building between the 1730s and 1752, so this may well give us the normal capacity for Fielding's day. Applying the usual Little Haymarket prices to these figures, we may deduce a maximum box-office take of £57 10*s*.

[38] For a detailed analysis of theatrical competition and the repertories of the various theatres, see Robert D. Hume, 'The London Theatre from *The Beggar's Opera* to the Licensing Act', ch. 9 of *The Rakish Stage* (Carbondale, 1983).

[39] Loftis, *Politics of Drama*, p. 106.

[40] Rogers, p. 51.

the *New Theatre* in the *Hay-Market*) . . . told me, Nothing must be play'd there till a Gentleman of the *Treasury*, and another of the *Exchequer*, had read and approv'd it.' Aston duly sought permission, and thought he had it. 'I distributed the Parts, printed Bills and Tickets, and had it rehearsed thrice; but unexpectedly a *Message* came, to stop the Performance; for the Actors should be all taken up.'[41] This passage has been noticed in connection with censorship, but the managerial implications have been ignored. Managers normally accepted or refused plays and took responsibility for getting them to the stage, but in this case the author was left to negotiate with the authorities. Authors generally advised on the assignment of parts and attended rehearsals, but Aston clearly implies that he not only called rehearsals himself (a managerial function) but arranged for the printing of playbills and tickets—hardly a part of the author's usual duties at the other theatres.

Did the Little Haymarket have any kind of resident staff in the 1730s? A benefit was advertised for 'Mr Green, Prompter' on 2 June 1731, but we have no other certain reference to the gentleman, and hence no way of knowing whether he was part of a permanent staff employed by Potter (*ipso facto* not very likely) or if he was simply a member of the *ad hoc* troupe that had been enjoying a success with *The Tragedy of Tragedies* and *The Fall of Mortimer* that spring. I do note what might be a reference to the same man in an advertisement for a single performance at the Little Haymarket, Wednesday 26 January 1737. 'As Mr Green could not possibly be sure of the House till Monday Night late, he hopes the Shortness of Time will plead his Excuse for not waiting on his Friends, and that they will favour him with their Company notwithstanding.'[42] This suggests that the three little pieces making up the bill were simply jobbed into the theatre on short notice when Mr Green was able to arrange a date, presumably with Potter. A resident company with a manager would not operate this way.

One could easily collect a multitude of modern scholarly references to 'the young company at the Little Haymarket'. This phrase obscures our lack of evidence that the theatre was ever occupied by a regular repertory company in these years. Advertisements that omit casts make analysis maddeningly vague, but the facts that we have suggest two conclusions. First, different 'companies' used the Haymarket

[41] *The Restauration of King Charles II* (London, 1732), pp. ii–iii.

[42] *The London Stage*, Part 3, II, 633.

each season.[43] Second, the principal 'company' generally consisted of a handful of regulars plus others drawn from a large pool of fringe actors at liberty. Even the regulars changed with disconcerting frequency.

For the latter part of 1727–28, for example, analysis of advertised casts reveals that the following distinct groups were using the Little Haymarket: (*a*) Mme Violante's mimes and tumblers; (*b*) a musical group that mounted *Penelope*; (*c*) a 'New Company of English Comedians'; (*d*) a 'New Company' that mounted *The Beggar's Opera*; (*e*) a group of actors—Giffard, Reynolds, Miss Mann, *et al.*—who prove to be the nucleus of the principal 'company' using the theatre in 1728–29. Or consider the season of 1732–33, more typical of these years. In September a temporary summer company occupied the theatre. During the regular season most performances were by groups drawn from a mixed bag of minor professionals, though an English opera company also used the premises occasionally. On 28 May the Goodman's Fields company used the Little Haymarket for a benefit (possibly because management had refused the benefit at Goodman's Fields?). In June a company drawing personnel from both the English opera group and the 'extended company' pool started a summer season. At least once (12 July) 'a Company of Gentlemen' took over the house for a performance of *The Fair Penitent*. Late in July a few of the winter regulars staged a performance with a group of unknowns.

After surveying the distinct groups that used the Little Haymarket between 1728 and 1737, I am convinced that it was always a road house. Potter appears to have rented it night by night (probably longer on some occasions) to any group that wanted it. We simply do not know how the 'extended company' (if we may call it such) that used the house most often chose plays, bargained with authors, and made casting decisions. Could it use Potter's scanty set of scenes and costumes? Was use of them an optional extra? Did each performer provide his or her own clothes? We do not know. The repertory of the 'extended company' is suggestive—a mixture of war-horses (*The Beaux Stratagem*, *Venice Preserv'd*) and contemporary drama, much of it brand

[43] The editors of *The London Stage* imply this when they give the composite season rosters of the Little Haymarket as 'all companies', though they do not discuss the problem in the introductions and make no attempt to distinguish the different groups that used the theatre each season. For such an attempt, see William J. Burling and Robert D. Hume, 'Theatrical Companies at the Little Haymarket, 1720–1737', *Essays in Theatre*, 4 (1986), 98–118.

new. I would hypothesize that the actors put on a few sure-fire pieces and also struck bargains with authors for new plays, the terms doubtless varying with the author and the play. The large number of author benefits on the first or second night suggests an arrangement quite different from the third-night author benefit long traditional at the patent houses. An author who had underwritten the costs of a production might well have been able to claim any profit beyond the expenses and salaries he or she had guaranteed to cover.

The 'extended company' deserves a further word of explanation. In most seasons a handful of regulars reappear in many of the productions for which we have casts. In 1729–30, for example, Wells, Mullart, Lacy, Stoppelaer, Dove, Hicks, Mrs Mullart, Mrs Clarke, Mrs Nokes, and a few others seem to have been the heart of the group. They were joined by an ever-shifting succession of others, most of whom worked at the Little Haymarket only once, or very occasionally. Sometimes a performer would come over temporarily from another theatre (Mrs Kilby from Lincoln's Inn Fields), or a newcomer from Dublin would be snapped up (Paget, who arrived in June 1730). Most seasons a small, fairly stable core of performers and a large pool of interchangeable parts are drawn on as needed and available. The amount of recasting done within a single month is evidence that this group did not operate as a repertory company. The best modern comparison I can offer is the difference between a group like the New York Philharmonic and the pick-up orchestras assembled in New York for anything from a new musical to a morning of work on television commercials. The Drury Lane and Lincoln's Inn Fields actors were almost invariably hired for the season, and this was also the case at Goodman's Fields. The Little Haymarket performers seem to have been freelancing. A hit like *The Author's Farce* or *Pasquin* gave the lucky ones hired for that show a spell of prosperity, but the norm was short-term work.[44]

Logic tells us that there must have been someone among the freelancers each season who co-ordinated the productions of old plays and helped cast and stage the new ones. In 1728–29 this was

[44] How did the actors communicate? At a guess, I would say at a conventional hang-out, a 'theatrical tavern' of the sort described by Philip H. Highfill, jun. for the period around 1790 at which impresarios from town and country could strike bargains with performers at liberty. See Highfill, 'Performers and Performing', in *The London Theatre World*, pp. 154–5. Joseph Wechsberg describes a modern musical equivalent in the Café des Quat'z' Arts in Paris during the 1920s and 1930s. See *Looking for a Bluebird* (New York, 1945), ch. 3.

apparently Mr Reynolds, or so I would deduce from the title-page of Coffey's *Southwark Fair* (1729) and controversy in the papers over Mr Charke's obligations for the fair season of 1729.[45] Fielding's dislike of his treatment at the hands of the 'Great Moguls' at Drury Lane and Lincoln's Inn Fields—a dislike shared by a high percentage of his fellow authors—probably explains his readiness to deal with a theatre whose *modus operandi* seems to have been do-it-yourself, even in the mid-1730s when he had become an established writer.

Our sense of the Little Haymarket's offerings would be distinctly more solid if we could be certain that we possessed complete performance records. Unfortunately, an examination of the offerings recorded in *The London Stage* raises some qualms. Three patterns emerge clearly. Very occasionally, the theatre had a smash hit like *Pasquin*, at which time it operated five or six days a week. The more normal pattern in times of relatively frequent advertisements is two or three performances each week. But for significant stretches every season we find blanks of many days and sometimes weeks. Conceivably the theatre was dark most of these nights. (Potter did book in non-theatrical entertainments not recorded in *The London Stage*.) But we have to allow for the possibility that handbills and a 'house bill' were sometimes regarded as sufficient advertising. This idea is reinforced by an examination of the extant advertisements: an astonishing number are for benefits. There are two possible explanations. (1) The 'extended company' of fringe professionals who used the theatre tended not to advertise unless a benefit was involved or a poor turnout feared. (2) The 'extended company' treated benefits as the principal component of each actor's income, not as a special bonus. Whatever the truth of the matter, we would be rash to assume that we have complete performance records for the theatre.

What we know of the repertory contradicts clichés about 'topical satire' and 'anti-Establishment theater of ideas'. If, for example, we consider the season of 1735–36, during which *Pasquin* enjoyed its phenomenal run, we find the following: *Jane Shore* (1714), *Love and a Bottle* (1698), *A Bold Stroke for a Wife* (1718), *The Recruiting Officer* (1706), *The Inconstant* (1702), *The Beaux Stratagem* (1707), *The Spanish Fryar* (1680), *The Twin-Rivals* (1702), Young's *Revenge* (1721), *The Careless Husband* (1704), *Aesop* (1697), and *The Beggar's Opera* (1728). Most of these plays were standard fare at the patent theatres.

[45] See particularly the *Daily Post* for 14 Aug. 1729. I owe this reference to the kindness of William J. Burling.

What distinguishes the Little Haymarket's offerings of old plays from those at other theatres is its heavy bias towards post-1700 works. At this time more than 50 per cent of the repertory plays at Drury Lane and Covent Garden were pre-1695, and more than 80 per cent were pre-1708. Of course the Little Haymarket also mounted a flock of new plays during 1735–36: Charke, *The Carnival*; Drury, *The Rival Milliners*; Haywood (?), *Arden of Feversham*; anon., *The Contract*; anon., *The Heroick Footman*; Dorman (?), *The Female Rake*; Cooper, *The Nobleman*; Phillips, *The Rival Captains*; Lillo, *Fatal Curiosity*; anon., *The Comical Disappointment*; 'Jack Juniper', *The Deposing and Death of Queen Gin*—as well as Fielding's *Pasquin* and *Tumble-Down Dick*. While most of these works proved entirely ephemeral, we can legitimately say that the Little Haymarket was the venue for far more new plays than any other theatre during the 1730s, and that many of those plays were topical. Reading the Little Haymarket plays that have survived quickly establishes that few of them qualify as 'theater of ideas' or even as 'anti-Establishment'. One could more accurately characterize the Little Haymarket plays as an odd combination of earnest amateur efforts and rollicking farces, most of them very lightweight indeed. The Little Haymarket did launch some genuinely experimental drama at a time when other houses tended to be unreceptive. Lillo's *Fatal Curiosity* (1736) springs to mind, though that case must be credited to Fielding's judgement. But one fact is obvious: the Little Haymarket repertory is far less political than has been assumed.

How much influence the Little Haymarket exerted on 'the kind of writing' Fielding undertook is hard to say. Obviously the actors could not compete with the personnel of the major houses in heavyweight repertory, but they must have been good enough to offer presentable productions of standard mainpieces. Since the Little Haymarket did not have a 'Great Mogul' making script decisions, Fielding did not have to tailor his pieces to anyone else's preconceptions or preferences. If we survey the new plays staged before *The Author's Farce*, we find little inspiration for Fielding. Samuel Johnson of Cheshire's *Hurlothrumbo* (1729) might have given him a notion towards *Tom Thumb*. But just about all the other new plays of 1728–30 fall into standard categories—from Wandesford's dreary *Fatal Love* and Hatchett's *The Rival Father: or, The Death of Achilles* to ballad operas like Coffey's *The Beggar's Wedding* and farces like Mottley's *The Craftsman*. Such works were staged at all the theatres.

We do not know with whom Fielding bargained for performance at the Little Haymarket in 1730, or on what terms *The Author's Farce* was produced. No one seems to have commented on the lack of an advertisement for an author's benefit the third night. Fielding duly received a benefit the third night of *Tom Thumb*, and again the ninth night (which was the seventeenth of *The Author's Farce*), but these remained the only advertised author benefits, despite the astonishing forty nights achieved by *The Author's Farce* this season. The peculiarity is reinforced when we note that Fielding received the standard third- and sixth-night benefits for his *Rape upon Rape*, premièred 23 June. What financial arrangements Fielding made for *The Author's Farce* we can only speculate. He might have accepted a profit-sharing arrangement in place of a benefit, perhaps because he had no cash to invest, or was unable to guarantee expenses. The 'usual' benefit arrangement for *Rape upon Rape* I would interpret as a sign of the actors' confidence in the young author.

IV. EXPERIMENTS IN SATIRE (1730)

The author of *The Temple Beau* is an earnest but uninspired apprentice. The writer of *The Author's Farce* and *Tom Thumb* is a budding genius. These plays are not great literature, but they are brilliant theatre, and superlatively effective performance vehicles. The difference in both genre and quality is startling, and a few words about this sudden leap forward seem in order.

In writing *Love in Several Masques*, *The Wedding-Day*, and *The Temple Beau*, Fielding had been working imitatively in the intrigue-comedy form. In *Don Quixote in England* he was less formulaic, but he had little idea how to control the technical problems his choices created. All four plays lack purpose beyond simple entertainment. Their design is borrowed, and though they express Fielding's ideology clearly enough, they have no urgency of any sort, no genuine feeling. When he writes *The Author's Farce* and *Tom Thumb*, Fielding is suddenly expressing his own views—his animus against the Drury Lane management; his disdain for heroic tragedy; his reactions to being a hackney writer.

When Fielding sat down to vent his feelings about the Drury Lane managers, he found his *métier*. Like many another Harlequin with ambitions to play Hamlet, he cherished the idea that he should write other sorts of work as well, and he tried to do so. Fielding tried his hand at various sorts of straight mimesis (*The Modern Husband* is a particularly interesting example)—but mimesis was never to be his strength. His genius was for burlesque. In saying this I do not mean to denigrate Fielding in any way. I enjoy Hogarth more than I do any 'serious' painter of the day. But just as a brilliant caricaturist will usually fall into mediocrity and flatness when trying to do straight portrait painting, so Fielding's work loses its life and spirit when he abandons the mannered presentation that lends bite and savour to his view of his subjects. This is as true of his fiction as of his plays. Fielding infuses *Tom Jones* with an irony almost vanished from *Amelia*. Whatever the reason for the difference, the results are hard to deny. Much as there may be to admire in its design, moral, characters, and details, *Amelia* is rather flat. Sincerely meant and felt, without question, but lacking the special style and angle of vision that make Fielding's best works what they are. To understand Fielding we must try to see why he wished to write *The Universal Gallant* and *Amelia*, but we need not pretend that they are, for us, as successful and effective as *Pasquin* and *Joseph Andrews*. That Fielding cherished a special affection for *Amelia* is true, but so did Sir Arthur Sullivan for his *Ivanhoe*.

Fielding's best creations are always artificial. He is a puppet-master of dazzling skill, and a deliciously effective stylist. His travesties are glorious, whether of Cibber or of the type encapsulated in Squire Western. But in truth Fielding was never more than routinely competent at three-dimensional psychological development, even in fiction. Much as I prefer Fielding to Richardson, I would admit without argument that against Clarissa and Lovelace all of Fielding's characters seem thin, contrived, and unreal. The fascination of *Tom Jones* is the way the story is told, not the story or the characters. From any other teller the story and characters would hold no special charms.[46]

[46] We need a book on Fielding's theory of literature. For the most helpful studies to date in relation to his drama, see W. R. Irwin, 'Satire and Comedy in the Works of Henry Fielding', *ELH* 13 (1946), 168–88; A. E. Dyson, 'Satiric and Comic Theory in Relation to Fielding', *Modern Language Quarterly*, 18 (1957), 225–37; William B. Coley, 'The Background of Fielding's Laughter', *ELH* 26 (1959), 229–52. For a more specific account of Fielding's development of a satiric form in his plays, see Jean B. Kern, 'Fielding's Dramatic Satire', *Philological Quarterly*, 54 (1975), 239–57.

The Author's Farce

When Fielding sat down to write *The Author's Farce*, he had something to say. He was obviously furious about the rejection of his plays at Drury Lane, and particularly irked by the behaviour of Colley Cibber. His presentation of the woes of the impecunious author is formulaic enough for him to be promptly accused of plagiarizing from Farquhar's *Love and a Bottle* (1698),[47] but it has the crisp bite of actuality so lacking in the intrigue comedies. Likewise Fielding knew the entertainments of the town at first hand, did not think much of them, and set about debunking them with enthusiasm.

Critical perceptions of *The Author's Farce* have been clouded by an accident of textual history. Fielding revised the play drastically in 1734: he had to remove Wilks (who had died in the intervening period) and add Theophilus Cibber (who had become prominent). The revision had a short and inglorious life on stage and did not find its way into print until 1750. But because the 1750 edition served as the basis for all reprints until 1966,[48] most accounts of the play have treated the revision rather than the original. Dudden, for example, mentions the original, but promptly proceeds to a description of the later version, even though it comes badly out of place chronologically. By 1734 Fielding was a more expert playwright, and his construction is naturally tighter, despite the difficulties posed by enforced changes—but let us leave the revision for its place.

Fielding's design for the original *Author's Farce* is ramshackle but effective. Acts I and II present the 'realistic' story of the playwright Luckless, beset by duns, unable to pay his landlady, and madly in love with his landlady's beautiful daughter. Act III takes us into the Little Haymarket for a performance of a puppet play (enacted by humans) that Luckless has contrived.[49] He is embarrassed at producing

[47] See *The Candidates for the Bays*, a poem by 'Scriblerus Tertius' (London, 1730), pp. 9–10. The author of the poem calls Fielding a mad and drunken plagiarist who is too hot tempered to accept criticism from anyone. Farquhar's play had been performed a number of times at Lincoln's Inn Fields in 1724 and 1725, and revived as recently as May 1728. It was of course regularly reprinted in collections of Farquhar's plays. Fielding may have taken some hints from Farquhar, but the specifics of his play do not seem to owe much to Lyrick's confrontations with his landlady, Widow Bullfinch, and the publisher, Pamphlet. The parallels seem inherent in the situation.

[48] Ed. Charles B. Woods (Lincoln, Nebr., 1966), an edn. completed and seen through the press by Curt A. Zimansky.

[49] On Fielding's use of puppets, see Anthony J. Hassall, 'Fielding's Puppet Image', *Philological Quarterly*, 53 (1974), 71–83.

something 'beneath the Dignity of the Stage' as the Player calls it, but rejoins: 'who would not . . . rather Eat by his Nonsense, than Starve by his Wit'? (28)[50] The play-within-a-play, set in the underworld, has a plot of sorts: the Goddess of Nonsense has fallen in love with the ghost of Signior Opera, and so forth, but it is really just an excuse for pot-shots at a gallery of transparently identifiable representatives of popular entertainments. These are Don Tragedio (Lewis Theobald), Sir Farcical Comick (Colley Cibber), Dr Orator (John Henley), Signior Opera (the celebrated castrato Senesino), Monsieur Panto-mime (John Rich), and Mrs Novel (Eliza Haywood). Fielding stands them up one after another to make fools of themselves. Most of the barbs are reasonably good-humoured, but we cannot wonder that Fielding ruffled some feathers. John Rich had thick skin, and Senesino little reason to care, but Henley's stinging attacks on Fielding in *The Hyp Doctor* in the next few years—which Fielding minded very much—probably have their origin in this lampoon.

How to end such a medley is always a problem, and Fielding hit on a surprisingly effective fantasy device. Luckless—who has been suffering from amnesia—turns out to be the King of Bantam, and his landlady proves to be the deposed Queen of Brentford (and mother of Punch!), so Luckless can marry her daughter, Harriot. Luckless graciously pardons all offenders. The Constable who tried to arrest him for libelling diversions of people of quality (52) is made Chief Constable of Bantam, and Luckless goes on:

> You, Mr. *Murder-text*, shall be my Chaplain; you, Sir [Henley], my Orator; you [Witmore?] my Poet-Laureat; you [Bookweight] my Bookseller; you *Don Tragedio*, Sir *Farcical* and *Signior Opera*, shall entertain the City of *Bantam* with your Performances; Mrs. *Novel*, you shall be a Romance Writer; and to shew my Generosity, *Marplay* and *Sparkish* [Cibber and Wilks] shall superintend my Theatres—All proper Servants for the King of *Bantam*. (57–8)

This cheerful distribution of rewards collapses satiric distinctions, mingling the deserving Witmore with Fielding's butts, but the play is a spoof, not an allegorical fable. Luckless spends two and three-quarters acts denouncing the taste of the town, and then sees only good in Cibber and Henley and Rich. Perhaps this is a plot convenience, or perhaps Fielding is mocking those who sell out to the establishment when they find themselves welcomed into it. One does

[50] Citations are to the second Roberts edn. of 1730 (not so labelled), designated 'O2' by Woods, p. xi.

not expect rigorous consistency in such entertainment, and of course the whole finale is a send up. Fielding's parody of recognition scenes is done with verve: the hat Luckless pawns in Act I in order to buy a dinner ('my Head must always provide for my Belly' (7)) is recognized at the pawnshop by 'Gonsalvo', his former tutor, who has come in search of him. Luckless's rejoicing in this 'Prodigious Fortune!' is interrupted by a post-horn, and the arrival of a messenger from Bantam with the news that his father is dead and he is now king. (How comfortable, we may wonder, had Fielding been when he concocted the recognition-scene finale for *The Wedding-Day*?) The conclusion of *The Author's Farce* manages to be good-humoured while consigning Fielding's catalogue of aversions to the realm of Bantam.[51]

The 'realistic' part of the show is a clever combination of the straightforward and the ironic. The Landlady's loud complaints are predictable ('Never tell me, Mr. *Luckless*, of your Play . . . I would no more depend on a Benefit-Night of an un-acted Play, than I wou'd on a Benefit-Ticket in an un-drawn Lottery' (1)), but her declaration of passion for the unfortunate poet is a neat twist. Luckless's exalted romantic love for Harriot bursts forth into ludicrous ringing verse (5): as in Act III, Fielding uses Luckless as a satiric tool, but is perfectly willing to ridicule his puppet.

The difficulties of the aspirant author are amusingly communicated. Luckless cannot get 'his Lordship' to listen to his play and cannot even get a refusal to hear it from 'Mr. *Keyber*' (yet another whack at Colley Cibber). Act II opens with Luckless reading his play to Marplay (Cibber) and Sparkish (Wilks) in a tavern. Cibber suggests alterations for the worse, and Wilks repeats his comments like a parrot.[52] Most of Fielding's animus is clearly against Cibber, but we can easily believe that a 'slight Pique' between Wilks and himself prevented the submission of *The Wedding-Day* to Drury Lane. The other really fine scene in the play is the set piece displaying the unfortunate hack writers who work for the publisher, Mr Bookweight. The tricks of the trade are exhibited with glee: authors answer their

[51] For discussion, see Valerie C. Rudolph, 'People and Puppets: Fielding's Burlesque of the "Recognition Scene" in *The Author's Farce*', *Papers on Language and Literature*, 11 (1975), 31–8.

[52] For a sour view of the triumvirate's treatment of authors, see anon., *The Laureat; or, the Right Side of Colley Cibber* (London, 1740), esp. pp. 94–5. For discussion, see Charles B. Woods, 'Cibber in Fielding's *Author's Farce*: Three Notes', *Philological Quarterly*, 44 (1965), 145–51. For a broader consideration of Fielding's relations with Colley Cibber, see Houghton W. Taylor, 'Fielding upon Cibber', *Modern Philology*, 29 (1931), 73–90.

own pamphlets; the advantages of false imprints are savoured; the judicious use of the dash is commended; Virgil can be translated out of Dryden.

Scrappy and cheerful as *The Author's Farce* is, it conveys with zest its author's caustic view of the profession of writing and the state of English culture. As Fielding has his poet say in Act III: 'Authors starve and Booksellers grow fat, *Grub-Street* harbours as many Pirats as ever *Algiers* did—They have more Theatres than are at *Paris*, and just as much Wit as there is at *Amsterdam*; they have ransack'd all *Italy* for Singers, and all *France* for Dancers' (35–6). But grumpy as Fielding was about Cibber and Drury Lane, the play fairly bubbles with high spirits. The use of the cat in the epilogue is the sort of device that keeps one from believing that Fielding's view of the world in which he hoped to earn his living was altogether despondent.

One issue needs to be raised and dismissed: political import. Some twenty-five years ago Sheridan Baker proposed a systematic political reading that found favour in many quarters.[53] His case has, however, been very effectively answered. Bertrand Goldgar points out that 'there is not the slightest scrap of evidence which suggests that . . . [*The Author's Farce*, *Tom Thumb*, and *Rape upon Rape*] were read or viewed at the time as satirizing Walpole'.[54] This is a very powerful argument: the newspapers of 1730 were quick to descry political meanings, either to gloat over them or denounce them. If the 'hits' Baker expounds were intended, we none the less lack evidence that anyone apprehended them aright. As Charles Woods observes, 'if Professor Baker's line of reasoning were followed, every stage production of the Walpole era that presents Punch and Joan or Harlequin would be politically suspect.'[55] Unlike Fielding's earlier plays, *The Author's Farce* is topical and full of allusions to current events and real people. But references to 'a Libel against the Ministry' (21), and lines like 'When you cry he is Rich, you cry a Great Man' (41) do not add up to a political position. Cleary's careful analysis turns up virtually no political substance. I have to agree with him that '*The Author's Farce* of 1730 is the play of a young man without a real stake in politics or real animus.'[56]

[53] Sheridan Baker, 'Political Allusion in Fielding's *Author's Farce*, *Mock Doctor*, and *Tumble-Down Dick*', *PMLA* 77 (1962), 221–31.

[54] Goldgar, p. 102.

[55] Woods edn., p. xv.

[56] Cleary, p. 30.

To get a sense of Fielding's play as it appeared in 1730, we may usefully glance at two works with which it directly competed. Fielding's play received its première on 30 March; so did Gabriel Odingsells' *Bayes's Opera* at Drury Lane. Three days later James Ralph's *The Fashionable Lady, or Harlequin's Opera* appeared at Goodman's Fields. All three are ballad operas aimed at debunking the popular entertainments of the town. *Bayes's Opera* was the most ambitious and the least successful (three nights)—a systematic allegory with commentary *à la* Buckingham from the 'author', addressed to Belinda and Arabella, a pair of society ladies. The 'Lawful Heir' Tragedio has been confined by the usurper Cantato (i.e., opera), and the kingdom is besieged by the pretender Pantomime. General Briton's taste turns out to be of the worst, and when Pantomime triumphs, Briton bargains to marry Pantomime's daughter, Farcia, even though both of them are already married. Pantomime coolly gives tragedy and opera their freedom: 'Go and enjoy free Liberty to starve' (67). As Edmond Gagey has said, the allegory is too involved and human interest is lacking, but the piece is intelligently constructed, the music well integrated, and the symbolism logical and consistent.[57] The unhappy author's preface tells us that the audience failed to keep track of the allegory and that offence was taken over General Briton. Fielding's Bookweight observes that 'There are your Acting Plays, and your Reading Plays' (10), and *Bayes's Opera* would seem to be one of the latter.

Ralph's *The Fashionable Lady* is a strange pot-pourri, a mixed-genre spoof.[58] He mingles comedy of manners, pantomime, opera, farce, and rehearsal in a sometimes bewildering way, and the sixty-eight songs often slow action to a crawl. But it is an effective and enjoyable travesty, despite its length and disjointedness. It ran nine nights (with three author benefits), and was performed four more times its first season, three of them actor benefits (a sign of popularity).

Fielding's play is, in short, part of a salvo of protests by 'serious' writers against Italian opera, farce, and pantomime—couched in ballad opera form, and in Fielding's case, in farce form. *The Author's*

[57] Edmond McAdoo Gagey, *Ballad Opera* (New York, 1937), pp. 152–4.

[58] Ralph's sober critical views on the entertainments of the town are expressed at length in *The Touch-Stone* (London, 1728). For a plausible argument that this work influenced Fielding (and specifically that it affected his design of *The Author's Farce* and *Tom Thumb*), see Helen Sard Hughes, 'Fielding's Indebtedness to James Ralph', *Modern Philology*, 20 (1922), 19–34.

Farce is the least ambitious of the three; perhaps not coincidentally, it was also the most successful in the theatre. It enjoyed forty-one performances in less than half a season (aided by the popularity of *Tom Thumb*)—the greatest hit since *The Beggar's Opera*.[59]

Tom Thumb

The delicious little burlesque that Fielding added to *The Author's Farce* as an afterpiece on 24 April 1730 is rarely studied in its own right. Critical attention is almost always given to the radically revamped version of 1731, *The Tragedy of Tragedies; or the Life and Death of Tom Thumb the Great*. They are works so different that any attempt to consider them together here seems unwise. Unlike its successor, *Tom Thumb* is a very general burlesque of heroic tragedy form. It seems not to have been written with particular targets in mind, and it altogether lacks the heavy overlay of verbal detail drawn from some forty plays that is so prominent a feature of its successor. Nor does it have any of the mock-scholarly footnote apparatus Fielding added to document his particular digs in the revision. *Tom Thumb* is a much simpler and less ambitious play, and in some respects a more nearly perfect one, especially for performance.

Tom Thumb might easily have been conceived, written, and polished in a week. In its first form it comprises only sixteen pages of text—a *jeu d'esprit* written as a makeweight for *The Author's Farce*. It was published as '*Tom Thumb*. A TRAGEDY. As it is Acted at the Theatre in the Hay-Market'.[60] The design is simplicity itself: the work masquerades as a tragedy and is fitted out with the semblance of heroic apparatus—King, Queen, Princess, conquering general, courtiers. The pigmy hero (played by a Miss Jones)[61] might alone have served to undercut the pro forma genre, but Fielding stuffs the text with anti-heroic rhetoric of a sort that has a radically deflationary effect. This technique is in full evidence in the opening lines:

> Sure, such a Day as this was never seen!
> The Sun himself, on this auspicious Day,

[59] *The Author's Farce* had only nine performances between 30 March and 24 April. I presume that the Little Haymarket was already booked for the other productions staged in that time, including Hatchett's *The Rival Father; or, The Death of Achilles*, in which Eliza Haywood (ridiculed in Fielding's play) took a principal part.

[60] Citations are to the first Roberts edn. of 1730 (BL C.131.de.5).

[61] A petite teenager, to judge from the account in the *Biographical Dictionary*, VIII, 226–8.

Shines like a Beau in a new Birth-Day Suit:
All Nature, O my *Noodle*! grins for Joy.

The victorious Tom Thumb is likened to a cock sparrow hopping at the head of a flock of turkeys and said to be but 'a Lump of Gristle'—in the first two pages. The King pronounces a day of rejoicing and exclaims 'To-day it is our Pleasure to be drunk, / And this our Queen shall be as drunk as Us' (2). The mighty Thumb constantly concludes heroic pronouncements with inappropriate similitudes: 'So when some Chimney-Sweeper . . .' (4), 'So when two Dogs are fighting in the Streets . . .' (6). Many of the felicitous touches are so well known as hardly to need recitation: 'wherefore art thou *Tom Thumb*?' (8); the false report of Tom's death (a monkey has been poisoned by mistake instead of Tom (12)); the quart of rum under Princess Huncamunca's bed (10); Tom's demise when swallowed by 'A Cow of larger than the usual Size'—a catastrophe seen by Noodle from his 'Garret' (15); Grizzle obtaining his vengeance by killing Tom's ghost (15); and the gory finale with eight more deaths in almost the same number of lines, the King having to kill himself for want of anyone else to do it. The outlines of the story and the constituent elements are more or less those of heroic tragedy, but the style and characters produce the clanging discords that render the whole production deliciously absurd.

All the signs point to a riotous success in the theatre. The Prince of Wales attended the second night and commanded a performance two weeks later. By 6 May (when the Fielding double bill began to be offered daily) the advertisements were explaining that because the boxes were 'not equal to the great Demand for Places', at the 'Desire of several Persons of Quality, Pit and Boxes will be put together'—i.e. that top price would be charged for all places in the pit, as well as the boxes. On 8 June the bills announced that 'Tom Thumb and his Retinue are entirely new dress'd'—a nearly unique case of new costumes added in the middle of a run.

As with *The Author's Farce*, critics have espied political meaning in *Tom Thumb*. And once again, the evidence will not support such a reading. Goldgar points out that the opposition press actually attacked the play, and that *Fog's Journal* of 1 August 1730 sneered at Walpole for attending three times. As late as 1733 *Fog's* was calling it an innocent and frivolous entertainment.[62] Cleary concludes that the

[62] Goldgar, p. 105.

idea that the farce is directed against Walpole 'must be dismissed' and says flatly that as with *The Author's Farce* the anti-ministerial reading is entirely a creation of modern critics,[63] a view with which I entirely concur. Fielding's target is perfectly obvious, but 'target' is perhaps a misleading term. *Tom Thumb* is a burlesque satire, but its object is more entertainment through simple incongruity than effective ridicule of heroic tragedy, whether general or particular. One need not be well read in Dryden or his 1720s' successors to be amused.

On 1 May, Fielding provided a prologue and epilogue, and on the 6th he added 'two New Scenes' (so advertised on the 7th)—the beginning of Act II in the second edition of 1730. They concern a bailiff and his 'Follower' who attempt to arrest Noodle for a debt to his tailor and who are killed by Tom Thumb, striking a blow for the dignity of the nobility—a pleasantly silly business. Fielding seized the occasion offered by the second edition to incorporate not only his new scenes but an exuberant preface, dropping all sorts of names (Longinus, Lucian, Locke, Plato, Cicero), responding with pseudo-solemnity to critical objections (particularly to the killing of the ghost), and congratulating his 'Cotemporary Writers [*sic*], for their having enlarged the Sphere of Tragedy ... to provoke the Mirth and Laughter of the Spectators, to join the Sock to the Buskin, is a Praise only due to Modern Tragedy'.[64] The self-satisfied style, the confused allusions, and some of the verbal particularities are a clear burlesque of Colley Cibber's prefatorial style, and specifically of his notorious preface and prologue for *The Provok'd Husband*. Such jabs as '*Paraphonalia*' and '*when the People of our Age shall be Ancestors*' would not have been missed by many readers of plays in 1730.

Tom Thumb is a very simple kind of travesty indeed, and requires virtually no prior knowledge to be enjoyed. Its point is amusement, and it proved superlatively effective, creating the public interest that every young playwright dreams of. Neither *The Author's Farce* nor *Tom Thumb* was the sort of work to be easily repeated: Fielding would have to find fresh targets and other modes. But with these hits he had made a tremendous step forward as a would-be professional dramatist.

[63] Cleary, pp. 32–5.

[64] Quotations are from BL Ashley 717, which is not labelled 'The Second Edition' on the title-page but is otherwise identical to copies so designated (e.g. BL 11775.c.79).

Rape upon Rape

Fielding's third Little Haymarket play of the spring is an odd amalgam of social satire, intrigue comedy, and romance. Dudden is quite wrong in saying that it is 'modelled on the lines of the Jonsonian "comedy of humours"'.[65] Politick, the old merchant run mad after news and newspapers, is certainly a humours character, and so is Sotmore (who says he would turn a daughter out of doors for drinking tea (45)).[66] But despite the emblematic nature of some characters (Worthy the good justice; Quill the clerk; Faithful the honest servant), they are not conceived as humours in the Jonsonian sense. As in his apprentice plays, Fielding sets up contrasts: Worthy against the corrupt Justice Squeezum; Ramble the gay blade against Constant the true lover. But the central thrust of the play is its satire of Politick and Squeezum. Unfortunately—and this is a significant weakness in the play's design—the two characters have virtually nothing to do with each other, and so the satiric force of the play is vitiated.

As in the intrigue comedies, the plot is creaky. Politick's daughter Hilaret, trying to elope with Constant, meets Ramble in the street and is taken for a whore (10–13). He assaults her; she cries 'Rape'; and they are both taken up by the watch and hauled before Justice Squeezum. The ensuing complications take up most of the next four acts. Constant, meanwhile, has been seized on a mistaken charge of rape in the course of rescuing Worthy's sister Isabella—who turns out to be Ramble's lost wife (supposed dead). And Ramble turns out to be Politick's long-estranged son. The happy ending—Constant gets Hilaret, Ramble recovers both Isabella and her £80,000 fortune—is rather less plausible than that of *The Gondoliers*, but then Fielding's 'story' is really only an excuse on which to hang the double-barrelled satire and a way of engineering amusing situations.

Justice Squeezum is a grotesquely depraved character, and if the other characters were more real he would be disgusting and upsetting rather than amusing. Squeezum extorts protection money from madams; rigs juries; gives gamesters 'licences' that exempt them from gaming-house raids (14–15). He sees every miscreant brought before him as nothing more than a potential payer of a bribe. Squeezum is frightened only by his wife, who blackmails large sums out of him by

[65] Dudden, I, 69.

[66] Citations are to the 'Wats' edn. of 1730.

threatening exposure: 'I'll blow you up, I'll discover all your midnight Intrigues, your protecting Ill Houses, your bribing Juries, your snacking Fees, your whole Train of Rogueries' (18). Squeezum examines Hilaret 'in private', and promptly offers to take her into keeping, pointing out the advantages of his position: 'You are as safe with a Justice in *England*, as a Priest abroad; Gravity is the best Cloak for Sin, in all Countries' (23). Mrs Squeezum, meanwhile, is doing her best to get herself into bed with Ramble.

Fielding's views about corrupt justices were always strong, and the problem of seeing the truth is real even for the most honest of men. Squeezum is presented with more humour and larkiness than Justice Thrasher (in *Amelia*), but the genuine indignation behind the satire is the same. That Fielding is not attacking justices *per se* is made explicit in the portrait of Worthy, and in Worthy's appalled response to Squeezum's claim that 'the Makers of Laws, and the Executors of them, should be free of them; as Authors and Actors are free of the Playhouse' (69). Worthy is a sawdust-stuffed dramatic contrivance, but a significant part of the play's ideology.

Much less space is devoted to Politick. He and his news-mad friends Dabble and Porer are entertaining, though Fielding's satire lacks any serious point. He can hardly claim that London's merchants are abandoning commerce *en masse* for the delights of news and 'Projects'. A father too worried about the Grand Turk to absorb the news of his daughter's disappearance is amusing (6–7, 27 ff.)—and might have been more so if Fielding had been able to refrain from having Worthy deliver a moral soliloquy on the subject (30). The catalogue of the seventeen genuine newspapers that Politick has read is delicious, especially when he is then in haste to see what the *Lying Post* has to say (63). But there is not much that Fielding can do with Politick: the humour is entertaining, but static.

Generically, *Rape upon Rape* is a muddle of satire and romance. In recent years critics have suggested that the muddle is thinly camouflaged political satire. Goldgar points out that in the spring of 1730 allusions to 'rape' would inevitably bring the notorious Charteris case to mind. Cleary wonders if the references in the prologue to 'Publick *Villany*', '*Mighty Villain*', justice preserving rogues, '*Vice*, cloath'd with Pow'r', and 'the Heroick *Muse* . . . dares the *Lyon* in his Den' are a hint at anti-ministerial aims. Because of the satire on news mania, there are frequent references to topical matters, some of them touchy from the government's point of view. I think there can be little doubt that

Fielding alludes harshly to Charteris' pardon in Worthy's lament that 'Golden Sands too often clog the Wheels of Justice, and obstruct her Course: The very Riches which were the greatest Evidence of his Villany, have too often declared the Guilty innocent; and Gold hath been found to cut a Halter surer than the sharpest Steel' (67). But I see no systematic reference to the Charteris case, or the allusion is ineffective if Fielding intended it. A play concerning false accusations of rape is not an ideal vehicle for paralleling a genuine case of rape. And unlike Constant, Charteris was convicted before he was pardoned: in his case the fault lay in the government, not in the court.

As with Fielding's other plays this spring, we have no evidence that his contemporaries saw politics in *Rape upon Rape*: the newspapers are silent. Backing off his earlier argument for 'genuine commitment', Goldgar admits that there is 'no way to prove' specific political purpose in the play.[67] Cleary reviews the evidence in the text itself and rather reluctantly concludes that '*Rape upon Rape* is not a very partisan play.'[68] My own view is that by comparison with Fielding's earlier plays it is much more topical and politicized, but that it is not in any sense a systematic political satire or a concealed allegory. And it is certainly not partisan in a party sense. The opposition made political capital out of the pardon to Charteris, but disgust over that case was hardly confined to the opposition. I suspect that Fielding had simply come to realize that he could make a good thing out of topicality. *Rape upon Rape* is an uneven piece of work, but it has a lot more life and vitality than the intrigue comedies.

Possibilities for the Future

Cross says that Fielding's 'farces' must 'have enabled him to live like a gentleman',[69] but in fact we do not know what Fielding made out of his Little Haymarket plays in the spring of 1730. Nor have we any idea of his future plans. Since an educated guess can be made about the proceeds from authors' benefits at Goodman's Fields, and because the Little Haymarket is unlikely to have been any more lucrative, we might speculate that Fielding's two benefits for *Rape upon Rape* netted him £40–£60, and the two for his double bill something like £30 each, plus gifts from friends (which might have amounted to nothing or to

[67] Cf. 'The Politics of Fielding's *Coffee-House Politician*', *Philological Quarterly*, 49 (1970), 424–9, and *Walpole and the Wits*, pp. 105–10, and 235 n. 52.

[68] Cleary, pp. 36–41.

[69] Cross, I, 93.

quite a bit). But since the financial arrangements for *The Author's Farce* and *Tom Thumb* are unknown, no estimate of Fielding's income is possible. From the four plays he had seen staged in six months, he must certainly have made enough to live on comfortably for a year, *if* he were reasonably prudent. We have, however, no particular grounds for assuming prudence.

We know that Fielding must soon have been at work on a new and ambitious play, for on 4 September he wrote a letter to Lady Mary Wortley Montagu:

> I hope your Ladyship will honour the Scenes which I presume to lay before you with your Perusal. As they are written on a Model I never yet attempted, I am exceedingly anxious least they should find less Mercy from you than my lighter Productions. It will be a slight compensation to the Modern Husband, that your Ladyship's Censure will defend him from the Possibility of any other Reproof, Since your least approbation will always give me a Pleasure infinitely superiour to the loudest Applauses of a theatre. For whatever has past your Judgment may, I think, without any Imputation of Immodesty, refer Want of Success to Want of Judgment in an Audience. I shall do my self the Honour of waiting on your Ladyship at Twickenham next Monday to receive my Sentence, and am, Madam, with the most devoted Respect, Your Ladyship's most obedient, most humble Servant,
>
> London, 7br 4 Henry ffielding.[70]

The Modern Husband was not staged until 1732, but the text of this epistle leaves no doubt that it was the work at issue, though the play was not necessarily complete at the time. That the year was 1730 rather than 1731 is made highly probable by a puff which appeared in the *Craftsman* on 19 September 1730: 'We hear that the Town will shortly be diverted by a Comedy of Mr. *Fielding*'s, call'd, The *Modern Husband*, which is said to bear a great Reputation.' And on the 24th the *Grub-street Journal*, already exhibiting its inveterate hostility to Fielding, reprinted this little puff with a sneering comment: '*I don't understand how* a Comedy *so* little known *can be* said to bear a great reputation.'

I will deal with *The Modern Husband* when we get to its production in 1732, but we must observe that in the summer of 1730 Fielding was hard at work on what Charles Woods rightly terms 'a comedy of social purpose', which is indeed a model Fielding had never yet attempted and very different indeed from his 'lighter Productions'. Why it did

[70] *Letters of Lady Mary Wortley Montagu*, II, 93.

not come on the stage in the season of 1730–31 we do not know. Possibly it was not finished to Fielding's satisfaction, or perhaps the players were chary of its subject. Cross asserts that 'why the comedy ... had never yet been performed [in 1732] is quite apparent. The company at the Haymarket could have done nothing with it.'[71] This I doubt: they could apparently do presentable performances of *The Provok'd Husband*. The delay in performance is a fact; explanations are conjectural. The importance of the letter to Lady Mary and the *Craftsman* puff is simply the proof that Fielding was already aiming at a much more serious and disturbing kind of satire than he had previously attempted.

Given what he had just done to Colley Cibber—and to a lesser degree to Wilks—Fielding can scarcely have imagined that his work would be welcomed at Drury Lane the next season. He may have approached the management at Goodman's Fields, but their lack of interest in new plays is clearly signalled by what they actually performed in 1730–31.[72] We have one potent piece of evidence, however, that Fielding did not simply assume that he would take his work to the Little Haymarket. That Fielding should consider associating himself with John Rich may seem surprising, but the proof is beyond reasonable doubt.[73]

On 4 December 1730 *Rape upon Rape* was produced at Lincoln's Inn Fields under the title *The Coffee-House Politician*.[74] We might presume that this was nothing more than simple piracy, except that Fielding received an author's benefit on the third night. Such a benefit is quite extraordinary: Rich had no obligation whatever to pay Fielding a penny, and he was famous for his parsimony. The only plausible explanation for this anomaly would seem to be that Rich and Fielding were exploring the possibilities of an association between Fielding

[71] Cross, I, 119.

[72] Goodman's Fields mounted only two new mainpieces, James Ralph's *The Fall of the Earl of Essex* and an anonymous piece called *The Cynick* (not printed; lost).

[73] On this curious episode, ignored or misunderstood until very recently, see William J. Burling, 'Fielding, His Publishers, and John Rich in 1730', *Theatre Survey*, 26 (1985), 39–46.

[74] Although *The Coffee-House Politician* was advertised as 'Revis'd by the Author', the text published by Watts in December 1730 under that title is identical to the first edn. Cross—followed, as usual, by Dudden, *et al*.—says that the title was changed 'owing to objections' against *Rape upon Rape* (I, 90), but I can find no evidence of such objections. I would guess that the title was changed because Rich wished to give the impression that the play was altered. Many critics have assumed that the work was rewritten, but this is not true. In fact, the B–F gatherings of *The Coffee-House Politician* consist of sheets remaining from the June printing of *Rape upon Rape*.

and Lincoln's Inn Fields. Rich was impervious enough to personal attacks that he probably cared not a whit about Fielding's portrayal of him in *The Author's Farce*, and the prospect of securing the right of first refusal to scripts from a writer as successful as Fielding had been in 1730 probably seemed well worth a benefit.

Nothing further came of this dalliance with Lincoln's Inn Fields. The new production of *Rape upon Rape* was not a success.[75] It grossed £39 5*s*. the first night, £59 13*s*. the second, and £77 18*s*. the third.[76] When Rich tried it again ten days later, it managed only a wretched £28 9*s*. This may have soured the relationship. In all likelihood, this was when Fielding 'read' *The Wedding-Day* to Rich, and he might have offered *The Modern Husband*. Rich may have disliked both of them, or Fielding may have developed an immediate antipathy to Rich. Whatever the reasons, Fielding returned to the Little Haymarket in the spring of 1731, and there is a strong probability that he did so because he had no alternative.[77]

V. THE EMERGENT PROFESSIONAL (1731)

JUPITER. I doubt you have been dabling in Defamation.
MOMUS. In none but what was wrapt up. Blame them that open'd it.

Forrest, *Momus Turn'd Fabulist* (1729), p. 62

[75] A long-standing puzzle about this production is the major differences between the cast advertised in the newspapers and that listed in what turns out to be the first state of the Dec. edn. of *The Coffee-House Politician* (reported in *The London Stage*, Part 3, I, 99). Radical recasting during the short run seems inconceivable. The octavo evidently contains an intended cast that no one remembered to alter—an explanation borne out by the amended cast in the revised prelims of the second state of the December 1730 edition, which confirms Worthy—Ogden; Politick—Chapman; Constant—Milward; Hilaret—Mrs Younger; Isabella—Mrs Boheme. Exemplars of the two states of the Dec. edn. are the Yale and Penn State copies respectively.

[76] The third-night take comprised £54 13*s*. in cash and only £23 5*s*. in 'tickets'—i.e. Fielding's friends apparently did not turn out in force, or he did not yet have many friends of the sort who took benefit tickets.

[77] We have one piece of evidence that the Little Haymarket actors were irked by his attempt to establish himself at Lincoln's Inn Fields. On 30 Nov., just four days before the production of *The Coffee-House Politician* opened at Lincoln's Inn Fields, the play was revived at the Little Haymarket, under the new title, recast as necessary, with *Tom Thumb* as afterpiece. That Fielding had nothing to do with this collision is proved by the addition of a new act to *Tom Thumb* called *The Battle of the Poets*, a satire on the contenders for the Laureateship. Uncharacteristically, Fielding was not amused, and published a disclaimer in the *Daily Journal* of 30 November: 'Whereas it hath been advertized, That an entire New Act, called, *The Battle of the Poets*, is introduced into the Tragedy of *Tom Thumb*; This is to assure the Town, that I have never seen this additional Act, nor am any ways concerned therein. *Henry Fielding*.'

During 1731 Fielding produced two new plays and two revisions. *The Letter Writers* neither deserved favour nor found it, and *The Grub-Street Opera* was never performed, but even so we may fairly say that Fielding began to prove that he was more than a flash in the pan: he had the makings of a professional playwright. With the works of 1731 we must confront the problem of political meaning, and a brief survey of the political (or arguably political) plays of the time will be necessary.

Political Drama in the 1730s

How do we prove that a play was written to make a political point? What are the different types of political plays? Did the different London theatres have demonstrably different political stances? To assess the politicality of Fielding's plays, we need answers to these questions.

What counts as a 'political' play? This question is by no means semantic or pedantic. If Wilbur Cross and a host of his successors see *Tom Thumb* as a systematic debunking of Walpole and make out a very plausible set of parallels, but nothing in contemporary newspapers, letters, and diaries suggests that anyone took the play this way at the time, then the play would seem to be *de facto* non-political, regardless of any argument we might care to make about Fielding's intentions. Even if we had a letter from Fielding saying outright that he meant to ridicule Walpole, we would have to admit that he apparently failed to make his point. At an earlier date, lack of evidence about audience response would mean much less, but the aggressive newspapers of the 1720s and 1730s were quick to crow or sling mud. With a play that failed outright and fell into instant oblivion, we might not be certain of either authorial aim or audience perception (Odell's *The Patron* is an example). Unhappily, neither apparent authorial intention nor audience reaction is an altogether reliable criterion. A harmless play could upon occasion be 'explained into a satire', as I would say happened with Mallet's *Eurydice* (1731)—and as Walpole's propagandists claimed was done with *The Beggar's Opera*. Less than three weeks after the première of Gay's play, the *Craftsman* published a gleeful, tongue-in-cheek denunciation of it as 'the most venemous *allegorical Libel* against the *G——t* that hath appeared for many Years past'.[78]

[78] 17 February 1728. It was reprinted as *A Key to the Beggar's Opera in a Letter to Caleb*

The kinds of real-life specifics that can be written into a play are bewilderingly diverse—from ideology and allegory to personation and topical allusion.[79] For present purposes I have simply surveyed the plays treated as political by Loftis, Goldgar, and Kern.[80] Considering these plays (some forty of which are extant), I would suggest a basic distinction between *topical allusion plays* and *application plays*. Most of the former are comedies, most of the latter tragedies, though the generic distinction is not absolute. The topical allusion plays refer openly to current events (and sometimes to real people, thinly disguised), generally in an insinuating or hostile way. *Pasquin* is a good example. Application plays invite the audience to draw parallels and see connections, 'applying' the lessons of Scanderbeg, the Earl of Essex, and Charles I to the times and court of George II—as in Havard's *Scanderbeg*, Ralph's *The Fall of the Earl of Essex*, and Havard's *King Charles the First*. The difference between the two types is usefully illustrated by comparing *The Beggar's Opera* (which caused a flap, but did Walpole little harm) with *Polly* (which was firmly suppressed).[81] Both censorship and journalistic uproar in the 1730s suggest that the application plays were taken a great deal more seriously. Why this should be so is hard to say, especially since the 'topical' plays often refer directly and unmistakably to their targets while the 'application' plays generally purport to be something else. Most of the topical plays, however, are written in a spirit of fun and mockery, while the application plays (ostensibly more remote) tend to deal in more serious issues and handle them in less frivolous ways.

Another important distinction is between *politicized* plays and *partisan* plays. We have already encountered this distinction in *Rape upon Rape*, which is liberally stuffed with topical allusions but does not systematically attack either the ministry or the opposition. Because Walpole was more recognizable than anyone else, and because the party in power almost always presents the more inviting target, topical/politicized plays tend to snipe more at the ministry than at the

Danvers, Esq; and appended to the 1728 edition of Christopher Bullock's *Woman's Revenge* (London, 1728), pp. 69–76.

[79] For an attempt at a theoretical and methodological disentanglement of types of 'content' in plays and valid ways of analysing them, see Hume, *The Rakish Stage*, ch. 1.

[80] Loftis, *Politics of Drama*; Goldgar, *Walpole and the Wits*; Kern, *Dramatic Satire in the Age of Walpole*.

[81] For an excellent explanation of the 'application' of *Polly* (a far less harmless work than has generally been supposed), see Vincent J. Liesenfeld (ed.), *The Stage and the Licensing Act 1729–1739* (New York, 1981), Introduction, pp. x–xiii.

opposition. In a similar way today a political cartoonist will get more mileage out of the President or the Prime Minister than out of the relatively faceless opposition leaders, and the public will enjoy the put-down of the figure in power. But this does not mean that digs at Mr Reagan and Mrs Thatcher are necessarily motivated by genuine malice and hostility. There are cartoonists with ideological and party commitments, but not many of them.[82] A willingness to ridicule the person in power need not imply partisan commitment on the part of the cartoonist—or the playwright. To forget this is to ignore important distinctions in the plays of the 1730s. We need not only to ask whether a play contains political material, but also to consider the degree of malice and party spirit behind it.

Just how political were the offerings at the Little Haymarket? And to what degree did the venue affect Fielding's writing? Pat Rogers sums up the usual view of the theatre and its supposed political commitments when he says that 'the management . . . sailed closer to the wind than any other house, and so the theatre was closed by the authorities at regular intervals'.[83] In fact there was no 'management' in the usual sense, and the Little Haymarket was closed by authority only once—in the summer of 1731. We will examine this episode in detail in due course. A survey of particular titles reveals that with the freak exception of *Don Quixote in England* (staged in April 1734), all of the 'political' plays mounted at the Little Haymarket fall into two periods, 1728–1731 and 1736–1737.

Since such 'significant control' as the Little Haymarket may have exerted over Fielding must have derived from expectations generated by plays in the early period, let us consider them. Aside from Fielding's own plays, only three titles are germane. Curiously enough, they suggest to Loftis that the Little Haymarket was 'sympathetic to Walpole in the season of 1728–9'.[84] Mottley's *The Craftsman* (October 1728) is a very lightweight afterpiece farce built on a love-plot and incidentally ridiculing, as Loftis says, 'the journal of that name, its fictional author, Caleb D'Anvers, and the bumpkin squires who read it'. The tone is so light and good-humoured that one can hardly see the play (an afterpiece that limped through six nights) as much of a satire. Odell's double-bill, *The Smugglers* and *The Patron*, apparently

[82] When Carter was President, Oliphant savaged him; when Reagan took over, Oliphant turned his fire in that direction. And his cartoons have been enjoyed by all but the stuffiest die-hard supporters of both presidents as well as by their opponents.

[83] Rogers, p. 34.

[84] Loftis, *Politics of Drama*, p. 103.

ran only a single night in May 1729. The former is a romantic farce that capitalizes on the taste for low-life engendered by *The Beggar's Opera* and tries to expose illegal practices that hurt the public, as the author explains in his dedication to George Doddington, 'One of the Lords Commissioners of His Majesty's Treasury'. The depiction of the noble Trusty, an honest exciseman, would certainly have pleased Walpole. I do not know what to make of *The Patron: or, The Statesman's Opera*. As Loftis observes, the piece 'seems to be rich in political innuendo, though the butt of its satire is not at all clear'.[85] Lord Falcon, 'a Minister of State', is a lying scoundrel, bamboozled into giving the deserving Merit a government post of £400 per annum in return for the favours of a prostitute posing as Merit's wife. From someone other than Odell one might take this as a nasty hit at the way business was done in Walpole's administration. But Odell was a Walpole loyalist (or later became one) who was appointed Deputy Examiner of Plays after 1737. If this damp squib was meant as a hit at the administration, it found no audience favour, and it was either forgotten or forgiven. Loftis somewhat misleadingly calls these three plays evidence of a 'flirtation between the Little Theatre in the Haymarket and the Minister'. The only other pre-1731 Little Haymarket plays in which significant political content has been discerned are Fielding's own *Author's Farce*, *Tom Thumb*, and *Rape upon Rape*. What kind of politics we find in *The Tragedy of Tragedies*, *The Welsh Opera*, and *The Grub-Street Opera* is a problem to be taken up in due course, but clearly we have no reason to believe that Fielding wrote anti-Walpole plays because the audience at the Little Haymarket expected and demanded them. There is simply no evidence to support such a contention.

The one indisputably partisan political play actually performed at the Little Haymarket between 1728 and 1731 is *The Fall of Mortimer* (staged 12 May 1731), and it immediately generated fierce public controversy. The authorities found themselves unable to suppress it quickly and cleanly, but they harassed the theatre into silence. *The Fall of Mortimer* is an 'application' play created by altering 'Mountfort's' *King Edward the Third* (published in 1691) to make it aim very clearly at Walpole.[86] Like other 'Majesty Misled' plays, this one relies

[85] Ibid.

[86] The adaptation was anonymous; Lowndes credits [William] Hatchett, plausibly, but without explanation. See William Thomas Lowndes, *The Bibliographer's Manual*, rev. Henry G. Bohn, 6 vols. (London, 1857–64), III, 1619.

on an application drawn from a safely remote subject. Some bits of the prologue will give the idea. 'We change the ancient for the modern Dress. . . . The *British* Constitution . . . by *one bad Man* was almost sacrific'd . . . foul Corruption was become a Trade. . . . The Monster is cast down. . . . A *Villain-Statesman*, not the *King* to *blame*.' The King finally orders Mortimer (i.e., Walpole) executed for his crimes (thereby becoming 'a King indeed!'), and says: 'Such be the Fate of all, who dare abuse / The Ministerial Function' (61). Sometime in May or June appeared a pamphlet entitled *Remarks on an Historical Play, Called, The Fall of Mortimer*, 'Shewing Wherein the said Play may be term'd a Libel against the present Administration'.[87] It is written as a horrified denunciation of such 'Poyson', and prints the most scurrilous bits 'from the very Words of the Play, as I took 'em down in short Hand the 2d time of the Performance'. This was promptly answered by another pamphlet, *The History of Mortimer*, 'being a vindication of *The Fall of Mortimer*. Occasioned by it's having been presented as a treasonable libel.'[88] Studying the *Remarks*, I am inclined to think it either a remarkably inept protest or an ironic one. The author manages, deliberately or not, to rub the reader's nose in all the nastiest parts of the play. This exchange of pamphlets could well be a practical demonstration of Bookweightean policy of the sort Fielding satirized in *The Author's Farce*.

We can hardly be surprised that so flagrant a smear as *The Fall of Mortimer* aroused the wrath of the authorities. Even so, it managed fifteen performances. By 20 June someone was collecting formal depositions about performances,[89] and on 24 June the *Grub-street Journal* carried a report that 'The Company of Comedians at the New Theatre in the Hay Market, have been forbid acting any more *The fall of Mortimer*'—without explanation of who forbade performance or on what authority. Evidently some of the actors got scared. An advertisement for a sixteenth performance, on 30 June, states: 'The Company of Comedians have determined to play notwithstanding the Opposition made by some of the Company to prevent this Performance.' At this point the authorities got tough and included the play in a Grand Jury warrant against libellous and seditious books and pamphlets (reported in the *Daily Courant*, 8 July). When the play was next announced on 21

[87] E. Rayner (London, n.d.). Arnott and Robinson, no. 3892.

[88] (London, 1731). Arnott and Robinson, no. 3891.

[89] See the sworn testimony by John Ibbutt, stationer, Folger MS T.b. 3 (transcription by J. Payne Collier).

July constables showed up to arrest the actors, who 'all made their Escapes'.[90] On 20 August the actors tried to resume business, advertising the safely non-political *Hurlothrumbo*, but once again constables appeared with a warrant for their arrest, and they had to take to their heels.[91] Thus ended the first 'political' phase of the Little Haymarket.

Scholars have sometimes wondered if politics lurk even in the zany *Hurlothrumbo*,[92] but this is far-fetched. *Hurlothrumbo* had been through three dozen performances since its première in March 1729. It was stopped in August 1731 because the company had made itself obnoxious to the authorities, including both the ministry and the Justices of Westminster. We may deduce, however, that there was no effective mechanism for censorship. The actors must have been warned or threatened (hence the notice of 30 June), but their defiance produced not a formal prosecution for operating an unlicensed theatre, but a more indirect kind of harassment. Apparently the local JPs issued warrants for the arrest of the actors as 'Rogues and Vagabonds'—on whose complaint we do not know. To judge by the events of 1733 the actors might have got off if brought into court on this charge, but they did not choose to stand and fight. They probably lacked the financial resources, and perhaps they assumed the worst. The actors fled, and the *de facto* result of *The Fall of Mortimer* was the silencing of the theatre. Formally, the theatre was never shut by court or government order, and it was never officially allowed to reopen. Potter evidently complained about losing the business his actor-tenants had given him and was told (perhaps late in the autumn of 1731) that they could resume operations unmolested, but only if he would see to it that they did not stage plays obnoxious to the government. Or so I would deduce from Aston's indignant preface to *The Restauration of King Charles II*. Aston's play strikes me as both inept and harmless, but tales of restoring Stuart kings to their rightful thrones were not popular with Georgian governments.

[90] A letter of 21 July by Nicholas Paxton (evidently to Walpole) reports both a meeting of the 20th by the Justices of Westminster about how to suppress the Little Haymarket and the attempt to arrest the actors (PRO SP 36/23, fols. 252–3). Paxton's claim for expenses in connection with the harassment of the Little Haymarket performers was submitted to the government on 20 Oct. 1731. See PRO T 27/25, p. 76.

[91] See the *Daily Post* and *Daily Advertiser* of 23 Aug. and the *Daily Courant* of 25 Aug.

[92] See Cross, I, 112; Loftis, *Politics of Drama*, p. 106. For mockery of the idea that 'the silly Character of Lord Flame is meant as a Satyr upon anybody', see *Fog's Weekly Journal* of 28 Aug.

Aware of the political potentialities of 'application', the opposition press sought to stimulate this habit of mind in the audience. A particularly good example of this sort of journalism appeared in a lead article (signed 'Dramaticus') in the *Craftsman* of 8 March 1728/9. The author solemnly agrees that 'it is the Duty of *Men in Authority* to take particular Care that *Scandal* and *Sedition* be not exhibited to the People', and ironically proposes that 'a large INDEX EXPURGATORIUS' be erected by 'a *Committee of learned Gentlemen*' who should be appointed and given '*proper Salaries*, to inspect and examine all *Dramatical Performances, antient* as well as *modern* . . . to *obliterate* or *soften* all such Passages as appear *offensive*, or which They shall apprehend the *present Circumstances* of the Times may render subject, in any Manner, to *bad Interpretations*'. (Cibber is proposed as a member, on the condition that he refrain from writing any more himself.) Pointing to offending passages in *The What d'ye Call It*, *Henry the Fourth*, *Sejanus*, *Henry the Eighth*, *The Sophy*, *The Spanish Fryar*, and *Cato*, the author concludes that playwrights can 'be as *free* and *satyrical* as They please upon the *Vices of Princes*', but that they must 'remember that Characters of *Ministers*, however *wicked*, ought always to be *inviolable*'.

Obviously we have found far less political satire at the Little Haymarket than its reputation would lead us to expect. What of the other theatres? Were they even more politically toothless? On the contrary, we will find that many of the political plays of the thirties appeared elsewhere.

Drury Lane was widely viewed as a Whig stronghold during the long reign of the triumvirate, a truism borne out by their plays prior to September 1732. Martyn's *Timoleon* (1730) is an allegorical justification of William III and the Revolution of 1688, a still timely salvo for 'Revolution Principles'.[93] Lillo's *The London Merchant* (1731) is political largely in ideology, but as a trumpeting of Whig mercantilism it does not seem out of place at Drury Lane, though it arrived via the back door of the summer company. Mallet's *Eurydice* (1731) was accused of Jacobitism in a contemporary pamphlet (apparently seriously), but I must agree with Loftis that if there are any politics in the play they are thoroughly swamped by neoclassical clutter.[94]

[93] See J. P. Kenyon, *Revolution Principles: The Politics of Party 1689–1720* (Cambridge, 1977), for relevant background.

[94] Loftis, *Politics of Drama*, p. 108. For the charge of Jacobitism, see the anonymous *Remarks on the Tragedy of Eurydice* (London, 1731). Arnott and Robinson, no. 3979.

Following the advent of new management in 1732 Drury Lane produced occasional plays with significant opposition sympathies. Kelly's *Timon in Love* (1733) has as much social as political satire, but it does hammer away at the theme that gold corrupts, apparently a comment on the Walpole administration.[95] Duncombe's *Junius Brutus* (1734) is yet another defence of the Revolution and William III, but it hits hard at Walpole via Tarquin's subversion of Roman law. Lillo's *The Christian Hero* (1735), like other 'Scanderbeg' plays, preaches resistance to tyranny—opposition code for 'down with Walpole!' Dodsley's *The King and the Miller of Mansfield* (1737) shows its opposition colours in its fervent presentation of 'country' ideology.

None of these plays is political in the fashion of *The Fall of Mortimer*, but with the probable exception of *Eurydice* all of them would pretty clearly have been understood as political statements. To express the principles and ideology of the opposition was within the unwritten rules; to point a finger too directly at Walpole (much less at the King) would almost certainly have got a theatre in real trouble, as *The Fall of Mortimer* had proved. No one really knew what the government's powers of censorship were, but Goodman's Fields existed in a precarious legal limbo, while Drury Lane and Lincoln's Inn Fields operated on Royal patents that could be suspended, if not easily revoked. A great many theatre people must have remembered that in 1709 the Lord Chamberlain had been able to silence Christopher Rich and make it stick. No theatre manager would have risked producing something like the anonymous *Majesty Misled; Or, The Overthrow of Evil Ministers*, published in 1734 as 'intended to be Acted ... But ... refus'd for Certain Reasons'.

The story at the other theatres is similar. John Loftis is quite right in saying that 'John Rich showed restraint in the plays he produced—he clearly wished to avoid trouble', but Lincoln's Inn Fields had consistently demonstrated a Tory/opposition bias between 1714 and 1728, and Rich continued to produce plays whose 'political overtones ... could not be misunderstood'.[96] *The Beggar's Opera* is the only important instance of a topical allusion play there, but in four cases Rich was prepared to mount 'application' plays with clear-cut opposition messages. *Polly* was suppressed in 1729. Madden's

[95] *Timon in Love* was staged by Highmore's 'loyal' company, not by the regular Drury Lane acting company, then at the Little Haymarket.

[96] Loftis, *Politics of Drama*, p. 107. On Lincoln's Inn Fields' Tory bias between 1714 and 1728, see ibid., ch. 4.

Themistocles (1729; dedicated to the Prince of Wales) uses Greek history to make a rather general comment, and Jeffreys' *Merope* (1731) spouts the usual opposition stuff about patriotism and liberty. Tracy's *Periander* (1731), however, is exactly what Loftis calls it—a blatant 'propaganda' play denouncing Whig 'luxury' and tyranny, and proposing the restoration of the 'ancient' form of government in the best Bolingbrokean fashion. No one seems to have called attention to the point, but Rich never again mounted a genuinely political play. I would deduce that he observed the results of *The Fall of Mortimer* at the Little Haymarket and got the message. Bond's *The Tuscan Treaty* (1733), an account of Tarquin's overthrow with much vaguer parallels to contemporary England than Duncombe's *Junius Brutus*, is about as political a play as Rich cared to venture after the spring of 1731.

At Goodman's Fields the politic Giffard went to considerable pains to advertise his 'loyalty' to George II, and he is generally described as a political non-combatant.[97] He was none the less willing to produce political plays of any stripe within the limits of safety. Walker's (?) *The Fate of Villany* (1730) is a rather general criticism of courtiers who abuse their power, but Ralph's *The Fall of the Earl of Essex* (1731) comes much closer to Walpole, especially in his relations with Queen Caroline. Havard's *Scanderbeg* (1733) is quite bland. Three political plays produced by Giffard at Lincoln's Inn Fields in 1737 span the whole spectrum. Hewitt's *A Tutor for the Beaus* (dedicated to Molly Skerret) feebly ridicules the opposition. Lynch's *The Independent Patriot* is an oddly impartial hit at the world of London politics, freely damning all parties. Havard's *King Charles the First* suggests that bad ministers can lead to the downfall of kings. Havard's play was softened in performance to smudge his clear parallels with George II, and small wonder.

From this survey we learn several things. (1) After *The Beggar's Opera* only the Little Haymarket does much with topical allusion plays of the comic sort—and most of them are Fielding's. (2) Rich staged some opposition propaganda until he took fright in 1731. (3) After the demise of the triumvirate Drury Lane was perfectly willing to stage anti-ministerial works of the 'application play' variety. (4) Giffard was surprisingly ready to do political pieces, including a couple of flagrant opposition allegories. (5) The offerings of the Little Haymarket prior to 1736 are a great deal less political than its reputation would lead one

[97] See *The London Stage*, Part 3, I, lxxxii–lxxxiii, and Loftis, *Politics of Drama*, p. 106.

to believe. (6) The two openly obnoxious 'application plays' were both suppressed—*Polly* and *The Fall of Mortimer*. (7) Most broadly, we may say that after 1731 the theatres did not stage 'application plays' unless they stuck to fairly general parallels and ideology. Walpole probably did not like some of the plays that were produced, but the London theatre of the early 1730s was hardly a hotbed of partisan political activity. With this background in mind, we are ready to consider Fielding's much-disputed plays of 1731.

The Tragedy of Tragedies

Fielding's decision to rewrite *Tom Thumb* probably stemmed from several factors. He hoped to get more mileage out of it as a mainpiece; he wanted to improve it as a 'reading play'; and he saw untapped possibilities in the subject-matter that he was evidently anxious to exploit. The result is a very different work. Most of the words of *Tom Thumb* are retained, but his alterations radically change the work.[98]

The spoken text is doubled in length. The piece remains a bit scanty for a mainpiece, but it sufficed—especially with afterpieces more substantial than usual. Fielding went to some trouble to complicate his plot: Glumdalca is introduced to burlesque the captive princess so common in heroic drama; the King is made to fall in love with her; competition between Tom Thumb and Lord Grizzle for Huncamunca is played up; Merlin introduces the conjuror found in some of the plays under attack; and Foodle mocks the out-of-place courtier and provides an element of court intrigue. In themselves, these additions are not particularly desirable, but the expansion of scale permits the large number of additional speeches needed to carry out Fielding's new plan.

Tom Thumb mocks a genre; *The Tragedy of Tragedies* parodies that genre's verbal style. But in neither case, as T. W. Craik observes, is the result essentially a work of 'ridicule': Fielding has written not with animosity but with gusto.[99] Much of the burlesque impact of the

[98] The work was altered yet again two years later when it appeared as *The Opera of Operas* at the Little Haymarket (31 May 1733). Fielding has no known connection with this version, traditionally ascribed to Eliza Haywood and William Hatchett, with music by Arne. 33 songs are added, and Merlin contrives an operatic happy ending, but the alterations are mere hackwork. It was sufficiently popular that Highmore's Drury Lane mounted it in November 1733, with a score by Lampe.

[99] T. W. Craik, 'Fielding's "Tom Thumb" Plays', *Augustan Worlds*, ed. J. C. Hilson, M. M. B. Jones, and J. R. Watson (New York, 1978), pp. 165–74. Since I first wrote this chapter Nancy Mace has discovered that Fielding was systematically travestying the

original comes from the low-life incongruities with which Fielding fills the work. Most of these remain in the revision, but they are made to coexist—not always comfortably—with a veritable catalogue of high-flown lines culled from particular heroic plays. *Tom Thumb* could have been tossed together in a few hours, but as Hillhouse has observed, 'the composition of [*The Tragedy of Tragedies*] must have taken considerable time and a good deal of drudgery. The citations and references with which the notes are thickly scattered are practically all correct ... the innumerable quotations from plays necessarily imply real work.'[100] In performance the audience merely senses the flavour added by these carefully selected lines, but for the reader, inundated with footnotes, the stylistic self-burlesque becomes the single most prominent feature of the work. The best of these additions have proved memorable, particularly 'Oh *Huncamunca*, *Huncamunca*! oh!' (26),[101] inspired by Thomson's *Sophonisba* (1730).

The apparatus that Fielding concocted for his reader is a delight.[102] If, as critics complain, the footnotes sometimes partake of the tedium they parody, they none the less effectively document the target sources and simulate scholarly clutter, while enjoying a horrid fascination of their own. The celebrated heroic plays of the preceding seventy years really do contain the sort of bombast Fielding quarries and displays, and he spells it out with the gleeful air of one who assures the reader that he isn't making it all up.

The preface is a little masterpiece of pseudo-scholarly style, and one cannot help being disarmed by the self-mockery of the opening lines: 'The Town hath seldom been more divided in its Opinion, than concerning the Merit of the following Scenes. Whilst some publickly affirmed, That no Author could produce so fine a Piece but Mr. *P*—, others have with as much Vehemence insisted, That no one could write any thing so bad, but Mr. *F*—.' Fielding cleverly dismisses *Tom Thumb* as a 'surreptitious and piratical Copy', though granting

works of Lewis Theobald, though without calling attention to the fact in his notes. See her 'Fielding, Theobald, and *The Tragedy of Tragedies*', forthcoming in *Philological Quarterly*.

[100] *The Tragedy of Tragedies*, ed. James T. Hillhouse (New Haven, Conn., 1918), pp. 9–10. Although corrected and supplemented by L. J. Morrissey's edn. (Edinburgh, 1970) in a variety of ways, the Hillhouse edn. remains a remarkably good one.

[101] Citations are to the Roberts edn. of 1731.

[102] For a reading of '*The Tragedy of Tragedies* as Literary Hoax', see Robert F. Willson, jun., *'Their Form Confounded': Studies in the Burlesque Play from Udall to Sheridan* (The Hague, 1975), ch. 5.

that it contained 'sufficient Beauties to give it a Run of upwards of Forty Nights'. The conceit that *The Tragedy of Tragedies* is Elizabethan (possibly by Shakespeare) and much plundered by later authors is a superb excuse for the footnotes documenting these unacknowledged borrowings. The critical jargon so deftly fabricated must be a delight to anyone familiar with Dryden and Dennis. By comparison, Fielding's preface to the second edition of *Tom Thumb* less than a year earlier seems schoolboyish.

To find any point beyond amusing incongruity in *Tom Thumb* is probably misguided, but *The Tragedy of Tragedies* is a different matter. In the best critical analysis of the work to date, J. Paul Hunter argues that it 'suggests with surprising accuracy the directions and extent of Fielding's talent. Here, in rather simple form, is his account of the manners and ideals of the times; his sense of a heroic, inapplicable past; his method of judging action by commentary and vice versa; and his genial sense of life's vitality. And here too is his hatred of the pompous, the pedantic, and the grave . . . no matter how insistently they pretend to be sponsored by higher commitments.'[103] The immediate objects of *The Tragedy of Tragedies* are obvious enough, and Fielding's ridicule of stylistic inflation and pretension in tragedy is highly effective. But this is not a new *Rehearsal*: as many commentators have observed, usually with surprise, most of Fielding's targets are more than thirty years old. A handful of the plays cited were still occasionally revived (e.g. *Aureng-Zebe*, *Don Sebastian*, *The Indian Emperour*, *The Unhappy Favourite*), but why should Fielding set out to flog so sickly a horse as heroic tragedy?

The answer is complex. *Tom Thumb* burlesques heroic tragedy because it is burlesquable. Pseudo-classic tragedy would hardly have done. But when Fielding revamped his playlet, he introduced three major new centres of interest: (1) language *per se*—in the flood of lines adapted into the text and cited in the notes; (2) Dryden—whose work figures very prominently in the apparatus; and (3) false scholarship.

Literary style and verbal precision were to be lifelong preoccupations with Fielding, and his hatred for affectation and inflation never abated. And if this satire was not especially topical, it was certainly entertaining. As for Dryden, who had died in 1700, I suspect that Hunter is correct in suggesting that Fielding's hostility is based both on scorn for the laureateship and the poetic establishment, and on

[103] Hunter, p. 23.

temperamental incompatibility with Dryden's well-advertised faith in progress. Like Pope and Swift, the young Fielding, Grub Street hack though he was, had espoused the cause of the ancients. This preoccupation is likewise apparent in the pseudo-scholarship, in which Fielding's debt to the *Dunciad* is evident. Given the Theobald–Pope controversy over the editing of Shakespeare, the learned fool of an editor must clearly have seemed a swipe at Lewis Theobald. And of course Fielding works in a superb joke: the editor finds all sorts of obscure plays to cite, but is virtually blind to the stream of Shakespeare-allusions with which Fielding studs his text, including speeches as flagrant as 'Your *Huncamunca*. *Tom Thumb*'s *Huncamunca*, every Man's *Huncamunca*' (37) and 'wherefore art thou *Tom Thumb*?' (22).[104]

I would guess that in performance *The Tragedy of Tragedies* remained pretty much what *Tom Thumb* had been, a travesty of heroic drama to be enjoyed for its sheer silliness. Production history suggests some rather gross devices. When Drury Lane staged the play in May 1732, for example, John Harper (the most notable Falstaff of the day) was cast as Huncamunca. Harper made something of a specialty of skirts' roles, taking such parts as Mrs Midnight in *The Twin-Rivals* and Lady Termagant in *The Boarding School*. The effect of his presence as Huncamunca must have been pleasantly grotesque but decidedly unsubtle. Even without such additional touches, *The Tragedy of Tragedies* invites flagrant overacting. Its effect on the reader is naturally very different. On the page, Fielding's inflated editorial machinery so swamps the text that the play is overshadowed: the apparatus becomes the point, and modern learning becomes a satiric target at least as important as the plays whose style is displayed for ridicule.

I have left for last the vexed question of political import. Cross, Dudden, and Morrissey have read the work as a systematic political attack on Walpole, with incidental sniping at the King and Queen. Hillhouse flatly denies it; Goldgar considers *Tom Thumb* 'innocent of political innuendo' and sees nothing any more political about the

[104] The latter is probably a complicated joke. Modern scholars generally suppose that the editor's note to Otway's *Caius Marius* (which uses *Romeo and Juliet* in a sub-plot) is a piece of blind duncery. But we have no definite record of performance of *Romeo and Juliet* later than the early 1660s, while *Caius Marius* was revived regularly in the 1720s. Fielding presumably knew that 'Shakespeare' is the right source, and meant the reader of Shakespeare to pick it up.

revision; Cleary sees a drastic distinction between the two, finding *Tom Thumb* non-political but *The Tragedy of Tragedies* surrounded with 'new hints, external to its action or dialogue, that would have primed audiences or readers in 1731 to look for political satire in patterns, characterizations, dialogue, and details that would have seemed politically innocent in 1730'.[105] The evidence, such as it is, lies in the addition of the epithet '*the Great*' to the subtitle; performance with *The Welsh Opera* in late April 1731 (a month after the première of *The Tragedy of Tragedies*); descriptions of the dramatis personae added to the printed edition of 1731; and in some scattered references—e.g., to foxhunting (16), and ''fore *George*' (7).

Against the political reading, as Cleary admits, is 'the total absence of known contemporary comments implying that the play was so interpreted'.[106] The politicality of *The Tragedy of Tragedies* is a problem not susceptible of clear proof. My own view is that political interpretation depends on over-reading of disjunct details that are largely outside the spoken text. Tom Thumb is a very unsatisfactory 'Walpole', being a warrior, not a courtier (much less a parliamentarian). In performance, I suspect that the obvious literary targets and the hurly-burly of travesty acting would sufficiently distract the audience that only much blunter political parallels would have been noticed. When Cleary speaks of 'audiences or readers', he blurs an important distinction.[107] The reading version presents a very different experience. The most suggestive evidence for topical application is the dramatis personae descriptions of the King and Queen:

King *Arthur*, A passionate sort of King, Husband to Queen *Dollallolla*, of whom he stands a little in Fear; Father to *Huncamunca*, whom he is very fond of; and in Love with *Glumdalca*.

[105] Cross, I, 103; Dudden, I, 67–9; Morrissey, Fountainwell edn., and 'Fielding's First Political Satire', *Anglia*, 93 (1972), 325–48; Goldgar, pp. 104–5; Cleary, pp. 41–5. The most detailed political reading is Morrissey's, but ingenious as his explication is, I suspect that one could get allegory out of practically any text by applying his methods.

[106] The one such piece of evidence that has been adduced is an article in the *Daily* Post of 29 March 1742 (see, e.g. Dudden, I, 68). This article is, however, clearly a spoof of allegorical readings written to mock the Licenser. The author 'explicates' *The Tragedy of Tragedies* with a flood of tantalizing dashes and concludes, 'I hope the L— C— will, for the future, prohibit it, as dangerous to the State.' The rest of the article (concerning *The Double-Dealer* and some French dancers) is even more overtly preposterous.

[107] Craik (p. 172) points out, for example, that 'Foodle is never addressed by name in the dialogue: he is named for Fielding's own pleasure and the reader's.'

Queen *Dollallolla*, Wife to King *Arthur*, and Mother to *Huncamunca*, a Woman entirely faultless, saving that she is a little given to Drink; a little too much a *Virago* towards her Husband, and in Love with *Tom Thumb*.

As Cleary expounds these characters, they do 'apply' quite well to George II and Queen Caroline. 'Books of the Tragedy' containing these descriptions were sold at the theatre from the opening night (*Daily Post*, 22 March), and in April and May *The Tragedy of Tragedies* was on five occasions part of a double bill with *The Welsh Opera*, a work in which Fielding unquestionably personates the King and Queen. I would conclude that Fielding may well have realized—perhaps as late as March 1731 when preparing *The Tragedy of Tragedies* for press—that he could link the work to his new burlesque. But the result seems more an in-joke than an attempt to redefine *The Tragedy of Tragedies* as a political satire. And if any sort of satiric reading was being invited, the target is more the court than the Prime Minister.

The Letter-Writers

The three-act farce Fielding concocted to serve as afterpiece for *The Tragedy of Tragedies* managed only four performances and is of interest largely because it shows us Fielding trying his hand at another formulaic genre. The results are not bad, but Fielding was little more at home in contretemps farce than in intrigue comedy. The gimmick is a good one: Mr Wisdom and Mr Softly, a pair of elderly merchants with young wives, write threatening letters to each other's spouses, hoping to frighten them into staying at home.[108] Mrs Softly continues to parade about the town—ostentatiously carrying a blunderbuss and guarded by footmen (12)—while Mrs Wisdom carries on her love intrigues at home.[109] The dashing Rakel, an officer on leave, is pursuing both of them. In Act I Mrs Wisdom has to hide him in a closet when her husband returns unexpectedly; in Act II Mrs Softly, for want of a closet, has to spin a tale to allay her husband's suspicions

[108] Charles B. Woods, 'Notes on Three of Fielding's Plays', *PMLA* 52 (1937), 359–73, has shown that Fielding got the idea from a rash of blackmailing letters from 'incendiaries and murderers' in the autumn of 1730 and the winter–spring of 1731. Woods quotes the *Monthly Chronicle* for Oct. 1730 which gives an account of a letter to Lady Diana Fielding (Henry Fielding's second cousin) 'threatning Death, &c. in case she did not send a certain Sum of Money to a Place in the said Letter specified'. The problem was serious enough for the King to issue a Royal proclamation on 20 Nov., offering a reward for information about the writers of such letters and forbidding compliance with their demands.

[109] Citations are to the Roberts edn. of 1731.

when he finds them together. Later in Act II Mrs Softly interrupts Rakel and Mrs Wisdom; he leaps under a table and is discovered when it is upset by the drunken Commons. This is standard fare for the genre, though executed without the verve of Durfey or Ravenscroft at their best. And despite the ostensible sexual motivations, actual adultery is even less likely than in Feydeau.

Compared with the lumbering intrigue comedies, *The Letter-Writers: Or, a New Way to Keep A Wife at Home* moves briskly. Something actually happens in Act I, and Fielding keeps the cast of characters small enough to avoid dispersion of focus. The gimmick, alas, is ineptly handled. Fielding imparts the design at page 12; introduces a largely redundant explanation to Mrs Softly at page 26; and then at the end has Mrs Softly announce that she 'over-heard your fine Plot' (46) without telling us *when* she overheard the plot or what difference that made. Neither wife ever seems at all impressed by her supposed danger, belying Cross's assertion that the play 'depicts the effect of these letters upon wives of different temperament'.[110] The two women are rather feebly developed, and their husbands are silly but not hateful, which reduces the marital and sexual tensions of the play to the vanishing-point. The old men's argument over how to govern a wife is a pale imitation of a sex-comedy commonplace: Fielding simply cannot bring the cliché to life.

Once again Fielding employs emblematic names (clearly ironic in the case of Mr Wisdom). Rakel is a likeable scapegrace. His servant Risque is one of the better touches in the play, a genuine rogue quite prepared to swear that his master is a burglar and a highwayman when the two of them are caught in Mr Wisdom's house. The most interesting character is Commons, a brother in iniquity of Rakel in town for one final fling before he goes off to take orders. When Rakel laughingly asks him if he has 'the Impudence to pretend to a Call', Commons coolly replies, 'Ay, Sir; the usual Call: I have the Promise of a good Living. Lookee, Captain, my Call of Piety is much the same as yours of Honour—You will fight, and I shall pray for the same Reasons I assure you' (7). This bluntness about matters pertaining to the church is unusual and effective.

Despite its good ideas, the play ultimately fails because Fielding has no real zest for the clichés he is relying on. Rakel is a very tame rake; the wives are merely playing games, not trying to commit adultery, and

[110] Cross, I, 102.

there is no sting in the marital exchanges. Fielding gets the contretemps more or less right, but he seems to derive no delight from plot manipulation. Mr Wisdom's discovery of Rakel near the end of Act I falls very flat, and the window-breaking scheme Rakel dreams up at the start of Act II to clear Mrs Wisdom from suspicion smells of the author's lamp. Commons' scene with whores and musicians in Act II is an irrelevant digression, and not very amusing in any case. Fielding mercifully avoids excessive moralizing at the end, but the cheerful forgiveness of Risque (who threatens blackmail) is hard to justify after the self-serving lies he has told, and it trivializes the whole arrest and prison scene. I am baffled by Allardyce Nicoll's belief that 'of all eighteenth century farces' this one 'is perhaps the best'.[111] At this stage Fielding lacks the plot control, sense of timing, and zest for formulaic confrontation that first-rate farce requires. His skill in handling the ancillary details is unquestionable, and we will find that when he borrows his structure from Molière, he can develop it successfully. The verdict of the eighteenth-century audience seems correct: there is no serious comparison between *The Letter-Writers* and *The Mock Doctor* or *The Intriguing Chambermaid*.

The Welsh Opera and *The Grub-Street Opera*

In *The Welsh Opera* (first staged 22 April 1731 as an afterpiece for *The Tragedy of Tragedies*) Fielding daringly vented his penchant for burlesque. Its politicality has often been overestimated, but its audacity is beyond question. The design of the piece is simplicity itself. Fielding exhibits King George, Queen Caroline, the Prince of Wales, Walpole, and Pulteney as master, mistress, not-so-hopeful heir, and principal servants in the disorganized household of Squire Ap-Shinken, an amiable Welsh squire whose only wish is peace and quiet in which to smoke and drink.

Fielding draws parallels sufficently precise to remove any possible doubt of what he is doing, but he does not extend them so far that he would be unable to plead injured innocence if need be. Squire Ap-Shinken is George II, quite under the thumb of Madam Ap-Shinken (Queen Caroline), and not inclined to dispute her authority. ('If she interfereth not with my Pipe, I am resolv'd not to interfere with her Family—let her govern while I Smoke' (4).)[112] His son Master Owen

[111] Nicoll, II, 215.
[112] Citations are to the edn. 'Printed by *E. Rayner*, and sold by *H. Cook*', n.d. (1731).

Ap-Shinken is the egregious Prince of Wales, who is making himself 'too familiar with the Maids' (3). Parson Puzzletext has been variously identified with Dr Samuel Clarke (d. 1729), Bishop Hoadly, and Francis Hare, Dean of St Paul's,[113] but I agree with Cleary that attempts at particular identification are misguided. Fielding is not attacking an eminent churchman; he is pointing to the Queen's well-publicized taste for theological controversy (promptly alluded to on page 4). Robin the Butler is obviously Walpole; John the Coachman is Walpole's ally John, Lord Hervey (Vice-chamberlain of the Household); William the Groom is William Pulteney, leader of the opposition (and hence 'Enemy to *Robin*'). Thomas the gardener is a problem: the obvious candidate for a 'Thomas' in the Royal establishment is Thomas Pelham-Holles, Duke of Newcastle, formerly Lord Chamberlain and now Secretary of State for the Southern Department. But he was an ally of Walpole's, not an enemy. Morrissey proposes Thomas Wyndham, a member of the opposition,[114] but I doubt that he would have been recognizable enough to make an effective point. We need see him merely as a cohort of William. Sweetissa is always identified as Molly Skerret, but this makes little sense: she is presented as Robin's sweetheart and a virtuous woman, not as his mistress. The other women do not seem to represent anyone in particular, despite a variety of wild guesses by critics.

The story is very slight indeed. Owen forges letters—simply to make mischief—and thereby creates a breach between Robin and Sweetissa. Despite his extremely pacific nature, Robin challenges William to a duel for alienating Sweetissa's affections. The duel turns out to be a boxing match that does not come off. Presumably Hervey's duel with Pulteney in January 1731 is glanced at, though here assigned to 'Walpole'. The happy ending, a deliberately improbable piece of grafting, is achieved by Goody Scratch, a witch the Parson has been pursuing with greyhounds while she had the form of a hare. The witch cheerfully announces that all the male servants are sons of 'Sir *Geo. Wealthy*' (proved by swellings behind their ears) and the women are daughters of 'Lord *Truelove*' (proved by stars on their arms), and that she is a widow with £500 a year—but that she must marry a parson in order to dissolve the spell that has been cast on her. Puzzletext

[113] *The Grub-Street Opera*, ed. Edgar V. Roberts (Lincoln, Nebr., 1968), pp. xvii–xviii.

[114] *The Grub-Street Opera*, ed. L. J. Morrissey (Edinburgh, 1973), p. 105. As alternatives, Morrissey offers Thomas Hamilton, Sixth Earl of Haddington, and Thomas Villiers, First Earl of Clarendon. Neither seems very plausible.

volunteers with enthusiasm. Owen meanwhile has eloped with Molly, the virtuous daughter of one of the tenants, and at her husband's urging ('ply him with Songs 'till he forgives us' (37)) she sings so charmingly that the Squire and even Madam Ap-Shinken give way at once. By comparison *Iolanthe* seems a model of plausibility, and this is Fielding's point. The ending is a gross travesty of fortunate-discovery comedy endings, though in truth not a very good one. Fielding was later to mingle literary and political satire much more skilfully. Here the literary part does not come off.

The scenes between the Squire and his wife are quite funny in themselves and genuinely hilarious to anyone who knows something of the court of George II. Loftis comments that Fielding might almost be dramatizing Lord Hervey's *Memoirs*.[115] The parents' sour view of their heir ('Nature . . . hath left his Head unfurnish'd' (4)) is absolutely true to life, and their marvellous quarrel scene (35–6) shows that Fielding was learning the difference between the scalpel and the bludgeon.

'Politics' enter principally in the charges William levels against Robin/Walpole:

> I will tell my Master of two Silver Spoons you stole—I'll discover your Tricks—Your selling Glasses, and pretending that the Frost broke them. Making your Master brew more Beer than he needed, and then giving it away to your own Family—especially to feed that great swollen Belly of that pot-gutted Brother of your's—who gets drunk twice a Day at Master's Expence . . . then there's your filing the Plate, and when it was found lighter, pretending that it wasted in Cleaning. . . . (26)

Robin maintains that William simply wants to supplant him (27). Fielding's non-partisan stance is made even clearer, however, in Susan's reply to William's charges: 'what have we to do with Master's Losses, he is rich and can afford it.—Don't let us Quarrel among our Selves.—Let us stand by one another; for let me tell you if Matters were to be too nicely examin'd into, I am afraid it would go hard with us all' (26). This is as much as Fielding does with politics: *The Welsh Opera* is cynical, but hardly partisan. A genuine opposition allegory would presumably have set a Thomas Trusty against a much more thieving Robin Robber the Butler.

The Welsh Opera is a lively, scrappy, rather inconsequential little ballad opera. The *lèse-majesté* is quite amusing, but does not go

[115] Loftis, *Politics of Drama*, p. 105.

anywhere. The Goody Scratch ending fails to work, and there are signs of undeveloped complexities, notably the Squire's cryptic speech in the penultimate scene, when he reports that Owen is really the tenant's son, and Molly 'our own Daughter'—but his wife does not know it, and he chooses to 'defer' the discovery to 'some other Opportunity' (38). We must wonder whether this speech belongs in the text, since it seems to fit nothing else in the play as we have it.

After its première on 22 April 1731, *The Welsh Opera* was performed on 23, 26, and 28 April, and then not again until 19 May. At this point the history of the play becomes extremely confusing, and for the sake of clarity a close chronological survey of the events of the next three months may help clarify exactly what happened.

12 May: Première of *The Fall of Mortimer* (performed again, by itself, 13, 14, 17, 21, and 24 May).

19 May: *The Welsh Opera* revived 'With several Alterations and Additions' (as afterpiece for *The Tragedy of Tragedies*).

21 May: The *Daily Post* prints a puff for a forthcoming revision of *The Welsh Opera*: 'We hear that the Grubstreet Opera, written by Scriblerus Secundus, which was to have been postponed till next Season, will, at the particular Request of several Persons of Quality, be perform'd within a Fortnight, being now in Rehearsal at the New Theatre in the Hay-market. This is the Welch Opera alter'd and enlarg'd to three Acts. It is now in the Press, and will be sold at the Theatre with the Musick prefix'd to the Songs (being about sixty in Number) on the first Night of Performance.' No such edition was ever published.

26 May: *The Welsh Opera* performed as afterpiece for *The Fall of Mortimer* (and again 27 May, and 1, 2 and 4 June).

29 May: *The Fall of Mortimer* published. Advertised in the *Daily Post* of 28 May, with a nasty quotation from Shakespeare's *Richard II*: '. . . England that was wont to conquer others, / Hath made a shameful Conquest of herself.'

5 June: Notice in the *Daily Post*: 'There being a great Demand for the *Welch Opera*, we are obliged to advertise the Town, that it being now made into a whole Night's Entertainment, intituled, The *Grub-Street Opera*, now in Rehearsal, it cannot possibly be performed any longer with this Play' (i.e., *The Fall of Mortimer*).

11 June: *The Grub-Street Opera* advertised but deferred: 'The Principal

Performer having been taken violently ill was the Occasion of putting off the Opera till Monday next' (*Daily Post*, 12 June).[116]

14 June: The company advertised an indefinite postponement without explanation: 'We are oblig'd to defer the *Grubstreet Opera* till further Notice' (*Daily Post*). The company evidently played *The Fall of Mortimer* on this day, but nothing further until 30 June, except *The Author's Farce* and *The Tragedy of Tragedies* on the 18th.

20 June: By this date either the ministry or magistrates were collecting depositions about *The Fall of Mortimer*, evidently part of a systematic effort to shut it down.[117]

24 June: The *Grub-street Journal* reported that the company had been 'forbid acting any more *The fall of Mortimer*'.

26 June: *The Welsh Opera* was published by E. Rayner and H. Cook (*Daily Journal*).

28 June: A notice appeared in the *Daily Post*: 'Whereas one Rayner hath publish'd a strange Medley of Nonsense, under the Title of the *Welch Opera*, said to be written by the Author of the Tragedy of Tragedies; and also hath impudently affirm'd that this was the great Part of the Grub-Street Opera, which he attempts to insinuate was stopt by Authority: This is to assure the Town, that what he hath publish'd is a very incorrect and spurious Edition of the Welch Opera, a very small Part of which was originally written by the said Author; and that it contains scarce any thing of the Grub-street Opera, excepting the Names of some of the Characters and a few of the Songs: This latter Piece hath in it above fifty entire new Songs; and is so far from having been stopt by Authority (for which there could be no manner of Reason) that it is only postponed to a proper Time, when it is not doubted but the Town will be convinced how little that Performance agrees with the intolerable and scandalous Nonsense of this notorious Paper Pyrate.'

116 Morrissey (*Grub-Street Opera*, p. 5) identifies the 'Principal Performer' as William Mullart (Robin), but on Monday the 12th he was apparently well enough to perform the title role in *The Fall of Mortimer*. If the report of illness is genuine then I would guess that Stoppalaer (Owen) might have been the actor taken sick. Especially for musical reasons, his part in the revised play is a major one, and he had no part in *The Fall of Mortimer*.

117 Folger MS T.b.3 includes a transcription by J. P. Collier of sworn testimony of John Ibbutt, stationer, that on 2 or 3 June he paid to attend a performance at the Little Haymarket, where he saw Peterson, Mullart, and ten other actors (named) perform various specified roles in a play called *King Edward III or the Fall of Mortimer*. Collier adds a note that 'On the same day Francis Higginson . . . Barber-surgeon, made a similar affidavit regarding the same performance.'

30 June: *The Fall of Mortimer* was advertised with the comment: 'The Company of Comedians have determined to play notwithstanding the Opposition made by some of the Company to prevent the Performance.'

8 July: *The Fall of Mortimer* was included in a Grand Jury warrant against seditious works (reported in the *Daily Courant*).

21 July: *The Fall of Mortimer* was advertised, but the *Daily Journal* of 22 July reported that 'when the Company . . . was going to perform . . . the High Constable . . . came with a Warrant from several Justices of the Peace, to seize Mr. Mullet [Mullart], who play'd the Part of Mortimer, and the rest of the Performers; but they all made their Escapes.'

[early August] *The Genuine Grub-Street Opera* was published, at least ostensibly 'for the Benefit of the Comedians of the New Theatre in the Hay-market' (title page). Publication was advertised in the *Grub-street Journal* of 19 August. Morrissey identifies the printer as Rayner from printer's ornaments and an advertisement on A2r of *The Fate of Corsica* (1732).[118]

12 August: The *Daily Journal* reported that 'the genuine Grub-street Opera, which was to have been acted at the New Theatre in the Hay-Market, but suppressed, is printed for the Benefit of the Comedians of the said Theatre, and handed about privately.'

16 August: The *Daily Journal* printed a retraction of its notice of 12 August. 'This is to inform the Publick, that we were imposed on in the said Account; and we are since well assured that the said Company are no ways concerned in the printing or publishing thereof: And as to its being suppressed, the said Company knows no more than that the Author desired it might not be performed.'

20 August: *Hurlothrumbo* was advertised, but the *Daily Courant* of 25 August reported that 'On Friday Night last the Constables of Middlesex and Westminster went to the New Theatre in the Hay-Market, in order to apprehend the Actors and Players there, upon a Warrant signed by several of his Majesty's Justices of the Peace against them, as Rogues and Vagabonds, but they all made their Escapes.'

[1755?] *The Grub-Street Opera* was printed (probably by Millar) with a fictitious imprint reading 'J. Roberts . . . MDCCXXXI'.

[118] Morrissey edn., pp. 16–17.

From this tangle emerge a few facts and a lot of questions. *The Welsh Opera* showed no signs of special popularity in April and May, even after Fielding made the alterations and additions advertised on 19 May. None the less, by 5 June the company was evidently rehearsing a new mainpiece version to be called *The Grub-Street Opera*. This was delayed on 11 June; indefinitely deferred on 14 June; and then silently suppressed. By whom? We do not know. The publication of *The Welsh Opera* in late June was clearly unauthorized. Rayner was a shady publisher with opposition ties, and certainly not one of Fielding's usual outlets. How literally we can take the public disavowal of his text on 28 June (evidently by Fielding) might be debated indefinitely.

The preface published with *The Welsh Opera* (by Rayner or someone in his pay?) informs us that 'the Performance of the *Grubstreet* Opera has been prevented, by a certain Influence which has been very *prevailing* of late Years'. We do not, however, know who prevented performance, or exactly how. Clearly the Little Haymarket actors were in very hot water over *The Fall of Mortimer* by 24 June, and with the possible exception of 30 June they apparently did not perform after 18 June. Throughout this time there was no fuss in the papers over either *The Welsh Opera* or *The Grub-Street Opera*, other than the denial on 28 June that the latter 'was stopt by Authority . . . for which there could be no manner of reason'. Orator Henley attacked the 'Hedge-Actors' in his pro-government paper *The Hyp Doctor* on 15 and 22 June, suggesting that their next performance would be a one-act ballad opera by 'Doeg Fielding' to be called 'Tyburn in Glory, or Thespis in a Cart, tying in one knot the beginning and end of tragedy'. But this has no definite connection to either version of *The Welsh Opera*: by now Fielding was very prominently associated with the Little Haymarket actors.

Scholars have differed about the political content of *The Welsh Opera*, though most have concerned themselves principally with *The Grub-Street Opera*, its lack of performance notwithstanding. The revision is admittedly a great improvement. Analysis of what was performed or intended to be performed is complicated because the texts we have are unauthorized. We possess a pirate edition of *The Welsh Opera*, though whether of the first version or the revision of 19 May we cannot tell. *The Genuine Grub-Street Opera* is again a pirate edition, perhaps a rehearsal copy peddled on the sly by one of the actors. That Fielding made some further revisions is proved by the fictitious '1731' edition published by 'J. Roberts'.[119] Morrissey rightly raises the possibility, however, that some of the revisions could have been made as late as the 1750s, particularly a couple of those that seem especially friendly to Walpole. As a working hypothesis we might guess that the printed *Welsh Opera* is the first text (22 April); *The Genuine Grub-Street Opera* the rehearsal text of the major revision (around 5 June); *The Grub-Street Opera* a version Fielding polished in late June while waiting for the *Fall of Mortimer* uproar to blow over. He may honestly have believed (as the notice of 28 June claims) that *The Grub-Street Opera* could be staged when the situation cooled.

In the notice of 16 August, the actors denied that *The Grub-Street Opera* had been suppressed, and claimed that Fielding 'desired it might not be performed'. If so, this 'desire' must have been expressed in June, since the company had been unable to act since then. Was Fielding threatened, and if so, by whom? Was he bought off? Did he simply take fright from the *Fall of Mortimer* fracas and decide that the game was not worth the risks? We do not know.

The Welsh Opera seems to have created no recorded fuss. Is there anything in *The Grub-Street Opera* that made it markedly more obnoxious to the authorities? The differences between the two versions are substantial. Fielding deleted Goody Scratch and his botched ending; vastly expanded the music;[120] added a new act; strengthened the story; and developed the characters. Owen's letter-writing is now motivated by his pursuit of Sweetissa, and his pursuit of Molly (and eventual marriage to her) are improved by the addition of her father, the tenant Apshones. Fielding works in a nasty reference to Prince Frederick's buying the sexual services of a musician's daughter for £1,500 (20); makes Owen's slimy rakishness much more explicit and unpleasant (23); has Mr Apshones reject Owen even as a husband for his daughter because he 'had rather have a set of fine healthy grand-children . . . than a poor puny breed of half-begotten brats—

[119] For a brilliant disentanglement of the printing history, see Morrissey's 'A Note on the Text', pp. 13–23.

[120] 31 songs became 65. L. J. Morrissey points out that a third of the added airs had been used in James Ralph's *The Fashionable Lady* the previous year, and comments: 'It would appear that Fielding, hurrying his revision, relied heavily on his friend Ralph's sure musical sense and perhaps on more.' Morrissey also documents the degree to which John Watts monopolized publication of ballad operas with music, and suggests that an author who wanted to sell his play to Watts was well advised to use music that Watts already had available in wood-block. See Morrissey, 'Henry Fielding and the Ballad Opera', *Eighteenth-Century Studies*, 4 (1971), 386–402.

that inherit the diseases as well as the titles of their parents' (33). Many of Fielding's additions are directed against the Prince of Wales.

The new third act allows a much better working out of the story, both the Owen–Molly plot and the servants' quarrel. Fielding adds references to Walpole's peaceableness (e.g. 29, 51) and conspicuous allusions to his being a favourite of the Queen (e.g. 'Mr. Robin, you are safe enough—her ladyship is your friend' (43)), but at least two of the additions are relatively pro-Walpole. Sweetissa replies to complaints about Robin with a brief and telling speech: 'an upper servant's honesty is never so conspicuous, as when he is abused by the under servants.—They must rail at some one, and if they abuse him, he preserves his master and mistress from abuse' (8). And after the accusation scene, Puzzletext comments: 'I think it is a difficult matter to determine which deserves to be hang'd most; and if Robin the butler hath cheated more than other people, I see no other reason for it, but because he hath had more opportunity to cheat' (52). This is cynical, but not partisan.

Surveying *The Grub-Street Opera*, we may wonder at Fielding's daring to personate the Royal family in such cutting terms, but we will find little partisan politics. We cannot even be sure whether some of the more striking touches in the edition of *The Welsh Opera* are Fielding's. Did Rayner, for example, add the subtitle and the title-page epigraph? *The Gray Mare the better Horse* really underscores the nasty implications about George II and Queen Caroline, as a passage in the relevant song makes clear:

> For where the grey mare
> Is the better horse, there
> The horse is but an ass, sir.

We should note, however, that this song ('Good madam cook') does *not* appear in *The Welsh Opera*; it was added as Air XXXIV in *The Grub-Street Opera*. The epigraph ('. . . a Batchelor Cobler, is happier than a Hen-peck'd Prince') points very directly to the mockery of the Royal family, as do several passages in the unsigned preface.[121] Cleary says that these are 'surely by Fielding',[122] but we cannot be certain.

[121] '. . . a *domineering Wife, who will aspire at wearing the Breeches*'; 'G—d help the Men whose hard Lot it is to fall under *Petticoat Government*'; '*Sovereign Princes* have not been exempted from such *Female Furies*; even one of the most arbitrary Emperors of *Turkey* had a *Roxolana* that held his Nose to the Grindstone.'

[122] Cleary, p. 47.

The subtitle does not appear in the theatre's bills in the *Daily Post*, and Rayner may have been trying to make trouble.

Scholarly views of *The Welsh Opera* and its revision have been warped by preconceptions. McCrea calls *The Welsh Opera* an 'attack on Walpole'.[123] Moss terms *The Grub-Street Opera* Fielding's 'first venture into party politics'; assumes that he could have been prosecuted for libel (highly questionable, given the indirectness of the satire); and treats the work as a key link in 'the progressively bitter political satire that led eventually to the Licensing Act'.[124] But in neither work does Walpole emerge so badly, and in neither is he the primary satiric target. Scholars not committed to the political reading find the satire lightweight and randomly directed, communicating more 'political cynicism than political commitment', as Goldgar says. Jack Richard Brown, in what remains one of the best accounts of the work, notes the 'tone of light-hearted banter' and concludes 'that Fielding was far more interested in writing a clever play than in carrying the flag for any political faction'.[125]

Dismissing preconceptions, we need to be clear on exactly what Fielding was doing in these works. Cleary's account, for example, while it is generally helpful, muddies the waters on several points. '*The Welsh Opera* ... was the culmination of his first, increasingly daring experiment with strong political ingredients. ... He satirized the royal family (as well as the politicians) so openly and pungently ... that the Lord Chamberlain, *ex officio* censor of the stage, prevented the performance of the revision of the play.'[126] 'Political ingredients' seems misleading. The point is not politics but burlesque ridicule of prominent persons, royalty included. And we have no evidence of the Lord Chamberlain's involvement in preventing performance of *The Grub-Street Opera*. But I agree with Cleary that *The Welsh Opera* is 'too balanced to be termed an opposition play', and that its servant plot expresses 'contempt for both the opposition and the ministry'. I would agree further that 'Fielding's preference for the corrupt Prime Minister over his opponents ... became patent in *The Grub-Street Opera*.' But Cleary confuses his case when he says that 'Even at the

[123] McCrea, p. 67.

[124] Harold Gene Moss, 'Satire and Travesty in Fielding's *The Grub-Street Opera*', *Theatre Survey*, 15 (May 1974), 38–50.

[125] Jack Richard Brown, 'Henry Fielding's *Grub-Street Opera*', *Modern Language Quarterly*, 16 (1955), 32–41.

[126] Cleary, pp. 45–53; quotation from p. 45.

height of his first flurry of anti-ministerial satire, Fielding was not drifting toward opposition allegiance.' By Cleary's own testimony neither form of the play is genuinely anti-ministerial. Impudent, cynical, and irreverent about royalty, yes; anti-ministerial, no. The point is the shock value of clever low burlesque, not politics or ideology.

If *The Grub-Street Opera* is politically harmless, why was it not performed? And why did Fielding not immediately publish it? McCrea observes that 'Fielding let his *Grub-Street Opera* die without complaint or protest', and speculates on his reasons for not authorizing publication and trying to 'profit from its banishment *à la* Gay'. McCrea suggests that 'he was eager to curry both the literary and political favor of the Whig establishment'.[127] This does not quite square with the facts, and it treats Fielding as more of a twister than he was. *The Grub-Street Opera* is not the opposition tract McCrea makes it out to be, and so it would hardly have had the sort of sale enjoyed by *Polly*, especially since Fielding could probably not have claimed that it was suppressed by authority. Someone had twice published notices in the papers denying suppression.

We know that *The Grub-Street Opera* could not have been performed at the Little Haymarket after 1 July 1731 because nothing was performed there for several months. It was not picked up by another theatre for rather obvious reasons: Drury Lane and Lincoln's Inn Fields were both subject to the Lord Chamberlain's authority and were hardly likely to be allowed to stage so disrespectful a view of the household supervised by that official; the management at Goodman's Fields was far too cautious to risk such treatment of royalty, which ran counter to their policy of ostentatious support for George II. Fielding could presumably have staged the play at the Little Haymarket in 1736 or 1737, but by that time he was associated with an opposition faction allied to the Prince of Wales, and the picture of Owen in *The Grub-Street Opera* was not exactly what Fielding's friends wanted him to propagate.

Fielding's failure to publish the work could have resulted from any of several causes. He may have felt that the two pirated editions had spoiled the market. His usual publishers may have shied away from his treatment of royalty. He may have wanted to wait for performance. He may have decided that what he could make from publication would not be worth the risk of recriminations.

[127] McCrea, p. 221 n. 17.

We need, finally, to return to the statement in the notice of 16 August that 'the Author desired it might not be performed'. If true, this presumably means either that Fielding took fright (in mid-June when the *Fall of Mortimer* controversy was heating up?) or that he was bought off by the government. His statement a decade later about accepting money to suppress his work might conceivably apply to this case.[128] If whoever was bent on muzzling the Little Haymarket was willing to use both carrot and stick, Fielding may prudently have decided that he should take what he could and run. We need not postulate complex political motivations. Fielding was an ambitious young professional playwright who would undoubtedly have preferred to have his plays produced at Drury Lane or Lincoln's Inn Fields, and who was sensible enough to avoid a scandalous and damaging controversy. This is cowardice or political apostasy only if we imagine that Fielding was committed to the opposition in 1730–31, an interpretation for which I can find no evidence.

The disappearance of *The Grub-Street Opera* into limbo was probably inevitable, but is regrettable. It is one of the finest ballad operas of its time and a splendidly wicked mockery of its exalted subjects. It had no serious purpose, and the best light in which to see it is probably Fielding's distinction 'between Ridicule and Scurrility; between a Jest on a public Character, and the Murther of a private one'.[129] In itself, the squelching of *The Grub-Street Opera* was not especially important to Fielding, but the *de facto* silencing of the Little Haymarket that resulted from *The Fall of Mortimer* was very serious indeed. By August 1731, Fielding was without a venue for his plays.

VI. TRENDS IN NEW PLAYS

Between the opening of Goodman's Fields in 1729 and the summer of 1731 significant changes occurred in the circumstances in which playwrights worked in London. The effect of competition on the patent houses is obvious when we survey their offerings in the early

[128] 'I have been obliged with Money to silence my Productions, professedly and by Way of Bargain given me for that Purpose.' Preface to *Of True Greatness* (London, 1741); repr. in *Miscellanies by Henry Fielding, Esq;*, Volume I, ed. Henry Knight Miller (Oxford, 1972), p. 248. In the *Champion* of 4 Oct. 1740 Fielding admits to having accepted money 'to stop the Publication of a Book, which I had written against his Practice, and which he threaten'd to take the Law of me, if I publish'd'. For discussion, see Goldgar, pp. 197–8, who suggests that this probably refers to *Jonathan Wild*.

[129] Preface to *Miscellanies*, ed. Miller, p. 14.

thirties. In 1730–31 Drury Lane mounted sixty-seven mainpieces for a total of 192 nights; eight of the plays were new. Lincoln's Inn Fields did fifty-four mainpieces over 178 nights, six of them new. The fourteen new mainpieces at the two patent houses is by a large margin the largest total since well before the union of 1708. Of the new plays only *The London Merchant* (initially, a summer production at Drury Lane) was a major success, but David Mallet's *Eurydice* managed fourteen nights at Drury Lane. Lincoln's Inn Fields had less luck with new plays, but responded to changing circumstances by picking up recent plays from other theatres' repertories. For the first time Lincoln's Inn Fields staged *The Conscious Lovers* (1722), and of course it mounted Fielding's *The Coffee-House Politician*. In 1731–32 Drury Lane was to try five new mainpieces (two of them Fielding's), Lincoln's Inn Fields just one—but by that time Rich was putting his money and energy into building his new Covent Garden theatre.

The full significance of the competition inaugurated by the Little Haymarket in 1728, however, became visible only after 1730 and was not restricted to new plays. A brief analysis of the 1731–32 season suggests the great changes in the London theatre. Of the fifty-eight plays offered at Lincoln's Inn Fields, twenty-three were in the active repertory at Drury Lane this season—an increase of 50 per cent over the average for duplicated plays in the mid-1720s. Both companies performed *The Beggar's Opera* and *The Provok'd Husband*, and Lincoln's Inn Fields started doing *The London Merchant*, premièred at Drury Lane just the preceding summer. Both patent companies continued to rely heavily on pre-1708 classics, but the figures in Table 2 are significant. New plays constitute more than half the total of post-1720 mainpieces, and much of the balance represents a few plays repeated

TABLE 2: Post-1720 Mainpieces (Including New Plays) Offered Each Season by the Patent Companies

	DL	%	LIF	%	Total	%
1726–27	2	(3)	5	(10)	7	(6)
1727–28	4	(6)	4	(7)	8	(6.5)
1728–29	4	(6)	4	(8)	8	(7)
1729–30	6	(9.5)	6	(10.5)	12	(10)
1730–31	8	(12)	11	(20)	19	(16)
1731–32	10	(16)	7	(12)	17	(14)

each season. Even so, we learn that competition from the Little Haymarket and Goodman's Fields definitely pushed the patent houses to mount some new plays, and that concomitantly they increased the proportion of contemporary plays in the repertory. The absolute numbers are not great either in plays or performances, but the contrast with the mid-1720s is striking. In short, the effect of the non-patent theatres was exactly what a believer in free enterprise would predict. When pushed by competition, the patent houses bestirred themselves.[130]

Surveying the plays staged at all theatres since the inauguration of competition, we can see several trends. First, music had become a conspicuous element in a high proportion of the new plays. Nearly twenty-five ballad operas of various sorts had been mounted in just three years, and another half-dozen were to reach the stage in 1731–32.[131] After 1730 the trend was clearly away from musical mainpieces, which were relatively expensive and hence a greater risk in time, trouble, and money. The vogue for low-life subjects died quite quickly, and ballad opera moved towards pantomime and farce, as in *Momus Turn'd Fabulist* and *The Fashionable Lady*. This trend is evident in the major successes of 1731 and 1732: the Coffey–Mottley *The Devil to Pay* (DL, August 1731),[132] and Fielding's *The Lottery* and *The Mock Doctor* (DL, January and June 1732) are musicalized farce.

John Rich had made surprisingly little effort to follow up *The Beggar's Opera* with more ballad opera. Prior to 1730–31 Drury Lane and the Little Haymarket had each mounted six new ballad operas, and Lincoln's Inn Fields four; Goodman's Fields had tried just one.[133]

[130] Another clear indicator of increased competition is the rise in the number of afterpieces. Drury Lane offered 149 afterpieces in 197 nights, Lincoln's Inn Fields 131 in 172 during 1731–32. We must remember that as a rule neither house ordinarily played afterpieces during the first run of a new play; a few shows (e.g. *The Beggar's Opera*) normally stood by themselves; and benefits often added singing and dancing instead of an afterpiece.

[131] Ballad opera should not really be seen as a distinct genre, since very different sorts of plays employed the technique that Gay had pioneered. But in so far as it is a separable phenomenon, it has been particularly well discussed for the period 1728-36 by Roger Fiske, *English Theatre Music in the Eighteenth Century* (London, 1973), ch. 3.

[132] For a disentanglement of the complex history of this popular piece, see Arthur H. Scouten and Leo Hughes, '*The Devil to Pay*: A Preliminary Check List', *University of Pennsylvania Library Chronicle*, 16 (1948), 15–24.

[133] Fiske (p. 104) says that 'Goodman's Fields was not at first able to find enough singers', but began to stage ballad operas with vigour in 1732. In fact, Goodman's Fields mounted *The Fashionable Lady* in April 1730 (in its first season), and in July the company got up *The Beggar's Opera* and *The Stage Coach Opera*.

But in 1730–31 and 1731–32 Lincoln's Inn Fields, the Little Haymarket, and Goodman's Fields offered just two ballad operas apiece, while Drury Lane tried ten new ones, a couple of them ambitious mainpieces like *The Jovial Crew* and *Highland Fair*. One must grant that Drury Lane's persistence paid off: despite a string of disappointments, they found some popular and profitable afterpieces, Fielding's *The Lottery* and *The Mock Doctor* prominent among them. Rich's relative lack of interest in ballad opera probably reflects his understanding that it was increasingly aimed at the market he already reached with pantomime.

Second, pantomime continued its overwhelming popularity. The enormous and lasting success of several mid-1720s pantomimes (*Jupiter and Europa*, *The Necromancer*, *Harlequin a Sorcerer*, *Apollo and Daphne*, and *The Rape of Proserpine* at Lincoln's Inn Fields; *Harlequin Dr. Faustus*, another version of *Apollo and Daphne*, and *Harlequin's Triumph* at Drury Lane) naturally spawned more such pieces. There are two reasons that they did not inundate the stage. They were both expensive and complicated to produce, and hence a risk. Then too, audiences were so willing to see the same few over and over that managers did not often need to take such a risk. As with ballad operas we find Drury Lane far more aggressive than Lincoln's Inn Fields in trying new shows: eight versus three from 1728 to spring 1731. Goodman's Fields also tried three; one appeared at the Little Haymarket. The two versions of *Perseus and Andromeda* flourished; so did Drury Lane's *Cephalus and Procris*.

Third, tragedy was relatively easy to get staged, but seldom achieved much popularity. Dramatists, and to some degree managers, were caught in a bind. Critical precepts pointed in one direction, audience preferences in another. The abundant periodical criticism in these years demands moral seriousness, historicity, poetic justice, conformity to decorum and the rules, and so forth.[134] Critics held that writers ought to compose such pieces, and that managers should produce them. Audiences, however, rarely liked such plays when they were produced.

In practice, we can distinguish at least six types of serious drama being written at this time. The most numerous are (i) heroic-intrigue tragedies, and (ii) 'Roman' or pseudo-classical tragedies. By this time

134 For a convenient survey, see Charles Harold Gray, *Theatrical Criticism in London to 1795* (New York, 1931), chs. 1 and 2.

the heroic-intrigue mode was pretty tired, but authors still cranked out such works with great regularity. Barford's *The Virgin Queen*, Jeffreys' *Merope*, Walker's *The Fate of Villany*, and Ralph's *The Fall of the Earl of Essex* are examples. The Roman plays, in a genre much indebted to Addison's *Cato* (1713), include such pieces as Johnson's *The Tragedy of Medæa*, Mallet's *Eurydice*, and Sturmy's *Sesostris*. The best of them is undoubtedly Thomson's *The Tragedy of Sophonisba*. (iii) A subcategory of the Roman play is perhaps best termed 'patriot drama', a subgenre that grew more popular in the later years of the Walpole administration. Madden's *Themistocles* and Martyn's *Timoleon* are the principal examples. Political topicality (even just in theme) seems to have been a significant advantage with the audience. (iv) A few providential tragicomedies were still being written—for example, Theobald's *Double Falshood; or, The Distrest Lovers* (whose modest success was surely the result of its alleged Shakespearean origin) and Cooke's *Triumphs of Love and Honour*. (v) Pathetic plays by Southerne and Rowe remained extremely popular in the repertory, but new ones are few. Bellers's *Injur'd Innocence* is an instance. (vi) Finally, one promising new development is the 'fate play'. Wandesford's *Fatal Love*, Hill's *Athelwold*, and Lillo's *The London Merchant* are examples. This subgenre creates a psychological crisis for the leading characters. Its roots lie in pathetic drama; Southerne's *The Fatal Marriage* (1694), still popular on the stage in the 1730s, is an obvious ancestor. Roman plays tend to be emotionally frigid, the heroic-intrigue plays emptily heated. The purely pathetic plays depict misery simply to arouse sympathy. The fate plays are more interesting because of their greater emphasis on character. Unlike the Roman plays, they tend to have characters who are to some degree believable.[135]

A writer's best chance with a tragedy was Drury Lane or Lincoln's Inn Fields, which mounted nine and seven respectively between 1728 and 1732. By contrast, four appeared at the Little Haymarket, and just two at Goodman's Fields. Drury Lane (if we count the summer company) sponsored two of the fate plays, two providential tragicomedies, a pathetic play, a patriot drama, and three Roman plays. Drury Lane was, interestingly, the only house *not* to mount a heroic-intrigue play. Lincoln's Inn Fields tried four of them, along with a patriot drama and a pair of Roman plays. Thus in this period Drury Lane was

[135] For detailed accounts of the 'Roman', 'Othellean' (pathetic), and 'fate' genres, see Bonnie A. Nelson, *Serious Drama and the London Stage: 1729–1739* (Salzburg, 1981).

clearly the most adventurous and successful house for tragedy—not that it made any money for its pains. Whether Fielding avoided tragedy because he felt no inclination to write it, or because he recognized its limited popular appeal, he was probably wise to concentrate his efforts elsewhere.[136]

Fourth, comedy was not flourishing. With the riches of the seventeenth century to draw upon, the managers had little enthusiasm for bothering with new mainpieces, and since the most successful afterpieces were pantomimes and ballad operas, managers underwrote no great number of straight two-act comedies either. For such comedies as did get produced, however, we can see a clear distinction between theatres. 'London social comedy' was principally the province of Drury Lane, which had put on *The Provok'd Husband*, as well as lighter London comedies like *Love in Several Masques* and *The Lover*, and was to mount *The Modern Husband* and *The Modish Couple* in 1731–32. Some light comedies were staged at the Little Haymarket, but most of its comedies were more topical and farcical (*The Craftsman*, *Rape upon Rape*, *The Author's Farce*). Lincoln's Inn Fields, in clear contrast, had little use for new comedies of any sort. Rich tried just one London social comedy in these years (Kelly's *The Married Philosopher* in 1732) and a trio of undistinguished farces. Goodman's Fields mounted three London comedies (of which *The Temple Beau* was the most successful) and what appear to be a pair of afterpiece farces (lost). For a writer ambitious to try 'serious' comedy, Drury Lane was clearly the place to be, if possible.

Fifth, burlesque was flourishing. The Little Haymarket had done extremely well with *Hurlothrumbo*, *Tom Thumb*, and *The Tragedy of Tragedies*, and a flock of others had been produced there, including such works as *The Cheshire Comicks*, *Jack the Giant-Killer*, *The Welsh Opera*, and *The Blazing Comet*. The first major burlesque mounted elsewhere was Fielding's *Covent-Garden Tragedy*, put on at Drury Lane in June 1732. Its production was a sign that Drury Lane was ready to try to steal the thunder from troublesome non-patent competitors.

Overall, an ambitious young writer might reasonably have concluded that legitimate comedy was moribund, mainpiece ballad opera was *passé*, and tragedy needed a new twist to get away from its clichés. Burlesque and topical material had become good bets. Farcical ballad

[136] For comments by Fielding on tragedy, see Appendix IV.

opera afterpieces were in demand. For the writer with loftier literary aspirations, patriot drama and fate tragedy were the best possibilities.

Contemplating his prospects in the autumn of 1731, Fielding must have had a pretty good idea of the trends in new plays. But with the Little Haymarket indefinitely dark, where would he take his work? At Goodman's Fields, management had passed from Odell to Giffard,[137] but this seems to have made little practical difference to the management policy of the theatre. Goodman's Fields continued to be unadventurous in its choice of new plays, and did not care to mount many in any case. At Lincoln's Inn Fields Rich had mounted more new plays (especially in the realm of tragedy) than his reputation would lead one to expect, but he was both conservative in taste and a poor judge of quality. Granting that competition had been required to provide the necessary stimulus, this survey shows Drury Lane to have been surprisingly eclectic and forward-looking. Despite all the abuse and ridicule heaped on Colley Cibber (with Fielding contributing prominently to the chorus), the evidence suggests that Drury Lane was being intelligently managed between 1728 and 1732.[138] And to Cibber's credit, when Fielding needed a new venue in the autumn of 1731, the Drury Lane management was quite prepared to forget the past and produce his work.

[137] Reported in the *Daily Post* of 9 Sept. 1731.

[138] Many modern critics have ridiculed Cibber for rejecting *The Beggar's Opera*. We may reflect in his defence, however, that he was no fool, and cannot have been unaware of its anti-Whiggish tenor. Perhaps he would have swallowed his Whig principles and pocketed the cash had he anticipated its success, but in the circumstances one can hardly sneer at his turning down so very odd a work, especially one liberally freighted with matter obnoxious to Cibber's high-life friends.

3

The Drury Lane Years, 1732–1733

BETWEEN January 1732 and June 1733 Fielding was Drury Lane's leading playwright, mounting a total of seven new plays in just a season and a half. How this happened is not altogether clear. We know nothing of Fielding's thoughts or whereabouts between the suppression of the Little Haymarket in July 1731 and the première of *The Lottery* at Drury Lane on 1 January 1732, but plainly he reached some kind of accommodation with Cibber and Wilks. He reportedly made a great deal of money from *The Lottery* and *The Modern Husband* in the winter of 1732, and was seemingly launched on as secure and profitable a career as any playwright could hope for. But life was never to be easy for Fielding.

In June 1732 *The Covent-Garden Tragedy* was a total failure and *The Old Debauchees* no better than a marginal success, if that. Over the summer Fielding became embroiled in an ugly public dispute over the merits and morality of his plays. Worse was soon to come. By the end of the summer the long-stable triumvirate management of Drury Lane had vanished: Booth sold out, Wilks died, and Cibber prudently removed himself. Drury Lane fell into the hands of amateur dabblers, and, after an increasingly unhappy season of disputes, the actors rebelled; the patentees locked them out; and Fielding found himself in the midst of a frightful mess. Fielding backed the patentees—a surprising choice. If his motivation was venal, then he guessed wrong, for they were to be the losing party. But in the long run, backing the losers probably made no difference. The Drury Lane that had been a monument of stability since 1709 vanished with the triumvirs, and with it any prospect of security for Henry Fielding in a patent theatre.

I. THE RETURN TO DRURY LANE

Following the rejection of *Don Quixote in England* and *The Temple Beau* in 1729, Fielding had indulged himself in a fairly nasty and spectacularly successful satire of Colley Cibber and Robert Wilks in *The Author's Farce*. How did he restore friendly relations with the triumvirate? Dudden says magisterially that because of the closure of the Little Haymarket, 'Fielding determined to transfer himself to Drury Lane'.[1] But the matter hardly lay in Fielding's determination. Cross more sensibly says that 'In the circumstances the natural course for Fielding was to make peace with the managers of Drury Lane', but then adds that Colley Cibber was preparing to quit the stage (for which we have no evidence) and that he 'had already delegated his office as one of the managers of Drury Lane' to his son Theophilus (which is untrue). Cross also says that with Fielding 'migrated the best actors of the Haymarket theatre. . . . The two companies . . . went on harmoniously.' Ducrocq repeats these errors.[2] The facts are a bit different. Colley Cibber and Robert Wilks remained in charge of Drury Lane (Booth was ill and largely inactive), and among the Little Haymarket regulars only Mr and Mrs Mullart were employed at Drury Lane in 1731–32.[3] In no sense did two companies coexist at Drury Lane. The question remains: why was Fielding now welcome there? What had changed in the course of two years?

The answer is partly that Fielding's smash hits of 1730 and 1731 had made him, at the age of twenty-four, the most successful living playwright. In itself, this might not have softened the triumvirs, but faced with increasingly vigorous and successful competition, they now needed new plays. In Table 2 ('Post-1720 Mainpieces') at the end of the last chapter we see the managers' reluctant decision to fight fire with fire. Colley Cibber was a ruthless pragmatist. If Fielding's plays could put money in management's pocket, then management would stage his plays, past piques notwithstanding. On Fielding's side, there was little choice.

Fielding's move to Drury Lane in the season of 1731–32 is almost always treated as a momentous matter, a kind of public announcement of a change in his political views. Thus, Goldgar says that 'in the move to Drury Lane, the dedication to *The Modern Husband*, and the epilogue to *The Modish Couple* Fielding unmistakably and publicly

[1] Dudden, I, 95.

[2] Cross, I, 115; Ducrocq, p. 177.

[3] Both are carelessly omitted from the *London Stage* roster for Drury Lane in 1731–32. Whether Seedo had been a 'regular' at the Little Haymarket is uncertain; a benefit on 9 June 1732 *may* indicate regular employment at Drury Lane in 1731–32. Stoppelaer worked at several theatres in the early 1730s. A certain number of transfers occurred every year. Quite a few of the Little Haymarket's old regulars were back there with the 'extended company' in the spring of 1732. See Burling and Hume, 'Theatrical Companies at the Little Haymarket'.

aligned himself with the Walpole camp.'[4] Passing over the dedication and the epilogue for a moment, we need to ask whether writing for Drury Lane amounted to a public endorsement of Walpole in 1732. The answer is clearly negative. Under the triumvirate (i.e. until September 1732) Drury Lane was certainly pro-Whig and pro-ministry. But as John Loftis rightly says, in practice this meant that the theatre 'did not present plays patently hostile to Walpole. . . . Drury Lane cannot be said to have actively supported Walpole or his policies.'[5]

The facts of Fielding's return to Drury Lane are extremely simple. First, Drury Lane was the best and most prestigious company. Every writer hoped to get plays staged at Drury Lane. Given a chance to have his work produced by a wealthy, apparently stable, and celebrated management, rather than by a fringe theatre, any ambitious author would be foolish not to seize the opportunity. And second, what were Fielding's options? The Little Haymarket was harassed into silence in July 1731, and when he came to town that autumn (at an unknown date), he had no way to know when, if ever, it might reopen.[6] Fielding's possibilities for 1731–32 were Lincoln's Inn Fields, where a year earlier he had evidently not hit it off with Rich; Goodman's Fields, whose management was little disposed to mount new plays; and Drury Lane. We have no reason to suppose that there was any special intrigue involved in Fielding's return to Drury Lane. Whether the ministry paid him off in July 1731 or not, it certainly had no way to dictate his acceptance at a patent theatre—and no reason to wish to do so. No contemporary commentator found any oddity in Drury Lane's wishing to have the work of so successful a writer or in his being glad to work for so distinguished a company.

On what terms did Fielding take his work to Drury Lane? We do not know. We have virtually no evidence suggesting that he became a salaried 'house poet', and he received the usual benefits for his mainpieces. That he was paid any sort of retainer (as had been the custom in the seventeenth century) seems unlikely. The chance to have his work staged at Drury Lane was ample lure: a successful benefit could bring him five times the maximum possible at the Little Haymarket, roughly £150 rather than £30. We need not marvel at Fielding's willingness to forget old grievances.

[4] Goldgar, p. 113.

[5] Loftis, *Politics of Drama*, p. 108.

[6] The first legitimate drama performance did not occur until 10 February 1732.

Did Fielding have to write a different sort of play for Drury Lane? Yes and no. Modern scholars anxious to differentiate the Drury Lane repertory from that of the Little Haymarket cite the lack of revivals of Fielding's early shows when he moved to Drury Lane. But the matter is not so simple. *The Author's Farce* was not revived at Drury Lane in 1732 for the good reason that it satirized Wilks and Cibber. *Rape upon Rape* and *The Letter-Writers* had basically failed (though Rich did try the former at Lincoln's Inn Fields). *The Welsh Opera* was full of dangerous personations. *The Tragedy of Tragedies* was produced at Drury Lane in May 1732 and revived a year later. It was also staged at Lincoln's Inn Fields in 1732, and Goodman's Fields added *Tom Thumb* to its repertory as early as March 1731. We may deduce from performance records that these plays did not transplant very successfully, but the record does not show a tidy distinction between Fielding's plays staged at Drury Lane and those produced at the Little Haymarket.

As far as we know, Drury Lane continued to refuse to submit new scripts to the Master of the Revels, a state of affairs unchanged since February 1715. The theatre operated, however, under a patent specifying that the 'said Company shall be our Servants' (i.e. subject to regulation by the Lord Chamberlain), and specifically directing the management to show 'the Strictest regard to such Representations as any Way concern Civil Polity or the Constitution of our Government & That these may Contribute to the Support of our Sacred Authority and the preservation of Order and good Government'.[7] This certainly gave the government leverage, and in the season of 1731–32 the triumvirs must have been acutely conscious that their patent was in its last year. They were negotiating to get it renewed for another twenty-one years in their own names. We can be certain that they would not have staged anything likely to offend King or ministry in the spring of 1732. No *Welsh Opera* or *Fall of Mortimer* would grace their boards.

Fielding must have known this when a *rapprochement* was discussed. But he had no reason to feel that he would become a pawn of the ministry by returning to Drury Lane. Drury Lane had been no hotbed of pro-ministry propaganda, and it remained politically inert in 1732 and 1733, even in the midst of growing uproar over Walpole's Excise Bill. Cleary rightly concludes that Fielding's acceptance at Drury Lane necessitated a 'retreat' from politics that 'was near-total,

[7] PRO C66/3501, no. 13.

conscious, and obvious'.[8] We have, however, no evidence that Fielding wished to write political satire. He had enjoyed success with impudent personations in *The Author's Farce* and *The Welsh Opera*, but none of his early plays was genuinely political. Various forms of topical and social satire would be welcomed by the triumvirate, and Fielding had every reason to believe that he could adapt successfully to their needs and wishes. The plays he wrote for Drury Lane are far less distinct from his earlier work than most commentators have implied.

Fielding and Walpole

Other than Fielding's return to Drury Lane, his epilogue for *The Modish Couple* (Drury Lane, 10 January 1732) and his dedication of *The Modern Husband* to Sir Robert Walpole have usually been deemed politically significant. Both require reconsideration, and together they provide an occasion to consider Fielding's attitude towards Walpole.[9]

The Modish Couple is a competent, apolitical marriage-problem comedy. It was brought to the theatre (and subsequently published) by Captain Charles Bodens, a member of the Coldstream Guards and pimp to the Prince of Wales. The play met a fiercely hostile reception in the theatre, and was dismissed on its fourth night. Egmont reports a rumour that it was actually written by Lord Hervey and the Prince of Wales. Charles Woods's long-standard account of the play attributes its stormy reception to opposition knowledge of the authorship. But a recent manuscript discovery by Calhoun Winton proves that the actual author was almost certainly the Revd James Miller, an attribution confirmed by the anonymous but apparently knowledgeable author of *The Dramatick Sessions* (1734).[10] How Hervey and the Prince of Wales were involved, or thought to be involved, is now obscure.

What of Fielding in all this? Martin Battestin succinctly summarizes the orthodox view: '. . . so thick was Fielding with the Court Party

[8] Cleary, p. 54.

[9] See W. B. Coley's judicious review of unsatisfactory evidence, 'Henry Fielding and the Two Walpoles', *Philological Quarterly*, 45 (1966), 157–78.

[10] *Diary of Viscount Percival Afterwards First Earl of Egmont* (London, 1920–23), I, 216; *Daily Journal*, 14 Jan. 1732; Charles B. Woods, '"Captain B—'s Play"', *Harvard Studies and Notes in Philology and Literature*, 15 (1933), 243–55; Calhoun Winton, 'Benjamin Victor, James Miller, and the Authorship of *The Modish Couple*', *Philological Quarterly*, 64 (1985), 121–30.

at this time that he could be counted on to supply the epilogue'.[11] But there are problems with this interpretation. Did Fielding know that Miller was the author? Did he believe that Hervey and Prince Frederick were the authors? We have no idea. Why, in any case, would Walpole and the 'Court Party' want to do favours for the egregious Frederick, even if they supposed him part-author? Fielding's epilogue is cheerful and conventional: he commends the play for purity and twits the portly Bodens about the sweating agonies an author suffers while he awaits the verdict of the audience. Fielding disliked the prologue–epilogue convention and rarely supplied such pieces for other authors.[12] We do not know who asked him in this case, but there is a very real possibility that Fielding's writing the epilogue was nothing more than a routine chore carried out to oblige management. He may well have been paid for the job, and happy to pick up £5 or so. Without evidence of what Fielding knew about the situation, we have no reason to suppose that the episode has special significance.[13]

The dedication of *The Modern Husband* requires more explanation. Let us approach it by briefly surveying Fielding's view of Walpole in these years. (1) In the summer of 1728 Fielding may have published a pair of satiric squibs directed at Walpole, one of which ('The Norfolk Lanthorn') considerably riled the opposition press. Two more such efforts, arguably his, appeared in summer and autumn 1730.[14] (2) In 1729, under the influence of Lady Mary Wortley Montagu, Fielding wrote an unpublished mock-epic fragment rightly described by Cleary as 'blunt, slanderously partisan ministerial propaganda'.[15] (3) According to dates given in the 1743 *Miscellanies*, in 1730 and 1731 Fielding wrote but did not then publish a pair of comic verse epistles to Walpole, requesting patronage. Hugh Amory has argued that the correct date is 1738 and that both pieces are ironic, but though his case

[11] Battestin, 'Four New Fielding Attributions', p. 72.

[12] For a helpful discussion of the epilogue Fielding wrote for Theobald's *Orestes* (Lincoln's Inn Fields, April 1731), see Charles B. Woods, 'Fielding's Epilogue for Theobald', *Philological Quarterly*, 28 (1949), 419–24. This epilogue may, of course, have been the result of Fielding's flirtation with Rich the previous winter.

[13] I can find no evidence to support Cross's offhand suggestion (I, 118) that Fielding 'perhaps touched [the play] up here and there'. A writer in the *Grub-street Journal* of 24 Feb. 1731[/2] says he was 'told' that it 'was lick'd into the form it now bears, and had the last touches given it' by Colley Cibber, which seems likely enough.

[14] See Battestin, 'Four New Fielding Attributions'. The cases for attribution are circumstantial but plausible.

[15] Cleary, p. 21. This poem was first published by Isobel M. Grundy, 'New Verse by Henry Fielding', *PMLA* 87 (1972), 213–45.

is ingenious, the refutations by Goldgar and Cleary seem convincing.[16] Whether the poems are anything but playful *jeux d'esprit* I am inclined to doubt. (4) Fielding's mocking picture of Robin the Butler in *The Welsh Opera* (April 1731) and *The Grub-Street Opera* has been discussed in Chapter 2. (5) In February 1732 Fielding chose to dedicate *The Modern Husband* to Walpole, and did so in terms of ringing panegyric.[17]

This evidence shows no clear progression in Fielding's attitude towards Walpole. If we want to be literal, we find Fielding 'anti' in 1728; wildly 'pro' in 1729; hostile on one occasion in 1730 and fulsomely begging for patronage on another. The next year (1731) finds Fielding equally unsettled in his outlook, but in 1732 he becomes an apparently rapturous admirer of the Prime Minister. But could the dedication be ironic? Much in *The Modern Husband* itself can be 'applied' to Walpole in a hostile way, as Hunter has demonstrated.[18] Perhaps the dedication is a sly trick, designed to bring Walpole to the reader's attention? Against this interpretation must be set the lack of confirmation from any eighteenth-century source, and also our knowledge that Lady Mary (not to mention the managers of Drury Lane) would certainly have objected if they had thought Fielding was playing any such game. Whether his intentions were ironic we cannot be sure; probably the dedication really is, as John Loftis has read it, 'an effort to secure Walpole's patronage'.[19] We can, however, hardly suppose that Fielding was seeking a position as a political hack-writer on a government paper: such jobs tended to be badly paid.[20] Was he so naïve as to suppose that a bit of flattery would get him a government sinecure?

[16] The poems are 'To the Right Honourable Sir Robert Walpole . . . Written in the Year 1730', and 'To the same. *Anno* 1731', *Miscellanies*, vol. I, ed. Miller, pp. 56–9. For discussion, see Hugh Amory, 'Henry Fielding's *Epistles to Walpole*: A Reexamination', *Philological Quarterly*, 46 (1967), 236–47; Goldgar, pp. 100, 233 n. 27; Cleary, pp. 25, 117, 180, 306 n. 10. For Amory's reconsiderations on the matter, see his 'The Evidence of Things Not Seen: Concealed Proofs of Fielding's Juvenal', *Papers of the Bibliographical Society of America*, 80 (1986), esp. pp. 30–1.

[17] Cross states that Walpole 'accepted the dedication' (I, 121), but I can find no evidence for this.

[18] Hunter, pp. 56–7. I once took this position myself: see *The Rakish Stage*, pp. 209–10.

[19] Loftis, *Politics of Drama*, p. 130.

[20] Fielding may have been paid as little as '*a Crown a-piece*' for his *Champion* papers in 1739–40. See Thomas Lockwood, 'New Facts and Writings from an Unknown Magazine by Henry Fielding, *The History of our Own Times*', *Review of English Studies*, NS 35 (1984), 466 n. Lockwood concludes that 'in its best days the *Champion* brought him a trickling payment of ten or maybe fifteen shillings a week', and that 'this payment is consistent with what we know independently of the amounts paid to journalists'.

Our understanding of the matter has been skewed by Cross's belief that Fielding viewed Walpole with a fierce hostility that only occasionally wavered. The evidence we now possess does not support such a view. Fielding clearly enjoyed tugging the great man's tail when paid for doing so, but nowhere before 1737 does he display fundamental disapproval of Walpole, either moral or ideological. As McCrea and Cleary have amply demonstrated, Fielding was a Whig. The bulk of the effective opposition consisted of Whigs, most of whom would gladly have accepted government office if given the opportunity. When Fielding's parliamentary friends moved seriously into opposition in 1734, he drifted in the same direction. Until then, Fielding displays no very serious convictions either about politics in general or Sir Robert Walpole in particular.

If Fielding planned *The Modern Husband* as a sly blow at Walpole, it plainly did not work. If he hoped for lavish patronage, he must have been disappointed. Fielding did know Walpole. In 1740 a pamphleteer charged that back in 1728, or thereabouts, Walpole had bailed Fielding out of a country jail and was repaid by Fielding's libelling him in a satire.[21] And Walpole may even have given Fielding a present in response to the dedication in 1732. A writer in the *Grub-street Journal* (26 September 1734) lists Fielding among writers who have received bounty from the great man.[22] We have, however, no good reason to believe that Fielding's return to Drury Lane was politically motivated, or that it was connected in any way with his view of Walpole. He wanted a first-rate company to stage his work, and Drury Lane provided one.

The Lottery

Fielding's first new effort for Drury Lane was a rollicking little ballad opera afterpiece called *The Lottery*, which was premièred 1 January 1732 (added to Addison's *Cato*). The first edition totals just thirty-one pages of text, including words and music for nineteen songs.[23] The

[21] See Battestin, 'Four New Fielding Attributions', p. 74. The satire was probably 'The Norfolk Lanthorn'. Walpole was presumably just doing a favour for a kinsman of Lady Mary's.

[22] I owe this reference to William J. Burling. The writer might, of course, just have assumed from the dedication that Fielding was paid for it.

[23] *The Lottery* was Fielding's first definite ballad-opera collaboration with the shadowy Mr Seedo. See Edgar V. Roberts, 'Mr. Seedo's London Career and His Work with Henry Fielding', *Philological Quarterly*, 45 (1966), 179–90. Roberts speculates that they may have worked together at the Little Haymarket as early as 1730. For a general

subject was highly topical: the government lottery of autumn 1731 had generated tremendous public attention. Fielding mocks the hopes of buyers and vividly illustrates the deceptions practised by jobbers who rented 'Horses'—that is, temporary rights to tickets for a single drawing. (Drawings went on over a period of many weeks, and tickets were often resold, split, and rented.)[24] The plot is exceedingly slight. Lovemore has pursued Chloe to town, his intentions left discreetly vague. A dizzy chit, she is convinced she will win £10,000 with her lottery ticket, and gives herself out as a fortune. The impecunious Jack Stocks pretends to be Lord Lace and marries her. When her ticket proves to be her fortune and comes up blank, he is happy to resign all interest in her to Lovemore for £1,000.

The songs are well integrated. Some directly advance the action; others make tart comments on it. Fielding's avoidance of the usual marriage-ending cliché is surprising and effective: folly and avarice remain uppermost in our minds and are not obliterated by saccharine convention. The cast was superb, including John Harper as a crooked renter of tickets, Theophilus Cibber as Jack Stocks, Miss Raftor (Kitty Clive) as the feckless Chloe, and Stoppelaer as Lovemore. The play was an immediate success, enjoying fifteen performances in January alone.

Despite this considerable popularity, Fielding felt that he could improve the work, and promptly did so. On 1 February the piece was advertised 'With Alterations and an Additional Scene representing the Drawing of the Lottery in Guild-hall'. Revision of a successful new play was uncommon, but was to be characteristic of Fielding. (We have already encountered his habit of immediate revision in *Tom Thumb*, even before he thought of *The Tragedy of Tragedies*, and *The Welsh Opera*.) Comparison of the first edition with the second (both published by John Watts in 1732), shows that the text is identical up to

discussion of Fielding's technique in ballad-opera form, see Roberts, 'The Songs and Tunes in Henry Fielding's Ballad Operas', *The Eighteenth-Century English Stage*, ed. Kenneth Richards and Peter Thomson (London, 1972), pp. 29–49.

[24] For an excellent account of the historical background, see Edgar V. Roberts, 'Fielding's Ballad Opera *The Lottery* (1732) and the English State Lottery of 1731', *Huntington Library Quarterly*, 27 (1963), 39–52. Roberts makes the important point that each £10 ticket entitled the owner to a £7 10*s*. share of stock on which 3% would be paid (as well as the chance for large and small prizes). Fielding's scepticism notwithstanding, the lottery appears to have been honestly conducted, and only renters of tickets were simply gambling their money away.

page 18. Fielding then cut four songs[25] and inserted seven new ones.[26] He also added the new scene advertised on 1 February.

The revision is a major improvement. In the original, Chloe learns by letter that she has a blank, and this 'catastrophe' is abrupt and unprepared for (27–8). In the revision Fielding uses the local colour of the drawing to good effect; introduces a flock of hopeful purchasers; shows two of them discovering that they have rented the same ticket; and satirically displays the happy Lord and heiress. To have them watch the drawing heightens the effect of her ticket's coming up blank. Fielding also strengthens the denouement with two new songs. Air XX ('Now, my dear *Chloe*, behold a true Lover') allows Lovemore to lay more effective claim to the lady than the vapid 'Smile, smile, my *Chloe*' it replaces, while also letting him say that free love is better than marriage.[27] And Air XXI ('Since you whom I lov'd, / So cruel have prov'd') gives Chloe the opportunity to reject Jack Stocks and accept 'Gallant' in place of 'dull Husband'. Clearly her fate will be to go into keeping.

In revamped form, *The Lottery* managed another fourteen performances during its first spring, or twenty-nine in all, which must have delighted the Drury Lane managers. Its popularity proved lasting: the piece was performed every year to 1740; virtually every year until 1760; and occasionally until 1783—often many times per season. Such 'living plays' (as the old prompter John Downes had termed them) were rare, and they were exactly what the triumvirs hoped to get from Fielding. What he made from this play we do not know. No benefit seems to have been advertised, though 'Rich's Register' noted succinctly on 21 January (the tenth night) 'Benefit Author of Afterpiece'. If this is correct, we might guess that Fielding got both a flat fee plus the profits of a performance. The mainpiece that night was Betterton's *The Amorous Widow* (*c*.1669) with Wilks in the lead role. How much Fielding netted is unknown. But this success was an auspicious beginning for his new relationship with London's leading theatre.

[25] 1st edn.: 11. 'Nice Honour, by a private Man'; 15. 'Whom do not Debts inthral'; 17. 'Heav'n fear'd, when first it Woman made'; 18. 'Smile, smile, my *Chloe*, smile'.

[26] 2nd edn.: 14. 'Oh how charming my Life will be'; 16. 'The Lottery just is beginning'; 17. 'In all Trades we've had'; 18. 'Number One Hundred Thirty-Two!'; 19. 'Number Six Thousand Eighty Two'; 20. 'Now, my dear *Chloe*, behold a true Lover'; 21. 'Since you whom I lov'd'.

[27] The song concludes: 'Love shall hold thee / Dearer than Wife. / What Joys in Chains of dull Marriage can be? / Love's only happy, when Liking is free.'

II. *THE MODERN HUSBAND*

By Fielding's own account in the prologue, *The Modern Husband* was a major effort, and a deliberate attempt to try new directions. Forswearing the 'unshap'd Monsters of a wanton Brain' and 'repenting Frolick Flights of Youth', the twenty-five year-old author announces that 'he flies to Nature, and to Truth'. The title-page epigraph is from Juvenal, and Fielding states his determination to show 'detestable' modern vice, and to draw the 'Town' as 'vicious, as it is'.[28] Claims to satiric purpose are a commonplace part of prologue rhetoric; only very rarely are they borne out by the play that follows. In this instance, Fielding exaggerates not a whit. Even those modern critics who have most disliked the play have usually not questioned what Cross calls Fielding's 'serious purpose' in writing it.[29] This play was no sudden vagary on Fielding's part: a draft was extant by September 1730, when he submitted it to Lady Mary for her judgement (see pp. 74–5, above). His letter to her refers to 'a Model I never yet attempted' and differentiates the piece from his 'lighter Productions'.[30]

Determined to write a harsh and serious satire, Fielding selected three principal targets: Mr and Mrs Modern, who live on her immoral earnings; her paramour, Lord Richly, a vicious womanizer; and the 'crim. con.' law that enabled a man to collect damages for his wife's adultery. Fielding may well have got the idea of an attack on 'crim. con.' from a case that came before Lord Chief Justice Eyre in February

[28] All quotations are from the Penn State copy, which is an exemplar of the corrected form of the first edn. printed by Watts in 1732. Fielding appears to have made numerous substantive changes in the text after a significant number of copies were printed. Most of them do not affect pagination, but pp. 7–9 had to be revamped considerably to squeeze in several new lines, and in the process 'not' was dropped from 'it will be a Language not understood by the Great' on p. 9. BL Ashley 719 and 643.h.19(6) show the first state; 11775.e.25 is the corrected state, identical to 643.h.19(7) except for a reset title-page in the latter dubbing it 'The Second Edition'.

[29] Cross, I, 121.

[30] A second letter to Lady Mary is generally held to apply to this play and is dated '[*Feb*. 1732]' by Halsband (*Letters of Lady Mary Wortley Montagu*, II, 96). But the letter has no date, and says merely 'I have presum'd to send your Ladyship a Copy of the Play which you did me the Honour of reading three Acts of last spring, and hope it may meet as light a Censure from your Ladyship's Judgment as then.' This has been taken as referring to the printed book of *The Modern Husband*. However, Lady Mary saw some sort of draft in Sept. 1730, and this letter says that only three acts were submitted 'last spring' (i.e. 1731, if this is Feb. 1732). And we cannot tell whether Fielding was sending a printed book or a complete manuscript copy of a work in progress. Any of his five-act plays could be the work involved.

1730.[31] Odd as the law seems to twentieth-century sensibilities, it was not repealed until 1857. The gist of the matter was simple. If husband and wife were indeed one flesh, the wife could not (in legal theory) consent to adultery, so that a husband could sue her paramour for compensatory damages if he could prove 'criminal conversation' with her body. This process was a particularly obnoxious part of eighteenth-century divorce proceedings. Most readers will have derived their familiarity with the notion of crim. con. from Theophilus Cibber's suit against William Sloper in 1738, a striking instance of life imitating art. Theophilus Cibber performed Captain Bellamant in this play, and if he learned from it, he did not learn enough. Much like Fielding's Mr Modern, he first sold his wife's sexual favours to her lover, attempted to increase his profits with a crim. con. action, and then found himself frustrated by witnesses who could attest to his collusion in the adultery. Whether London was as full of willing cuckolds living off their wives' lovers as Fielding would have us believe,[32] Theophilus Cibber's later career is proof that Fielding was not departing from the bounds of possibility.

The Modern Husband is a strikingly original play. As John Loftis points out, Fielding breaks sharply with the 'Restoration stereotypes' on which he had relied in *Love in Several Masques* and *The Temple Beau*.[33] *The Modern Husband* is a genuine satire (a rarity in English comedy), and it offers one of the darkest comic visions of society since Otway's bitter *Friendship in Fashion* (1678). Many of Fielding's ideas in the play derive from the tradition of marriage-problem comedies popular in England during the early eighteenth century.[34] Southerne and Vanbrugh had attacked the position of women under English divorce law in such plays as *The Wives Excuse, or Cuckolds Make Themselves* (1691) and *The Provok'd Wife* (1697). Farquhar had presented a kind of fantasy-solution in the illegal 'divorce' at the end of *The Beaux Stratagem* (1707). A long stream of 'reform' comedies was initiated by Colley Cibber's *Love's Last Shift* (1696) and continued in

[31] This source was first suggested by Woods, 'Notes on Three of Fielding's Plays', p. 364. Several contemporary pamphlets were published concerning the case, *Lord Abergavenny* v. *Richard Liddell, Esq*.

[32] 'Many Husbands in this Town . . . live very comfortably by being content with their Infamy. . . . It is a modern Trade. . . . Marriage is Traffick throughout; as most of us bargain to be Husbands, so some of us bargain to be Cuckolds.' (23)

[33] Loftis, *Comedy and Society*, p. 119.

[34] For a survey and analysis of such works, see my 'Marital Discord in English Comedy from Dryden to Fielding', *Modern Philology*, 74 (1977), 248–72.

such plays as Cibber's *The Careless Husband* (1704), Steele's *The Tender Husband* (1705), and Charles Johnson's *The Generous Husband* (1711) and *The Masquerade* (1719). The Vanbrugh–Cibber *Provok'd Husband* (1728) was an extraordinarily successful marriage-problem comedy with a contrasting romance plot, and in all likelihood it gave Fielding some of his ideas. Even the notion of the complacent cuckold selling his wife had precedent—as for example in Mrs Haywood's *A Wife to be Lett* (1723), in which the husband takes £2,000 but his virtuous wife refuses to co-operate and sees that the money is returned.

Fielding's passionate belief in marriage is clearly expressed in *The Modern Husband*, a work whose parallels to *Amelia* twenty years later need not be detailed here.[35] Fielding's strategy was to convey a harsh and ugly picture of vice, a warmly attractive picture of virtue, and a sympathetic analysis of human frailty. In Fielding's view of human nature almost everyone is reclaimable, but he is no sunny optimist. Unlike Cibber, he waves no magic wand to bring about miraculous reformations. The Moderns and Lord Richly will remain as they are, and Fielding knows it. He is realist enough to understand that a good marriage does not preclude infatuation with a Mrs Modern, but insists that such infatuation need not destroy the marriage.

Despite the originality and seriousness of Fielding's design, the play itself is badly flawed. Once again, Fielding has problems with integration of plot. Against the Moderns he balances Mr and Mrs Bellamant, whose good marriage is threatened by Mr Bellamant's covert affair with Mrs Modern. Mr Modern 'surprises' his wife with Mr Bellamant, and Mrs Bellamant promptly forgives her erring husband. With little for his principals to do but talk, Fielding fills out a very long mainpiece with two subsidiary romance plots. In one, the Bellamants' son, an army Captain and socialite, marries Lady Charlotte Gaywit, a vivacious flapper. In the other, the Bellamants' sensible daughter Emilia agrees to marry Lord Richly's nephew, Mr Gaywit, who turns out to be the only lover for whom Mrs Modern has truly cared (76–7). Both sub-plots disappear from view for long periods.

If plot cohesion is inadequate, character psychology does little to redeem the play. The Moderns and Lord Richly are simplistic monsters, really just objects of detestation. Fielding does not manage

[35] For an account of Fielding's views of marriage, see Murial Brittain Williams, *Marriage: Fielding's Mirror of Morality* (University, Ala., 1973).

to make very clear why a husband otherwise so sensible and devoted as Mr Bellamant should be in the toils of a boring harpy. Even his self-reproaches about deceiving his wife seem formulaic (43). Captain Bellamant and Lady Charlotte constitute a late version of the 'gay couple', and the scene in which he wins her by spurning her (71–5) strikes me as quite entertaining. A critic in the *Grub-street Journal* (30 March) condemned her as unnatural; Fielding was to imply in *Tom Jones* VIII. i. that Lady Mary Wortley Montagu praised her as 'the Picture of half the young People of her Acquaintance'. Exaggerated she certainly is, disconcertingly so in a generally sober and 'realistic' picture of London life. The Captain Bellamant–Lady Charlotte plot seems inadequately connected to the rest of the play. The Gaywit–Emilia plot serves as a positive standard of romance and marriage, but their courtship is woefully underdeveloped.

Twentieth-century views of *The Modern Husband* have inevitably been coloured by the moral prejudices of Cross and Dudden. Cross manages to be fairly factual in his account, though he does say that Modern and Richly are 'unendurable on the stage'. Dudden's quasi-Victorian sensibility leads him to employ such terms as 'disagreeable', 'abominable', 'sordid', 'calculated crudity', 'highly offensive', and 'revolting'. He grants that the play was 'written with a moral intention', but only grudgingly.

So distressing have many critics found the subject-matter that they have assumed that the eighteenth-century audience shared their disgust and condemned the play on that basis. Banerji calls it 'a complete failure'; Cross reports that it was hissed the first night;[36] Dudden tells us that '*The Modern Husband* did not please the public . . . though it managed to struggle through fifteen [*recte* fourteen] performances.'[37] Fifty years ago Woods attempted to scotch this nonsense, and whatever our judgement of the play, we cannot accurately say that it was anything but a conspicuous success.

A play might 'struggle through' six nights, but not many more than that. *The Modern Husband* enjoyed an unbroken initial run of thirteen nights, which was highly unusual for a mainpiece. The only Drury Lane mainpiece to do better in recent history had been the phenomenal *Provok'd Husband*; the only later play with a better initial

[36] True, by Fielding's admission in the satiric front matter to *The Covent-Garden Tragedy*.

[37] H. K. Banerji, *Henry Fielding: Playwright, Journalist and Master of the Art of Fiction* (Oxford, 1929), p. 36; Cross, I, 120; Dudden, I, 105.

run before the Licensing Act was Hill's *Zara* in 1736, which lasted fourteen consecutive nights. The managers would hardly have kept *The Modern Husband* on (and given Fielding at least four benefits) if it had not been making money. A clear sign of its appeal is the managers' use of this play as a benefit on 2 March for Mrs Porter, who had broken her 'Thigh Bone' the previous summer in a chaise accident. This performance is described in the *Daily Post* on 3 March: 'Last Night their Majesties, his Royal Highness the Prince of Wales, their Highnesses the Princesses, and the whole Royal Family, were to see the new Comedy, call'd, The *Modern Husband*, acted to a splendid crowded Audience, for the Benefit of Mrs. *Porter*. This play has been performed thirteen Nights with Applause, to very good Audiences, but is now discontinued, on account of the Indisposition of a principal Actress.' There may be some puffery here, but Woods points out that 'the harshest contemporary criticism of the play' (in the *Grub-street Journal*, 30 March) 'begins with these words: "The favourable reception *The Modern Husband* has met with from the Town . . . ."'

To this potent testimony we can add two more pieces of evidence. A hostile writer in the *Grub-street Journal* of 29 June, who derides Fielding's most recent plays, refers to 'the vast encouragement he met with last winter'. Even better, the pseudonymous author of a topical pamphlet tells us that

> *Fielding* has had very good and very bad Success, a *Farce* of his call'd the *Lottery* And a Comedy intituled the *Modern Husband*, have both met with extraordinary Success; and, between both, he has made little less than a thousand Pounds, but the poor Author has fall'n into the Jaws of *Rattle-snakes*, His Elbows have destroy'd the Off-spring of his Brain; and in Spight of all his good Sense he has been stript at Play by Sharpers.[38]

'Extraordinary Success' seems consistent with the performance records. And the assertion that young Fielding promptly lost his earnings by gambling ties in with an odd passage in a satire of 1734:

> Where is *F-ld-ng*, She [*the Goddess*] cries, with his *heavy Quixote*?
> A biting his Audience, one said, he was got:

[38] 'Lord B—', *See and Seem Blind: Or, A Critical Dissertation on the Publick Diversions*, *&c* (London [1732]), pp. 7–8. This work was apparently written in May 1732; I suspect that the very knowledgeable author may have been Aaron Hill. For discussion, see my Introduction to the Augustan Reprint Society facsimile (Los Angeles, 1986).

> Hold there, cries another, he's now at *All-fours*,
> With a parcel of *Dam-me Boys*, and *bob-tail'd Whores*.[39]

As many readers have suspected, the tales of Mr Wilson and The Man of the Hill would seem to have foundation in hard personal experience.

Can we accept the claim that Fielding 'made little less than a thousand Pounds' from *The Lottery* and *The Modern Husband*? This is a startlingly high figure. According to 'Rich's Register', Fielding received a benefit for the former on 21 January. *The Modern Husband* ran from 14 February to 2 March, with Fielding receiving author benefits the third, sixth, and ninth nights. It was revived for one more night on 18 March, again advertised as an author benefit. Perhaps Fielding also received a benefit the twelfth night, or perhaps it was postponed because of the planned benefit for Mrs Porter. We can be certain that Fielding enjoyed five (possibly six) benefits for these two plays; presumably he paid the usual £50 house charges. We cannot suppose capacity audiences for all benefits, but Fielding could have averaged £100 from each. I would guess that he also received an initial cash fee for *The Lottery*, and of course he sold publication rights for both plays to John Watts. A thousand pounds seems high, but £600–£700 seems entirely possible, and if Fielding sold some benefit tickets above par, then £1,000 or close to it is conceivable.

Whatever our critical estimation of *The Modern Husband*, all evidence points to 'extraordinary Success' in February and March 1732. Why then was it never revived? This question takes us into the realm of speculation. The initial popularity may have reflected interest in Fielding more than approbation for the play. Two of the principals were dead within a year. The subject-matter was probably grounds for concern, and few actors like to play truly repellent characters. And, finally, *The Modern Husband* is just not a very good play. Questions about its quality have tended to get lost in the fuss over its subject, but if we simply consider the work as a dramatic vehicle, its shortcomings are all too apparent.

Fielding scholars, inevitably partisan, have almost unanimously decried the analysis published by 'Dramaticus' in the *Grub-street Journal* of 30 March, and it is regularly cited as evidence of the ill-natured attacks with which Fielding was soon inundated. Dramaticus was the disappointed author of a play recently rejected by Drury Lane,

[39] *The Dramatick Sessions* (London, 1734), p. 11.

as he informs us in a previous article (24 February). None the less, his critique is worth our consideration. It is no offhand slam but more than two thousand words of carefully reasoned analysis, liberally freighted with quotations from Fielding's text.

Dramaticus's most fundamental objections stem from his belief that 'Comedy chuses such characters, as having nothing absolutely ill in them, render themselves nevertheless ridiculous by their follies.' He allows for both exemplary and satiric comedy, but holds that the latter must offer the possibility of reform for the 'vicious', or there can be no 'instruction'. Mr and Mrs Modern and Lord Richly he finds 'such wretches, that they are as much below Comedy, as they are our pity'. Dramaticus's second basic objection is to inadequacies of design and cohesion. Fielding 'seems to have thought, that the assembling of a certain number of characters together, under the titles of Husbands and Wives, Sons and Daughters', is sufficient to establish the connections among them, 'and that the making of them talk together, is enough to form the dialogue'. These are not unfounded charges: the secondary characters have at best marginal relevance to the 'main action', and a large part of the endless conversation could be dropped without loss to either the plot or the satiric aims of the play. A third complaint—that Lady Charlotte is so frivolous as to be unnatural—smacks of pomposity, though how well she fits in this context is a legitimate question. Dramaticus approves of the Bellamants, and Gaywit and Emilia, but points out (justly enough) that they are essentially 'imitations from much better Plays than this', citing Lady Grace and Manly in *The Provok'd Husband* and Sir Charles and Lady Easy in *The Careless Husband*.

When Fielding's friend Thomas Cooke answered Dramaticus in *The Comedian* (June 1732), he granted that it had 'some Scenes independent of the main Busyness of the Play', but defended it for its 'Wit, Humour, Satire, and moral Reflections not unworthy the Pen of the best Stoic'. He also instanced haste as a reason for imperfections—not, as we now know, a valid claim. The argument boils down to the objection that *The Modern Husband* is badly designed and written against the answer that it is redeemed by its serious satiric purpose.

Fielding's great difficulty arises from his satirizing people he depicts as heartless fiends, and doing so in 'A Comedy'. Charles Woods suggests parallels to Shaw and Ibsen, arguing that *The Modern Husband* should be judged as a 'comedy of social purpose'. But Fielding merely offers us objects of contempt. The subject-matter is seriously presented, but the awkward, stunted plot and minimal psychology reduce the play to a tract. I do not gladly agree with either Dramaticus or Dudden, but their strictures are just. When Dudden stops fulminating over the 'offensive subject' and analyses the bad construction, the superficial psychology, and the padded, often irrelevant dialogue, he is, in a word, right. Fielding's reiterated partiality for this play is no credit to his judgement.

If *The Modern Husband* is so unsatisfactory, why was its first (and only) run so successful? The answer probably lies in Fielding's soaring reputation and the quality of the production Drury Lane was able to mount. Dramaticus prefaced his critique with a long paragraph reminding his readers that the trappings of performance can disguise defects in a play that are obvious 'when we see it divested of all these exterior helps; and take it, as we would a fine woman, naked of all its ornamental drapery'. The cast was magnificent. Colley Cibber was Lord Richly, and no doubt his genius for obnoxious fops breathed life into Fielding's simplistic monster. Robert Wilks took Mr Bellamant (it proved his last new role), and the best Sir Charles Easy of the age was the ideal man for the part. Mr Modern was taken by the journeyman Bridgwater, but the part demands little more than uniform unpleasantness. Captain Bellamant and Gaywit were done by Theophilus Cibber and Mills, jun. Even tiny parts could be afforded the likes of John Boman for Lord Lazy and John Harper for Mr Woodall. Lord Richly's Porter was Mr Mullart, an actor who would probably have been Mr Bellamant if the play had been produced at the Little Haymarket. The women were slightly less stellar, with Oldfield dead and Mrs Porter incapacitated, but still outstanding. Jane Cibber was the fizzy Lady Charlotte; Mrs Horton took Mrs Bellamant;[40] and Mrs Heron had the rather thankless task of trying to make Mrs Modern believable. To this group of performers Fielding probably owed much of the play's success.

The Modern Husband shows Fielding trying to be a Juvenalian satirist. Even a friendly reader cannot reasonably deny the play's basic defects of design and execution. We can certainly admire Fielding's originality and daring and his passionately serious view of marriage. But to pretend that satiric intent and moral fervour make a good play would be idle. Fielding was lucky to emerge from this production with

[40] Mrs Horton may be relatively unfamiliar, but for some idea of her considerable range of strengths, see *An Apology for the Life of Mr. T......... C....., Comedian*, pp. 141–2. She must have been highly effective as the injured but forgiving wife.

a profitable success, for, shorn of its glossy production, the play appears clearly as the prentice work it was. Fielding's commitment to what he was trying to do was real, and in due course he would attempt such a work again in *The Universal Gallant*. But neither character psychology nor social satire in high life was ever to be Fielding's forte, and for him in 1732 *The Modern Husband* was a relic of an earlier phase.

III. THE PROLIFIC AND CONTROVERSIAL PROFESSIONAL

Becoming Drury Lane's principal supplier of new plays was an immense step up in the literary world for Fielding, but it gave him a dangerous prominence. He was probably due for a conspicuous flop or two in any case, but having his work produced by Cibber & Co. could only arouse jealousy among the many less successful authors the triumvirs had trodden upon. Dedicating *The Modern Husband* to Walpole was a red flag to the opposition press, and at least an irritant to the *Grub-street Journal*, which in any case had a special venom reserved for everything associated with Colley Cibber.[41] Any failure on Fielding's part would be exploited by envious detractors. He got away with *The Modern Husband*, which evidently overcame some first-night hisses and was attacked only after the fact. With his next ventures his luck ran out. And unused to malicious personal attacks, Fielding reacted with an offended fury that simply provoked his detractors to respond with yet more scurrilous reprisals.

The Old Debauchees and *The Covent-Garden Tragedy*

On Thursday, 1 June 1732, Drury Lane premièred a new double-bill by Fielding—with disastrous results. Whatever served as publicity department (perhaps Fielding himself) had evidently prepared to trumpet yet another triumph, for on 2 June the *Daily Post* reported 'Last night the new Comedy call'd, The *Old Debauchees*, and The *Covent-Garden Tragedy* were acted for the first Time . . . with universal Applause.' On 5 June the *Daily Post* had to print an awkward retraction: 'We were partly misinform'd as to the Reception of the two Pieces play'd on Thursday Night. . . . We are assured the Comedy call'd *The Old Debauchees*, did meet with universal Applause; but the *Covent Garden Tragedy* will be Acted no more, both the Author and the

[41] On this periodical, see James T. Hillhouse, *The Grub-street Journal* (Durham, NC, 1928).

Actors being unwilling to continue any Piece contrary to the Opinion of the Town.' This the *Grub-street Journal* reprinted with the sneering comment, '*For* unwilling *read* unable' (8 June). By the 15th the *Grub-street Journal* was in full cry against '*The Common Garden Tragedy*', assuring its readers that 'It would be ridiculous to aim any sort of criticism upon so shameful a Piece.' Fielding foolishly rose to the bait, and the ensuing controversy rumbled on for the whole summer, its fires regularly refuelled by the delighted editors of the *Grub-street Journal*. The critical brawl (which will be examined in due course) has overshadowed the plays themselves.

The two plays were evidently planned as a double bill, and were apparently ready nearly two months before the première, when Fielding signed a publication agreement with John Watts.

April 4th 1732

Recd then of Mr John Watts the sum of twenty Guineas for the Copies of a Farce of three acts called the despairing Debauchee and a Tragedy called the Covent-Garden-Tragedy or by whatever other names they shall be called which I promise to assign over to the said John Watts.

Henry ffielding[42]

The price seems surprisingly modest, especially for plays that had not yet failed. If the plays were indeed ready, why was performance delayed until June? I would hazard the guess that management wanted to keep them clear of the benefit season. Or perhaps Fielding wrote them specifically for Theophilus Cibber, who was manager of the summer season that opened 25 May and starred in both pieces.

The Old Debauchees is almost invariably said to represent the celebrated case of Father Girard, Director of a Jesuit seminary in Toulon, brought to trial in October 1731 for employing sorcery to seduce Catherine Cadiere, a virtuous girl to whom he was confessor.[43] This account is misleading. The Girard case probably stimulated Fielding's imagination, but the specifics of his play are so remote from Girard and Cadiere as to be almost unrecognizable. The Girard case could certainly have been dramatized in a literal way—as indeed it was. To see how little Fielding owes to history,

[42] Printed in facsimile by Cross, opposite III, 360, from the original then in the R. B. Adam Collection. Now in the collection of Viscountess Eccles (formerly Mary Hyde).

[43] For a report of the verdict in the case, see the *Craftsman*, 16 Oct. 1731.

we may compare his play with *The Wanton Jesuit: or, Innocence Seduced*, staged at the Little Haymarket 17 March 1732. The anonymous author milks the situation for all the sexual titillation it is worth, and the results are good gutter journalism, if poor dramaturgy.[44] The crux of the story, naturally, is that the wicked Jesuit uses dark arts to seduce the poor innocent girl. Fielding, in sharp contrast, makes the girl smart and worldly-wise enough to see right through the plot and foil it. Fielding's Jesuit is a sorry dog, not a dangerous and successful villain. In keeping with his design, Fielding's tone is boisterous, appropriate to broad farce, not to shilling-shocker melodrama.

The focus and structure of Fielding's plot are his own. He contrasts two 'old debauchees'—Old Laroon, an unrepentant whoremaster and mocker of the Church, and Jourdain, a guilt-haunted sinner now become priest-ridden to the point of simplemindedness.[45] Young Laroon is engaged to Jourdain's daughter Isabel; her confessor Father Martin delays the marriage while he tries to seduce her. Much of the plot (such as it is) turns on Jourdain's panic-stricken determination to do anything any priest tells him, however idiotic. From Fielding's early title, *The Despairing Debauchee*, we may guess that he originally saw Jourdain as the central humours character in the play, perhaps intending to develop him psychologically in the fashion of Molière's Bourgeois Gentleman or Imaginary Invalid. For whatever reasons, the play did not come out that way.

Fielding indulges in his favourite trick of contrasting two exaggerated humours in his father figures. The priest is a stock villain; Young Laroon a stock lover. Isabel is a fine, lively young woman, an excellent vehicle for the popular Kitty Clive (still Miss Raftor at this date). The plot devices are predictable. At various times both Old Laroon and his son disguise themselves as priests in order to manipulate Jourdain; Isabel pretends to be all innocent compliance in order to trap Father Martin before witnesses, which duly happens. At

[44] (London, 1731[/2]). Only the one performance is recorded. On 2 Feb. 1732 Goodman's Fields had mounted an anonymous afterpiece on the subject (lost), called *Father Girard the Sorcerer; or, The Amours of Harlequin and Miss Cadiere* and described as 'a Tragi-Comi-Farcical Opera'. It enjoyed eleven performances.

[45] The designation 'A Comedy' on the title-page is misleading, and promptly drew fire from critics, who maintained that such gross caricatures as Old Laroon and Jourdain 'might have passed in a Farce; but are altogether inconsistent with Comedy'. (See 'Prosaicus' in the *Grub-street Journal* of 24 August 1732.) Fielding himself had designated the work a 'Farce' in his contract with John Watts.

the end the priest is dispatched to be ducked in a 'Horse-pond' and tossed 'dry in a Blanket' (39).[46]

Intermixed with this standard farce fare is a long string of scorchingly hostile references to Catholicism.[47] Cleary refers to this prominent element in the play as 'bigoted scurrility', which is a fair description.[48] Fielding's deep-seated detestation of the Catholic Church is obvious in much of his later writing, and this is not the place either to analyse it or apologize for it. Priest-baiting was an established game in English comedy: Dryden's *The Spanish Fryar* remained a repertory staple, and Shadwell's *The Lancashire Witches* was performed at Drury Lane as late as 1729. But to put most of the anti-papist speeches in the mouth of a ranting buffoon like Old Laroon is strange. A critic may want to think that Fielding is satirizing both priest-haters and priest-worshippers, but the play itself does not support such a reading. The stream of anti-papist speeches is rarely funny, and only a dedicated hater of Romanism could rejoice in it for the sake of the abuse. Whether part of the audience liked it, we do not know, but as Fielding was soon to discover, some members found sneering mockery of religion distasteful.

How well *The Old Debauchees* succeeded in the theatre was warmly debated in the newspapers over the summer. The *Daily Post* of 16 June reiterated its assertion that the work was received with 'great Applause', a claim disputed in the *Grub-street Journal* of 29 June, which stated that 'the 3d night's audience on June 13th was dismissed, as not being sufficient to pay half the charges'. On 31 July 'Philalethes' (usually taken as Fielding himself) replied angrily in the *Daily Post* that the play 'was received with as *great Applause* as was ever given on the Theatre'; that 'The Audience ... was as numerous as hath been known at that Season of the Year'; and that 'except on the first Night, and ev'n then in one particular Scence [*scene?*], there never was one Hiss in the House'.[49] The known performance history suggests considerable exaggeration here. The company was performing twice a

[46] Citations are to the Roberts edn. of 1732.

[47] They are catalogued by Dudden, I, 108.

[48] Cleary, p. 59.

[49] We do not know which scene was hissed the first night. I assume that this passage is the basis for Cross's undocumented statement (I, 130) that Fielding 'cut from "The Old Debauchees" the passages which displeased the public so that by the next week the comedy was being received with "universal applause"'. I am aware of no definite proof that Fielding made any cuts in response to first-night hisses, any more than he did for *The Modern Husband*.

week, and between 1 June and 7 July *The Old Debauchees* managed just six actual performances, the last of them advertised as an author benefit. The third scheduled performance (13 June) was indeed dismissed,[50] and all succeeding performances were part of a double bill with *The Mock Doctor*, which was well received. This record, coupled with the lack of revival at Drury Lane in the next decade, does not suggest a success.[51]

The Old Debauchees is an unusual combination of farcical buffoonery and harsh invective, and not an effective one. A pattern is emerging, however. Fielding clearly wants to write something more than commercial pap, and he is experimenting (awkwardly at times) with ways to incorporate serious commentary in standard generic frameworks. *The Lottery*, *The Modern Husband*, and *The Old Debauchees* all have a good deal more bite and satiric substance than is usual in the forms Fielding was employing—ballad opera, social comedy, and humour-intrigue farce. His moral indignation in these works is not new. Ducrocq rightly identifies parallels between the treatment of Justice Squeezum in *Rape upon Rape* and Father Martin in *The Old Debauchees*: humours characters and farce trappings notwithstanding, Fielding's harsh disapproval comes through in a way that is not comic at all.[52] He is not laughing at follies but reprehending vices. This harsh view is again evident in the second half of Fielding's ill-fated double bill.

The Covent-Garden Tragedy died its first night. The cliché about the work is that the audience simply would not stand for the representation of a brothel.[53] Certainly the first-night audience must have

[50] Although *The London Stage* does not say so, the cancelled performance was advertised in the *Daily Post* of 12 and 13 June as 'For the Benefit of the Author'.

[51] The Little Haymarket actors tried the work for one night a year later (27 March 1733). In 1745–46 it was revived for more than 20 performances at Drury Lane (and for several at Goodman's Fields as well) at the height of anti-Jacobite hysteria. It was shortened and cleaned up a bit in performance, and was republished at that time as *The Debauchees*, with the cuts indicated in the new edn. Two performances at Drury Lane in 1748 ended the work's stage history.

[52] Ducrocq, p. 220.

[53] As Fielding complains in the *Daily Post* of 31 July, however, the audience continued to tolerate *The Humorous Lieutenant*. And of course Hogarth's *The Harlot's Progress*, pub. in April 1732, was a runaway success. Robert Etheridge Moore goes so far as to suggest that 'it seems certain . . . that the sensation caused by Hogarth's series gave Fielding the whole idea for his play'. See *Hogarth's Literary Relationships* (Minneapolis, 1948), p. 96. Moore lists parallels, but unless Fielding knew *The Harlot's Progress* before publication (as is possible) it could not have served as inspiration for *The Covent-Garden Tragedy*, which was apparently extant by 4 April. Ironically, Hogarth's work served as

made its objections plain. The usual assertion that 'the next performance in a legitimate theatre was a revival by the National Theatre in 1968',[54] is, however, quite untrue. The work was revived with *Don Quixote in England* at the Little Haymarket in 1734, ran four nights, and was revived a fifth night by the summer company that year. It was used by the 'extended company' at York Buildings on 21 March 1735, and for a single night at the Little Haymarket as late as 28 December 1778.[55] Obviously the work never caught on, but it was not anathema to the eighteenth-century audience, as most critics have assumed.

The Covent-Garden Tragedy attempts to duplicate in travesty of pseudo-classic tragedy the success that *Tom Thumb* had enjoyed as a burlesque of heroic tragedy. Fielding's principal target is usually said to be Ambrose Philips's *The Distrest Mother* (1712). The parallels are real, but so are the divergencies (both are usefully outlined by Peter Lewis).[56] I doubt that even an inveterate playgoer would have made the connection unprompted at a performance of Fielding's play. Philips's play remained a repertory staple,[57] but the distance between the elevated agonies of Racine's *Andromaque* (Philips's source) and Fielding's brothel is quite a jump.

Since Fielding gives no hint of a specific target in either prologue or text, we must presume that he thought *The Covent-Garden Tragedy* would work as a more general travesty of classic tragedy. The travesty is genuinely brilliant in both conception and details, and there is much to relish here if one is not automatically disgusted by a play whose characters are a madam, her porter, her whores, and their customers. One need not go back to the text of *The Distrest Mother* or other such plays to enjoy Fielding's quarrel scene and demand for revenge (24–5), reported deaths (27), mad scene (30), and happy-ending mockery of catastrophe.[58] *The Covent-Garden Tragedy* does not,

the basis for Theophilus Cibber's very popular *The Harlot's Progress; or, The Ridotto Al' Fresco* (March 1733). Nor is any objection recorded to Henry Potter's ballad-opera, *The Decoy; or, The Harlot's Progress*, performed four nights at Goodman's Fields in Feb. 1733.

[54] Rogers, p. 55.

[55] Fielding scholars seem to have ignored its adaptation by the highly moral Holcroft in *The Rival Queens*, staged at Covent Garden on 15 Sept. 1794 (Larpent MS 1039).

[56] The best critical account of the play is Peter Lewis, 'Fielding's *The Covent-Garden Tragedy* and Philips's *The Distrest Mother*', *Durham University Journal*, NS 37 (1975), 33–46.

[57] It had been performed at Drury Lane on 13 May 1731 and at Goodman's Fields on 7 December 1731, and was put on at Drury Lane the week following Fielding's fiasco (9 June 1732) and again the following 7 Nov. and 10 Jan.

[58] Citations are to the Watts and Roberts edn. of 1732.

however, enjoy the high spirits of *Tom Thumb*. The characters and setting are decidedly more 'real', and Fielding's numerous references to real life seem designed to reinforce this sense of degraded actuality. Covent Garden was five minutes' walk from Drury Lane. The clear allusion to Elizabeth Needham (a madam killed in the pillory in 1731), a real porter named Leathercoat, the bully Edward Braddock, and his sister Fanny's suicide—all contribute to an oppressive refusal to let the audience take the whole business as literary fun.[59] The material is extremely funny, but in his anxiety to make the piece a serious satire, Fielding did not allow his audience sufficient 'distance' for comfort. Evidence of this, I think, is the work's success as a puppet show.[60]

Tom Thumb is a joke. *The Covent-Garden Tragedy* is a harshly unsympathetic travesty of contemporary tragedy. The one mocks, the other degrades. The later work has no jokey exuberance, but an all-too-evident distaste for both the object of the satire and its vehicle. The results are closer to Thomas Duffett's *The Empress of Morocco* (1673) and *The Mock-Tempest* (1674) than to something like Gay's *The What d'ye Call It* (1715).[61] Fielding's prologue closely echoes the rhetoric of Rowe's prologue for the ever-popular *Fair Penitent* (1703), with its assertion of the remoteness of examples of the great. But Fielding's final tag-moral, delivered by Lovegirlo, bluntly expresses his contempt for such drama: 'From such Examples as of this and that, / We all are taught to know I know not what.'

The Covent-Garden Tragedy was not published until 24 June, so Fielding had plenty of time to respond to its failure in the theatre. The eleven pages of 'Prolegomena' he provided are brilliantly funny satire on his enemies, but also a provocation that Fielding might have been wise to forego. Fielding provides a letter from a dolt, who says wonderingly that 'One wou'd have guess'd from the Audience, It had been a Comedy.' Even better is the 'Criticism . . . originally intended for the *Grub-street Journal*.' Here the degree to which 'Dramaticus' had stung Fielding's vanity is all too clear. The fatuous critic, citing 'Aristuttle' and 'Horase', flourishes a silly definition of tragedy and displays his ignorant malice in denouncing Fielding's play. Fielding

[59] See Cross, I, 128–9.

[60] See George Speaight, *The History of the English Puppet Theatre* (London, 1955), pp. 104, 106, 108, 331.

[61] As Lewis notes, we have no evidence that Fielding was familiar with Duffett's coarse, harsh, effective travesties, but the parallels are numerous. *The Mock-Tempest* (a smear aimed at the highly successful new 'operatic' *Tempest* of 1674) even employs a crowd of apprentices attacking a brothel in place of the opening storm.

takes care to have him stumble across the parallels between his characters and those in *The Distrest Mother*: this is as close as he comes to providing any sort of key. Coupled with his having the semi-literate porter Leathersides write dramatic criticism for the *Grub-street Journal* in the play itself (2), this seems an open invitation to retaliate in kind. And unhappily for Fielding, the challenge was accepted with glee.

The Mock Doctor

Just three weeks after the disastrous double bill, Drury Lane gave the delayed third performance of *The Old Debauchees* with a new afterpiece, *The Mock Doctor: or The Dumb Lady Cur'd*, 'Done from *Moliere*' as the title-page informs us. Fielding's preface says that 'The *English* Theatre owes this Farce to an Accident not unlike that which gave it to the *French*' (i.e., to the failure of another of the author's plays), adding that he translated it in less time even than Molière wrote it.[62] Perhaps this is the literal truth, but it is an odd tale. Why should the summer company be frantically anxious for a new piece to be learned in a great hurry when they had all sorts of proven afterpieces at their disposal? Why should Fielding, shocked by a distressing public rebuff, rush to produce an adaptation? Possibly he did, but we cannot scout the idea that he was simply making rhetorical use of a complimentary parallel between Molière and himself.[63] Whatever the history of the piece, it proved an immediate success. It was performed eleven times during the summer, seven times in September, and another six times during the autumn.[64] Its popularity proved lasting: it was revived regularly into the nineteenth century.

Fielding's method in concocting the piece is simple. For the most part, he follows Molière's text closely speech by speech. But instead of providing a verbal translation, he adapts Molière's speeches into vigorous, colloquial English, in the process making his play 'a

[62] Quotations are from the first Watts edn. of 1732.

[63] A puff in the *Daily Post* of 16 June says that the author 'has permitted this Performance to come on at a more disadvantageous Season than he at first intended' in order to avoid bringing on some 'old worn-out Entertainments'—a claim that contradicts the tale about Fielding getting the piece written and produced in three weeks.

[64] The degree of its success is indicated by a pirate performance at Tottenham Court as early as 4 Aug. The success of the Drury Lane summer season as a whole in 1732 is stressed in *A Letter from Theophilus Cibber, Comedian, To John Highmore, Esq;* (London, 1733), p. 1, where the company is said to have paid the exceptionally high fee of £150 for the 'use of their Stock, and the Privilege of Acting'.

thorough adaptation, English in setting and in sentiment'.[65] Fielding streamlined it a bit, trimming speeches and dropping the sex scene between Sganarelle and Jacqueline in Act III. In its place he substitutes Gregory's sexual encounter with his wife, in which the woodman is disguised as a 'French doctor'—i.e., Dr John Misaubin, the celebrated quack of St Martin's Lane, to whom Fielding dedicated the play in mock-reverent terms. Fielding added a little scene in which the disguised Gregory turns his wife over to Dr Helebore as a mad person in need of treatment. The most conspicuous and significant additions, however, are the nine songs, which make the work a kind of miniature ballad opera.

Though the play is structurally Molière's, Fielding's contribution is significant. If one compares his springy, colloquial speeches with the more careful rendering of Molière's words in eighteenth-century English translations, the theatrical effectiveness of Fielding's version is instantly evident. Taking the overall design from Molière, however, solved the technical problems of plot control that Fielding had so often failed to solve.

How Fielding came to adapt Molière we do not know. He says in his preface that 'any *English* Reader' can see how he carried out his adaptation 'by examining an exact literal Translation of the *Medecin malgré Lui*, which is . . . in . . . *Select Comedies of Moliere*, just published by *John Watts*'. Cross leaps to the conclusion that Fielding was among the 'several gentlemen' involved in this venture, and offers 'the conjecture that Fielding's "Miser" and "Mock Doctor" were adaptations which he made from Molière while engaged upon the laborious task of more literal translations of these very plays'.[66] Despite two sober rebuttals, this airy speculation has been taken far too seriously by later scholars. Joseph Tucker provides good evidence to show that the 1732 translation was primarily the work of James Miller, with help from Henry Baker, and *Tartuffe* provided by Martin Clare.[67] L. P. Goggin, in a close comparison of Fielding's text with the original, the Ozell translation of 1714, and the 1732 translation, concludes that 'Fielding most probably worked on his adaptation with only a French text before him', and that differences in idiom make 'it seem extremely improbable that one person did both' the 1732 translation and *The*

[65] Cross, I, 130.

[66] Ibid., I, 144–5.

[67] Joseph E. Tucker, 'The Eighteenth-Century English Translations of Molière', *Modern Language Quarterly*, 3 (1942), 83–103.

Mock Doctor. Goggin suggests, sensibly, that Fielding knew of the forthcoming translation and mentioned it 'as a favor to Watts'—his own publisher.[68] Unless fresh evidence turns up, we should assume that Fielding had no part in the *Select Comedies* translation.

With *The Mock Doctor* we see once again Fielding's habit of improving upon a success. The performance of 16 November 1732 was advertised as 'Revised by the Author', and the changes are to be found in Watts's 'Second Edition, With Additional Songs and Alterations'.[69] Interestingly, Fielding broke the text into formal scenes: the first edition was likewise a single act, but with unnumbered scene breaks when location changed. Most of the verbal changes are small, but Fielding dropped four of the original songs and replaced them with new ones, two of them specially set by Mr Seedo. The object of the rearrangement was evidently to strengthen the latter part of the show, which had been rather short of music, without increasing the length.[70]

Even Fielding's detractors admitted that the original version was well received by the town, though they were inclined to credit Molière for the merits of the piece and the skills of Theophilus Cibber and Miss Raftor for its success.[71] Unlike Fielding's other plays of 1732, *The Mock Doctor* has no pretensions to serious purpose of any sort.[72] Fielding benefited greatly from taking over the well-crafted frame of Molière's play, but what he provided by way of adaptation and additions he handled with great skill.

[68] L. P. Goggin, 'Fielding and the *Select Comedies of Mr. de Moliere*', *Philological Quarterly*, 31 (1952), 344–50.

[69] London, 1732.

[70] From the first edn. Fielding cut 3. ''Tis true, my good Dear, I am Bone of your Bone'; 5. 'In formal dull Schools'; 8. 'The Soldier, who bravely goes'; and 9. 'Alas! how unhappy is that Woman's Fate'. The first two are good songs, well-integrated in the show; the third is rather inorganic; the fourth fits into Gregory's 'test' of Dorcas' virtue and perhaps pulls the show off centre. In the revision, Fielding added: 6. 'A Fig for the dainty civil Spouse'; 7. 'Thus, lovely Patient, *Charlotte* sees'; 8. 'If you hope by your Skill'; and 9. 'When tender young Virgins look pale and complain'. The first aptly adds to the marital conflict theme; the second develops the romance between the 'dumb' girl and her lover; the third adds to the Dr Helebore episode; the fourth constitutes a rousing new finale.

[71] See, e.g. 'Prosaicus' in the *Grub-street Journal* of 24 Aug. 1732.

[72] Nor, in my opinion, does it have political allusions that make it a sly dig at Walpole. Sheridan Baker has argued such a case ('Political Allusion in Fielding's *Author's Farce*, *Mock Doctor*, and *Tumble-Down Dick*'), but I have to agree with Cleary's objection that such subtle and complex associations as Baker discerns would not have been apparent to the audience. Certainly there is not a hint of political 'application' in any of the newspapers I have read.

The Feud with the *Grub-street Journal*

A word needs to be said about the critical disputes into which Fielding entered in the summer of 1732. He had been phenomenally lucky not to be attacked in his first two seasons of conspicuous success. Perhaps because his hits were lightweight entertainment, the critics treated him with indulgence. 'Bavius' (John Martyn) published a little parody of *Tom Thumb*, and 'a young Gentleman of Cambridge' handled him dismissively in an imitation of Horace, but these are not serious *examens* of Fielding's plays, and they have no personal venom.[73] When Fielding unveiled his pretensions to Juvenalian status in *The Modern Husband*, he was inviting judgement by different standards, and he got it. The stinging dismissal of that play by 'Dramaticus' in the *Grub-street Journal* of 30 March plainly cut Fielding to the quick, and he responded with a gratuitous swipe at the *Journal* in the text of *The Covent-Garden Tragedy*. The failure of that work, and its subject matter, were just the opening his envious detractors needed, and they pounced. These attacks—and Fielding's angry, ineffectual replies—are well known and need no extensive quotation or analysis here.[74] A brief list of the principal items, however, suggests just how bruised and embattled the twenty-five-year-old author must have felt. All of the attacks were lengthy (and most of them front-page) affairs.

(1) 8 June *Grub-street Journal*. 'Prosaicus' attacks the depravity of *The Covent-Garden Tragedy*.

(2) 15 June *Grub-street Journal*. 'Dramaticus' attacks *The Covent-Garden Tragedy* ('Such a scene of infamous lewdness, was never brought ... before on any Stage ... No Company ... can justify the turning the Stage into a rank Bawdy-house').

(3) 21 June *Daily Post*. 'Mr. Wm. Hint, Candle-Snuffer'[75] (i.e. Fielding?) objects to these attacks in huffy terms and defies the critics to 'wrest one Word ... into an indecent Meaning ... Methinks it is

[73] See the *Grub-street Journal* of 11 June 1730 and 18 Nov. 1731.

[74] The most important of them have been conveniently reprinted in *Henry Fielding: The Critical Heritage*, ed. Ronald Paulson and Thomas Lockwood (London, 1969). For a general summary of the controversy, see Hillhouse, *The Grub-street Journal*, pp. 173–85.

[75] Presumably working from refs. in the *Grub-street Journal* of 29 June and 10 Aug., Cross suggests that this letter was written by Fielding and Theophilus Cibber in collaboration (I, 133). For a plausible argument that Fielding alone wrote the letter, see William J. Burling, 'Henry Fielding and the "William Hint" Letter: A Reconsideration', *Notes and Queries*, 231 (1986), 498–9.

incumbent on every Man who affirms a Play to be bad, indecent and infamous, to give some Quotations from it, or mention some particular Scene or Incident which are so.'

(4) 29 June *Grub-street Journal*. 'Prosaicus', 'A.B.', and 'Dramaticus' heap abuse on Fielding and ridicule 'Hint's' defence, with Dramaticus taking the opportunity to 'whisper' to Fielding that *The Mock Doctor* is 'miserable stuff'.

(5) 13 July *Grub-street Journal*. 'Dramaticus' falls nastily upon Cooke's defence of *The Modern Husband* (in the June *Comedian*); 'Miso-cleros' objects heatedly (with plenty of textual citations) to the presentation of churches and clergy in *The Old Debauchees*.

(6) 20 July *Grub-street Journal*. 'Publicus' devotes a long leader to moral and literary objections to *The Old Debauchees* and *The Covent-Garden Tragedy*, with copious quotations, and concludes with a sneering complaint about Fielding's debasement of Molière in *The Mock Doctor* and his misunderstanding of its very title.

(7) 31 July *Daily Post*. 'Philalethes' (i.e. Fielding?) denounces the detractors: 'I have read, with the Detestation it deserves, *an infamous Paper* call'd *the Grubstreet Journal* . . .' He complains bitterly that *The Old Debauchees*, far from being 'met with the *universal Detestation of the Town* . . . was received with as *great Applause* as was ever given on the Theatre'. *The Covent-Garden Tragedy* he defends on the ground that it exposes vice. Affronted dignity is evident in every paragraph, and the author is so unwise as to object to grammatical strictures by referring to 'the Education which the Author of the Debauchees is known to have had', a piece of old Etonian snobbery that the critics did not allow to pass in silence.

(8) 3 August *Grub-street Journal*. Inspired by a limping defence in the *Daily Courant* of 29 July, 'Dramaticus' again denounces *The Modern Husband*.

(9) 10 August *Grub-street Journal*. 'Bavius' makes a cool and cutting reply to the *Daily Post* protest of 31 July, dubbing Fielding 'a venal and venereal Poet' who writes 'lewd dramatical entertainments'.

(10) 24 August *Grub-street Journal*. 'Prosaicus' returns to the attack, with a contemptuous dismissal of *The Old Debauchees*.

(11) 10 September *Grub-street Journal*. 'Bavius' summarizes the whole controversy, cutting Fielding to pieces with the skill of a veteran journalist. His point-by-point rebuttal of the *Daily Post* letter of 31 July is rhetorically devastating.

Fielding finally had the sense to realize—or perhaps his friends convinced him—that silence was the best response to malicious criticism, and the uproar eventually ceased. Cooke published an epigram in the September issue of *The Comedian* (p. 32), justifying Fielding's silence: 'When *Grubs*, and *Grublings*, censure *Fielding*'s Scenes, / He cannot answer that which Nothing means . . .' But Fielding's desire to answer is plain, and he must have been mightily frustrated by his inability to do so effectively. Our scanty evidence suggests that Fielding was greatly distressed by this storm of abuse. Indeed, although he was to suffer such attacks (and worse) the rest of his life, he never learned to be indifferent to them. Fielding was not crushed, but he probably felt badly bruised.[76] As Rogers observes, 'less hostile criticism has silenced major talents'.[77] Fielding could not afford to be silenced—he needed to eat—but he must have been discouraged by his failures and uncertain what to try next. And at this inauspicious moment, the Drury Lane management disintegrated.

IV. THE CHANGING THEATRE SCENE

While Fielding was taking his drubbing from the critics, the London theatre world was undergoing rapid change. Just as the triumvirate management was in the process of disappearing (leaving Drury Lane in a perilous state), their competitors seemed to be prospering. Goodman's Fields had done well enough that its new owner erected a new theatre for the company, and John Rich was completing his elegant new Covent Garden playhouse. This would make the serviceable Lincoln's Inn Fields theatre available for someone else—and still more new buildings were rumoured. We may presume that while Fielding watched Drury Lane dissolve into chaos, he was eyeing developments elsewhere with keen interest.

[76] Cooke's assertion in the June *Comedian* that Fielding 'laughs, without Anger, at those who expose themselves by a fruitless Endeavour to expose him' does not ring true. And it is sarcastically answered by 'Dramaticus' in his critique of 13 July: 'I have received an account of a transaction at a certain Bookseller's shop near Temple-bar, which directly contradicts this: for there two celebrated Captains quarrelled about this affair, and were likely to have come to blows.' Hillhouse interprets this as a threatened assault by Fielding upon Gilliver, the publisher of the *Grub-street Journal* (see Hillhouse, *The Grub-street Journal*, p. 178). Whether Fielding was threatening Gilliver or one of his writers, the threat of physical violence seems the more plausible when we recall that Fielding had been sued for assault in 1726 (see Battestin, 'Four New Fielding Attributions', p. 74 n. 8). Fielding's touchiness and bluster are nastily depicted by the author of *The Dramatick Sessions* (1734), who calls him 'a *mad blust'ring Fool*'.

[77] Rogers, p. 56.

The 1732 Patent and the New Management of Drury Lane

The death of Sir Richard Steele on 1 September 1729 meant that the Drury Lane patent would expire exactly three years after that date. Steele had taken no active part in management for nearly a decade, but the triumvirs had rested secure because of his patent. With his death, the government was faced with a very awkward question: who should own and operate the company? A variety of investors owned the building. The actors worked under informal contracts to the three managers, who owned the company's 'stock'—i.e. its scenes, costumes, prompt-books, etc. If the government gave a new patent to a ministerial favourite, could the actors be compelled to work for him and the building sharers to rent to him? Could the owners of the 'stock' simply remain *in situ*, letting the new patentee hunt for a venue and scrounge for actors as best he could? No one knew. The success of Goodman's Fields and the Little Haymarket proved that a company could operate without a patent, or even a licence. But to operate without formal authority was a risky way to run a substantial business, and even a limited-term patent must have been regarded as highly desirable.

We have little information about the infighting that went on behind the scenes in the government. Presumably, the triumvirs pulled every string they could to get a new patent in their own names; who objected and who competed with them we do not know. On 3 November 1730 the *Daily Journal* reported that 'a Patent for the Theatre-Royal in Drury-Lane, is order'd to pass the Seals in Favour of Mr. Wilks, Mr. Booth, and Mr. Cibber. A Patent for the said Theatre was granted to Mrs. Oldfield, deceas'd, upon the Death of the late Sir Richard Steele.' I have found no other evidence about a grant to Anne Oldfield (who died 23 October 1730), but if she was promised the patent, that must have thrown a scare into the triumvirs. Even after Oldfield's death, however, the matter seems to have been complex.

On 1 April 1731 the Lord Chamberlain ordered the Attorney General to 'prepare a Bill for His Majesty's Royal Signature' for a twenty-one-year patent to be granted to Wilks, Cibber, and Booth, commencing 1 September 1732. This order was cancelled, and written again 15 May 1731.[78] On 3 July 1731 the patent was drafted,[79] but then seems to have stuck in the government machinery, where it remained

[78] PRO LC 5/160, pp. 175, 179.

[79] PRO LC 5/202, pp. 407–9.

nine months. On 27 April 1732 the *Daily Post* reported: 'On Tuesday last came on a Hearing before the Lord Chancellor, assisted by the Lord Chief Justice Raymond and Mr. Baron Comyns, touching the Validity of the Patent granted by his Majesty to R. Wilks, C. Cibber, and Barton Booth, Esqs. for the Playhouse in Drury-lane; and the Court unanimously agreed, that the said Patent was a lawful Grant; and it passed the Broad Seal accordingly.' This was reprinted in the *Grub-street Journal* on 4 May, with the additional information that 'The Patent is for 21 years to the longer liver, and assignable.' The last word is the key: Wilks and Cibber were both past sixty, and Booth was in bad health. But together with their 'stock', a patent had considerable cash value.

When the formal patent was issued is not known, but it took effect from 1 September 1732.[80] The text was taken almost verbatim from Steele's patent of 1715. It states that the company is 'under the regulation hereinafter mentioned'; specifies that no abuse of church or government will be tolerated; and orders 'the said Governors' to purge both new and revived plays of any 'Expressions Offensive to Piety and good manners'. Beyond 'the Governors', the regulatory apparatus is vague, but the government's intention to forbid plays it found obnoxious is clear.

Why the government gave the patent to the actors we can only guess. Colley Cibber, recently become Poet Laureate, had friends in high places. Perhaps someone remembered the perpetual nuisance caused by Christopher Rich's battles with his performers. And perhaps possession was regarded as a powerful claim: any outsider receiving the patent might have had great difficulty taking control of the company, the building, and the stock. Whatever the reasons, the unpopular triumvirs got their bonanza, and the ailing Booth lost no time cashing in on it. On 13 July 1732 the *Daily Courant* reported: 'Mr. Booth of Drury Lane Playhouse hath sold his Share and Interest in the Stock and Management of that Playhouse to John Highmore of Hampton Court, Esq.' This is not the whole story. Benjamin Victor (an intimate of Booth) tells us that Highmore paid £2,500 'for *one half* only of Mr. *Booth*'s third Share', though he received 'all the Power, as he was to act for Mr. *Booth* in the Management'.[81] This purchase

[80] The official roll-copy is PRO C66/3586, no. 5. The only internal date is 3 July (without year or regnal year), but this is taken over from the draft in LC 5/202.

[81] Victor, I, 7. Victor states that he was the go-between in arranging the sale, and we have no reason to disbelieve him.

precipitated a strange situation. Wilks and Cibber abruptly found themselves with an equal partner who was a court socialite, one whose entire theatrical experience consisted of having played Lothario, Hotspur, and Torrismond as a gentleman amateur.[82] Though they could outvote him, what useful service he might perform in return for several hundred pounds' profit is hard to imagine.

In the event, the experiment was not tried. Wilks fell ill and died on 27 September 1732. His widow appointed as her deputy in the management the painter John Ellys, a most peculiar choice. The wily Cibber, not liking the situation, thereupon 'rented' his interest in the management to his son Theophilus for the season of 1732–33 at a charge of £442, contracting himself to the company as an actor at the handsome salary of two guineas every time any play was acted.[83] The changes in management were reported in the *Grub-street Journal* on 2 November 1732: 'John Ellys Esq; the eminent painter, succeeds Mr. Wilks in the management of Drury-lane play-house; . . . Mr. Cibber, jun. succeeds his father, who has resigned to him.' As of November 1732 Drury Lane had an entirely new, untried, and unstable management. The competence of Highmore and Ellys was extremely suspect, and how well they could work with the arrogant and volatile Theophilus Cibber remained to be seen. What Fielding thought of these developments is not recorded, but alarm and dismay would have been very much in order. Unpopular as the triumvirs had been, they were professional men of the theatre, distinguished actors whose skilful management had kept the theatre stable and profitable for more than twenty years. What the future might hold for Drury Lane was anyone's guess, but the signs were profoundly unsettling.

Covent Garden and the Second Goodman's Fields

Why John Rich built Covent Garden to replace Lincoln's Inn Fields no one has ever really been able to explain. As rebuilt in 1714, Lincoln's Inn Fields was a modern and commodious theatre rigged for the kind of pantomime spectaculars in which Rich specialized. The new theatre does not seem to have had an appreciably larger auditorium, and in many details it was closely modelled on the older

[82] On Highmore, see the *Biographical Dictionary*, VII, 288–91. Victor, I, 4–7, is scathing about Highmore's theatrical knowledge, abilities, and unfounded pretensions.

[83] Colley Cibber's terms are stated in Theophilus Cibber's letter to Highmore of June 1733. See p. 155 n. 110 below.

one.[84] Rich may have decided that the public demand for entertainment was such that he could operate companies in both, or rent the old one out to another entrepreneur without damaging the receipts of his own company.[85] Rich experimented with running performances at both theatres during the Christmas and Easter seasons in 1732–33; he was able to rent Lincoln's Inn Fields to various opera companies and nonce troupes; and Giffard occupied the theatre full-time in 1736–37—after which the Licensing Act made the second theatre something of a white elephant.[86] There is testimony from summer 1732 that 'some of the Sharers at *Lincolns-Inn-Fields*, are Malecontent, and Law is like to be the Upshot'.[87] They were naturally alarmed at the prospect of losing their daily fee when the theatre was used, a problem Rich had to solve by agreeing to pay the 'building sharers' in both of his theatres, regardless of which building was actually used.

Very possibly one reason that Covent Garden was built was that Rich could raise the money. Indeed, Rich not only raised the money, he made a large profit in the process. Rich's statement of terms for prospective investors says that he has obtained a sixty-one-year lease from the Duke of Bedford on a piece of ground 120 by 100 feet on which a theatre is now being erected by Edward Shepherd. Rich offers to sell fifty shares for £300 each (£100 immediately, £100 on Lady Day 1732; £100 on completion). Each subscriber is to lease his share back to Rich for a rent of 2*s*. per acting night anywhere performances are given under Rich's patent and 'the Liberty to see plays in the New Theatre (without paying any thing for the same) in any part of ye House Excepting behind the scenes'.[88] The prospectus does not mention that Rich's contract with Shepherd called for a construction price of £5,600, though he was offering £15,000 worth of shares. Because of the complexity of Rich's banking arrangements, scholars

[84] Rich sued his architect, Edward Shepherd, and their testimony (never printed in full) gives many helpful details about Covent Garden and the parallels between the two theatres. See PRO C11/2662/1.

[85] Rich may also have had a deal for the old theatre fall through. The *Daily Courant* of 12 Jan. 1730/1, reporting plans for Covent Garden, adds: 'the other House in Lincoln's-Fields will be disposed of to the Crown, for the Use of the Commissioners of his Majesty's Stamp Duties.'

[86] See Leo Hughes and A. H. Scouten, 'John Rich and the Holiday Seasons of 1732–3', *Review of English Studies*, 21 (1945), 46–52; Paul Sawyer, *The New Theatre in Lincoln's Inn Fields* (London, 1979).

[87] *See and Seem Blind*, p. 24.

[88] BL Add. MS 32,428. The copy is dated 11 Dec. 1731, but apparently most of the investors had already signed on.

long believed that 'the subscribers barely paid in enough to satisfy the amount of the building contract',[89] but this is quite untrue. Rich collected the whole £15,000 and pocketed the difference.[90]

In essence, Rich financed his new theatre by adding £5 to his 'constant charge' (2*s*. × 50 = £5). He also had to pay his remaining 'renters' at Lincoln's Inn Fields, and of course he lost some expensive seats to as many of the investors as cared to come. But supposing that the company continued to draw as it had in the previous decade, Rich could well afford the addition to his daily costs. His investors stood to collect about £18 per annum, plus whatever benefit free admission gave them—i.e. they would get their money back in roughly seventeen years. Given the perpetual patent, they could assume that the company would stay in business. A less secure enterprise might need a shorter payback period. We may note that if Rich had contented himself with raising the actual cost of the building, the increment in his daily charge would have come to just about £2.

The opening of Covent Garden made little immediate difference to the London theatre: a new building did not appreciably change Rich's repertory. It did make Lincoln's Inn Fields available for rent night-by-night in competition with the Little Haymarket. The fee seems to have varied between £10 and £15 15*s*.[91] Fielding was never to make any use of it, but this figure is perhaps some hint of what John Potter received for the use of the Little Haymarket.

Both Rich and the triumvirs had been flourishing, but so had their principal competitor, Goodman's Fields. After surviving the legal challenge from city authorities in April 1730, the company continued to prosper. In September 1731 the actor Henry Giffard bought out Odell.[92] At an unknown date (probably during the autumn), Giffard ambitiously decided to try to raise the capital to build a new and better theatre. The prospectus he issued to attract investors is a document of sufficient interest that I have reprinted it in full in Appendix I. In many respects, it closely parallels John Rich's proposals. Giffard

[89] *The London Stage*, Part 3, I, xxviii.

[90] For details of the financing of Covent Garden, see the *Survey of London*, vol. XXXV (London, 1970), pp. 71–5.

[91] Particulars of a dozen nights' rental in 1736 are given on fo. 186 in the extracts from John Rich's account books preserved in BL 11791.dd.18 (vol. 3).

[92] The *Daily Post* of 9 Sept. reports that Giffard has 'taken' the theatre and is 'beautifying' it and acquiring 'new Cloaths and Scenes'. Rumours of Giffard's buying out Odell, and of his plan to build a new playhouse, were circulating as early as 2 June 1731 (*Daily Advertiser*).

planned to raise the modest sum of £1,500 by selling twenty-five shares of £60 each for a term of at least forty-one years. An investor would receive 1*s*. per acting day (with the annual season estimated as 'at least ... a Hundred and Sixty [performances] ... but more frequently a Hundred and Eighty'.[93] As at Covent Garden, investors were to have the right to free admission to all performances. On this basis Giffard would pay each investor £8–£9 per annum, making payback time about eight years. The 'constant charge' thus incurred would be a mere £1 5*s*.

Giffard fared even better than he hoped. According to *The Case of the several Persons upon whose Subscription the Theatre at Goodman's-Fields hath been built* (1735), 'twenty-three Persons became Subscribers at One hundred Pounds', each entitled to a daily rent of 'One Shilling and Sixpence for every acting Day'.[94] *The Case of Henry Giffard* informs us that the term was sixty-one years. Pay-back time on the investors' capital remained about eight years, making this an excellent investment if the company stayed in business. But the key figure for Giffard was his constant charge to 'building renters', which remained well under £2 per acting day. Even allowing for ground-rent and upkeep, this represents a very substantial advantage when compared to the £10 or more John Rich wanted for use of Lincoln's Inn Fields (admittedly a much larger theatre).

We do not know when construction started, but evidently it proceeded quickly. On 14 July 1732 the *Daily Post* printed a little puff: 'The Roof of the Theatre now erecting in Goodman's-Fields, by Direction of Mr. Edward Shepherd, Surveyor, is putting on, and tis thought by Architects it will be as commodious and finish'd a Building as any of the Theatres, and ready to open at the usual Season.' The architect, we should note, was the same man Rich was employing for Covent Garden. The theatre actually opened (on time) on 2 October, elegantly decorated.[95]

Giffard got a lot for his money. Because William Capon studied the

[93] Guildhall Broadside 7.57. Arnott and Robinson, no. 159. For the full text, see Appendix I.

[94] Petition against the Barnard Playhouse bill. Arnott and Robinson, no. 168. BL 11795.k.31(12).

[95] The *Daily Advertiser* of 4 Oct. 1732 describes a large ceiling-painting of the King trampling 'Tyranny and Oppression', surrounded by the heads of Shakespeare, Dryden, Congreve, and Betterton. Other painting included Cato, Julius Caesar, and Antony with Octavia and their children (in *All for Love*). Above the proscenium arch was 'an handsome Piece of Painting of Apollo and the Nine Muses'.

structure with considerable care in 1786 and 1802 and recorded his findings, we know quite a lot about its dimensions and ground plan.[96] The exterior dimensions were around 90 feet by 52 feet, and the total depth of the stage a surprising 50 feet. The width of the proscenium arch was only about 23 feet. The auditorium was shallow and fan-shaped, with only seven rows in the pit and a single gallery. Establishing audience capacity involves some estimates and guess-work, but between 700 and 750 is likely; perhaps a few more could be squeezed in.[97] At ordinary prices, a full house would have yielded about £70. At 'advanced prices', and with boxes built on stage to accommodate fifty people (a favourite device of Giffard's), the maximum take would have been close to £100.

The importance of Goodman's Fields to Fielding is obvious. If an actor-entrepreneur like Giffard could raise the money to erect a handsome and highly functional theatre and make it operational within half a year, then so could a playwright-entrepreneur. In 1732 Fielding probably had not the faintest intention of building a theatre or managing his own company, but the example was there to be drawn upon. Better yet, the company showed every sign of flourishing. Giffard seems to have been an outstanding manager. He believed in rigorous training for young performers, aggressive promotion, good public relations, changing casts until a play was at its best, and so forth.[98] These things do not show up in a performance calendar, but they go a long way towards explaining how Goodman's Fields could compete with the giants.

Goodman's Fields' repertory policy continued to be arch-conservative. The company's initial strategy was to offer a repertory essentially similar to that of the patent houses, but to do it in a location where a well-drilled company of beginners and journeymen would have an audience to itself. In their first season, all but two of their thirty-four old plays were in the current repertory at Drury Lane, Lincoln's Inn Fields, or both. Goodman's Fields simply took the most attractive of the patent theatres' shows and made them available to city residents closer to home. Recent hits like *The Beggar's Opera* and *The Provok'd Husband* were performed six and

[96] See Robert Eddison, 'Capon and Goodman's Fields', *Theatre Notebook*, 14 (1960), 127–32. Capon's ground-plan is reproduced in *The London Stage*, Part 3, I, following p. 224.

[97] For a detailed estimate of capacity, see *The London Stage*, Part 3, I, xxv–xxvi.

[98] See *The London Stage*, Part 3, I, lxxx–lxxxv.

seven nights respectively. Instead of running plays like *Hamlet* or *The Recruiting Officer* once or twice or four times in a season, Goodman's Fields ran them eight or nine, and they gave far fewer plays just once or twice. The company preferred the more modern part of the patent theatres' repertory. They ran some old favourites (*Hamlet*, *Merry Wives*, *Othello*) and some Restoration staples (*The Old Batchelour*, *Venice Preserv'd*), but the figures show a clear tilt towards the eighteenth century. After the initial season, new plays are rare and mostly unsuccessful.[99] Goodman's Fields offered no hope for Fielding.

The success of Goodman's Fields tells us that the patent theatres were not exhausting the audience demand for traditional dramatic entertainment. In these circumstances, London must have seemed ripe for still more theatres. A new 'fringe' theatre opened on 26 December on the Bowling Green, Southwark,[100] and there were rumours of more competition for the patent theatres closer to home. On 6 January 1733 the *Daily Courant* reported, 'We hear that a new Playhouse will be built by Subscription in St. Martin's le Grand, towards which the Sum of 1500*l*. is already subscribed.' Nothing came of this venture, but the idea of new theatres and accelerating competition was definitely in the air. Licking his wounds and wondering what to write next, Fielding was doubtless more concerned with the new management of Drury Lane than with developments elsewhere. But the events of 1732 suggest a vigour in the London theatre that boded well for the future.

V. THE PLAYS OF 1733

Accounts of the season of 1732–33 at Drury Lane inevitably stress dissension within the new management. How quickly Highmore, Ellys, and Theophilus Cibber fell foul of one another we do not know; probably for some time they jockeyed for position, schemed in private, and kept up a public show of affability. Fielding's position must have been awkward. He can barely have known Highmore; he was

[99] In 1730–31 Goodman's Fields mounted *The Cynick* (3 nights) and *The Fall of the Earl of Essex* (4); in 1731–32 *The Footman* (5) and *The Jealous Husband* (3); in 1732–33 *The Decoy* (4) and *Scanderbeg* (2); in 1733–34 and 1734–35 no new mainpieces; in 1735–36 *The Parricide* (4). Only when he moved his company to Lincoln's Inn Fields in 1736–37 did Giffard modify his repertory policy.

[100] Puffed in the *Daily Post*, 18 December 1732.

apparently friendly with 'Jack' Ellys;[101] and he had worked closely (not necessarily happily) with Theophilus Cibber. We do not know if Fielding went into the country in the summer or early autumn of 1732, but he was evidently in town by November, presumably sounding out the new managers and assessing his prospects.

One sign that the new management was anxious to secure his favour and scripts is a benefit on 16 November 1732—a performance of *The Relapse* with the 'revised' *Mock Doctor* as afterpiece. This is a highly unusual author benefit: mere improvements would not ordinarily have been recompensed so extravagantly.[102] Fielding might have netted a lot, a little, or nothing, but he presumably found the benefit encouraging. His other known connection with Drury Lane during the autumn was his epilogue for Charles Johnson's *Cælia*, which failed in one night on 11 December. This play is remembered almost entirely because it anticipates Richardson's *Clarissa* in important and interesting ways, *sans* rape but plus pregnancy. Wronglove lodges Cælia in Mrs Lupine's brothel; she pines and dies; he is killed in a duel. Like most of Johnson's plays it is obtrusively didactic, but it is without doubt one of the most impressive and interesting tragedies of the 1730s. Unlike the high-flown tragedies Fielding had mocked in *The Tragedy of Tragedies* and *The Covent-Garden Tragedy*, *Cælia* is astonishingly 'realistic' in its presentation of the foolish girl, the lying lover, and the madam and her girls. From Johnson's 'Advertisement to the Reader' we learn that once again the audience had taken exception to the brothel, despite its necessity in showing 'the Distress of *Cælia*' and the author's care 'that nothing indecent shou'd be said'. Fielding's view of this work is hard to judge from his flippantly ironic epilogue ('Lud! what a Fuss is here! what Blood and Slaughter! / Because poor Miss has prov'd her Mother's Daughter'), but we may guess that he approved Johnson's design. *Cælia* is a play Fielding might easily have written had he ever ventured upon tragedy.

The Miser

In his first season at Drury Lane Fielding's two greatest successes had been afterpieces—a topical ballad opera and a Molière translation

[101] Both Martin Battestin and Thomas Lockwood believe that Fielding was the author of 'An Epistle to Mr. *Ellys* the Painter' (printed by Cooke in *The Comedian* in Aug. 1732). Their arguments in attribution—as yet unpublished—seem cogent.

[102] This benefit might represent a retainer paid to Fielding for first rights to his plays. I offer this speculation with hesitation, but it is a possibility.

with a substantial infusion of songs. Both had become stock plays. Fielding's ambition was probably to write comedy of social purpose, but the abuse heaped *ex post facto* on *The Modern Husband*, the death of Wilks, and the need to establish himself on a firm footing with new managers evidently convinced him that he should opt for safety first. Given his comment in the preface to *The Mock Doctor* that he hoped to 'transplant' some 'others' of Molière, the appearance of *The Miser* on 17 February 1733 is no surprise.

The Miser is an altogether different kind of enterprise from *The Mock Doctor*. For one thing, it is a five-act mainpiece; for another, it employs no songs; for a third, it departs substantially from Molière's plot. As in the earlier play, Fielding does a thorough job of making the characters and setting English, moving the scene to London. *The Mock Doctor* is a mistaken-identity farce; *The Miser* is vigorous satire on a reprehensible vice, a satire whose title-page epigraph from Juvenal should not be ignored. Molière's Harpagon is comically awful; Fielding's Lovegold is amusing but much more repulsive. *The Miser* is far from being the kind of comedy of social purpose Fielding had essayed in *The Modern Husband* and was soon to try again in *The Universal Gallant*.[103] However, it is probably as close to such comedy as Fielding thought he could safely come.

Fielding greatly expanded the roles of the servants. The part of the adventuress Frosine is subsumed into that of Harriet's scheming maid, Lappet, and she is made foil to Frederick's servant Ramilie. Fielding's motive was probably just to take advantage of the available performers, but the changes increase the play's sense of class structure and add significantly to its social breadth and solidity. He also radically revamps the character of Mariana, who becomes a major figure in the play. Instead of Molière's virtuous, rather colourless young woman, Fielding supplies a card-loving socialite and accomplished coquette (7).[104] Frederick woos her with difficulty, and her wit is responsible for the ultimate discomfiture of the miser and the happy ending.

Fielding wisely abandoned Molière's recognition-scene basis for the happy ending. Molière has Valère and Marianne discover that they are brother and sister, long-lost children to the wealthy Anselme, whose benevolent generosity makes possible the marriages of Cléante

[103] Not performed until 10 Feb. 1735, but ready for the stage by Dec. 1733. See pp. 169–70, below.

[104] Refs. are to the Watts edn. of 1733.

and Marianne, Valère and Élise. Fielding had botched such finales in *The Wedding-Day* and *Rape upon Rape*, and satirized them in *The Author's Farce*. For a social comedy of the sort he concocted here, it would have been a disconcertingly self-indulgent departure from reality.

The altered finale is brilliantly conceived. Fielding has Lovegold sign a promise of marriage with a performance bond of £10,000 (56, 77). Several schemes to make him back out fail, but Mariana's stratagem (carefully concealed from the audience) works beautifully. In the miser's name she orders expensive food and drink; invites 'above five Hundred People to Supper' (76), hires the Drury Lane orchestra to entertain them, and arranges for a steady stream of fashionable tradesmen to bring goods she intends to buy. Upholsterer, mercer, tailor, and a pair of jewellers duly arrive and book fabulous orders while Lovegold nearly goes berserk. Fabric at £12 a yard, not to mention a necklace and earrings for 3,000 guineas, leave him in no doubt that this is a wife he does not want—though the thought of forfeiting £10,000 to be rid of her is so awful that Lovegold says 'I'll marry her first, and hang my self afterward to save my Money' (77). Fielding builds his situation with the skill and patience of the Marx Brothers overstuffing a stateroom. Tradesman follows tradesman; Mariana exhibits enthusiastic determination to marry Lovegold and be a great lady in town; Lovegold rages and laments. The joke is cruel, but Lovegold deserves no sympathy and gets none. Lest anyone take the miser's side, Fielding has Lovegold order Lappet to swear that Mariana has robbed him (83). Lappet naturally reneges and tells the truth (85), opening the way for a happy ending. Lovegold storms off, but between the £10,000 and the 3,000 guineas Ramilie has stolen from the miser on behalf of his master (an episode retained from Molière), the miser's children have enough leverage that they can be confident of making a 'Peace with the old Gentleman' on terms that will allow them to marry in comfort.

I would not claim that Fielding has improved upon Molière: the two plays are markedly different. L. P. Goggin points out that verbal resemblances prove that Fielding worked from the recently published dual-language edition, drawing freely on the words of both the original and the translation.[105] Molière's elegant display of character with its improbable happy ending is expertly transformed into a

[105] Goggin, 'Fielding and the *Select Comedies of Mr. de Moliere*', pp. 345–8.

social-intrigue comedy with a broader array of vivid characters and a richer social setting. Fielding pillories his miser, but comes closer than Molière to confronting the unappetizing fact that such avarice is not merely a 'humour' and is not corrigible. Fielding took over many of Molière's speeches and deft touches, but the resulting play is a very free adaptation, not an anglicized translation.

Once again, Fielding deserves high praise for the vehicles he provided particular actors. The scheming maid Lappet is a gem of a role for Miss Raftor, and her witty feud with her valet-counterpart Ramilie (Theophilus Cibber) is contrived with skill. In Lovegold Fielding gave the veteran character actor Benjamin Griffin a fine display piece. The miser's son and daughter, and her suitor Clermont, remain stock lovers and were taken by second-rank actors (Bridgwater, Mrs Butler, and Mills jun.), but Mariana is a striking improvement on her original, and a fine part for the talented Mrs Horton. Fielding was never at his best with conventional lovers, but then Drury Lane no longer had the personnel to make the most of such parts, and he could hardly have bettered his use of the resources available to him.

The Miser was a resounding success. Between its première in February and the untimely closing of Drury Lane on 28 May, it enjoyed twenty-three performances.[106] Its initial run was interrupted by command performances and actor benefits, but Fielding received author benefits the third, sixth, ninth, and twentieth nights, and every sign points to the kind of success that endears a playwright to management. The fourth benefit, coming as late as 3 May, seems clear evidence of favoured status for Fielding. Nor was this success illusory: *The Miser* was performed regularly for the rest of the century. Over the decades it did not run up the fabulous totals of Fielding's most successful afterpieces (*The Mock Doctor* and *The Virgin Unmask'd*), but by a large margin it was Fielding's most enduring mainpiece, as a glance at *The London Stage Index* quickly shows. Fielding himself prudently claimed no great credit, leaving others 'to decide what Share the Translator merits in the Applause' (Dedication to the Duke of Richmond and Lenox). But he was far more than a translator, and *The Miser* demonstrates Fielding working at a high level of professional competence.

[106] Cross (I, 143) and Rogers (p. 63) say 26 performances, but I can document only 23—or 24, if 'Rich's Register' is correct in recording *The Miser* as a replacement for *The Provok'd Husband* on 7 April.

Deborah

Fielding's only other new play this season survived just one night and was not printed. Hard facts about it are in short supply. The newspaper bill for 6 April 1733 calls the work *Deborah; or, A Wife For You All*; describes it as 'A Farce of one Act' by the author of *The Miser*; and lists as performers Johnson, Griffin, Miller, Shepard, Stoppelaer, Miss Raftor, Mrs Mullart, and Miss Mann. The work served as afterpiece for *The Miser* on Miss Raftor's benefit night. Genest, evidently working from a playbill or newspaper bill unknown to modern scholars, names four of the parts and their performers: Justice Mittimus—Griffin; Lawyer Trouble—Johnson; Alexander Whittle—Miller; Deborah—Miss Raftor.[107] Beyond this we are into the realm of conjecture.[108]

Unless the title is a surprising coincidence, reference was presumably intended to Handel's oratorio *Deborah*, premièred 17 March 1733 at the King's Theatre, Haymarket. Handel's attempt to double prices the first night (to a guinea, and half a guinea in the gallery) enraged his audience and produced a storm of negative publicity.[109] What Fielding was taking off we cannot be certain. Deutsch suggests that Fielding's afterpiece 'may have been a burlesque of Humphreys' word-book' for the oratorio, but would Fielding have risked overt parody of a biblical story? Unflattering allusion to Handel's prices and the foreign singers' difficulties with English seems more likely.

The character names reported by Genest strongly suggest a courtroom scene, and the subtitle implies that Fielding's Deborah was a woman of less than perfect virtue. If Fielding meant to mock Senesino (the celebrated castrato), Signora Strada, and other foreign singers, he had suitable performers in the versatile Stoppelaer and Miss Raftor (who became particularly noted for such take-offs). From Fielding's practice in his numerous trial scenes in plays and novels, Edgar

[107] John Genest, *Some Account of the English Stage*, 10 vols. (Bath, 1832), III, 371.

[108] For a speculative attempt to reconstruct *Deborah* 'in the light of Fielding's usual artistic practices', see Edgar V. Roberts, 'Henry Fielding's Lost Play *Deborah, or A Wife for You All* (1733)', *Bulletin of the New York Public Library*, 66 (1962), 576–88. I am indebted to Roberts' conjectures in the discussion that follows.

[109] See the famous attack on Handel in the *Craftsman* of 7 April 1733. This and other relevant documents, including the celebrated epigram linking Handel's ticket prices and Walpole's excise scheme (Handel asking 'Of what Use are *Sheep*, if the *Shepherd* can't shear them?') are printed in Otto Erich Deutsch, *Handel: A Documentary Biography* (New York, 1955), pp. 308–13.

Roberts guesses that Deborah, though guilty, was found innocent by a corrupt or corruptible court, which seems highly likely. That outrageously raised prices entered somewhere also seems probable.

We do not know why the work died its first night or why it was not published. A vehicle for the popular Miss Raftor on her benefit night ought to have been received with reasonable indulgence. If offence was taken over allusion to the biblical background, no hint of such objection has come down to us in newspapers or theatrical anecdotes. Supposing that Handel's oratorio and the fuss over raised prices gave Fielding the idea, he must have got the piece up and produced it in exactly twenty days. It was presumably very short, and (as Roberts suggests) Fielding might have plundered earlier ballad operas for the music. Perhaps he withheld it from publication in 1733 because he remembered the way his critics had jumped on *The Covent-Garden Tragedy*. But why *Deborah* was not resurrected for the *Miscellanies* in 1743 remains a mystery.

During the season of 1732–33 Fielding had seen to the stage one successful mainpiece, one failed afterpiece, and a revised afterpiece. From Drury Lane he had received a total of five benefits. What he made from them is anyone's guess, but probably not less than £200 or much more than £500. If he stayed away from gaming tables, this would have been sufficient to live upon in comfort. His buffeting of the previous summer notwithstanding, he had continued to make his way as a professional playwright. But whatever his hopes, plans, or expectations, they must have received a rude shock at the end of May 1733, when Drury Lane suffered an earthquake beside which all previous upsets seemed mere premonitory tremors.

VI. THE ACTOR REBELLION OF 1733

By January 1733 Theophilus Cibber and his amateur co-managers were feuding vigorously.[110] The instability of the management must have been obvious to every insider. The actors seem to have been disgusted by the ignorant interference of gentlemen dabblers, but what they thought they could do about it is not recorded. To interested outsiders, the situation offered possibilities. Thus on 22

[110] See Theophilus Cibber's letter to Highmore and Ellys of January 1733, printed in *A Letter from Theophilus Cibber, Comedian, To John Highmore, Esq;* (hereafter *Cibber to Highmore*), p. 3, published around late June 1733. Arnott and Robinson, no. 1325. BL 1889.d.1(32). His letter to Highmore in February (ibid.) is openly offensive.

March 1732/3 Aaron Hill wrote to Benjamin Victor, criticizing Theophilus Cibber and expressing regret that he could not afford to buy a half-interest in the patent and become Highmore's partner.[111] Hill had wanted to get back into the Drury Lane management ever since (as William Collier's deputy) he had been thrown out in the actor riot of June 1710. He was a gentleman; a playwright of some distinction; a noted trainer of young actors; and an erudite if opinionated critic. How well he would have got on with the actors is hard to say. Hill did not abandon hope. On 5 April he wrote again to Victor, saying he would prefer 'to unite my Endeavours with Mr. *Highmore*'s . . . than to open a new House, (and to that End either enlarging the little one in the *Haymarket*, or building another in a better Place)'. Hill suggests that he farm Booth's remaining half-share for three years at £300 per annum, and Mrs Wilks' share for £600 per annum.[112] This proposal must have been met with the counter-suggestion that he purchase a half-interest in the patent, for on 9 April Hill wrote to Victor, again regretting that he could not afford to do so, but raising his offer to £1,000 per annum for a half-share in management and profits. Nothing came of this, and in May we find Hill asking Alexander Pope about the possibility of buying one of the original 1660s' patents.[113]

Many insiders must have known that shares in the patent could be bought: the question was price. Booth had proved his willingness to sell; Mrs Wilks and her deputy Ellys had no strong reason to remain involved; Colley Cibber plainly wanted out. But Highmore had bought a one-sixth interest for £2,500, which by implication made each full share worth £5,000 or the whole patent £15,000, a staggering sum.[114] We can easily see why Aaron Hill did not want to raise half of this price, and of course even a one-third interest was totally beyond Fielding's means. But the company had a bad season in 1732–33, and the price might come down. In February 1733 Colley Cibber agreed to farm his share to Theophilus for 1733–34 for just £300. Before this agreement was actually signed, however, Highmore 'eagerly pursued

[111] Printed in Victor, II, 185–8.

[112] Ibid., II, 188–91. Following quotation from II, 192–5.

[113] See Pope's letter of 22 May 1733, *A Collection of Letters . . . By Alexander Pope . . . To the Late Aaron Hill* (London, 1751), p. 27.

[114] Of this putative figure something like £9,000 must be assigned to the patent. According to figures evidently supplied by the patentees, the 'stock' was 'valued at no less than 6000*l*. and insur'd at 4000*l*'. See *An Impartial State of the Present Dispute between the Patent and Players* [London, 1733], p. 5. Arnott and Robinson, no. 1328.

Mr. *Cibber* Senior, and with a large Sum tempted him to sell' (as Theophilus phrases the matter).[115] The *Daily Post* of 27 March 1733 reports: 'Colley Cibber, Esq; ... has sold his intire Share of the Cloaths, Scenes, and Patent, to John Highmore, Esq; At the End of this Season he quits the Stage altogether'. Victor gives the price as 3,000 guineas for the full share; other sources imply that it was £3,500.[116]

This sale naturally enraged Theophilus Cibber, who regarded the patent as his 'Birthright' and incautiously said so in print. But had the other actors been passably content with the new managers (or with actor-deputies, if some had been appointed), Theophilus's disappointment would have been laughed at and the company would have continued as it was. Many scholars have been puzzled by the senior actors' willingness to unite behind the leadership of 'Pistol' (as Theophilus was popularly known), an arrogant, unpleasant, and unstable person. We must remember, however, that his days of 'crim. con.' notoriety were years ahead. He was pushy and obnoxious, but he was an excellent actor in non-romantic and non-heroic 'lines', and he had successfully managed four summer seasons. As he loudly claimed in *Cibber to Highmore*, he had learned about management from his father, Wilks, and Booth. Theophilus was probably no more unpleasant than his father; given favourable circumstances, he might well have flourished as his father had done.

Theophilus's first step, having politely congratulated Highmore on his purchase, was to propose himself as principal deputy and head of daily operations.[117] This proposal refused, he set about organizing a revolution. How much fomenting it took, we do not know. The plan appears to have been as follows. In phase one a group of actors would secretly lease the Drury Lane theatre in their own names, thus depriving the patentees of the use of the building. In phase two, with the building secured, the actors would offer to rent the patent and stock for 900 guineas per annum, an offer later increased to 1,200 guineas.[118] The actors, functioning as a co-operative, would then set their own salaries and manage their own affairs. This would not have

[115] *Cibber to Highmore*, p. 2.

[116] Victor, I, 8; *Daily Post*, 4 June 1733; *Craftsman*, 9 June 1733.

[117] His letter of congratulation is printed in *An Impartial State of the Present Dispute*, p. 4, together with an account of his subsequent meeting with Highmore.

[118] These figures come from *An Impartial State*, p. 4; *Cibber to Highmore*, p. 4; and the *Daily Journal* of 26 Sept. 1733.

been a bad deal for the patentees. Highmore, for example, would have recovered his £6,000 in ten years, or just half the remaining time the patent had to run. But plainly the actors did not expect such a proposal to be accepted willingly, or they would not have started by secretly securing rights to the building as a way of pressuring the patentees.

Phase one almost worked. The patentees had no formal lease on the theatre, and a large majority of the building sharers were quite willing to rent to the actors on improved terms.[119] Inevitably, however, the patentees got wind of this manœuvre, and they moved to counter it by putting guards in the building and locking the actors out. The *Daily Post* of 29 May 1733 reports:

We hear that there was Yesterday no Play acted ... the Occasion we are inform'd was, that at Midnight on Saturday last several Persons arm'd took Possession of the same, by Direction from some of the Patentees, and lock'd up and barricado'd all the Doors and Entrances thereunto, against the whole Company of his Majesty's Comedians, as also against Mr. Cibber, jun. notwithstanding he had paid to one of the Patentees several Hundred Pounds for one third Part of the Patent, Cloaths, Scenes, &c. and all Rights and Privileges thereunto annexed, for a certain Term not yet expired. Mr. Cibber, jun. and the rest of the Company of Comedians, are this Morning to wait upon his Grace the Duke of Grafton, Lord Chamberlain of his Majesty's Houshold, with their humble Petition, and the Representation of their Case ...

As far as I am aware, the actors' petition is not preserved. The Lord Chamberlain appears to have shrugged his shoulders and wished a plague on both factions: neither got any help from him.

About 1 June, the two parties were caught in an awkward deadlock. The actors held a lease on the theatre, but the patentees continued to occupy it. The actors sued for ejectment and possession, and the matter disappeared into the courts, whence it would emerge in the distant future.[120] The managers had no company, the performers no theatre.

[119] The actors involved were John Mills, Benjamin Johnson, Josias Miller, Theophilus Cibber, John Harper, Benjamin Griffin, William Mills, William Milward, Mary Heron, and Elizabeth Butler. The lease was for 15 years at £920 per annum, plus taxes and repairs. See *The Case of John Mills . . . [et al.] and the Rest of the Comedians of the Theatres-Royal of Drury-Lane and Covent-Garden*, presented to parliament against the Barnard playhouse bill in 1735, BL 11795.k.31(8). Arnott and Robinson, no. 166. The daily rent on the theatre amounted to more than £5, a considerable increase from the £3 12*s*. the patentees had been paying.

[120] See PRO C11/778/28 (Giffard's suit against Fleetwood in 1735) for some relevant details.

So spectacular a civil war naturally produced a great flurry of commentary in the papers, most of it highly partisan. Public opinion divided sharply. The *Craftsman*, for example, described the situation as follows: 'We have ... received undoubted Intelligence from the Theatre-Royal in *Drury-Lane*, that a considerable Body of *malecontent Players*, under the Command of that puissant Captain, Mr. *The---lus C----r*, have lately enter'd into a mutinous Association against their Masters, the *Patentees*, and still continue in a State of Hostility; which hath prevented any Plays being acted there this Week' (2 June). On 7 June the *Grub-street Journal* published two opposed views of the situation. 'Musæus' praised the new patentees for treating playwrights genteelly; denounced Theophilus Cibber as a selfish 'little creature'; and ridiculed the idea that outside owners are unfair to the performers. 'Philo Dramaticus' argued that managers should be qualified for the job; objected to owners who are interested only in profits; and likened the purchase of the patent to buying 'a plantation, and all the Negroes together', a proceeding inappropriate to 'the free-born subjects of Great Britain'. A high proportion of the newspaper controversy follows one or the other of these lines. On the one side, denunciation of rebellion against authority; on the other, protest against 'bondage' and 'slavery'.

Both sides published official justifications of their positions. The patentees were first in the field. All broadside copies of their 'Case' appear to be lost, but it was reprinted in the *Daily Post* of 4 June 1733. It is a dry but huffy document. The patentees recite the history of the 1732 patent and its sale and charge the actors with having 'clandestinely contracted with some of the Lessees' for the theatre. To rebut 'fictitious Stories of Hardships' they print a list of weekly salaries of principal performers, ranging from £3 to £5. And they loudly insist that never before was there any 'other Instance of Actors being at the Head of his Majesty's Company of Comedians', an obvious thrust against the actors' demand for self-government.[121]

The players' answer was *A Letter from Theophilus Cibber, Comedian, To John Highmore, Esq;* (late June 1733?). This long and windy document spends far too much time exhibiting Theophilus Cibber's personal grievances and inflated ego, but amidst its irrelevancies and verbosities three important points emerge. First, the actors consider

[121] Cibber promptly printed a copy of James I's 1603 licence to Shakespeare, Burbage, *et al*. (*Cibber to Highmore*, p. 4); 'Musæus' rejoined by asking him if he thought he was Shakespeare (*Grub-street Journal*, 16 July).

Highmore and Ellys incompetent and object to being ruled by them. Second, the actors believe that the patentees have renewed the dreaded 'cartel' agreement with John Rich, and point to the summary discharge of Benjamin Griffin as evidence of arbitrary tyranny.[122] Third, the actors have offered the patentees 1,200 guineas per annum to farm the patent to them, with half a year's advance payment guaranteed.

Disentangled from a great deal of hot rhetoric and particular detail, the gist is that the actors are willing to pay the patentees 1,200 guineas a year to let them manage their own affairs—and the patentees will hear nothing of it. How fair the offer was is hard to determine. We do not know what profit Drury Lane had been making. Victor says vaguely that 'for the preceding twenty Years' they had 'enjoyed such uninterrupted Success . . . [that] their Shares had amounted to Fifteen Hundred, and never less than a Thousand Pounds a Year'.[123] Presumably he means that each of the three managers had been making such a sum, but at least £600 per annum each was in essence salary as actor and manager.[124] If they had actually been collecting double that or more as a total income, they had earned it as experienced, competent, and hard-working managers. Whether someone else could make the theatre as profitable was uncertain: Highmore was greatly disappointed with the profits in 1732–33.[125] The new patentees, however, may well have felt entitled to such sums just by their possession of the patent. But whether unrealistic financial expectations or offended pride was the reason, they refused to farm the patent.

How genuine and legitimate was the actors' fear of tyranny and a new cartel? Some evidence suggests that they had genuine grounds for alarm. On 18 May 1733 (a week and a half before the lock-out) the Lord Chamberlain had issued 'Orders to the Managers' of the two patent theatres, forbidding them to 'admit, or receive any Actor, Actress, Singer or Dancer' from the other house 'without especial leave' from

[122] On the cartel as it functioned in the 1720s, see ch. 1, pp. 13–14, above.
[123] Victor, I, 7–8.
[124] The triumvirs allowed themselves £1 13*s*. 4*d*. 'for every acting Day to Each of us' (or £10 for a full week) for management. See Trinity College, Cambridge, MS Collum H28(1), dated 23 Sept. 1721, and a similar memorandum in Folger Y.d. 467, dated 29 Sept. 1722. This practice was upheld in Chancery against a complaint by Steele. See PRO C11/2416/49 and C33/350 (Chancery Decrees and Orders, 1727B), p. 224.
[125] This point is addressed in *Cibber to Highmore*, p. 4.

his office.[126] That Grafton cared who worked where seems very unlikely: the patentees had probably requested renewal of this prohibition as a step towards capping or reducing performers' salaries.

One clear sign of the patentees' vindictive spirit was their 'discharge' of 4 June 1733 to Benjamin Griffin, a popular and useful actor who had scored a great success as Lovegold in *The Miser* that same spring. On 11 June the *Daily Post* published 'The Humble Appeal to the Publick of *Benjamin Griffin*, Comedian'. Griffin rehearses in detail the way the triumvirs hired him in 1721 and then broke their promises and reduced his salary in 1724, using the cartel to force him to submit to harsh and arbitrary treatment. And he points out that though the discharge *says* '... and give you full Liberty to engage yourself to Mr. *Rich*', this is untrue: under the terms of the cartel he would be free to work for Rich, but Rich would not be free to employ him. Josias Miller had been forced into unemployment for two years in exactly this way, as both Griffin and Theophilus Cibber loudly complain.

Griffin was evidently picked as an example to other 'mutinous persons' to submit or face like punishment. Griffin had made his contempt for Highmore public during the previous season,[127] and he reiterated it in his 'Humble Appeal'. 'I could give the Publick a great many Instances of the *Gentlemen*'s Mismanagement and of Injuries done to the Company this Season in their Direction. But when I affirm that they have no Experience, no Knowledge, no Capacity, *For Gathering together, Forming, Entertaining, Governing, Privileging, and Keeping a Company of Comedians* ... more than the being able to purchase the *Patent*, Clothes and Scenes, it is a Truth that if any one does not now believe, I am positive they will in a very little Time be thoroughly convinced of.' If this was common opinion among the actors, we can see how young Cibber found supporters for a libertarian revolution.

Public debate over the rebellion raged all summer. The actors were accused of rebelling against authority in order to form a 'Commonwealth' (still a bugbear term), and the relevant parts of Vanbrugh's *Aesop* were reprinted.[128] 'Musæus' vehemently attacked Theophilus

[126] PRO LC 5/160, p. 230.

[127] See *An Impartial State of the Present Dispute*, p. 2.

[128] *Grub-street Journal*, 14 June 1733. Part 2 of *Aesop* is an attack on the actor rebellion of 1695. *Aesop* (with the addition) was duly staged at Drury Lane when it reopened with a scratch company in Sept.

Cibber's letter to Highmore, maintaining that actors were scum unfit to be managers, but also making the telling point that the monsters of iniquity who had made the original cartel were all actors, not gentleman-investors (*Grub-street Journal*, 26 July). Covent Garden tried to capitalize on the fuss by staging a silly little afterpiece called *The Stage-Mutineers* (27 July).[129]

The last major exchange in the first round of this affair was provoked by an anonymous pamphlet called *An Impartial State of the Present Dispute between the Patent and Players* (late July/August? 1733).[130] Far from being what the title claims, it is a ferocious diatribe on the side of the patentees. It commences: 'Tho' all Men of Sense and Integrity seem to be entirely convinced that the *Patentees* of the *Theatre-Royal* in *Drury-Lane*, have had great Injustice done them by the late Attempt of Part of their own Company to defraud them of their Property, and set aside his Majesty's especial Grant in their Favour . . .' Its biases notwithstanding, *An Impartial State* formulates the pro-patent case with helpful clarity and adds some useful facts. The author takes the position that since theatres are obnoxious public nuisances, 'nothing but a Patent from the Crown can authorize Dramatical Entertainments, or screen the Performers from the Lash of the Law' (1). Once again, we return to the issue of 'who should operate a theatre?' The patentees' opinion that the actors are mutinous wretches is evident in their contemptuous refusal of the proposal that they farm the patent (printed on page 5). By this time the patentees had realized that their former actors intended to set up shop for themselves in the Little Haymarket (5). This fact was probably the motive for their proposal (dated 16 July, and printed on page 5) that an arbitrator be appointed to hear grievances, and that the salaries of Theophilus Cibber, William Mills, and A. Hallam be raised. In return, the patentees ask that the actors cancel their lease on the Drury Lane theatre and 'enter into Articles' with the patentees—i.e., sign contracts for set salaries over a given term of years. And the patentees specifically declare the cartel 'void'. Made on the first of May, such a proposal would probably have been welcomed. Even on the first of

[129] By Edward Phillips. It managed twelve performances. Theophilus Cibber is recognizably satirized, but other characters seem to be generalized butts, including the playwright 'Crambo'. Despite 'Philo-Musus's' angry denunciation of the piece as a 'malicious' personal satire (*Grub-street Journal*, 9 Aug.), it is harmless stuff, and the managers come off as badly as the actors.

[130] A vigorous reply appeared anonymously in the *Daily Journal* of 26 Sept.

June it might have worked. By 16 July tempers were too high and the battle-lines too clearly drawn.

The issues can be stated in a series of questions.

Were theatrical performances legal without a patent or licence? The continued operation of Goodman's Fields and the Little Haymarket seemed to imply so, but the matter had not been fully tested at law. The rebel actors plainly did not want to bring the issue to court and risk losing. They were prepared to pay £1,200 per annum for the use of the stock and whatever legitimacy and protection the patent afforded.[131]

Could the Drury Lane building sharers rent the theatre to any group they chose for a set term of years? The issue was before the Court of Chancery. The answer was ultimately affirmative.

What control could the Lord Chamberlain exercise over the actors? A great deal if they claimed to perform by virtue of a Royal patent, perhaps none if they did not. Victor reports that Highmore had great hopes of the Lord Chamberlain, but that several weeks of 'Levee-haunting' got him only the advice 'that he must apply to the Law for the Support of his Patent'.[132]

Were actors fit people to govern their own affairs? Fierce prejudice against actors is evident in the newspaper controversy. Many of the patentees' supporters seem to have been hostile to the theatre, and regarded unregulated companies as a probable source of sedition and public debauchery. A writer in the *Grub-street Journal* of 14 June asks, sarcastically, but in genuine alarm, what is to keep fifty new theatres from springing up?

Did the actors' walk-out violate the patentees' property rights? This was certainly the patentees' position, and conservative elements in society shared their view. The *Craftsman* of 9 June accuses Theophilus Cibber of maintaining that '*picking a Gentleman's Pocket of six thousand Pounds* is perfectly consistent with the Principles of Liberty'. Despite such rhetoric, the actors actually offered the patentees a reasonable return on their investment.

What protection did the actors have against a new cartel? Virtually none. Scholars have paid too little attention to this issue, but the actors had reason to fear the effect of a cartel on salaries. And the threat of being

[131] Interestingly, they valued the use of the patent at only £300 per year (*Daily Journal*, 26 Sept.). Aaron Hill says in a letter of 31 Aug. 1733 that he has been offered a 'patent' for a fee of £400 per annum (*Works*, I, 135–8).

[132] Victor, I, 20–2.

blacklisted was real. True, an actor might go to Goodman's Fields or the Little Haymarket. But Giffard was just about to buy into the Drury Lane patent; he too could sign the cartel. And Little Haymarket actors cannot have made more than a fraction of Drury Lane salaries.

From the standpoint of the patentees, the actors were guilty of rebellion against the King's authority. In the eyes of the actors, the patentees were moneyed intruders, incompetent to run the business they had bought and determined to reduce their performers to servitude. By twentieth-century standards, the actors had more justice on their side. In the context of eighteenth-century English law, the situation was both complex and not easily resolved.

Drury Lane remained closed until 24 September, when it reopened with a scratch company of loyalists, recruits from the pool of freelance actors, and some imported strollers and beginners. On the 26th the rebel company opened at the Little Haymarket. Where all this would end was anyone's guess.

The relevance of the actors' rebellion to Henry Fielding has been insufficiently understood. Cross mentions the rebellion only in passing; Dudden hardly refers to it at all. To be sure, we are dismally ignorant of Fielding's part in it, if any. We do not even know whether he stayed in London over the summer, much less whether he was invited to join the rebels. But to a playwright in Fielding's position, the collapse of Drury Lane as he had known it must have been utterly dismaying. Since 1709—when Fielding had been two years old—the triumvirate had managed the theatre. Drury Lane had seemed the epitome of stability—and in a few brief months, all that was gone, and with it the bright future Fielding must have been rejoicing in. He needed an outlet for his plays. Should he stick with the patentees and their patchwork company at Drury Lane, trusting that authority would prevail and that the company would continue to want his services? Or should he offer his work to the rebel actors, hoping they would triumph and that he could coexist with Theophilus Cibber? Neither Covent Garden nor Goodman's Fields offered any refuge. Backing the wrong party in the Drury Lane dispute could virtually put Fielding out of business as a professional playwright. And even if he backed the winner, he had no guarantee that either party would reconstruct a strong and stable company and choose to stage new plays.

4

The Years of Uncertainty, 1734–1735

AT the start of the season of 1733–34 the future was murky indeed. Whether the rebel actors could survive financially at the Little Haymarket was doubtful, but so was Drury Lane's ability to remain open and pay its expenses with a makeshift company assembled over the summer. The rebel actors would try to get the patentees turned out of the Drury Lane theatre while the patentees attempted to have the rebel actors shut down by the courts.

Deprived of virtually all their front-line performers (and probably most of their staff), the patentees were desperate enough to consider the possibility of a union with Covent Garden.[1] Whether out of angry pride or because Rich would not offer attractive terms, they decided to fight on. At what date Fielding unequivocally made plain his support of the 'loyal' company, we do not know. His attack on Theophilus Cibber in the revised *Author's Farce* did not reach the stage until 15 January 1734, by which time the war was lost. That work, however, and his printed dedication to *The Intriguing Chambermaid*, put him in an awkward situation in February when the rebels won. *Don Quixote in England*, which had been in rehearsal at Drury Lane, was dropped from its production schedule and had to be moved to the Little Haymarket (an episode which has been greatly misunderstood). Worse, Fielding found himself an unpopular outsider at Drury Lane. In 1734–35 the Fleetwood regime staged two of his plays, but *The Universal Gallant* was a disastrous failure, and Fielding must have realized that he would find little favour from a management in which Theophilus Cibber was one of the powers.

To compound Fielding's worries, the introduction of the Barnard playhouse bill in Parliament in the spring of 1735 threatened to put the non-patent theatres out of business. The bill did not pass, but it failed only by a fluke. Furthermore, new signs of an anti-competitive *modus vivendi* between the patent theatres boded ill for a playwright who had just married and who needed to support a family on his earnings from

[1] Writing to Victor on 18 Aug. 1733, Aaron Hill says he is 'glad Mrs. *Booth* is resolved against a Union' (Victor, II, 196).

the theatre. In the spring of 1735 Fielding was clearly alarmed and discouraged, and he had reason to be. His career as a playwright appeared to be dwindling into failure.

I. FIELDING AT HIGHMORE'S DRURY LANE (1733–34)

The patent company that reopened in September 1733 was Drury Lane in name and building only. Of forty-five actors and actresses who had constituted the company in 1732–33, only fifteen returned, most of them negligible. Kitty Clive and Mrs Horton were front-line performers; Stoppelaer was a useful man, and Mullart was a reliable journeyman. But, as Victor says, 'Highmore . . . was reduced to the Necessity of beating his Drum for Volunteers: Several Recruits offered from the Strolling Companies; but I remember none of any Promise but Mr. *Macklin*.'[2] Major recruitment was necessary for the company to perform any plays at all. The patentees hired a pair of nonentities (Giles and Hyde) from Goodman's Fields, and three women (Mason, Morse, and Palms) from the pool of former Little Haymarket performers, but no fewer than fifteen performers were new or had not recently been employed in London. This stopgap troupe was probably the weakest that had ever mounted a season at Drury Lane, less capable even than the group left to Christopher Rich in 1695.

We do not know who handled day-to-day management and actually got plays on the stage. Obviously, every production had to be recast and newly rehearsed, with attendant costs in time, trouble, and money. Simply learning new parts must have been a tremendous strain on the hastily assembled company. Drury Lane somehow managed to offer a nearly full schedule of performances during the autumn, but they could not possibly have been on the level of the offerings at Covent Garden and Goodman's Fields, let alone those of the rebels' at the Little Haymarket. The inevitable result was heavy losses, as Victor testifies.

In this maimed Condition the Business of Course went lamely on; for a very middling Company of Players could be expected to bring but thin losing Audiences, especially while Party prevailed, and those very Plays were acted much better in the *Haymarket*. The unavoidable and melancholy Consequence of this Proceeding was, that there was a Ballance every *Saturday*

[2] Victor, I, 19.

Morning in the Office against the Manager, of Fifty or Sixty Pounds; and his Pride, as well as his Honour, were too nearly concerned not to produce the Deficiency every Week with the utmost Exactness. My Reader will easily see, that a constant Deficiency of something near the above Sums, upon an Average every Week, must, in Thirty Weeks, amount to a considerable Sum. (I, 19–20)

Even a very well-to-do young gentleman would not be pleased at the prospect of losing £1,500 in a year after having just invested £6,000 in the business. Drury Lane could not go on like this forever.

Even before the start of the season Mrs Booth prudently took what she could get and sold out. The *London Evening-Post* of 18–20 September 1733 reported: 'We hear Mrs. Booth . . . resolves to leave the Stage, having sold her Share in the Patent to Mr. Giffard, the Master of Goodman's-Fields Theatre.'[3] She received £1,350 for the half-share (one-sixth interest) remaining to her, a surprisingly good price, considering the state of the business.[4] Giffard's willingness to buy indicates the value he placed on the Drury Lane stock and patent. He 'made his Purchase in *Drury-lane* Patent (I heard him say) as a good Stake in an Establishment, he thought much surer than his own.'[5] Victor tells us, however, that the management of the theatre was left solely to Highmore, 'with only Mr. *Ellis* as Agent for the Widow *Wilks*, to aid and assist him'.

The ever-hopeful Aaron Hill had written to Highmore on 5 July 1733, denouncing 'The late revolt of your *mercenaries*' and offering to 'execute a scheme for your company, from the opening, to *Christmas* next, without any benefit, consideration, or claim, of any kind, further than a fourth part of the clear profits . . . and, as to apprehension of loss, I will indemnify you against any'.[6] Highmore doubtless came to regret his rejection of this rash offer. Hill did coach some of the Drury Lane actors during the autumn, and as late as 1 December he was offering his managerial services for the winter.[7] Despite such offers of amateur assistance, Highmore's company was doomed unless the

[3] Hester Booth, unlike Wilks' widow, had been a performer and knew a good deal about the theatre.

[4] Testimony in PRO C11/778/28. Victor says he was 'told, she got Fifteen Hundred Pounds' (I, 11).

[5] Victor, I, 11.

[6] Hill, *Works*, I, 129–34.

[7] Hill to Highmore, 1 December 1733 (*Works*, 187–90). For Hill's letters to various performers about their parts, see *Works*, I, 138–45, 149–70.

rebellion could be quashed in the courts, an endeavour that had decisively failed by the end of November (see Section II below).

Why Fielding banded himself with the patentees, and when he did so, are interesting, if unanswerable, questions. Most scholars have simply ignored these issues, despite their obvious relevance to the health and trajectory of Fielding's career. The principal exception is Cross, who delivers a one-sentence *ex cathedra* explanation: 'In accordance with his nature, he took the side of the distressed actors against the mutineers.'[8] This is a most peculiar interpretation. Fielding uses the phrase 'distrest Actors' in his preface to *Don Quixote in England*, and the ringing terms of his dedication of *The Intriguing Chambermaid* to Mrs Clive (discussed in Section II) demonstrate a fiercely partisan commitment. But disengaging ourselves from the rhetoric of the quarrel, we must remember that Fielding chose to side with management against virtually all of the senior actors. Why should 'his nature' not equally well lead him to sympathize with the rebel actors against an incompetent amateur management?

One possibility is that Fielding fancied himself a member of the property-holding class and agreed with the patentees' claim that their rights were being violated. Charles B. Woods states this hypothesis as fact when he says that 'Fielding sympathized [with the patentees] as people whose legitimate investments were being jeopardized.'[9] (The 'legitimacy' is, of course, open to question.) We may also wonder whether snobbery was involved. Highmore was a gentleman,[10] and if he treated Fielding as a social equal, the effect might have been potent. Social status plainly meant a lot to Fielding, whose insistence on putting 'Esq;' after his name on title-pages had evoked much derision in the press.[11] As a third hypothesis, we must consider the claims of self-interest. Fielding needed a management willing to stage his plays, and if he thought he had a receptive manager in Highmore,

[8] Cross, I, 149.

[9] Introduction to *The Author's Farce*, p. xiv.

[10] His status as such is relentlessly mocked in *Cibber to Highmore*.

[11] All plays until *The Modern Husband* are described as by 'Mr. Fielding' or 'Scriblerus Secundus' (except *Rape upon Rape* and *The Lottery*, which are anonymous). *The Modern Husband*, *The Miser*, *The Intriguing Chambermaid*, *Don Quixote in England*, *The Universal Gallant*, and *Pasquin* are all 'By Henry Fielding, Esq;'. *The Old Debauchees* is ascribed to 'the Author of the *Modern Husband*'. *The Covent-Garden Tragedy*, *The Mock Doctor*, the 1st edn. of *An Old Man taught Wisdom* (the 2nd is credited to 'Henry Fielding, Esq;'), and *Tumble-Down Dick* are anon. *The Historical Register* is ascribed to the author of *Pasquin*. For derogatory refs. to 'Esq;', see, e.g. *The Grub-street Journal* of 10 and 24 Aug. 1732.

that conviction might have been sufficient to command his loyalties. This is not discreditable. Fielding had to eat, and he can hardly be blamed if that necessity affected his judgement of the actor rebellion.

A fourth factor that may have affected Fielding is the presence of Theophilus Cibber at the head of the rebels. Fielding's view of 'Pistol' is hard to evaluate. Like Dryden, Fielding was prepared to lavish graceful public compliments where he thought they would do him the most good. In the summer of 1732 he had said in the 'Preface' to *The Mock Doctor*: 'The Applause our *Mock-Doctor* received on the Theatre admits of no Addition from my Pen. I shall only congratulate the Town on the lively Hope they may entertain of having the Loss, they are one Day to suffer in the Father, so well supply'd in the Son.' Eighteen months later he was to pillory Theophilus in his revision of *The Author's Farce*. We need not interpret this as insincerity on Fielding's part: Theophilus was a talented actor. A year's exposure to him as manager in 1732–33, however, may have convinced Fielding that Theophilus was impossible to work with. And, finally, Fielding's sympathies may have been swayed by friendly relations with John Ellys. Whatever his reasons, Fielding fiercely and publicly supported Highmore and the patentees.

The Revision of *The Author's Farce* and *The Intriguing Chambermaid*

In all probability, what Fielding intended to stage during 1733–34 was *The Universal Gallant* and *The Intriguing Chambermaid*. The former is a long social comedy cum satire in the tradition of *The Modern Husband*. The latter is yet another French-derived afterpiece vehicle for Kitty Clive. In the one Fielding indulged his determination to write serious drama; in the other he hedged his bets by providing sure-fire entertainment of the sort management would be certain to welcome.

On 8 December 1733 the *Daily Advertiser* ran a notice that Drury Lane would revive *The Author's Farce* 'immediately after Christmas with very great Additions, and that it will be succeeded by a New Comedy of the same Author's, call'd the Universal Gallant, or the Different Husbands'.[12] The reasons for the company's not attempting *The Universal Gallant* are not definitely known, but can be guessed. The makeshift troupe struggled just to mount repertory staples. Its first new

[12] Emmett Avery was the first person to notice that *The Universal Gallant* was ready for performance more than a year before its première. See 'Fielding's *Universal Gallant*', *Research Studies of the State College of Washington*, 6 (1938), 46. This notice was omitted from *The London Stage*.

play was Kelly's *Timon in Love* (5 December), which survived exactly three performances. On 3 January the company staged *The Cornish Squire* (by Fielding's friend James Ralph), which lasted only five nights (plus a single night two weeks later). Both were much more lightweight offerings than Fielding's, and we cannot wonder that management did not risk *The Universal Gallant*, even if no one had realized how poor a play it was. Had Highmore consulted Aaron Hill, for example, he would almost certainly have been advised to give it a miss.

When Fielding revamped his anti-Cibber hit of 1730 is impossible to guess, but evidently before 8 December 1733. The changes could not have taken more than a week or so (if that), and the topical application to Theophilus Cibber made the piece timely. Or rather, it would have been timely if it had come earlier in the autumn, for by 15 January the collapse of the Highmore management was inevitable, both for financial reasons and because the courts had ruled that the rebel actors held a valid lease on Drury Lane (see Section II below). The 'loyal company' struggled on, but it was doomed.

Charles Woods asserts that 'the revision is almost conscientiously thorough, scarcely a page being left untouched' and that the result 'is in effect a new play'.[13] But fewer than half of the pages have any substantive change at all, and the outline of the work is unaltered. Because Wilks had died, Fielding had to remove Sparkish. This he did by the simple expedient of rewriting II.i. and ii., replacing Sparkish with Marplay, *jun*. (Theophilus Cibber). Into Act I he inserted a short encounter between Luckless and Marplay, *jun*. (16–18).[14] The 'contest' of Act III is revamped slightly by making it concern 'the Election of an Arch-poet, or as others call him a Poet Laureat' (38). Several other small changes also snipe at Colley Cibber's having become Poet Laureate, notably 'Odes, Odes, a Man may be oblig'd to write those you know' (17).

Other than his cuts at the Cibbers, Fielding's alterations are minor. He elaborates Bookweight's scene with his hack writers (27–31); inserts passing allusions to 'the Players or the Patentees' (18), the 'other House' (34), and desertion by actors (38). Into Act III he interpolates the 'Ghost of a *Director*' ((43) a topical attack on fraud in the Charitable Corporation), Mynheer *Van-treble* (45),[15] a speech

[13] Woods edn., pp. xi, xv.

[14] Refs. are to 'The Third Edition', pub. by Watts in 1750.

[15] Evidently an attack on opera castrati. Unfortunately, the printed copy is defective, and no speech for the character is preserved.

about the Laureate (60), and a short scene involving 'Count Ugly' to mock Heidegger and masquerades (61). The rather irrelevant Murdertext is replaced by Sir John Bindover, a magistrate bent on stopping the abuse of nonsense (62).

The scene between the Cibbers (II.ii.) is in itself quite amusing: Colley gives sage advice on how to steal plays, suppress competition, and defy public disapprobation. Marplay *jun.* is vigorously mocked, but his substitution for Sparkish/Wilks is essentially unsatisfactory. In 1730 Fielding had ridiculed a real management, in 1734 a non-existent one. Colley and Theophilus Cibber never worked as equals in management, and Colley had retired from the stage in spring 1733. What had been an amusing satire on the unpopular if successful triumvirate became a personal swipe at the Cibbers. A few topical allusions do little to make the play relevant to the battle between patentees and actors. Little wonder it fell flat. Had Fielding written a better version of Covent Garden's topical farce, called something like *A Commonwealth in the Haymarket; or, The Mutineers*, and had he got it to the stage three months earlier, it might have been a much more effective piece of propaganda.[16]

Cross implies that Fielding significantly beefed up his 'burlesque of Italian opera', and offers the very strange comment that 'native drama was really suffering more this winter from the popularity of Italian opera than from the dissensions among the players'.[17] In fact, satire on Italian opera in the revision of *The Author's Farce* remains brief and incidental, and though a second Italian opera company opened at Lincoln's Inn Fields on 29 December 1733, both companies drew poor audiences and lost large sums of money.[18] Despite Fielding's growls in the epilogue at the popularity of '*Italian* Warblers', opera was irrelevant to the problems of English actors and playwrights. Neither Highmore's company nor Fielding's farce suffered because of Handel or even the posh new Opera of the Nobility.

The fate of Fielding's revision was not helped by a patchy cast. As in 1730, Mr Mullart took Luckless and his wife Mrs Moneywood. Kitty Clive was available as Harriot. The vital roles of Marplay *sen.*

[16] For an argument that the revision is aesthetically superior to the original version, see Marsha Kinder, 'The Improved *Author's Farce*: An Analysis of the 1734 Revisions', *Costerus*, 6 (1972), 35–43. Obviously I do not agree.

[17] Cross, I, 153.

[18] See Robert D. Hume, 'Handel and Opera Management in London in the 1730s', *Music and Letters*, 67 (1986), 347–62.

and *jun*. went respectively to Stoppelaer and Macklin. Cross tells us that Stoppelaer was 'a very good comedian' and that 'Macklin took off to the life the son',[19] but I suspect that this is idle puffery. I am aware of no testimony about their performances, and neither actor seems to me well suited to his part. The rest of the cast was wholly undistinguished.

The revised *Author's Farce* lasted six nights, only the third advertised as an author's benefit. The new prologue strikes a despondent note: 'our wretched Theatre'; 'this poor deserted Place'; 'Our Author ... aim'd to succour the Distress'd'; 'we're almost down'.[20] By 15 January, however, even a more topical satire would probably have died at birth at Drury Lane. Fielding did not even get the consolation of a few guineas from John Watts: the revision was not published until 1750.[21]

The second half of Fielding's double-bill of 15 January 1734 was *The Intriguing Chambermaid*. The source was Jean François Regnard's *Le Retour imprévu* (1700). As had become his custom, Fielding relied on the structure of the original while departing freely from it in many ways.[22] His most obvious change is turning the valet Merlin into the chambermaid Lettice. A dozen songs are added, all of them well integrated. The setting is, of course, moved to London and the characters are Anglicized.

The action is entirely farcical. Young Valentine has been living a wastrel's life in the company of Lords and Gentlemen. His merchant-father returns unexpectedly from abroad and is fended off as long as possible at his own door by Lettice, who assures him that the house is haunted (and so forth). Paternal forgiveness is obtained with unbelievable ease and speed, and the lovely, wealthy Charlotte is given to the undeserving but supposedly penitent Valentine.

The conclusion verges on self-burlesque, but the piece functions principally as a vehicle for the clever servant. Fielding did not even bother to write in a pro-forma rebuke and forgiveness scene for the chambermaid, who simply slips away and disappears. The extended

[19] Cross, I, 150.

[20] The new prologue and epilogue were printed with the afterpiece, Fielding's *The Intriguing Chambermaid* (London, 1734).

[21] Pub. then by Watts as 'The Third Edition' with the title-page explanation: 'This Piece was Originally Acted at the *Hay-Market*, and Revived some Years after at *Drury-Lane*, when it was Revised, and greatly Alter'd by the Author, as now Printed.'

[22] For comparison with Regnard, see A. E. H. Swaen, 'Fielding's *The Intriguing Chambermaid*', *Neophilologus*, 29 (1944), 117–20, and Ducrocq, pp. 289–95.

confrontation at the door (23–32) is well-sustained.[23] Curiously, having treated the merchant Goodall as a dupe, Fielding turns around and makes him an effective satiric spokesman against the gaggle of society companions whom Valentine has been entertaining at a drunken party. Lord Pride, Lord Puff, Col. Bluff, a French marquis, and their lady friends are shown up as heartless, sneering scoundrels (33–7). The mixture of formulaic farce reconciliation with harsh social satire is more than a little odd.

Considered as a piece of dramatic craftsmanship, *The Intriguing Chambermaid* is a splendid showcase for Kitty Clive, though a less well-wrought play than *The Lottery* or *The Mock Doctor*. Despite an undistinguished cast and the sorry circumstances of the company, it managed eight performances in short order, and four more after the return of the rebels. It never achieved the popularity of *The Mock Doctor* or *The Virgin Unmask'd*, but it was performed regularly to the end of the century. Fielding wrote it as a sure-fire formula piece, and he did not miscalculate. What he got for his pains is an interesting question. The author's night for the double bill is the only recorded benefit this winter. It may have been all Fielding got from the Highmore regime, and it is unlikely to have been lucrative.

II. THE VICTORY OF THE REBEL ACTORS

Before the 'loyal' company could bring Fielding's next offering to the stage, Highmore sold out—and his successor hurriedly made terms with the rebels. Exactly what happened in the autumn of 1733 has never been properly studied, and the legal phase of the actors' dispute with the patentees requires careful consideration. The triumph of the mutineers was enormously important to subsequent events: it made real the possibility that Fielding could run a permanent company of his own, but it also helped to bring about the Licensing Act.

In the summer of 1733, knowing that Highmore would try to get them suppressed, the rebels sought official authority to perform. According to Thomas Davies (writing many years after these events), Colley Cibber 'applied to the Duke of Grafton [then Lord Chamberlain] for a patent, in favour of his son Theophilus . . . . The duke saw through the injustice of the act, and peremptorily refused'.[24] In 1695

[23] Refs. are to the Watts edn. of 1734.

[24] Thomas Davies, *Dramatic Miscellanies* (London, 1784), III, 474. Davies says that he 'received' his information from Victor—evidently by personal communication, since Victor did not publish it.

the rebel actors had enjoyed better court connections than the patentees, but in 1733 Highmore's social standing made any application for a licence, let alone a patent, unlikely to succeed. The rebels did, however, obtain a licence of sorts from the Master of the Revels. They therefore advertised their performances as 'By the Company of Comedians of his Majesty's Revels'. The title was legitimate, but the authority spurious. In the anonymous pseudo-memoirs of Theophilus Cibber he is made to say: 'We had indeed got a specious Colour of a Licence, and put at the Top of our Bill, *By Licence of the Master of the Revels*; for which titular Honour we paid him handsomely; yet we did this rather to induce the Publick to think we play'd by a legal Authority, and under the Sanction of the Court, than for any Right which we thought it conferr'd on us.'[25] This may be pure guesswork, but it is highly probable. The office of Master of the Revels had atrophied, and its incumbent, Charles Lee, was a nonentity receiving just £10 per annum. Whether he was still licensing scripts for Covent Garden, we do not know, but he did not have the right to license a company to perform in London or Westminster. Strollers elsewhere were a different matter.[26] Lee was no doubt glad to collect a fee, and he issued a 'licence', but immediate objections were raised against it. A writer in the *Daily Post* of 29 September 1733, responding to the claim that Lee had 'Right to licence the Acting of Plays', printed 'A Translation of Mr. *Lee*'s Patent of Master of the Revels', a document that specifies no such authority.[27] The rebels' licence was nothing but a public relations ploy, and perhaps a device intended to buy time while the actors' suit to obtain possession of Drury Lane could be heard.[28]

The rebels can never have imagined that they could survive indefinitely in the Little Haymarket. Even if the courts ultimately held

[25] *An Apology For . . . Mr. T......... C....., Comedian*, p. 90.

[26] In a petition to Charles II in 1662, Davenant noted that a court had found that 'the master of Revels was allow'd the correction of Plaies, and Fees for soe doeing; but not to give Plaiers any licence or authoritie to play, it being prov'd that no Plaiers were ever authoriz'd in London or Westminster, to play by the Commession of the Master of Revels, but by authoritie immediately from the Crowne.' *The Dramatic Records of Sir Henry Herbert*, p. 119.

[27] No complete run of the *Daily Post* seems to exist, and I have not been able to locate a copy of the earlier issue containing 'The Case of *Charles Lee*'. The 'Case' was apparently a justification of the Master of the Revels' right to license the rebel company. But whatever arguments it advanced could not have been valid.

[28] Some details recorded in Lincoln's Inn Library Misc. MS 55, p. 335, show that the patentees tried to stall indefinitely, but found the court unsympathetic.

that what they were doing was legal, they were too expensive a troupe for so small a building. They had to acquire a rudimentary stock of scenery and costumes on tick, and though they charged normal patent theatre prices, a fairly full house would have been required every night just to pay their constant charge. But if the actors won their suit for possession of Drury Lane, they would have a powerful bargaining counter to use in negotiations with the patentees. Their strategy was clearly to hang on until they won their ejectment suit.

The strategy of the patentees is much less clear.[29] They persuaded John Rich to join their effort to intimidate the actors into returning to the patent companies.[30] On 30 October 1733, Mary Wilks, John Highmore, John Ellys, and John Rich dispatched a letter 'To Mr. *John Mills*, and the rest of the Persons, acting at the Theatre in the *Haymarket*, lately belonging to the Theatres at *Drury-Lane* and *Covent-Garden*'. The letter says that the patentees 'are well advised of the Unlawfulness as well as Unreasonableness of your Acting', and that unless the actors 'think fit to return' to their 'respective Companies', the patentees will 'be necessitated . . . to proceed in such a Manner as the Law directs, for supporting the Royal Patents under which we act'. The letter was returned, unopened, whereupon the patentees re-addressed it to Theophilus Cibber, who replied bluntly: '. . . I am well advis'd, that what I am about is legal, and I know 'tis reasonable; and therefore I do not think of changing my present Condition for Servitude.'[31]

Thus defied, the patentees, joined by John Rich, had the local JPs issue summonses 'against two of the Players of the Hay-market, and two of Goodman's-Fields, as *Vagrants within the Statute of* 12*th* of *Queen Anne*'. In other words, the patentees of Drury Lane and Covent Garden combined to try to get the courts to put both the Little Haymarket and Goodman's Fields out of business. A hearing was held on Monday 5 November, and was reported in the *London Evening-Post* in great detail. After some legal sparring, all parties (patentees and actors) agreed 'that an Action on a Feign'd Issue' should be tried at the end of the Michaelmas law term to determine 'whether they were *Vagrants, &c.* within that Act'. After further argument they agreed 'that

[29] They apparently did not understand that they were likely to lose possession of their theatre building.

[30] Milward and Harrington had deserted from Covent Garden to join the rebels.

[31] Both letters are printed in the *London Evening-Post* of 10–13 Nov. 1733. They also appear in the *Daily Post* of 13 Nov.

Mr. Highmore should be Plaintiff in an Action against Mr. Johnson, and Mr. Rich in another against Mr. Giffard; *and that in order to put the Case as strong as possible, both the Defendants were to be admitted settled Inhabitants in the Parishes wherein they Acted*' (emphasis added).

The point italicized is vital to understanding both this case and the Harper case that followed. Many historians have heaped contempt upon Highmore for his stupidity in arresting as a vagrant an actor who was a prosperous householder (and indeed a voter). This misunderstanding follows from Colley Cibber's confusion on the subject: Cibber says that *because* Harper was a householder he did not fall within the vagrancy act, and so was discharged and carried triumphantly out of the court.[32] But this is all wrong. As the earlier case makes explicit, the choice of a 'householder' was deliberate. Benjamin Victor explains that in the eyes of the law, 'it was in the Power of the greatest Subject in *England* to be guilty of an Action of Vagrancy; and that the only Point to be disputed there was, whether *Harper*'s performing in the *Haymarket* Theatre was committing that Act'.[33] The issue was not the solvency or domicile of the actors, but whether performing without a licence made them, legally speaking, vagrants.

The preliminary joint case, however, broke down before it started. When the lawyers tried to settle the terminology of the 'feigned suit', they could not do so. The patentees' counsel asked that the charge read 'Rogues *or* Vagabonds'; the actors' counsel insisted on 'Rogues *and* Vagabonds', the actual words of the statute—in which they were upheld by the chief magistrate. This technicality forced dismissal of the summonses with which the proceeding had started.[34] It also seems to have discouraged Rich, who dropped out of the affair at this point.

Exactly a week later, on 12 November, the players' suit for possession of the Drury Lane theatre came to trial in King's Bench before Chief Justice Yorke. Long delays notwithstanding, the case was extremely simple. The patentees occupied Drury Lane but held no lease on it. The actors had signed a valid lease with 'the two Trustees appointed by the Thirty-six Sharers of Drury-Lane House', and since holders of twenty-seven of the thirty-six shares approved the lease, the patentees did not have a leg to stand on.[35] The legal proceedings

[32] *Apology*, I, 283–4.

[33] Victor, I, 24 n. Victor understood the issues better than Cibber, but he has been much less read.

[34] *London Evening-Post*, 3–6 Nov. 1733.

[35] The trial is reported in the *London Evening-Post* of 10–13 Nov. Had a majority of the

continued to be slow, and the actors did not manage to take possession of the Drury Lane theatre until March 1734. But as of 12 November the rebels had backed Highmore against a wall: if he could not get them suppressed in a hurry, he would find himself and his sorry troupe occupying the Little Haymarket or Lincoln's Inn Fields.

Evidently anticipating defeat in King's Bench, Highmore had John Harper arrested as a vagrant on the morning of 12 November, and he was duly committed to Bridewell.[36] This was a dreadful error in public relations. Harper was a popular actor, and as the papers reported, the move seemed 'design'd . . . to prevent the Company acting last Night, by taking away so principal a Performer in the Play (Harper being to play the Part of Sir John Falstaff in Henry IV) . . . but the Audience being acquainted with this Prosecution, very kindly accepted of Mr. Cibber's reading the part'.[37] Public outcry was immediate. In the *Daily Post* of 16 November, for example, we find a long and indignant denunciation of the affair, pointing out that the vagrancy act was designed 'to prevent those, who want *Ability* to *maintain* themselves, from *wandring* about the *Country*, and becoming *Chargeable to Parishes*, where they have no Settlements'—hardly a case applicable to Harper. Since vagrants committed to confinement were presumed not to be bailable, the author also enquires sarcastically if the government intends to lock up every wealthy 'vagrant' it finds obnoxious. But on the same day habeas corpus was granted, and on Tuesday the 20th Harper was 'discharg'd out of Bridewell, on his own Recognizance, to appear the last Day of this Term; and an Action on a feign'd Issue is to be tried, whether he is a Vagrant within the Statute of the twelfth of Queen Anne, next Term'.[38]

At this point, we strike a snag in our analysis of the case. Harper was indeed freed (he was not, after all, a vagrant in the usual sense of the term), and scholars seem universally to believe that Harper 'won'. Liesenfeld, for example, says that Chief Justice Yorke 'found in his favor and dismissed the case', and refers to 'Harper's acquittal'.[39] But I

building sharers not supported their trustees, the patentees could probably not have been evicted, and certainly not without extended delays.

[36] A copy of Thomas Clarges's order for his commitment is in Lincoln's Inn Library Misc. MS 55, p. 363.

[37] *London Evening-Post*, 10–13 Nov. The following night 'a Party' tried to disrupt the performance at Drury Lane (*Daily Post*, 14 Nov.)—perhaps a response to the arrest of Harper.

[38] *London Evening-Post*, 15–17 and 17–20 Nov.

[39] Liesenfeld, p. 21.

can find no evidence of a definite resolution to the case. Harper duly appeared before the court on the last day of term (28 November). The *Daily Courant* of 29 November says that 'he was honourably acquitted'. However, the *Grub-street Journal* of 6 December reports that because the 'feigned issue' was not tried, 'the court continued Mr. Harper till the first day of next term'. And the relatively full report in the *London Evening-Post* of 27–29 November says that the case was continued and that the lawyers for both parties agreed again that at the end of the next term they would try the feigned issue, 'Mr. Highmore to be Plaintiff, and Mr. Harper Defendant'.[40] In short, the vagrancy case was never tried. What Harper 'won' was only 'the Trial of the Legality of his Commitment' to Bridewell, and on 20 November he was indeed 'discharg'd, and conducted through the Hall, amidst the triumphant Acclamations of his theatre Friends'.[41] But this did not mean that Harper and his fellow rebels were out of jeopardy on the issue of acting without authority.[42]

Why the 'feigned issue' was not tried on 28 November we can only guess. Perhaps Highmore's lawyers felt that they were insufficiently prepared and wanted more time to study the case and consult legal authorities. And since Highmore had sold the business before the end of Hilary term, the case never came on again.[43] That he could have won seems unlikely. If unlicensed actors could have been shut down by recourse to the vagrancy act of 12 Queen Anne, Goodman's Fields would not have survived its first season. As an anonymous writer said some years later:

Giffard's Company at *Goodman*'s *Fields* was then playing against all the Opposition that could be made to it, against the Power of the City of *London*, and even their Remonstrances to the Court that it was a Nusance. In short, it

[40] *The London Stage*, Part 3, I, xcii, erroneously cites this source as proof that 'Harper was acquitted on 28 November'.

[41] *An Apology For . . . Mr. T......... C....., Comedian*, p. 90.

[42] Four separate accounts of the case are preserved in various manuscripts in the Lincoln's Inn Library: Misc. MS 55, pp. 363–5; Hill MS 66 [Osborne 11], openings 135–8; Coxe MS 29, openings 101, 103–10; Coxe MS 47, pp. 296–8. Misc. MS 55 shows that Harper's lawyers initially fought the case on technicalities, but the lawyers' opinions most fully recorded in Coxe MS 29 (emphasizing the evident intent of the act at issue and the importance of 'wandering') suggest little hope of the patentees carrying their case.

[43] In a copy of a manuscript performance calendar in BL 11791.dd.18 (vol. 3, p. 135*v) is recorded under 12 Feb. 1734: 'This day Mr. Harper was discharged: neither Mr. Rich nor Mr. Highmore being willing to proceed to Tryal.'

was not then thought in the Power of the Crown to suppress a Playhouse, though acting without Royal Licence and Permission, because it was not evidently an illegal Thing. But the Case is now alter'd by a late Act of Parliament . . .[44]

The key phrase is *not evidently an illegal Thing*. An actor without fixed abode could be prosecuted. But could a person of fixed abode who was also an actor be prosecuted on the ground that being an actor made him (in legal theory) a vagrant? So Highmore's lawyers were endeavouring to prove, but their argument was born of desperation. Acting could not be an obviously 'illegal Thing', since the government had granted patents and licences permitting it. That laws could be enacted to regulate it was clearly true, but acting itself could not be held illegal.

After the rebels had won their suit for possession of the Drury Lane theatre and Highmore had failed to keep Harper in Bridewell, a settlement could only be a matter of time.[45] Nothing is known of the negotiations that must have occurred during December and January. According to *An Apology For the Life of Mr. T......... C....., Comedian*, the Little Haymarket company was in bad shape by winter, suffering from large debts and thin houses (which they were forced to paper), but they successfully concealed their problems from the despairing patentees.

On 24 January 1734 Charles Fleetwood purchased Highmore's half-interest for £2,250 and Mary Wilks' third for £1,500.[46] Thus, Highmore got less than half what he had paid, and Mary Wilks got little more for a third than Hester Booth had received for a sixth the previous September. The news of the purchase was public by 1 February, and on the 2nd the *Daily Courant* reported that Fleetwood had bought 'all the Shares of the Patentees', and that he 'will either keep them himself, or dispose of them to such Persons (Actors only) as shall be approved of by the Players themselves: On which Conditions, we hear that the Company from the Theatre in the Haymarket, are about to return to their Old House'.[47]

[44] *An Apology For . . . Mr. T......... C....., Comedian*, p. 90.

[45] The *Grub-street Journal* of 10 Jan. published a satiric set of 'articles of peace'. The best clause provides for 'establishing the peace and tranquillity of the Stage' by decreeing that 'the illustrious dowager *Hester Booth* shall be given in marriage to the most serene infant Don *Theophilus Cibber*'. But all foolery aside, compromise was in the air.

[46] PRO C11/778/28.

[47] Fleetwood did not buy all the shares: Giffard retained his one-sixth interest.

The author of 'Theophilus Cibber's' memoirs says that Fleetwood bought the Drury Lane stock and patent at John Rich's instigation, with the idea that the two companies would be run jointly and the actors kept firmly in their place—but this must be a mistake.[48] Rich and Fleetwood did indeed negotiate a quasi-union in autumn 1735, but in January 1734 the rebel actors held a valid lease on Drury Lane and could not easily have been coerced into terms they found objectionable.

Victor tells us that by winter the senior actors were 'ashamed' of being led by Theophilus Cibber, and anxious to make peace, but that Theophilus 'had Address enough to preserve his Station, and was not only principal, but alone, at the first Meeting for a Treaty of Peace with the new Manager; by which Means, it may be supposed, he made himself considerable, and got very advantageous Terms for himself and Favourites'.[49] The actors agreed to work for Fleetwood, and no doubt they insisted that the 'stock' they had acquired at the Little Haymarket be taken over (and paid for) by the patentee.[50] The patentee had the senior actors and the theatre; the actors got large raises and improved benefit terms, guaranteed in writing. Theophilus Cibber became deputy manager. On 8 March 'the Company of Comedians in the Hay-Market took possession of Drury Lane Theatre' (*Daily Advertiser*, 9 March), thus formally signalling their triumph. This settlement, however, left Henry Fielding in an extremely awkward position.

The Production and Publication of *Don Quixote in England*

The performance of *Don Quixote in England* at the Little Haymarket in April 1734 is one of the most widely misunderstood episodes in Fielding's career. Bertrand Goldgar summarizes the standard interpretation when he says that Fielding's 'return to the Haymarket with *Don Quixote in England* signaled a move toward the opposition as clearly as his earlier change of theaters . . . had signaled a move toward the court party'. Brian McCrea asserts simply that 'In 1734 he left Drury Lane and brought *Don Quixote in England* to the Haymarket theatre.'[51] But in fact the appearance of Fielding's play at the Little

[48] *An Apology For . . . Mr. T......... C....., Comedian*, pp. 96–7.

[49] Victor, I, 27.

[50] *An Apology For . . . Mr. T......... C....., Comedian*, p. 98, suggests that getting 'rid of our Stock-Debt' was part of the settlement.

[51] Goldgar, pp. 114–15; McCrea, p. 64.

Haymarket had nothing whatever to do with politics, and was not really a matter of his choice.

After writing *Don Quixote* in 1728, Fielding had been told by Wilks and Cibber that it would not do, and he laid it aside.[52] It would have remained on his 'Shelf', he says in his preface,

> had not the Solicitations of the distrest Actors in *Drury-Lane* prevail'd on me to revise it, at the same time that it came into my Head to add those Scenes concerning our Elections.
>
> Being thus altered, it was often rehearsed on that Theatre, and a particular Day appointed for its Action; but the Giant *Cajanus*, of a Race who were always Enemies to our poor *Don*, deferred his Appearance so long, that the Intervention of the Actor's Benefits would have put it off till the next Season, had I not brought it on where now it appears.

Fielding asserts that the play was accepted and rehearsed by the company at Drury Lane; that it was deferred on account of Cajanus (a Dutch 'giant'); and that the benefit season then forced indefinite postponement of his play. This is an unlikely tale. Cajanus was indeed performing at Drury Lane as an entr'acte attraction in February 1734, and he did put off his departure.[53] But why should his presence have interfered with performance of Fielding's play? The company was doing a flock of standard shows (*Rule a Wife*, *The Island Princess*, *The Miser*, *The Beaux Stratagem*) and could perfectly well have given *Don Quixote*. What Fielding does not say in his preface is that management was doing him no favours after 24 January. Not only had he lampooned the deputy-manager-to-be in *The Author's Farce*, but he had been so impolitic as to dedicate *The Intriguing Chambermaid* to Kitty Clive in highly partisan terms.[54] Dudden states that *Don Quixote* 'was accepted by Fleetwood', but this is highly improbable. Highmore's actors asked for it; Fleetwood appears to have stalled it off. The rebel actors began performing again at Drury Lane on 12 March, and benefits did indeed crowd the calendar into May. But Fleetwood

[52] For discussion of the play, see ch. 2, pp. 44–8, above.

[53] His last performance was advertised as 26 Feb., but on the 28th the papers reported that he 'is prevail'd upon . . . to stay a few Days longer in England'.

[54] 'The Part you have maintain'd in the present Dispute between the Players and the Patentees, is so full of Honour, that had it been in higher Life, it would have given you the Reputation of the greatest Heroine of the Age. You looked on the Cases of Mr. *Highmore* and Mrs. *Wilks* with Compassion, nor could any Promises or Views of Interest sway you to desert them; nor have you scrupled any Fatigue . . . to support the Cause of those whom you imagin'd injur'd and distress'd . . .'

could have let the play come on in February: Fielding had backed the wrong faction, and he was paying for it.

This episode provides occasion to remark that we must be clear about what labels signify. By 'Drury Lane' we can mean a building, a company of actors, or the current management. In autumn 1733 the Drury Lane acting company performed at the Little Haymarket, and the Drury Lane management had ceased to bear any resemblance to the triumvirate (of increasingly fair memory). That either Highmore or Fleetwood would have accepted plays obnoxious to the ministry seems highly unlikely, but we cannot make easy assumptions about the implications of venue. Scholars have read political significance into *Don Quixote in England* in part because it was staged at the Little Haymarket, but it appeared there *only* because it was forced out of Drury Lane by the return of the rebel actors.

Don Quixote in England received its première at the Little Haymarket on 5 April 1734, advertised as 'By the Persons who rehearsed it in Drury Lane before the Union of the Companies'. This is a bit misleading. Fleetwood evidently did have temporary contractual obligations to the 'loyal' actors, but most of them were dismissed at the end of the season. In the mean time, they performed occasionally at the Little Haymarket and Lincoln's Inn Fields.[55] And we must suppose that had *Don Quixote* premièred in February, Kitty Clive would have appeared in it—but she was of such value that the ex-rebels were glad to make use of her at Drury Lane.

Cross says that 'the piece was bound to succeed' and that it was acted 'night after night'.[56] The facts are less rosy. The play managed a total of eight performances in April, one the following August,[57] and one at Lincoln's Inn Fields in October. The première occurred the Friday before Passion Week, and the next three performances took place during Passion Week—not a good time, even though the patent theatres were closed. Fielding received no benefit as such. On 5 April the company advertised that 'Tickets for the Author's Night at Drury

[55] Ducrocq, p. 299, following Francis Aspry Congreve's *Authentic Memoirs of the Late Mr. Charles Macklin* (London, 1798), p. 13, supposes erroneously that Fielding 'collected' his own company and rented the Little Haymarket in April 1734, but that 'his Theatre was soon closed' owing to lack of success.

[56] Cross, I, 157–8.

[57] The advertisement for 21 August says 'In which are introduc'd two Scenes representing Don Quixote as a Candidate for Member of Parliament, which contain the Humours of Mayors and Corporations'. I take this as a special puff for the election scenes written for the original production, not as an announcement of further additions.

Lane will be taken here every Night of the Performance'. Perhaps so many tickets had been sold that the Little Haymarket could not have held the buyers on a single night, but this seems unlikely. The timing, the modest and discontinuous run, and the lack of a second benefit all suggest a mediocre reception.

Virtually every scholar since Cross has accepted his dictum that *Don Quixote* 'is noteworthy as marking Fielding's return to direct political satire, from which he was compelled to keep clear while writing for Drury Lane'.[58] Disregarding the muddle over Drury Lane, we need to ask how political the play really is. A number of allusions seem to mock Walpole (and may date from 1728),[59] but the 'election' scenes Fielding added for topicality in 1734 vigorously blast the dishonesties of both sides.[60] The mayor and his cohorts love elections because 'both Parties' spend 'as much as they are able' (19). But this very corrupt town supports Country (not Court) interest, and Guzzle's enthusiasm for the idea of annual elections (46) reflects unfavourably on the Country members, who kept demanding them. In short, I agree with Thomas Cleary's conclusion that 'Even the new election scenes can only be described as either non-partisan or slightly more biased *against* the opposition's Country wing than the ministry.'[61] *Don Quixote in England* is simply not a party play. Bertrand Goldgar arrived earlier at the same conclusion: 'the play itself . . . could certainly not have been considered anti-Walpole satire'. He suggests, however, that 'it is the dedication to the earl of Chesterfield which reveals Fielding's new direction'.[62]

Fielding's dedication to Chesterfield is hard to judge. The Earl had parted company with the ministry over the excise bill in 1733, and Fielding's references to Chesterfield's having 'distinguished Himself in the Cause of Liberty' and to 'the Corruption I have here endeavoured to expose' hint at anti-ministerial sentiments that are not

[58] Cross, I, 157.

[59] Notably Sancho's statement that if he is given an island, 'I'll act like other wise Governors, fall to plundering as fast as I can' (39), and Air V ('When mighty rost Beef') including the line, 'Our Soldiers were brave, and our Courtiers were good'. The history of the song is complex: Fielding used an earlier version in *The Genuine Grub-Street Opera* (Air XXXIX) and *The Grub-Street Opera* (Air XLV), and Richard Leveridge revamped it considerably in 1735. For a disentanglement, see Edgar V. Roberts, 'Henry Fielding and Richard Leveridge: Authorship of "The Roast Beef of Old England"', *Huntington Library Quarterly*, 27 (1964), 175–81.

[60] See particularly pp. 11, 18–19, 22–4.

[61] Cleary, p. 68.

[62] Goldgar, p. 150.

borne out in the text. The political signals in the published play are, as Cleary says, 'peculiarly mixed'. Whether the dedication was meant as an 'implied offer of service' to the leaders of the opposition is impossible to say.[63] Like *Rape upon Rape* and *The Welsh Opera*, *Don Quixote in England* is topical and satiric, but not genuinely partisan. Fielding's choice of Chesterfield as dedicatee need have no special political significance, and the allusions to 'Liberty' and 'Corruption' may be no more than the flattering rhetoric of dedications. Dudden says that Walpole's lack of response to the dedication of *The Modern Husband* convinced Fielding that 'no patronage was to be expected from that quarter. Now therefore he determined to try his luck with the Opposition.'[64] This cannot be disproved, but it seems unlikely. As recently as February 1734, when Fielding published *The Intriguing Chambermaid*, he included a complimentary poem 'occasioned by the Revival of the *Author's Farce*', said to be 'Sent to the Author by an unknown Hand'. The anonymous poet expresses the hope that Fielding's satiric labours will be suitably rewarded, and concludes:

> Or *Walpole*, studious still of *Britain's* Fame,
> Protect thy Labours, and prescribe the Theme,
> On which, in Ease and Affluence, thou may'st raise
> More noble Trophies to thy Country's Praise.

Fielding would hardly have printed this in February 1734 if he had definitely decided to become an anti-ministerial propagandist. I suspect that he would have been receptive to financial support from either quarter.[65]

Cross says at this point in his biography that though Fielding had no luck with patrons, he was 'not greatly disturbed by his ill fortune' with *Don Quixote in England*, and that 'his income from the stage . . .

[63] Dudden does say so (I, 134), adding without evidence that it was 'duly noted by the "Patriot" leaders, who were glad to avail themselves of it later on'.

[64] Dudden, I, 133.

[65] By spring 1736—two years later—Fielding was clearly in sympathy with the Broad Bottom faction in the opposition (see pp. 211–12, below). When he first allied himself with the opposition we do not know. By themselves, the election scenes and the dedication of *Don Quixote in England* do not seem conclusive. However, Martin Battestin and Michael Farringdon are about to publish a book in which they attribute some forty *Craftsman* essays to Fielding, the first as early as March 1734. If true, this association with the *Craftsman* would argue a sharp change in Fielding's outlook around January–March 1734. Professor Battestin also points out to me that Fielding's dedication of *The Universal Gallant* to the Duke of Marlborough in spring 1735 is politically significant: Charles Spencer, the third Duke, was at the time a prominent 'boy patriot' and member of the 'Liberty Club' formed in 1734 in opposition to the ministry.

must have been at least three hundred pounds a year'.[66] This may well be true, considered as an average between 1730 and 1734. But in 1733–34 Fielding apparently received just two benefits, and those from essentially unsuccessful plays. My best guess is that he would have been lucky to clear £100 from the season; £200 would be a wildly optimistic estimate. Pondering his circumstances and future in the spring of 1734, Fielding was probably both short of money and acutely aware that his relations with the new Drury Lane management were strained or worse.

III. FIELDING AT FLEETWOOD'S DRURY LANE (1734–35)

As usual, we know nothing of Fielding's thoughts or activities during the summer. On 28 November 1734 he married Charlotte Cradock in Bath, and by 6 January he was presumably in London for the première of a new afterpiece. He apparently expected to support a wife and children on his earnings as a playwright, but the prospects were increasingly dicey.

Relatively little is known about either Charles Fleetwood or the early years of his management at Drury Lane. Although Fleetwood inherited an estate reported at £6,000 per annum, he had gambled much of it away; Victor informs us that 'he came a ruined Man into the Management of the Theatre; and . . . was for some Years a Gainer by his Purchase there.'[67] Despite his ignorance of the business, Fleetwood got off to a good start.

> This Return of the capital Actors to their old well-accustomed Theatre, made a very visible Difference in the Audiences, to the Advantage of the new Manager, whose Unskilfulness in the Business of the Stage was by that Means the longer concealed; but though he was an entire Stranger to the Art of theatrical Navigation, he had Cunning enough to look out for a Pilot. *Theophilus Cibber* set out with him, his Favourite and first Minister; but did not long continue in that high Office. (I, 30–1)[68]

The London Stage points out, however, that Fleetwood took an active part in management, involving himself in performers' contracts and

[66] Cross, I, 157, 160.

[67] Victor, I, 33–4. Charlotte Charke describes him sourly as 'Squire Brainless, 'a Man of Fortune, who never appear'd but in a Side-Box, or behind the Scenes' before buying the business. *The Art of Management* (London, 1735), p. 20.

[68] *An Apology For . . . T......... C....., Comedian*, p. 107, confirms that 'The Company went on . . . with very great Success'.

the choice of new plays.[69] Obviously he could not handle stage production himself, and the *Biographical Dictionary* says that he 'was sensible enough to appoint Macklin to supervise the artistic business of the theatre'.[70] As far as I can determine, however, this did not occur until 1738. At the start of the regime Theophilus Cibber served as deputy manager.[71] Fielding presumably had to negotiate with Fleetwood for acceptance of his scripts; getting them staged meant working with the egregious Theophilus.

Some confusion has arisen over Fleetwood's plans as proprietor and the terms on which he settled with the mutineers. The *Biographical Dictionary*, for example, says that a plan for a 'committee of actors . . . to rent Drury Lane from Fleetwood for 15 years at £920 per year' was discussed, 'but this arrangement did not come into being'.[72] The actors may well have offered to 'rent' the patent and stock from Fleetwood on the terms they offered Highmore, but the *Biographical Dictionary* account appears to rest on confusion about the lease of Drury Lane. The actors held a fifteen-year lease on the building for £920 per annum, and part of the settlement of the rebellion was Fleetwood's agreement to take over the sublease of the theatre from the actors.[73]

Inveterate gambling and his increasing carelessness about theatrical business had Fleetwood in serious financial trouble by 1738,[74] but in 1734–35, and probably for some time thereafter, the company was apparently prosperous. It was not, however, especially receptive to new plays, whether by Henry Fielding or anyone else. A look at the performance calendar shows very heavy reliance on classics—*Rule a Wife*, *Venice Preserv'd*, *Love for Love*, *The Committee*, *Julius Caesar*, *The Alchemist*, *All for Love*, and other staples. Apart from Fielding's *The*

[69] *The London Stage*, Part 3, I, xciii. *The Prompter* of 11 March 1735 clearly implies that Fleetwood was choosing the new plays at Drury Lane. Four years later, when Aaron Hill was enraged by indefinite delays in the production of his *Caesar*, his letters show that Fleetwood was responsible for accepting and scheduling the play.

[70] *Biographical Dictionary*, V, 298.

[71] Victor is confirmed by the *Apology For. . . T......... C....., Comedian*, whose author says that in 1735 Theophilus was 'Prime Minister', though he had to compete with John Ellys for favour with Fleetwood (pp. 102–3). The *Apology* also says specifically that Theophilus led a 'Party' in opposition to Fleetwood in 1737–38, and about the time of his crim. con. trial found his 'Power clip'd in Relation of presiding over Rehearsals', leading to his celebrated quarrel with James Quin (pp. 108–9).

[72] *Biographical Dictionary*, V, 298.

[73] The matter is correctly explained in *Survey of London*, XXXV, 14.

[74] For a brief description of his troubles, see Paul Sawyer, 'Charles Fleetwood's Debts', *Theatre Notebook*, 39 (1985), 3–7.

Universal Gallant, Drury Lane premièred only three mainpieces this season.[75] Fleetwood was more interested in afterpieces, and the company mounted seven new ones during 1734–35. Fielding contributed one of them, and it scored a success. Unfortunately for him, however, his mainpiece was a total failure.

An Old Man taught Wisdom

On 6 January 1735 Fielding's new ballad-farce was staged as an afterpiece to *Venice Preserv'd*. Not a great deal need be said about the work. It was the fifth in a series of comic romps Fielding had written for Kitty Clive, all of which except *The Old Debauchees* were enormously successful. *The Lottery*, *The Mock Doctor*, and *The Intriguing Chambermaid* had become repertory staples. *An Old Man taught Wisdom* (usually staged in later years as *The Virgin Unmask'd*) tallied nearly three hundred performances by 1750 and was performed regularly through 1800.

The piece has almost no plot. Old Goodwill decides to marry off his daughter Lucy (a singularly silly fifteen-year-old) to one of five relations. Blister (an apothecary), Coupee (a dancing master), Bookish (an Oxford student), Quaver (a singing master), and Wormwood (a lawyer) address her in turn. She accepts Blister unwillingly, and then accepts Coupee and Quaver—and while her suitors are sorting this out, she marries Mr Thomas, a footman whose fine clothes and elegant *coiffure* have gone to her head.[76] The fatuous girl comes off better than she deserves. The footman turns out to be an intelligent and industrious person, and old Goodwill decides that his daughter has 'made a better choice, than she cou'd have done among her Booby Relations' (33).

Fielding mocks the suitors, but more in a spirit of contemptuous ridicule than serious satire. A note introduced at the bottom of the dramatis personae page of the first edition informs us that '. . . whereas the Audience at its first Performance seemed to think some Scenes too long, as well as to express a Dislike to one particular Character, to comply with their Opinion, that Character hath been since entirely omitted, and several Speeches and Songs left out in the Representation, which are to be found in the Printed Book.' The second

[75] Duncombe's *Junius Brutus* (7 nights in all); Lillo's *The Christian Hero* (4 nights); James Miller's *The Man of Taste* (27 nights' discontinuous run).

[76] 'His Head is so prettily drest, done all down upon the top with Sugar, like a frosted Cake, with three little Curls of each side . . .' (4). Refs. are to the first Watts edn. of 1735.

edition and later advertised casts tell us that the character who gave offence was the student, Bookish.[77] Whether the audience found the satire unfair or the portrait repulsive we do not know. Curiously, Bookish is the only suitor to say what several of them realize—that the girl is 'a most contemptible Creature' (31). To judge from the hasty deletion of the student, Fielding may have meant the virgin to be viewed with less sympathy than Mrs Clive elicited from the audience.

No description can do justice to the sheer fizziness with which Fielding invests Lucy, mad for a coach (2) and thrilled by a beau (21). On the printed page, *The Virgin Unmask'd* seems silly stuff, but as the performance history reminds us, it was written to display the talents of Kitty Clive, and it worked. As usual, Fielding integrated the songs skilfully, though the reduction from twenty to twelve after the première suggests that initially he overwrote the piece.[78]

An Old Man taught Wisdom—to give it the title of the first production—enjoyed a dozen performances in its first month, and its serviceability must have been obvious. We do not know what Fielding got for it. No benefit was advertised, and the probability is that the new management paid him a straight cash fee. Allowing ten guineas or so from John Watts for publication rights, I would guess that Fielding received no more than £50 or £60 for this bit of dramatic carpentry. The afterpiece was exactly the sort of thing the theatre wanted—but unless the fee was a lot higher than usual, we may deduce that Fielding was getting less generous treatment than he had received from the triumvirate.

The Universal Gallant

Fielding may well have been irritated by lack of a benefit for his afterpiece, but his hopes for the season must have been riding on his mainpiece, delayed for more than a year and finally performed on 10

[77] Cross (I, 170), followed as usual by Dudden (I, 151), says that particular exception was taken to Bookish's line, 'I shall throw my self at no Woman's Feet, for I look on my self as the Superior of the two' (20). This may be so, but I cannot find a source to verify the assertion.

[78] The 2nd edn. was also pub. by John Watts in 1735. From the 1st edn. it drops song 6 ('The Jokers have said'), 7 ('When our Wives deny'), 10 ('When you are like *Bateman*'), 11 ('What Virgin e'er wou'd marry'), 12 ('I never yet long'd'), 13 ('Go marry what Blockhead'), 14 ('I wou'd have you to know'), 15 ('O all ye Powers'), and 17 ('Dearest Creature'). Song 12 in the 2nd edn. ('Had your Daughter been physick'd well') was printed as an unnumbered afterthought at the end of the 1st edn.: I deduce that Fielding used it to replace his original prose ending very early on—perhaps during rehearsals. Copies of the 2nd edn. are relatively scarce: I have used BL Ashley 5311.

February 1735. He evidently had great expectations. *The Universal Gallant: or, The Different Husbands* is very long (five acts, eighty-two pages of text), a serious satire in the tradition of *The Modern Husband*, but rigorously limited in focus to avoid the objections to unrelated sub-plots that had been raised against the earlier piece.

The play's failure in the theatre devastated Fielding. His 'Advertisement' in the first edition starts as follows: 'The cruel Usage this poor Play hath met with, may justly surprize the Author, who in his whole Life never did an Injury to any one Person living. What could incense a Number of People to attack it with such an inveterate Prejudice, is not easy to determine; for Prejudice must be allowed, be the Play good or bad, when it is condemn'd unheard.' Against this assertion that the play was damned unheard by faction, we must consider William Popple's testimony in *The Prompter* of 18 February:

> The last piece brought on the stage this season was *The Universal Gallant or, Different Husbands*, wrote by the prolific Mr. Fielding. . . . If the Town had really the bad taste they are represented to have, this play would have run the remaining part of the season in an uninterrupted course of applause. I had likewise an opportunity of observing much more impartiality than I expected in the behaviour of the audience, for till almost the third act was over, they sat very quiet, in hopes it would mend, till finding it grew still worse and worse, they at length lost all patience and not an expression or sentiment afterwards passed without its deserved censure.

As Cross comments, 'each performance seems to have ended in a tumult of groans, catcalls, whistles, and horse-laughs. Remembering the scene, "The Prompter", when describing later a riot at Orator Henley's chapel, says there were "such hissings and clappings, that I thought myself, for a long time, at a representation of a new piece of Mr. F--l--g"'.[79] This was treatment of a sort Fielding had never before suffered. *The Covent-Garden Tragedy* was withdrawn after the first night, but the audience's objection was apparently to the setting. *The Universal Gallant* was his first mainpiece to fail outright on its own merits and to die with the third performance. This was a repulse as bad as that suffered by 'Bodens'' *The Modish Couple*.

Most modern critics have felt that the failure was deserved, and I regret to say that I agree with them. Pat Rogers is almost alone in finding the piece 'not such a bad comedy'. Cross says 'Never before had Fielding been so dull; never before had he put into the mouths of

[79] Cross, I, 171–2 (citing *The Prompter* of 22 Aug. 1735).

his characters so caustic remarks on the frailties of women; no scene until the fifth Act was really dramatic . . .' Dudden denounces its 'glut of cheap and shallow cynicisms' and calls it 'insufferably tedious and boring'.[80] Fielding would no doubt immediately object that the cynicism was put in the mouths of characters who were held up to ridicule and meant to be rejected, and this is true. But considered simply as a specimen of play construction, *The Universal Gallant* is a botched piece of work. Drury Lane found a very respectable cast for the play, but no cast imaginable could have breathed life into a work so long on sour talk and so short on action.

Fielding's design is built around character contrasts of a sort he had always favoured. The 'Different Husbands' of the sub-title are Sir Simon Raffler and Colonel Raffler, the one fanatically jealous of his primly virtuous wife, the other so foolishly trusting that his wife is finally shamed into being virtuous because he thinks her so (50).[81] The title character—Captain Spark, played by Theophilus Cibber—is curiously irrelevant and underdeveloped. He has little to do but boast about his imaginary affairs. Mondish—the principal character, title notwithstanding—is also woefully underemployed. The only characters of whom Fielding approves are Gaylove and Clarinda, who finally decide to get married (81), but of whose courtship we see practically nothing. They are yet another instance of his inability to write conventional romance.

Fielding's aim in *The Universal Gallant* was plainly to write a heavyweight social satire. Unfortunately, endless conversation and lack of action doom the play. The characters simply do not fill out and develop, and they are made neither attractive nor interesting. Mondish, Colonel Raffler, and Captain Spark are left untouched and unchanged, and the lesson against jealousy supposedly learned by Sir Simon is dismally pro forma. The sincerity of Fielding's condemnation of his characters cannot be doubted. But when he mounts his soap-box and claims the dignity of the serious satirist, he becomes shrill and dull. Fielding's genius was for the playful, for burlesque and irony, and without the leaven of such techniques, his work is thick, stodgy, and disagreeable. A worse-handled plot than that of *The Universal Gallant* would be hard to find among equivalent plays of the 1730s.

[80] Rogers, p. 78; Cross, I, 172; Dudden, I, 152.

[81] Citations are to the Watts edn. of 1735.

To suppose that Fielding wished to be Congreve or Vanbrugh would be quite wrong. His purposes are more overtly social and moral: he is trying to make comedy a vehicle for instruction. The closest parallel I can point to in his own day is the work of James Miller. Plays like *The Mother-in-Law* and *The Man of Taste*, almost totally ignored by modern critics, are essentially more competent versions of what Fielding appears to have had in mind. The form towards which Fielding was groping was something like the *drame*. Twenty-five years before Diderot defined *comédie sérieuse* in his essay on dramatic poetry attached to *Le Père de famille* (1758), Fielding was trying to write that sort of play.

The English dramatists most like Fielding in this respect all come much later—Holcroft, Inchbald, Frederick Reynolds. Fielding would surely have liked Holcroft's *Duplicity* (1781) or Inchbald's *Every One Has His Fault* (1793) and would have felt at home among the crusading 1790s' writers of what Dougald MacMillan has dubbed 'social comedy'.[82] *The Universal Gallant* is not a successful specimen of that type, but we must grant that Fielding was determined to write more than tidy little afterpieces for the commercial theatre.

The degree to which the 'unhappy Fate' of *The Universal Gallant* upset Fielding is evident in his 'Advertisement'. If the playwright, says Fielding, 'be so unfortunate to depend on the success of his Labours for his Bread', then only 'an inhuman Creature indeed . . . would out of sport and wantonness prevent a Man from getting a Livelihood in an honest and inoffensive Way, and make a jest of starving him and his Family'. Fielding sounds both hurt and frightened. When he was attacked in 1732, his vanity was wounded, but he had made a lot of money and probably had confidence that he could do so again. He was now more vulnerable. He had a wife to support, and doubtless he hated to suffer so dismal a failure before his bride of ten weeks.

We can only guess what he made out of his third night: someone must have been in the theatre to hiss. But for the second year in a row his income from the theatre was probably little more than £100, and in 1734–35 it may have been significantly less. Worse yet, the prospects of getting new mainpieces staged were increasingly poor. Drury Lane had gone sour for him—and was about to embark on a repertory policy that basically excluded new plays. Covent Garden and Goodman's

[82] Dougald MacMillan, 'The Rise of Social Comedy in the Eighteenth Century', *Philological Quarterly*, 41 (1962), 330–8.

Fields were headed in much the same direction. In 1734–35 not even the Little Haymarket could serve as a refuge: it was occupied the whole season by a visiting troupe of French comedians. Lincoln's Inn Fields was available, but fringe company activity had fallen to its lowest level since 1727–28.

In February 1735 Fielding felt battered, disillusioned, and ill-used. In practical terms, his position was alarming. He was, as Pat Rogers says, 'a high-living, hard-drinking London gentleman . . . committed to an insecure profession and lacking the funds to keep up the way of life he wanted to lead'.[83] Fielding was in a very nasty predicament.

At this juncture fate intervened. Fielding's mother-in-law, Mrs Cradock, died in February 1735, leaving everything to her recently married daughter. The value of the inheritance is unknown. Murphy—admittedly a treacherous source—says it 'did not exceed fifteen hundred pounds'.[84] Whatever the sum, it seems to have been enough for their immediate needs. Fielding and his young wife apparently went to East Stour around March 1735 and stayed there several months. Perhaps Fielding set to work on a new play, or he may just have licked his wounds and recuperated his spirits. Perhaps he contemplated other ways of life: his plans are unknown. His career as a playwright was virtually in ruins, and his prospects of continuing to earn his living from the theatre were poor.

IV. THE BARNARD PLAYHOUSE BILL OF 1735

While Fielding was in the country pondering his future, events in London further jeopardized his theatrical career. Indeed, only by a quirk of fate was there a non-patent theatre for him to work in when he came to town in 1736.

On 5 March 1735 Sir John Barnard rose in the House of Commons and 'mov'd for a Bill to restrain the Number and scandalous Abuses of the Play-Houses'. He objected particularly to their corrupting influence upon youth and stressed 'how much these Evils would be increas'd if another Play-House should be built, as projected, in St *Martins le Grand*'.[85] The *Gentleman's Magazine* reports that 'At this

[83] Rogers, p. 77.

[84] Murphy, I, 27.

[85] This and subsequent descriptions of Parliamentary debate are drawn from 'Proceedings in the present Parliament', *Gentleman's Magazine* (December 1735), pp. 777–8. Plans for a new theatre in St Martin's le Grand were again announced in the

Motion many in the House seem'd to smile', and that 'at first it seem'd to be receiv'd with a Sort of Disdain', but the idea quickly found support among a wide spectrum of members, and the house voted 'That Leave be given to bring in a Bill for the Restraining the Number of Houses for playing of Interludes', and that Barnard should be chairman of a committee appointed to 'prepare and bring in the same'. This news was reported in the *Daily Advertiser* of 6 March, and 'panic' promptly set in among 'common players of interludes' and others potentially affected by the legislation.[86]

The whole history of the Barnard bill has recently been told in detail by Vincent Liesenfeld, and I see no reason to duplicate his exemplary account.[87] My concern is not with the parliamentary history of the legislation (which did not become law), but with the issues it raised and their implications for the future of unlicensed theatres in London.

Barnard's bill—drafted with the assistance of Nicholas Paxton[88]—received its first reading on 3 April. It acknowledges the Davenant and Killigrew patents, as well as those issued to the Royal Academy in 1719 and the triumvirate in 1732, and states that 'diverse ill-disposed and disorderly Persons, have of late taken upon themselves, without any legal Authority, to act' plays, and that 'the Laws now in being, have been found insufficient for preventing this great and growing Evil'. 'For Remedy' whereof, the bill proposes the following restrictions.[89]

(1) Only persons acting under Royal patent may perform.
(2) The King can issue new patents when the current twenty-one year patents expire, but not additional ones.
(3) The 'Number' of playhouses 'shall not exceed [*blank*]'.

Daily Post of 21 Feb. 1735. In *The Prompter* of 13 May 1735 Aaron Hill mentions a 'report' that the advertisement 'was a manager's stratagem to alarm and incense . . . magistrates [in the City of London], and . . . establish his throne (and that of his brother monarch) . . . by a Parliamentary exclusion of all other pretenders'. Precisely the same suspicion was apparently voiced when Fielding advertised plans to build his own theatre in 1737 (see pp. 224–5, below): whether it was justified in this case we do not know.

86 *Grub-street Journal*, 27 March 1735.

87 See Liesenfeld, ch. 2. In his Appendix B, Liesenfeld helpfully prints the Barnard bill itself and eight of the petitions presented to Parliament against it. I am indebted to his study throughout this section.

88 Liesenfeld, p. 30. Paxton was Solicitor to the Treasury. He had co-ordinated the ministry's efforts to regulate the press for some years, and had been involved in the attempt to suppress the Little Haymarket in 1731.

89 This is my own (selective) summary.

(4) Nothing profane, obscene, or offensive to piety or good manners shall be performed.
(5) Anyone performing without authority is to be deemed a rogue, vagabond, and sturdy beggar, and dealt with accordingly.[90]
(6) Enforcement is to be handled by mayors, bailiffs, and Justices of the Peace. Any such officer failing to suppress illegal acting is to forfeit [*blank*].[91]
(7) No patent theatre is 'upon any Pretence or Occasion whatsoever' to charge prices higher than 'what hath hitherto been usually and customarily taken . . . upon common and ordinary Occasions'.

This is an odd agglomeration of provisions. Sir John Barnard was an alderman in the city and was to become Lord Mayor in 1737; he spoke for the aggrieved business community. The bill's intent, very simply, was to put Goodman's Fields out of business and prevent the erection of any new theatres in or near the City of London. Outright prohibition of plays and playhouses would have violated the terms of royal patents, but the framers came as close to total prohibition as they could. The bill significantly infringes Royal prerogative, forbidding the King to make grants of a kind his predecessors had made. The blank after 'Number' of playhouses to be allowed probably reflects doubt over the status of the original Davenant and Killigrew patents. John Rich held both of them, and owned two theatres. But in theory these patents had been 'united' in 1682: did Rich have the right to operate one theatre or two? And if two, could he sell the Killigrew patent to someone else, thereby conferring authority to perform on that person? Enforcement is to be by local authorities rather than by the Lord Chamberlain and the Master of the Revels—and, as written, the bill outlaws *all* performances outside of London, in the process depriving the Master of the Revels of his traditional right to license strollers. The stipulation about charging only 'ordinary' prices appears to be a sop thrown in for the benefit of those who did attend plays and objected to 'raised' prices.

The uproar caused by the bill was considerable. The theatrical community clamoured against it; people hostile to plays and play-

[90] The penalty is left blank in the original printed bill. It was filled in this way in ink in the Harvard copy, which was plainly the intent of the bill. Many blanks were left in the printed draft of the original bill, evidently to permit Parliament to debate appropriate specifics.

[91] '£50' is inked into the Harvard copy.

houses saw it as a blow for purity and social good; reformers protested that the bill did nothing to improve the theatres it left in place. Twentieth-century scholars have generally been surprised to discover that there was *no* public opposition to the bill in principle. No denunciations appeared in the newspapers, no passionate speeches were made in defence of a free theatre. The idea that theatres should be regulated, and their number limited, appears to have been accepted by almost everyone. Opposition was expressed only by those with special interests.

The shareholders in Goodman's Fields argued that the bill would 'destroy their *Legal Right*' by rendering their investment worthless, which is very much what Henry Giffard said in his petition to Parliament. Both petitions expressed the hope that if the theatre were shut, Parliament would grant 'Equivalent' compensation for this invasion of property right. The actors at Goodman's Fields protested that shutting the theatre 'would absolutely deprive above 300 Persons of the *Common Necessaries* of *Life*'. John Rich complained that unless he were allowed to operate both Lincoln's Inn Fields and Covent Garden he would suffer serious financial loss, since he was liable for rent on both. The Master of the Revels protested that his office had 'always Licensed and Authorized Players of Interludes'. The actors of Drury Lane and Covent Garden expressed fear that the bill would reduce them to '*abject Slavery*' if the patentees established a new cartel. And those who held the Drury Lane lease complained that if the patentee removed his company to other premises, 'the LESSEES will be forc'd to *pay* this *great Rent* [£920 per annum] without daring to make any Use of the Play-House, which must necessarily end in THEIR RUIN'.[92] The stroller Tony Aston hurried to town to point out that 'this Bill points directly at a total rural Extirpation: Whereas it is humbly to be presum'd, the prime Intention of it was only to destroy *Goodman's Field* Playhouse'.[93]

Obviously, these were self-serving arguments, but Giffard and the

[92] *The Case of the several Persons upon whose Subscription the Theatre at Goodman's Fields hath been built* (Arnott and Robinson, no. 168); *The Case of Henry Giffard* (Arnott and Robinson, no. 165); *The Case of the Comedians, &c. belonging to the Theatre in Goodman's Fields* (Arnott and Robinson, no. 167); *Mr. Rich's Case*; *The Case of Charles Lee . . . and Lestrange Symes*; *The Case of John Mills . . . and the Rest of the Comedians of the Theatres-Royal of Drury-Lane and Covent-Garden* (Arnott and Robinson, no. 166). All are reprinted by Liesenfeld. I have used the Harvard and Folger copies.

[93] *Tony Aston's Petition and Speech* (London, 1735). Arnott and Robinson, no. 2395. I have used the Folger copy (BL 11795.k.31[6] is defective).

owners of Goodman's Fields had indeed invested money in a venture that would simply be suppressed; John Rich owed money to the Lincoln's Inn Fields investors; Charles Lee's traditional rights of office as Master of the Revels were definitely infringed; the actors had every reason to fear a new cartel. But Parliament was deaf: many members evidently felt that no sympathy should be lavished on investors in incitements to vice, or on the rogues and vagabonds who worked in them. One of the speeches in the opening debate was a heated denunciation of the salaries paid to Italian opera singers and a complaint against 'the vast Gains which these Animals make by Presents, [and] by Benefit Nights'.[94] This was irrelevant to the point and content of the proposed bill, but it expressed the hostility of parliament men to highly paid entertainers whom they held in contempt.[95]

Most of the public support for Barnard's bill was predictable in source and content. Goodman's Fields was denounced as a public nuisance, a position endorsed by the Justices of Middlesex as well as the Lord Mayor, Aldermen, and Common Council of London.[96] The most interesting piece is *A Seasonable Examination of the Pleas and Pretensions of the Proprietors of, and Subscribers to, Playhouses, Erected in Defiance of the Royal Licence*, probably by Samuel Richardson.[97] It rehearses all the usual arguments against the corruption of youth and the risks of proximity to the city, and takes a heated view of what the author considers defiance of Royal authority. The author is in favour of restricting the number of theatres, but with equal passion he demands the imposition of censorship. The Barnard bill was designed to suppress non-patent *theatres*, but had virtually nothing to say about

[94] Quoted in the *Gentleman's Magazine* (Dec. 1735), p. 777.

[95] At the time of the actor rebellion of 1743 the performers encountered precisely this attitude on the part of the Lord Chamberlain. Thomas Davies tells us that 'They drew up a petition, in which they stated their grievances very exactly, and supported their claim to redress from a variety of facts which they offered to prove.' The Duke of Grafton, however, 'received the petition of the players with coldness: instead of examining into the merit of their complaints, he desired to know the amount of their annual stipends. He was much surprised to be informed, that a man could gain, merely by playing, the yearly salary of 500*l*. His Grace observed, that a near relation of his, who was then an inferior officer in the navy, exposed his life in behalf of his King and country for less than half that sum. All attempts to convince the Duke that justice and right were on the side of the petitioners, were to no purpose.' *Memoirs of Garrick*, I, 74–5.

[96] See the *Journal of the House of Commons*, 22 (1735), 450, 468–70.

[97] London, 1735. Arnott and Robinson, no. 170. On the authorship, see Alan D. McKillop, 'Richardson's Early Writings—Another Pamphlet', *Journal of English and Germanic Philology*, 53 (1954), 72–5.

plays, aside from the pro forma clause about acting nothing profane or offensive to piety and good manners. The author of *A Seasonable Examination* argues that the theatres should be supervised by an official board that would decide what plays should be performed, censor them, and enforce high standards of both quality and morality (29–30). Odd as this idea now seems to us, it was not new, and it had some supporters among proponents of the theatre—Aaron Hill, for instance.[98] There was public sentiment for a much closer regulation of the theatre than Barnard had proposed.[99]

Only an uncharacteristic piece of misjudgement by Walpole kept Parliament from putting Henry Fielding out of business as a playwright in spring 1735. All evidence suggests that Barnard's bill would have passed easily had Sir Robert Walpole not offered an amendment giving the Lord Chamberlain power to censor plays (21 April 1735). The *Gentleman's Magazine* reports:

> [The bill] was dropt . . . on Account of a Clause offer'd to be inserted therein, without which it was suggested his Majesty would not pass it: The Clause was to ratify and confirm (if not enlarge) the Power of the *Ld Chamberlain* of his Majesty's Houshold over the Players; which the worthy Gentlemen who promoted the Bill apprehended was either too great already, or had been too far exercis'd, in the Case of *Polly*, an Opera; and therefore they thought it more advisable to wait another Opportunity to get a Bill of this kind pass'd, rather than to establish by a Law a Power in a single Officer, so much under the Direction of the Crown, which Power might be exercis'd in an arbitrary Manner . . .

Sir John Barnard had been one of the principal opponents of the excise bill of 1733, and he was no friend to Walpole. He and his allies had no intention of putting regulatory power in the hands of the ministry.[100] Thus the Barnard bill failed, but the reasons for its failure

[98] See *The Prompter* of 21 March and 4 April 1735.

[99] e.g. in *The Grub-street Journal* of 17 April 1735 an anonymous correspondent proposes 'that one or more persons be appointed with a handsome salary to be pay'd by the state, who shall judge and determine betwixt the arbitrary proceedings of the managers of the Theatres, and the exorbitant claims of the actors. . . . That all plays, &c. be examined and authorized by the said officer, so that all plays, or such parts of them, as any way tend to corruption of manners, be excluded the Theatre. . . .' An even more sweeping proposal along such lines was made by 'Modulus' in the same journal on 27 March 1735. Back on 21 March 1734 the *Grub-street Journal* had published a proposal for the review of all plays by an 'academy' to be funded by Parliament and given £2,000 per annum for rewarding deserving authors. More such proposals could be cited.

[100] Whether George II really did demand that a censorship clause be added to the bill we do not know. It might have been his price for assenting to curtailment of the Royal prerogative, a subject on which he was extremely touchy.

should have been scant comfort to its opponents. Had Walpole simply let it go as drafted, we have every reason to believe that in September 1735 Drury Lane and Covent Garden would have been the only legal theatres in London, and perhaps in the whole of England.[101]

We should recognize that much of the zeal to suppress unlicensed theatres stemmed from bitter City opposition to Goodman's Fields. Had Giffard been a better politician, he might have made a tactful move to more distant quarters—as he was to do a year later in 1736–37, when he took his company to Lincoln's Inn Fields. But by 1735 the City was determined to get legislation passed that would protect it against any future incursion. Support for the unlicensed theatres seems to have been extremely limited. Edward Harley's parliamentary diary tells us that the bill was opposed 'by the young people of the House' and by friends of Sir William Lemmon ('ground Land-Lord of Goodmans fields playhouse'), but that 'The other Play Houses were for the Bill that They only might be established by law'.[102] From the standpoint of Fleetwood and Rich, the bill was a splendid idea, for it would give them a stranglehold monopoly enforced by law.

By all rights, the Barnard bill should have passed. Its failure was not proof that Parliament opposed censorship,[103] and it was anything but proof that Parliament would resist efforts to close non-patent theatres. Quite to the contrary, the bill had shown that there was widespread support for limiting the number of theatres. It was favoured by the City, by those opposed to the theatre on religious grounds, by the ministry, and by the patentees. The only real question was what kind of bill they could agree on. Liesenfeld seems to me essentially misleading, then, when he concludes that 'Parliament's refusal to control the playhouses meant that the only remaining threat against the nonpatent theaters had disappeared'.[104] The threat remained real and present.

Surprisingly, the vulnerability of non-patent theatres does not seem to have been apparent to theatrical insiders in 1735. Perhaps the failure of the patentees' efforts to quash the actor rebellion had made

[101] Depending on the final language of the bill, Lincoln's Inn Fields might have been tolerated under the Killigrew patent, and Liesenfeld raises the possibility that Tony Aston persuaded Parliament to reconsider the total ban proposed on theatrical activity outside Westminster (p. 45).

[102] Printed by Liesenfeld, p. 53.

[103] As has been claimed by Watson Nicholson, *The Struggle for a Free Stage in London* (London, 1906), p. 59.

[104] Liesenfeld, p. 58.

too deep an impression, even though the legal issue had never actually come to trial. Perhaps the actors counted too much on the solidity of the status quo. With the benefit of hindsight, we can see that the theatre was in a worse than precarious position. Paradoxically, the result of the ministry's failure to impose censorship was to encourage the theatres to be less cautious about what they presented—and the resulting plays were to help convince Parliament that censorship was needed. To this group of offending plays Fielding was to make some notable contributions.

5

Impresario at the Little Haymarket, 1736–1737

THE last and greatest phase of Fielding's career in the theatre was the result of simple necessity. In 1732 he had returned to Drury Lane as a prize catch, London's most popular playwright. Four seasons later he found himself just about where he had been in 1729–30—in need of a venue for his work. Indeed, his circumstances were actually worse, for the 'extended company' at the Little Haymarket had become moribund. In these inhospitable circumstances few options were available. Fielding became manager of his own company because that was the only way he could get his work performed.

We do not know if Fielding offered a new play to Drury Lane in the autumn of 1735, or whether he already knew that his work was not wanted there. He was desperate enough to approach John Rich about staging a play at Covent Garden. In the spring of 1736, following the triumph of *Pasquin*, Fielding dedicated *Tumble-Down Dick* to Rich, sneeringly expressing his gratitude for Rich's refusal of his proposals. '... as *Pasquin* has proved of greater Advantage to me, than it could have been at any other Play-House, under their present Regulations, I am oblig'd to you for the Indifference you shew'd at my Proposal to you of bringing a Play on your Stage this Winter, which immediately determin'd me against any further pursuing that Project....' Whether Fielding actually offered a manuscript or merely made an inquiry is not clear. All modern scholars seem to have accepted Cross's offhand assertion that the play Rich rejected was 'doubtless' *Pasquin*,[1] but I question this. *Pasquin* was not Rich's sort of play; Fielding implies that parts of it were composed at high speed;[2] and there is a good deal of venom against Rich in it. Perhaps this was added after the rejection of an early draft, but the probability is that *Pasquin* was a topical production written in the winter of 1736.

As an alternative hypothesis, I would suggest that the work Fielding had in mind was *The Good Natur'd Man*, which was not published in his

[1] Cross, I, 178.

[2] Pillage says in *Eurydice Hiss'd* (45) that the muse who bore *Pasquin* 'inspir'd my Pen / To write nine Scenes with Spirit in one Day'.

lifetime and was not performed until 1778. He mentions this play in his preface to the *Miscellanies*, where he says that when Garrick asked him in 1742

> if I had any Play by me ... I answered him, I had one almost finished. ... When I came to revise this Play, which had likewise [i.e. like *The Wedding-Day*] lain by me some Years, tho' formed on a much better Plan, and at an Age when I was much more equal to the Task, than the former; I found I had allowed myself too little Time for the perfecting it; but I was resolved to execute my Promise, and accordingly, at the appointed Day I produced five Acts, which were entitled, *The Good-natured Man*.[3]

Fielding goes on to explain that he was dissatisfied with it; that it lacked an appropriate part for Garrick; and that he suddenly remembered *The Wedding-Day* and substituted that. We can deduce that in 1742 *The Good-Natur'd Man* had been laid aside for some years, but that it does *not* date from around 1728–30, when Fielding wrote most of his original five-act plays.

The summer or autumn of 1735 seems to me a highly probable time for Fielding to have written *The Good-Natur'd Man*. He needed a couple of new pieces for the season of 1735–36, and the design of the play strongly suggests an attempt to get away from the satiric stance of *The Modern Husband* and *The Universal Gallant*, and to adopt a formula more agreeable to the town. Fielding was, I would guess, thinking about James Miller's recent successes and trying to move in that direction. But, since this is speculation on my part, I have relegated my discussion of *The Good-Natur'd Man* to Appendix II. We should not forget, however, that although Fielding's move into rehearsal plays seems natural and desirable to us, it was not what he wanted to do. As Pat Rogers says, 'If the Drury Lane management had gone on its accustomed way, he would very likely have continued to produce the mixture as before, with a special emphasis on the orthodox five-act comedies in which he obviously wished to excel.'[4] In *The Good-Natur'd Man* we see, I believe, Fielding's last attempt to do that kind of work.

The patent houses' lack of interest in new plays was not confined to those written by Henry Fielding. We have strong (if neglected) evidence that in the season of 1735–36 Drury Lane and Covent Garden tried a new kind of cartel. On 12 December 1735 Fleetwood and Rich signed the following agreement.

[3] *Miscellanies*, vol. I, ed. Miller, pp. 5–6.
[4] Rogers, p. 71.

Memorandum it is agreed on between Charles Fleetwood and Jno. Rich Esqrs That they agree to divide all moneys at Each play house (Viz the Theatre Royall in Drury Lane and the Theatre Royall in Convent-Garden [*sic*]) above Fifty pounds share and share like for the remainder part of this season, and to pay to Each other so much money as shall be wanting to make up fifty pounds Each Night, and to meet once a week to Ballance accounts Dec ye 12 1735 begining on Saterday the 13th: NB Wee agree if any difference should arise relating to the above agreement to be determined by W Greenwood Esqr

Wittness	Wallter Greenwood	Chas: Fleetwood
	John Ellys	Jno. Rich[5]

This agreement makes competition pointless. Each house is indemnified against loss if the other makes more than its £50 house charge, and profits are to be equally divided. This was probably intended as a first step towards a fuller union. The attractions of such co-operation for the patentees were obvious.[6] I suspect that at this time the two patentees seriously contemplated the idea that they should 'enter into a joint Partnership, and engage the best Actors, who should act occasionally at both Houses, performing always a Comedy at one House and a Tragedy at the other'.[7] The scheme was dropped because of 'a Breach . . . between Mr. *R--h* and Mr. *Fl--t---d*'. Dates and details remain cloudy, but the profit-sharing agreement tells us just how unreceptive the patent houses were to new plays in the winter of 1735–36.

If any confirmation is needed, it is evident in the statistics for these years.[8] See Table 3. In 1732–33 the five London theatres mounted 14 new mainpieces and 13 new afterpieces. After 1714 the patent companies had never been enormously receptive to new scripts, but between 1730 and 1732, under pressure of competition, they had accepted several each year. By 1735–36 they had clearly decided to adopt a different repertory policy. Fielding could not have known in

[5] Folger Y.d. 135. This is a facsimile of 1837. The Folger holds three other copies of the facsimile, but I do not know the whereabouts of the original. I have silently supplied a few missing letters in the text.

[6] Back in late July or Aug. 1733 Highmore *et al.* had denied that 'the Managers of both Houses' planned 'to play alternately three Times a Week, and, by that Artifice, reduce the Salaries of each Company to one Half of their present Value'. *An Impartial State of the Present Dispute*, p. 4.

[7] This plan is described by the author of *An Apology For . . . T......... C....., Comedian*, p. 97, who puts it in spring 1734. I have already explained why that date is unlikely (see p. 180, above), though of course such a scheme could have been discussed at that time.

[8] For fuller figs. and analysis, see Hume, *The Rakish Stage*, pp. 298–301.

TABLE 3: New Mainpieces

	Drury Lane	LIF/CG	Goodman's Fields	Other venues
1732–33	2	3	2	7
1733–34	3	2	0	3
1734–35	4	2	0	2
1735–36	1	0	1	5
1736–37	1	0	4*	7

* The Goodman's Fields company moved to Lincoln's Inn Fields this season.

the autumn of 1735 just how grim the figures were going to be, but looking at them now, we can understand his cold reception from the patentees. Nor did he have an alternative at Goodman's Fields. In 1735–36, for the first time in three years, Giffard did mount some almost 'new' mainpieces—exactly two of them: Aaron Hill's *King Henry the Fifth* and James Sterling's *The Parricide*. Interestingly, no author benefit was advertised for either. I strongly suspect that both plays were 'given' to the house by authors who could afford to be content with performance alone, a luxury not available to Fielding.

I. THE GREAT MOGUL'S COMPANY (1736)

We do not know when Fielding came to town, when he realized that he would have to produce his own plays, or how he went about doing so. The biographers have skated lightly over some formidable questions. Did Fielding plan a permanent company or a one-shot venture? How much capital did he need? Where did his actors come from? On what basis did the company occupy the Little Haymarket? What were its expenses and income? Hard evidence on these matters is in very short supply, but we can say a good deal more about them than has hitherto seemed possible.

Assembling a Company

The circumstances in which Fielding constituted and ran 'his company' in 1736 have always confused scholars. He did not exactly start from scratch, but he did not take over a going concern. Our difficulties are compounded by our not knowing when Fielding became responsible for performances at the Little Haymarket (or when he ceased to be so). Between summer and 10 December 1735 only four plays were given there. From December to February fourteen performances took place, all of them featuring old main-pieces, most of them from the classic repertory (*The Recruiting Officer*, *The Beaux Stratagem*, *The Spanish Fryar*, and the like). Pat Rogers assumes that Fielding put on this trickle of standard fare, and that in February he reorganized the troupe in preparation for the première of *Pasquin* on 5 March, an event that gave him the 'breakthrough' he needed.[9] I suspect, however, that most or all of the performances before 5 March were by a casual group unconnected with Fielding. The performance of 29 December was advertised as 'By a Company of Comedians under the Direction of Mr Odell'. Of thirty-nine advertised actors and actresses who performed at the Little Haymarket during the winter, only fourteen worked with Fielding in the spring. I hypothesize that Fielding returned to London around December 1735 or January 1736,[10] was rebuffed by John Rich (and perhaps by Fleetwood and Giffard as well), and decided that he must turn entrepreneur. The first clear reference to Fielding as 'Great Mogul' at the head of his 'Company of English Comedians' is in the *London Daily Post and General Advertiser* advertisement of 24 February, promising *Pasquin* for 5 March.

Why did Fielding not go to Odell, evidently the organizer of the group that was using the Little Haymarket from time to time? Two reasons are obvious. For one, Odell's 'company' was very feeble indeed. For another, Odell was politically conservative, and Fielding had probably already decided to present abrasive topical material. And for a third, we may wonder if he was sufficiently sick of managers that he was prepared to see what he could do for himself.

Fielding probably had no choice of venue. Lincoln's Inn Fields could be rented night by night, but his relations with John Rich were unfriendly, and *Pasquin* contains some nasty swipes at him. If Fielding did not want to risk getting evicted after the first night, he had to use the Little Haymarket.

How much capital was required to float the troupe? Probably very little. We may presume that the actors and house servants were paid stipulated sums out of the receipts for each performance. To judge

[9] Rogers, pp. 86–7.

[10] Aaron Hill says in *The Prompter* of 2 April 1736 that Fielding 'retired into the country [*i.e. in March 1735*] where he has continued ever since, till this winter'. To judge from his known theatrical activity, Fielding's normal pattern was to leave town in the early summer and return in late autumn.

from the general practice of the time, nothing was paid for rehearsals. Even if Fielding started preparations for *Pasquin* at the beginning of February, money owed for salaries should have been negligible. I would guess that both scenery and costumes were absolutely minimal. The scenic requirements of *Pasquin* are virtually nil—'The Play-House' and a 'room' or two.[11] The advertisement for the première says 'N.B. The Cloaths are old, but the Jokes intirely new.' I interpret this to mean that costumes were pulled from whatever minimal 'stock' the Little Haymarket maintained—or alternatively, that the actors provided their own. Judging from the practice at Lincoln's Inn Fields, Fielding probably had to put up house rent in advance. He must have paid a copyist to write out the actors' 'sides'. He may have had to pay something for rehearsal space in February. And provision of refreshments during rehearsals would no doubt have been well received. But nothing in the script implies significant incidental expense, and £25 would probably have seen so simple a play to the stage.

Fielding certainly had that, and no great risk was involved.[12] At worst, Fielding (and his partners, if any) might have lost three or four nights' expenses and a total of no more than £100. How much of the risk (and the potential profit) were Fielding's? Impossible to say. What little we know comes from an anecdote first published in 1780 by Thomas Davies, who had been a very junior actor with Fielding's troupe in 1736. 'About the year 1735', says Davies, James Ralph 'commenced a managing partner with Mr. Fielding in the Haymarket theatre', but 'poor Ralph, I believe, had no other share in the management than viewing and repining at the success of his partner. However, he espoused a play of Mrs. Cooper ... called The Nobleman, a comedy which I believe was acted at the Haymarket in May 1736, condemned the first night, and never afterwards resumed.'[13] Whether this means that James Ralph was co-owner, or friend and assistant, or dogsbody is anyone's guess. Because the company never advertised a benefit for Fielding, but did give *Pasquin* as a benefit for Ralph (31 March), I would imagine that Ralph was no

[11] The scenic demands of *Tumble-Down Dick* are more elaborate and specific. I suspect that they reflect the availability of cash to pay for them.

[12] Thomas Cleary points out that 'whatever remained' of Charlotte's inheritance 'no doubt helped Fielding to organize his own company' (p. 75). True, though Fielding probably needed money mostly to live on. In modern buying power, £25 represented anything between £1,000 and £2,000, depending on how one cares to calculate.

[13] Thomas Davies, *Memoirs of the Life of David Garrick*, I, 262–3. (Mrs Cooper's play was actually performed for 3 nights.)

more than assistant or junior partner, but the matter remains insoluble on present evidence.[14]

Exactly how Fielding went about assembling actors we will probably never know. We have no reason to believe that in February 1736 he was looking beyond an extremely limited set of offerings. The initial plan was probably to do *Pasquin* and Ralph's *The Astrologer*, and then see how the venture was faring.[15] As in 1730 and 1731, casts seem to have been hired for particular shows, with the assumption that the pool provided by the 'extended company' would supply additions and replacements as needed. Fielding may have recruited by word of mouth, or there may have been an actors' hang-out that served as a place to exchange information and solicit fringe performers. All Fielding needed was a single cast, not a repertory company.

Critics' assumptions about the troupe that Fielding put together for *Pasquin* do not square with the facts. Dudden tells us that Fielding 'took the Little Theatre in the Haymarket, and organized the players who were performing there into a troupe'[16]—but what 'organized' means he does not say. And in fact, the majority of Fielding's performers had not been at the theatre earlier in 1735–36. Even odder is Pat Rogers' assertion that the company was 'based on a nucleus of the younger players from Drury Lane'.[17] Probably only two (and no more than four) of the initial performers had ever been regularly employed at Drury Lane, even in bit parts.[18]

The company Fielding assembled in March 1736 was even more a scratch group than scholars have realized.[19] Of the forty-four named

[14] Benjamin Victor (I, 66) says that James 'Lacy, with many others, became Adventurers with the late Mr. *Fielding* at the little Theatre in the *Haymarket*'. This may imply profit-sharing, but there is no other evidence of that, and I am inclined to think Victor simply meant that the actors were freelancing with a speculative venture.

[15] *The Astrologer* was scheduled for 26 March but 'postponed by the run of *Pasquin*', according to the advertisement for 24 March. The company never did get around to staging Ralph's play, which was finally performed at Drury Lane in 1744. Such neglect seems unlikely if Ralph were an equal partner.

[16] Dudden, I, 170.

[17] Rogers, p. 86.

[18] John Roberts had worked at Drury Lane in 1732 and perhaps at other times (*The London Stage Index* confuses John and Ellis Roberts). The dancer Topham, jun., basically a freelancer, had performed there occasionally. The Messrs Jones active in the twenties and thirties cannot be disentangled with confidence. Mrs Egerton is known to have taken a minor role at Drury Lane in May 1729. The only genuine Drury Lane performer of any rank was Charlotte Charke, hired away in the second week of the run of *Pasquin* (see discussion below).

[19] For complete lists of the known personnel of Fielding's companies in 1736 and 1737, see Burling and Hume, 'Theatrical Companies at the Little Haymarket, 1720–

actors and actresses who appeared with the company between 5 March and 2 July, fourteen were veteran fringe performers.[20] Eight were fairly new fringe performers.[21] Three were established junior performers at other houses.[22] No fewer than seventeen were apparently new to the London theatre in 1735–36.[23] Moreover, not a single one was (or ever became) a front-line performer. I suspect that Mary Elmy and Miss Gerrard (two of the better-known names in the season roster) joined *only* for a performance of *The Beggar's Opera* on 26 June. And 'Chapman' was not (as is usually assumed) the well-known second-rank actor Thomas Chapman, who was earning 16*s*. 8*d*. per day at Covent Garden this year. The Haymarket Chapman, employed only as a walk-on in *Tumble-Down Dick*, appears to be otherwise unknown. (The *London Stage Index* confuses the two, and places Thomas Chapman at both Covent Garden and the Little Haymarket on the night of 29 April 1736.)

The list of performers hired for the première of *Pasquin* on 5 March 1736 can fairly be called dismal: it does not compare well with the personnel of Reynolds's day in 1730 and 1731. But of course *Pasquin* does not require subtle acting or depth of characterization. John Roberts was perhaps the best of the lot. Lacy, Machen, Pullen, and Miss Jones were at least thoroughly experienced, if undistinguished. Each of them had a benefit or shared in one, as did Elizabeth Burgess (evidently a success as Miss Stich) and Woodburn, who was advertised on 7 May as 'Treasurer'. His benefit was presumably a reward for administrative services, since he was a very minor performer.

I suspect that as soon as Fielding realized *Pasquin* would be a success, he hastened to improve his sorry band of actors. Within two weeks, he scored a coup, hiring Charlotte Charke (Colley Cibber's

1737'. *The London Stage* makes no effort to distinguish between different companies at the Little Haymarket, and its composite rosters for the theatre are disastrously incomplete and inaccurate. More than 300 actors' names are simply omitted between 1720 and 1737.

[20] Jones, Lacy, Machen, Pullen, Roberts, Topham, Turner, Williams, Yates, Mrs Egerton, Mrs Elmy, Mrs Jones, Miss J. Jones, Mrs Talbot.

[21] Boothby, Castiglione, Freeman, Lowder, Russell, Woodburn, Mrs Burgess, Mrs Ferguson, jun.

[22] Charlotte Charke (from Drury Lane); Mrs Gerrard and Miss Roberts (from Goodman's Fields).

[23] Adams, Blakes, Chapman, Collard, Davis [Thomas Davies], Phoenix, Rosamond, Master Sherwin, Smith, T. Smyth, Strensham, Wallis, Mlle Beaumaunt, Mrs Eaton, Miss Karver, Mrs Mills, Mrs Pile.

transvestite daughter) away from Drury Lane. This very odd young lady had quarrelled with her father and brother, and her satiric play *The Art of Management* (York Buildings, 24 September 1735) had presented so contemptuous a picture of Fleetwood that the Drury Lane management was glad to see the last of her, even without notice in mid-season. She joined the Little Haymarket troupe on either 18 or 19 March (the 11th or 12th night of *Pasquin*), replacing a nonentity (Yates) as Lord Place.

Even with the addition of Charke, the troupe was suggestive of hedgerows. But we must realize that in March 1736 Fielding was probably not looking beyond the immediate present. The 'company' was adequate for a satire like *Pasquin*. Did Fielding have plans for a more long-term repertory? Quite possibly he did not. At James Ralph's urging, the company mounted Mrs Cooper's *The Nobleman; or, Family Quarrel* (three nights; not printed). Lillo's *Fatal Curiosity* (seven nights in all) was an interesting and innovative choice.[24] An afterpiece (lost) by Thomas Phillips called *The Rival Captains* managed a total of eight performances late in the spring. Single performances of *The Tragedy of Tragedies* and *The London Merchant* were for benefits. The latter was paired with Joseph Dorman's (?) *The Female Rake*, which survived only one night.[25] Whether the company could have made its

[24] Thomas Davies's introduction to *The Works of Mr. George Lillo* (London, 1775) gives us a virtually unique picture of Fielding as manager. 'It cannot be doubted that *Lillo* applied to the managers of the more regular theatres, and had been rejected, so that he was reduced to the necessity of having his play acted at an inferior Play-house. . . . However, Mr. Fielding . . . treated *Lillo* with great politeness and friendship. He took upon himself the management of the play, and the instruction of the actors. . . . Fielding was not merely content to revise the *Fatal Curiosity*, and to instruct the actors how to do justice to their parts. He warmly recommended the play to his friends and to the public. Besides all this he presented the author with a well written prologue. . . . Notwithstanding all the friendly endeavours of Fielding, this play met with very little success at its first representation. . . . But it is with pleasure I observe that Fielding generously persisted to serve the man whom he had once espoused; he tacked the *Fatal Curiosity* to his Historical Register, which was played with great success in the ensuing winter. The tragedy was acted to more advantage than before, and was often repeated, to the emolument of the author, and with the approbation of the public.' (I, xv–xvii, xxxv–xxxvi) Fielding's puff for *Fatal Curiosity* is printed in Appendix IV.

[25] We cannot be certain that this performance, done for the benefit of the author of *The Female Rake*, was given under the auspices of Fielding's management, even though Charlotte Charke played George Barnwell in the mainpiece. Potter may have rented the house to another group for the night. *The Female Rake* was published anonymously in 1736, 'Printed for J. Dormer', and, as D. F. Foxon says, is 'generally attributed to [Joseph] Dorman'. *English Verse 1701–1750* (Cambridge, 1975), I, 194. Identical advertisements in the *Daily Post* of 23 April 1736 and the *London Daily Post, and General Advertiser* of 26 April for the one performance say that it is 'For the Benefit of Mr.

expenses without *Pasquin* is to be doubted. Happily for Fielding, the success of *Pasquin* was sensational. As Mrs Pendarves wrote to Swift on 22 April: 'When I went out of Town last autumn the reigning madness was Faranelli, I find it now turn'd on Pasquin. . . .'[26]

Pasquin and *Tumble-Down Dick*

The play with which Fielding triumphantly reclaimed the favour of the town represents a substantial departure from anything he had done previously. *Pasquin* is invariably linked to *The Author's Farce*, and rightly so, but the differences are at least as important as the parallels. The title-page describes Fielding's new play as 'A Dramatick Satire on the Times: being the Rehearsal of Two Plays, viz. A Comedy call'd, *The Election*; And a Tragedy call'd, *The Life and Death of Common-Sense*'. He may have got the idea for *The Election* from the additional scenes he wrote for *Don Quixote in England* two years earlier. *The Life and Death of Common-Sense* is an 'emblematic' play-within-a-play that functions as at least a two-level allegory. No one doubts that *Pasquin* is highly topical, but in what sense it is political is far less clear.

Fielding had used playhouse-performance-with-commentary in Act III of *The Author's Farce*, but had never before employed rehearsal format. Buckingham's *The Rehearsal* (1671) remained a repertory staple, and Fielding must have been familiar with a number of other plays representing rehearsals or performance—for example, Gay's *The What d'ye Call It*, Odingsells' *Bayes's Opera*, and James Ralph's *The Fashionable Lady*.[27] Fielding makes good use of playhouse jokes (actors squabbling, playwrights feuding, prologues 'sent by friends', and so forth), but he is not just ragging the theatre, and nor is he content simply to pillory recognizable butts, as he had been in 1730. *Pasquin* is an altogether more sophisticated satire.

Fielding says explicitly in Trapwit's prologue that he will 'maul' both '*Court* and *Country* Party' and he is as good as his word. When *The Election* gets under way, the audience quickly discovers that while the Court candidates (Lord Place and Colonel Promise) give cash

DORMER, Author of the *Female Rake*, &c'. I cannot determine whether 'Dormer' is the author or simply an error for 'J. Dorman'.

[26] *The Correspondence of Jonathan Swift*, ed. Harold Williams, 5 vols. (Oxford, 1963–65), IV, 475.

[27] See pp. 67–8, above. For a survey of such works, see Dane Farnsworth Smith, *Plays About the Theatre in England from 'The Rehearsal' in 1671 to the Licensing Act in 1737* (New York, 1936).

bribes, the Country candidates (Sir Harry Fox-Chace and Squire Tankard) reply with gifts and orders for goods that are even more valuable. As Sir Harry puts his case to the avaricious Mayor and Aldermen of the nameless town, topping his rival's offer: 'I hate Bribery and Corruption: if this Corporation will not suffer it self to be bribed, there shall not be a poor Man in it' (11).[28] Even Cross had difficulty seeing this as anti-ministerial satire. Goldgar rightly says that

> *Pasquin* contained nothing overtly objectionable to the government, and its popularity was not attributed at the time to any satire on Walpole which might have been suspected. The papers sympathetic to the opposition gave it no support and made no effort to capitalize upon it, with the [Tory] *Grub-street Journal*, in fact, launching its first full-scale attack on Fielding in several years. The *Journal*'s criticism . . . was directed at Fielding's cynical indictment of *all* parties as equally corrupt and at the very generality of his satire on lawyers, physicians, and divines.[29]

But though *The Election* is harsh on both parties, Fustian's 'tragedy' is a different matter. The tale of Queen Ignorance and her supporters invading the realm of Queen Common-Sense and killing her is a fairly abstract allegory whose particulars point to literary targets. That Fielding was directing fire at opera and pantomime is indisputable. But he had learned to 'superimpose' targets,[30] and to anyone so minded, the 'tragedy' is ripe for 'application'. Unlike *The Fall of Mortimer*, it is not a heavy-handed smear against Walpole, and coming after *The Election* it would not immediately have excited partisan suspicions. But as Thomas Cleary has demonstrated, *The Life and Death of Common-Sense* can 'be seen as a stringent, oblique criticism of Walpole's corruptive system and a plea for Bolingbrokean political sanity'.[31]

Pasquin is an odd combination of indignant satire and seeming non-partisanship. This position is emphasized in Fielding's jokey advertisement for the première:

> By the Great Mogul's *Company* of English *Comedians*, *Newly Imported*. . . . N.B. Mr. Pasquin intending to lay about him with great Impartiality, hopes the Town will all attend, and very civilly give their Neighbours what they find

[28] Citations are to the Watts edn. of 1736.
[29] Goldgar, pp. 152–3.
[30] Hunter, p. 63.
[31] Cleary, p. 87.

belongs to 'em. N.B. The Cloaths are old, but the Jokes intirely new. . . . To prevent any Interruption in the Movement of the Persons in the Drama (some of whom are Machines) no Person whatever can possibly be admitted behind the Scenes. (*London Daily Post, and General Advertiser*, 5 March 1736)

Fielding was a brilliant publicist: he wrote the best playbills of the age, going far beyond the usual dull titles and lists.

Pasquin is a highly political play, but not a party document. Far more than any of the earlier plays, it has genuine political bite. For the first time Fielding displays towards politics the intense conviction of his earlier satires against libertinism and corrupt justices. The election scenes in *Don Quixote* are strictly incidental, literally an afterthought. The politics of *The Welsh Opera*, and even *The Grub-Street Opera*, amount to little more than an adjunct to the joys of burlesque and *lèse-majesté*. *Pasquin*, as numerous commentators have observed, is raucous and high-spirited, but like the 1728 *Dunciad*, it attacks serious evils.[32]

Only very recently has anyone proferred a convincing explanation for the marked change in Fielding's outlook evident in his plays of 1736 and 1737. Thomas Cleary points out that Fielding became political when his school friends Lyttelton and Pitt entered the Commons and joined the 'Broad Bottom' faction in the opposition.[33] Like many truths, this seems obvious as soon as it is pointed out, but it had escaped previous scholars, myself included. Whatever details in Cleary's picture of Fielding future scholars may want to quibble over, challenging his basic picture of Fielding's Broad Bottom allegiance will be difficult. Fielding's serious commitment to political issues follows upon the formation of the Broad Bottoms in September 1735, and for the rest of his life his sometimes disconcerting political shifts mirror those of his parliamentary friends. Many points that have seemed baffling, especially in the years 1741 and 1742, make much better sense in light of Cleary's construct.

With the Broad Bottom alliance in mind, Fielding's point of view in *Pasquin* becomes a lot more comprehensible. Brian McCrea finds his attacks on both ministry and opposition evidence of 'ambivalence' and inability 'to create a political identity. . . . Fielding's political values and allegiances remained confused'.[34] But as Cleary observes, for

[32] On connections to Pope, see particularly George Sherburn, 'The *Dunciad*, Book IV', *Texas Studies in English 1944* [1945], 174–90.

[33] See Thomas R. Cleary, *Henry Fielding: Political Writer*, particularly chs. 1 and 3.

[34] McCrea, pp. 75–7. I am baffled by McCrea's statement that even in 1737 Fielding

Pasquin to be 'simply an assault on Court corruption ... would have been alien to Fielding and Broad-Bottom theory and rhetoric.... We must understand that balanced satire served *his* opposition, that it reflected a typical attitude of the Broad-Bottom faction.'[35]

How well Fielding's audience understood *Pasquin* in March 1736 is questionable. Aaron Hill tells us that

> it was a considerable time before the tragedy (tho' by much the finer performance of the two) made its way. I have heard it called stupid, dull, nonsensical, with other appellations modern critics give to what they don't understand, and that the comedy supported it. A short, humorous advertisement engaged a close attention and set it a going, and now I believe it supports the comedy, at least it loses nothing by coming after it. (*The Prompter*, 2 April 1736)

I presume that the 'advertisement' referred to was an early notice for James Lacy's benefit (6 April): 'Mr. Fustian desires the Audience ... to take particular Notice of the Tragedy, there being several New and very deep Things to be spoke by the Ghost of Tragedy'. 'Fresh Jokes' were likewise advertised for Trapwit's [Roberts'] night (5 April). Fielding did not publish *Pasquin* until 8 April (unusually long after the première), and these notices suggest that he followed his pattern of tinkering and improving. At a guess, he inserted some clarifications and hints. Sneerwell says, for example, 'This Tragedy of yours, Mr. *Fustian*, I observe to be Emblematical; do you think it will be understood by the Audience' (46)—a hint that might well not have been present on 5 March. The full version of Lacy's benefit advertisement (not printed in *The London Stage*) contains a neat double-meaning that seems a blunt hint. 'N.B. As Mr. *Fustian* is the first Poet that ever cared to own, that he brought Ignorance upon the Stage, he hopes all her Friends will excuse his calling in particular upon them, and favour him with their Company along with the Friends of Common Sense, which he hopes will be the Foundation of a Coalition of Parties.' As Cleary comments, the call for a coalition could hardly put the Broad Bottom bias more plainly.[36]

Pasquin is so rich in topical allusions and hints that it makes hard

was 'still uncertain whether he belonged with the Tories or with the Whigs'. I am aware of no evidence that Fielding ever flirted with the Tories.

[35] Cleary, pp. 82, 84.

[36] Ibid., p. 88.

going today except for a specialist.[37] The 1736 audience was free to seek sly digs or just to enjoy the fun. Fielding provides a steady flow of local and topical allusions—King's Coffee House, the 'Act against Witches',[38] 'Fairbelly' (the celebrated castrato, Farinelli), Cibber's odes, skirmishes between *Fog's Journal* and the ministry's *Daily Gazetteer*, and so forth—but though he intermixes some innuendoes (Firebrand = Walpole?), he is careful never to force the audience to make hostile identifications. The play quite clearly says that England is politically corrupt and culturally degenerate, but the message is conveyed in a roundabout way and softened by theatrical high jinks. As a direct satirist, Fielding is hopelessly shrill and preachy. He is altogether more successful when he has to communicate his indictment by way of a dunce's play in rehearsal. For Fielding, indirection and burlesque are always best. *Pasquin* manages to be funny, boisterous, pointed, subtle—and highly effective.

Fielding probably got the idea for a related afterpiece even before *Pasquin* opened. On 28 February Drury Lane staged a new pantomime called *The Fall of Phaeton*, 'Invented' by Mr Pritchard, with music by Arne and scenery painted by Hayman.[39] It is neither better nor worse than most of its brethren, but the issue of Phaeton's legitimacy (he being the result of Clymene's adultery with Apollo) made the work particularly vulnerable to Fielding's talent for travesty. *Tumble-Down Dick: or, Phaeton in the Suds* is a close and merciless burlesque of Pritchard's pantomime,[40] but entirely comprehensible on its own. Fielding despised the form, and the travesty allowed him a crack at both Drury Lane (staging pantomime in preference to Fielding) and John Rich. To reduce the setting to a round-house (a place of detention), and the sun to a watchman's lantern, is effectively ridiculous, and the irrelevancies Fielding interjects are true to John

[37] Pending publication of the Wesleyan edn., the reader may wish to consult the helpful student edn. by O. M. Brack, jun., William Kupersmith, and Curt A. Zimansky (Iowa City, 1973).

[38] Referring to 9 George II, c. 5 (passed 11 February 1736), which ended prosecution for witchcraft.

[39] Cross states (I, 192) that 'Rich bore a hand' in this piece, and he is followed by a host of later scholars, none of whom cites any evidence. Perhaps I am missing something obvious, but Rich's helping Drury Lane with a pantomime seems inherently implausible, even in a time of financial co-operation between the patent houses.

[40] 'Invented by the Ingenious Monsieur *Sans Esprit*. The Musick compos'd by the Harmonious Signior *Warblerini*. And the Scenes painted by the Prodigious Mynheer *Van Bottom-Flat*' (title-page). Quotations are from the Watts edn. of 1736.

Rich's patchy genre.[41] The rehearsal format (Mr Machine's 'Entertainment' follows the practice of Fustian's tragedy in *Pasquin*) allows Fielding to intermix bewildered questions and commentary with the pantomime, and of course this ties the work very neatly to the mainpiece.

Although *Tumble-Down Dick* was said to be 'now practising' when *Pasquin* was published, it was not brought on until 29 April. In the meantime John Rich had staged a hasty counterblast at *Pasquin*, no doubt hoping both to revenge himself and to capitalize on its success. On 10 April *Marforio* was played as an afterpiece to *All for Love*. The author is unknown, and the piece was not published. The playbill seems promising. The subtitle was *The Critick of Taste* (Aaron Hill?), and the characters include the Great Mogul (clearly Fielding), Common Sense, the Embryo of Common Sense, and many others. Rich cribbed Fielding's playbill style and added: 'N.B. Mr Marforio hopes those who have paid a Visit to his Brother Pasquin, will not refuse him the same Favour. His Clothes are as old, and the Jokes somewhat more New.' But the work must have fallen very flat in performance, for despite a take of £169 it was not tried a second night.

Fielding gloats over its failure in his dedication of *Tumble-Down Dick*, a sarcastically abusive address to Rich himself. Fielding says that he owes 'the Original Hint . . . of the contrasted Poets' in *Pasquin* to a play 'brought on' by Rich 'in the *May*-Month'. Previous scholars seem to have passed this by in silence; the reference is to John (and Benjamin?) Hoadly's *The Contrast: A Tragi-Comical Rehearsal of Two Modern Plays* (lost), performed at Lincoln's Inn Fields on 30 April 1731.[42] The *Daily Journal* of 30 April 1731 contains a puff for the play, describing it as 'a Rehearsal upon Modern Comedy and Tragedy' in which 'Simile and Fustian . . . imaginary Authors, are not meant to represent any particular Persons'. This disclaimer notwithstanding, we may wonder if Thomson's *Sophonisba* (1730) was in the author's sights. The only specific hit we know was reported in the *Grub-street*

[41] For analysis of this feature of *Tumble-Down Dick*, see Charles Washburn Nichols, 'Fielding's Satire on Pantomime', *PMLA* 46 (1931), 1107–12. Readers should note, however, that Nichols' association of *Pasquin* and its afterpiece with an attack on pantomime in the *Grub-street Journal* of 'March 3, 1736' is unsound: that attack actually appeared in the issue of 3 March 1737.

[42] See Hoadly's letter to Garrick, 3 June 1773, in *The Private Correspondence of David Garrick with the Most Celebrated Persons of His Time* (London, 1831–32), I, 542. I owe this identification and reference to the independent kindness of Martin Battestin and Thomas Lockwood.

Journal of 27 May, which quotes an objection to 'all Ghosts from the bloody Ghosts in Richard the 3d, to that in Tom Thumb'. Fielding was not offended, for in his dedication he delivers a flowery compliment to John Hoadly, 'any of whose Wit, if I have preserved entire, I shall think it my chief Merit to the Town'.

Pasquin scored a success on the scale of *The Beggar's Opera*. Fielding himself crowed that he had found *Pasquin* 'of greater Advantage . . . than it could have been at any other Play-House'. But in practical terms, what did this amount to? How much money did Fielding make, and could he realistically hope to support himself as a playwright/entrepreneur?

Finances at the Little Haymarket

We possess no account books for the Little Haymarket in the 1720s or 1730s. Even anecdotal testimony about financial matters is virtually non-existent. But to judge the realism of Fielding's plans to build and operate his own theatre, we must have some sense of his company's income and expenses in 1736. At this point we either beg the question or proceed to guesswork. Admitting the perils, I prefer to do the latter. We know a fair amount about the finances of other theatres in the 1730s, and that knowledge can be applied to what we know of the Little Haymarket. The results cannot be treated as fact, but I think they can fairly be called 'informed conjecture'.

To calculate the probable gross income of Fielding's company, let us make the following assumptions. For the capacity of the house we will use Francis Gentleman's figures of 1752—i.e. 150 places in the boxes, 200 in the pit, and 300 in the gallery.[43] Unlike previous companies at the Little Haymarket, this one advertised the same regular prices as the patent theatres: 4*s*. for the boxes, 2*s*. 6*d*. for the pit, and 1*s*. for the (single) gallery.[44] A full house at these rates would yield £70.[45] On the third night, though it was not advertised as an author benefit, prices were raised to 5*s*. for both boxes and pit, 2*s*. for

[43] On the capacity of the Little Haymarket, see ch. 2, pp. 54–5, above.

[44] For most of the benefits, prices were raised to 5*s*. for boxes, 3*s*. for the pit, and 1*s*. 6*d*. or 2*s*. for the gallery. As of 1 April the regular prices seem to have become 5*s*., 3*s*., and 1*s*. 6*d*.—an unprecedented instance of a price increase imposed more than 20 nights into a long run (not recorded in *The London Stage*). There could hardly be clearer proof of *Pasquin*'s extraordinary success.

[45] On 8 April 1736 the *Grub-street Journal* estimated the nightly take at £80. This would be perfectly possible at regular prices with some crowding—an extra 20 in the boxes, 30 in the pit, and 50 in the gallery would generate the additional £10.

the gallery, which could have generated as much as £117 10*s*. Obviously one cannot presume a full house every night throughout a sixty-day run, but we do have evidence that attendance was strong for many weeks. On the seventeenth night Egmont found the house 'extremely Crowded', and when the Prince of Wales attended on the twentieth night, the papers reported that the performance was given 'to a crowded Audience . . . and many thousands of People turn'd away for want of room'.[46] Fielding did not add his afterpiece until 29 April, when *Pasquin* had run forty nights. For the sake of financial calculations, let us estimate overall business at 80 per cent of capacity through sixty performances. In so doing, I am deliberately ignoring some performances of other works, particularly *The Nobleman* (three nights) and *Fatal Curiosity* (six nights). Rogers says the latter 'did extremely good business', but I am aware of no evidence on the point.[47] If it had been popular, I suspect that it would have run longer and been picked up by other houses. Fielding may have made a modest profit on Lillo's play, but for the sake of conservative calculations, I propose to discount it. After 2 June we cannot be certain that Fielding was involved in the occasional performances at the Little Haymarket. *Pasquin* was put on three times in June and once in July, but these might be performances by a separate summer company.

Of the sixty performances of *Pasquin* at issue, twelve were benefits. The probability is that management recovered house charges on virtually all of those nights.[48] We are probably safe in assuming forty-seven non-benefit nights at £56 each (80 per cent of a £70 house), plus £100 on the third night, or a gross of at least £2,700. Given that Fielding raised prices in mid-run, this seems an extremely conservative estimate.

The pattern of benefits is interesting. The company mounted a total of seventy-six performances between 5 March and 26 June.[49] Nineteen of these were benefits, eight of them for various members of the cast

[46] This sounds like an exaggeration, but may refer to the course of the run, not just to the night of 29 March.

[47] Rogers, p. 89.

[48] Charlotte Charke says that she was 'engaged at Four Guineas *per* Week, with an Indulgence in Point of Charges' at her benefit, at which she 'cleared Sixty Guineas'. This might mean a 'clear' benefit or only reduced charges. See *A Narrative of the Life of Mrs Charlotte Charke*, 2nd edn. (London, 1755), p. 63. The salary is plausible (she had been getting £3 per week at Drury Lane (p. 61)) and so is 'Sixty Guineas'.

[49] The last was *The Beggar's Opera* and *The Mock Doctor* for a 'Gentlewoman of Seventy Years of Age' who played Dye Trapes. This may have been an independent venture.

and one for James Ralph. Three were 'distress' benefits, one of them coming startlingly early, on 11 March.[50] Six of the benefits were for authors—Lillo (2), Phillips (2), Cooper, and 'Dormer'. Lack of any advertised benefit for Fielding suggests that he was getting his cut as proprietor.[51]

What of expenses? How much John Potter charged for use of the Little Haymarket is not known. John Rich seems to have collected a minimum of £10 for the use of Lincoln's Inn Fields for a single night, and more often £12 12*s*., though when Henry Giffard took the house for three or four nights at a time, the rate was cut to £5 per night.[52] The Little Haymarket was smaller and was surely no more expensive. Granting that we do not know exactly what such a fee entitled the renter to (use of a minimal 'stock'? the services of a skeleton staff?), we are probably safe in guessing that Fielding had to pay no more than £10 a night for the use of the theatre. And if he guaranteed use several nights a week, he may well have received a substantial discount. In the 1720s Aaron Hill had contracted to pay Potter £540 for two limited seasons (see Chapter 1, pp. 12–13, above). If Hill had mounted fifty performances each season, his daily charge for the house would have averaged slightly above £5, and he apparently hoped to perform much oftener.

Actor salaries take us into the realm of guesswork. Charlotte Charke is the only performer for whom we have a specific figure. To get some sense of scale, let us consider Rich's payroll for 1735–36.[53] Top actors were paid set totals for the whole season (£250 for Mrs Horton, £200 for Mr Stephens); others received a flat fee every night the company performed.[54] Stoppelaer got 13*s*. 4*d*.; Mullart 10*s*.; the prompter Stede 5*s*. 6*d*., and so forth. Solid performers like Mrs Hallam and Mrs Bullock got 16*s*. 8*d*., which makes the 14*s*. Fielding was paying Mrs Charke respectable, but not lavish. Most of the middle- and upper-rank actors also received benefits. The likes of Mr Bancroft got 3*s*. 4*d*.

[50] 11 March for a 'Gentlewoman in Distress'; 27 April for 'One who has wrote for the Stage'; 25 May for 'the Daughter of General Nugent, who was kill'd in the Defence of Gibraltar'. Cross comments that Fielding's 'generosity—and how fine it is!—appears in several benefits . . .' (I, 198). Perhaps this is the whole truth, or part of it, but Fielding was a superb publicist, and unlicensed theatres needed to look good when they could.

[51] Cross is in error in saying that the 60th performance of *Pasquin* was given for Fielding's benefit on 26 May (I, 187). That night was advertised as one of Thomas Phillips' benefits.

[52] See extracts from Rich's accounts preserved in BL 11791.dd.18, vol. 3, fo. 186.

[53] Ibid., fos. 177–83.

[54] In other words, if the company 'dismissed', the actor was not paid for that day.

(and no benefit), and salaries for both men and women range as low as 1*s*. 8*d*. with no benefit. The Covent Garden company performed 172 nights this season; for people like Edward Thompson and Su. Rogers this multiplies out to a total annual income from Covent Garden of £14 6*s*. 8*d*. And virtually all of Fielding's personnel, we must remember, were people who could not even get a job with a patent theatre.

Fielding was paying his best-known performer 14*s*. per night (plus a benefit). *Pasquin* requires about twenty actors (with some doubling), and *Tumble-Down Dick* about twenty-five. The company probably had some supers for padding the 'mob' scenes, and of course it needed some staff. Unlike the patent theatres, this company presumably kept no permanent tailor, carpenter, *et al*., on the payroll, and it probably had an absolute minimum of dressers and other servants. Even when the company was performing only *Pasquin*, however, Fielding must have had some thirty-five people on his daily payroll, and when *Tumble-Down Dick* (and other works) were added, the number must have risen. We know of forty-four named performers, though not all of them were necessarily paid every night.[55] By the standards of the Covent Garden company, Fielding would have been generous in giving 8*s*. or 10*s*. to his more experienced people, and the unknowns in minor parts would have been fairly paid at 2*s*. or 3*s*., as would house servants. If we assume that Fielding had to pay fifty people 5*s* for each performance as an overall average, we will probably be neither much too high nor much too low. This would amount to £12 10*s*. in salaries each night. By being as ruthless as John Rich, Fielding could probably have reduced that total by a third. To have paid much more would have been out of line with going rates at established theatres. About 'incident charges' (the day-to-day costs that were not part of the 'constant charge') we are wholly in the dark. Very little should have had to be rented or specially prepared.[56] Fielding might well have spent significant sums on the particular scenes called for in *Tumble-Down Dick*,[57] but I would judge that £100 for the whole production would have been wildly extravagant. To be generous, let us allot £5

[55] I am hypothesizing a difference from the patent theatres, which did pay all regular employees for every performance.

[56] Something like the cart in *Tumble-Down Dick* probably had to be rented for each performance.

[57] e.g. King's Coffee House, a barber's shop, and the exteriors of Covent Garden and Drury Lane.

per night for incident charges plus the cost of getting up new productions.

On this basis, we can estimate total daily costs at £27 10*s*. (£10 for the house, £12 10*s*. for salaries, £5 for incident charge and new production allowance). If my estimate of a £56 average gross is reasonable, then *Pasquin* was making something like an average profit of £28 10*s*. per night. Over forty-seven nights this would amount to some £1,300, and with the third night at a higher rate, a total of about £1,400. By comparison, we can note that if the house had been full every night, the total profit would have been about £2,100. If it had averaged only 60 per cent of capacity, the profit would still have been about £780.

By good fortune, we possess daily receipts for Covent Garden this season. Rich's company gave 114 regular performances (ignoring forty-six benefits, four dismissals, and nineteen nights on which Handel occupied the theatre). Rich grossed nearly £8,000 (or about £70 per night), and with a constant charge of £50 he must have netted some £2,300. Even after allowing for some extravagant investment in his fancy productions, Rich ought to have come away with more than £1,000.[58] Covent Garden was a vastly bigger theatre, but we should observe that its average gross in 1735–36 was just about exactly the take from a full house at the Little Haymarket with prices at 4*s*., 2*s*. 6*d*., and 1*s*.

Allowing very generously for expenses, I think the Little Haymarket company must have made a profit of between £1,000 and £1,400 between March and July 1736.[59] Even half of £1,400 would have been a spectacular income for Fielding, and he was probably entitled to more than half. If James Ralph got only a benefit, Fielding may have scooped a jackpot. This was certainly the public perception. An anonymous cartoon shows the Queen of Common Sense (from *Pasquin*) pouring gold into Fielding's lap while handing John Rich a halter with which to hang himself.[60] All signs indicate that Fielding's profit was even greater than in his fabulous spring of 1732. Better yet, the figures on theatrical expense and income suggest that if Fielding

[58] In addition to his benefits and the £593 6*s*. 8*d*. (£3 6*s*. 8*d*. per night) he allowed himself as a performer.

[59] More is possible. If Fielding kept his salaries under £10 and negotiated a lower fee for the house (say £5), then an additional £400 is thinkable, or a total of around £1,800.

[60] *Catalogue of Prints and Drawings in the British Museum*, no. 2283. Described in detail by Cross, I, 203–4, and reproduced in the Henley edition of Fielding, XI, 164.

could keep the Little Haymarket two-thirds full while holding costs down, he would have a decidedly profitable venture. No doubt he spent the summer and autumn of 1736 thinking hard about such matters.

II. FIELDING'S FINAL SEASON AT THE LITTLE HAYMARKET (1737)

Virtually all discussions of Fielding's activities in the spring of 1737 are warped by knowledge of impending doom. To see everything in relationship to the Licensing Act is natural but undesirable: we need to recreate Fielding's situation without regard to later developments. Another problem has been that when Emmett Avery wrote his standard account of the subject, he had not yet discovered Fielding's scheme to build his own theatre.[61] And when he did so, Avery buried this important find in a tiny *Notes and Queries* item during the Second World War, with the result that it has gone almost unnoticed. Neither Dudden nor Rogers appears to have been aware of it. We need, therefore, to enquire afresh not only into how Fielding operated his company in 1737, but also into his plans for the future.

We have no idea what Fielding had in mind at the end of the 1735–36 season.[62] His fat profit from *Pasquin* can hardly have disposed him to return to Drury Lane, even if he were offered the opportunity. In the summer of 1736 Giffard moved his company from Goodman's Fields to Lincoln's Inn Fields, effectively blocking Fielding out of that theatre.[63] That Fielding would return to the Little Haymarket was a foregone conclusion. So was his development of the satiric mode he had hit upon in *Pasquin*. There is no evidence, however, that Fielding took an exclusive lease on the Little Haymarket, or that he meant to

[61] Emmett L. Avery, 'Fielding's Last Season with the Haymarket Theatre', *Modern Philology*, 36 (1939), 283–92.

[62] We do not even know when his involvement with the Little Haymarket ended in the summer of 1736. Both Cross (I, 202–3) and Dudden (I, 193) assume that Fielding was managing the theatre when it produced 'Jack Juniper's' *The Deposing and Death of Queen Gin* (2 August), which seems to have lasted only one night as an afterpiece. But from the scrappy performance records after 2 July (the last night of *Pasquin*), I would guess that the company reverted to its usual *ad hoc* arrangements at that point (if not earlier), and consequently that Fielding is unlikely to have 'lent assistance' to the author of *Queen Gin*, as Cross supposes.

[63] Supposing that Rich would have allowed him there. But if Fielding had guaranteed extended use, he might have been able to strike a deal. Like the Cibbers, John Rich valued money above spite.

try to operate a repertory company there in the spring of 1737. Nor do we know when he actually commenced operations.

No plays were performed at the Little Haymarket between 2 August and 3 December 1736,[64] and the two performances in December were by 'a Company of Volunteers'. On 7 January 1737 the *Daily Advertiser* ran a puff:

> We are inform'd, that a certain Author, tir'd with the vain Attempts he has often made in the Political Way, has taken it into his Head, as unwilling to lay down the Character of a Reformer, to explode the reigning Taste for dumb Shew and Machinery, and has declar'd open War against Harlequin, Punch, Pierot, and all the Modern Poets, viz. Joiners, Dancing-Masters, and Scene-Painters. 'Tis said . . . he will open the Campaign next Week, having three new Pieces in Rehearsal on the Stage of the little Theatre in the Hay-Market . . .

This has been taken to be Fielding, but did he regard himself as a failed political writer? The venture commenced on 14 January with *The Defeat of Apollo; or Harlequin Triumphant* (anonymous, lost), described in the *Daily Advertiser* on 12 January as a satire on poetic rant and pantomime, and *The Fall of Bob, Alias Gin*, often said to be anonymous and lost, but actually by John Kelly and published (before performance) in 1736.[65] The double bill ran three nights, and the mainpiece again on the 21st. On the 26th a triple bill was advertised: *The Mirrour* (anonymous and lost; described as 'A Dramatic Satire on the Times'), *The Defeat of Apollo*, and *The Mob in Despair* (anonymous, lost; called 'A Farce of two Acts'). The newspaper bill adds: 'As Mr Green could not possibly be sure of the House till Monday Night late, he hopes the Shortness of Time will plead his Excuse for not waiting on his Friends. . . .' This sounds very *ad hoc*, and who is 'Mr Green'? Is he the prompter who was advertised on 2 June 1731? He appears to have been responsible for this performance.[66] Both Loftis and Lockwood assume that Fielding was in control of the Little Haymarket from the beginning of January 1737;[67] Avery regards this as questionable; and I consider it unlikely.

[64] Consequently Rogers's statement (p. 90) that 'the Haymarket company continued to do well in the early part of the season' baffles me. There was no 'company' and there were no performances.

[65] For an excellent account of this play and its authorship, see Thomas Lockwood, 'John Kelly's "Lost" Play *The Fall of Bob* (1736)', *English Language Notes*, 22 (1984), 27–32.

[66] A 'Green' is also advertised as Blunt in *The Defeat of Apollo* for 26 Jan. This may well be the same Mr Green noted in the *Biographical Dictionary* (VI, 324–5) as '*fl*. 1725?–1729'.

[67] Loftis, *Politics of Drama*, p. 136; Lockwood, 'Kelly's "Lost" Play'.

This January group announced in *Fog's Journal* on 1 January 'that nothing which has been already play'd will be exhibited', and sputtered out after five performances. In February some group used the theatre for single performances of *All for Love, The Orphan, Cato*, and *The Twin-Rivals* (*The Recruiting Officer* had to be dismissed). On 25 February *Pasquin* was given by its 'original Company' for the benefit of Jones and Dove.[68] On the 28th Matthew Gardiner staged a pair of his plays for his own benefit. This varied pattern continued until 14 March, when *A Rehearsal of Kings* appeared—the first play demonstrably connected with Fielding. I strongly suspect that no single group was responsible for the miscellaneous fare that appeared before mid-March. We do not know who the despondent political writer of early January was, but John Kelly seems a better candidate than Fielding.

From evidence about his plans to build a theatre, we know that Fielding was in London by 2 February—and, by implication, for some time before that. Not until the 19th did he start a press campaign puffing his plans for the current season. During this month Fielding was clearly busy with both his spring season and long-term plans. But in the midst of what must have been a very hectic time, he brought out a new afterpiece at Drury Lane.

Eurydice

On 19 February 1737 a work billed as '*Eurydice; or, The Devil Henpeck'd* . . . by the Author of Pasquin' was performed as afterpiece to *Cato* at Drury Lane. The timing was unlucky: a disturbance involving gallery footmen reached such proportions that the Riot Act had (literally) to be read by the 'High Constable of *Westminster*', and in the hullabaloo Fielding's play expired, never to be revived.[69] Apparently the audience did not like what it managed to see and hear: when Fielding finally published the play in 1743 in the *Miscellanies*, he called it '*Eurydice*, a Farce: As it was d—mned at the Theatre-Royal in Drury-Lane'.

Most scholars have seen *Eurydice* as Fielding's final attempt to re-establish himself at Drury Lane. Thus Cross tells us that upon its

[68] Oddly, Dove has no known connection with the 1736 troupe; he had been with Giffard's company.

[69] For details, see the *Daily Journal* of 22 Feb. 1737, and Fielding's *Eurydice Hiss'd*. Cross states that 'a second performance . . . was attempted on the following Monday', but I have found no corroborative evidence. Fielding's afterpiece was advertised in the *Daily Post* of 21 Feb., but it was replaced by *The King and the Miller of Mansfield*.

failure Fielding 'fell back upon' the Little Haymarket.[70] This is misleading. Fielding's first puff for his Haymarket company appeared the same day as the ill-fated première of *Eurydice*: obviously he was already well advanced with plans for another season on his own. Why then did *Eurydice* appear at Drury Lane?

Pat Rogers says dubiously that 'for some reason' Fielding offered the piece to Drury Lane, and that 'with conscious magnanimity Charles Fleetwood agreed to put [it] on'.[71] In fact, the evidence points strongly to its having been written for Drury Lane. As a spoof on Italian opera, the piece requires two stellar singers. Drury Lane had Stoppelaer and Kitty Clive for Orpheus and Eurydice; Fielding could not have hoped to make the piece a success at the Little Haymarket without such principals. And far from doing Fielding a favour in staging the work, Fleetwood almost undoubtedly commissioned it. We have two potent arguments for this. First, Fielding would hardly have written so specially tailored a piece without assurance of performance. And second, he received an author's benefit on the night of the première. None of this is surprising. Management evidently wanted another of Fielding's musical afterpieces featuring Mrs Clive, and Fielding was probably happy to pick up the money. Ironically, he may have made a tidy sum despite the fiasco: the house was apparently well-populated on the occasion of the riot, and Fielding should have been entitled to the profits, flop notwithstanding.

Eurydice itself is a very entertaining travesty-satire. Fielding makes the time and setting contemporary: Orpheus and Eurydice are society butterflies from London, and hell is populated by courtiers like Captain Weazel and Mr Spindle, as happy to attend Pluto as George II. Incredulity is expressed at someone wanting to recover his wife (her jointure would be another matter), and Proserpine is outraged at the idea. Eurydice, we quickly discover, is much happier *sans* spouse, and she tricks Orpheus into looking back (281–82), which allows her to return to the social whirl in hell.[72] Interspersed with the action is commentary from the 'Author' and a 'Critick', sitting 'between the Scenes' during the première. Fielding was plainly enamoured of the reflexive techniques that had served him so well the previous season,

[70] Cross, I, 207. Cleary echoes the idea, saying that 'Fielding retreated to the Haymarket' (p. 96).

[71] Rogers, p. 91.

[72] Citations are to the 1st edn., part of vol. II of the 1743 *Miscellanies*.

and he uses them here to deliver commentary that is sometimes very blunt indeed.[73]

Fielding gets good comic mileage out of his henpecked Pluto and from the almost Shavian conceit that high-society life in London and in hell are indistinguishable (286). Orpheus becomes a spoof on the castrato Farinelli, the reigning star of the Opera of the Nobility. Fielding's rancorous contempt for Italian opera and castrati is abundantly expressed, directly and indirectly. Nine airs and a 'Grand Dance' and 'Chorus' are included, the airs preceded by 'Recitativo' in English. The music is apparently lost (we do not even know who composed it), but if done right it might have been quite amusing. *Orfeo* (a *pasticcio* with a text by Rolli) had been the Nobility Opera's biggest hit of the previous season. That Fielding saw it and disliked it seems probable.

Why *Eurydice* was never revived we do not know. The tone is decidedly sour. Perhaps the music was poorly done. And Fielding implies in *Eurydice Hiss'd* (42) that the audience was offended by Captain Weazel, an 'Army-Beau' not to be 'mistaken . . . for a Soldier' (263). But though the combination of operatic travesty, social satire, and direct 'authorial' commentary is a bit unwieldy, the piece deserved a better fate.

Plans for the Future

Fielding must have been reconstructing his acting company by 15 February at latest.[74] For this season, he would occupy the Little Haymarket and attempt to duplicate his success of the previous year. But we definitely know that he had already decided to build a theatre to house a company of his own. On 4 February the *Daily Advertiser* published a notice dated 2 February:

> Whereas it is agreed on between several Gentlemen, to erect a New Theatre for the exhibiting of Plays, Farces, Pantomimes, &c. all such Persons as are willing to undertake the said Building, are desir'd to bring their Plans for the same by the 2d of May next ensuing, in order to be laid before the said

[73] '. . . for an *English* People to support an extravagent *Italian* Opera, of which they understand nor relish neither the Sense nor the Sound, is heartily as ridiculous and much of a piece with an Eunuch's keeping a Mistress: nor do I know whether his Ability is more despised by his Mistress, or our Taste by our Singers.' (285)

[74] A performance of *The Twin-Rivals* on 9 Feb. 'By the Original Company who performed Pasquin' may be a hint that Fielding was regathering his forces.

Gentlemen, the Time and Place of which Meeting will be advertis'd in this Paper on the last of April.

Proportions of the Ground:

The North side 120 Feet; the West, square with the North, 130 Feet; the South 110 Feet; and the East, on a Bevil, joining the Parallels.

Note, There must be a Passage left to go round the Building, and the Stage to be 30 Feet wide at the first Scene; the Distance between Wall and Wall 80 Feet; and the Scene-Rooms, Green and Dressing Rooms, to be on the outside of the last mention'd Measure.

The Stage to be either North or South.[75]

This is elucidated by a follow-up notice on the 19th:

In a late Paragraph . . . it was insinuated, that there was a Design on foot for erecting a New Theatre, which by some Wise Heads was suppos'd to come from a certain Manager, in order to revive the Playhouse Bill this Session of Parliament; I think it proper therefore, in Justice to the Gentleman levell'd at, to inform the Publick, that it is actually intended for a Company of Comedians every Day expected here, late Servants to their Majesties KOULI KAN and THEODORE, who in the mean time will entertain the Town in the true Eastern manner, at the New Theatre in the Hay-Market, with a celebrated Piece call'd *A Rehearsal of Kings*. I am, Sir, yours, &c. *Agent for the Company*.[76]

Obviously Fielding had acquired rights to a suitable site, presumably somewhere in Westminster.

We can make some deductions from the dimensions given. 'Between Wall and Wall 80 Feet' I take to mean that 80 feet is the combined depth of stage and auditorium, with scene-rooms, dressing-rooms, and green-room added to make the full length of the theatre. This is about the length of Goodman's Fields, which measured about 82 feet (Covent Garden was about 95, Drury Lane about 99). The width of 30 feet 'at the first Scene' I take to mean that there should be 30 feet of clear space at the first set of closable shutters when they were drawn off. This would imply a proscenium opening width of about 33 feet. By contrast, Drury Lane was 31 feet, 6 inches; Covent Garden about 25 feet; Goodman's Fields 23 feet. We may deduce good

[75] First noticed by Emmett L. Avery, 'Proposals for a New London Theatre in 1737', *Notes and Queries*, 182 (1942), 286–7.

[76] Cross (I, 207) explains the name: Kuli Khan was 'the reigning Shah of Persia, whose exploits were bringing consternation to the minds of coffee-house politicians lest he should invade and conquer Europe as well as Asia'. King Theodore of Corsica was 'a military adventurer who was also frightening these same politicians'. Fielding was playing with the idea that his invasion was terrorizing pantomime-minded theatres (and perhaps graft-minded ministries as well).

proportions for an attractive, fan-shaped auditorium.[77] Audience capacity is impossible to calculate with any precision from the data available, but we may note that Goodman's Fields probably held about 750. A slightly wider building might well have held 850–900. Drury Lane held about 1,000 and Covent Garden about 1,400, but they were seldom full.

To construct such a theatre, Fielding would need outside financing. If he issued a public prospectus, it has apparently not survived, and no word of it survives. Such a document would presumably have been similar to Giffard's (see Appendix I). Fielding probably meant to wait until he had a builder's plan to show potential investors. No follow-up advertisement appeared at the end of April, and we learn from the dedication to *The Historical Register* that by early May Fielding had decided to remodel the Little Haymarket instead of building a new theatre. But if he had chosen to proceed, and there had been no Licensing Act, his scheme ought to have been entirely feasible.

To build the second Goodman's Fields, Giffard had raised £2,300 by promising investors 1*s*. 6*d*. for each acting day, with an estimated season of at least 160 days.[78] Giffard already had some scenery and costumes. Fielding would have had to start from scratch, and we do not know what he would have had to pay for his site. The usual arrangement was to sign a term agreement (for example, sixty-one years), with the tenant paying a 'fine' (initiation fee) plus annual 'ground-rent'. The amounts varied wildly. Fielding might easily have had to pay £500 'fine' and annual rent of £100. If we presume construction costs of £2,500, £500 for the ground, and £1,000 to acquire a modest stock of scenery and costumes, then the venture would need £4,000 of capital.

I doubt that Fielding intended to operate his own company 160 nights each year. His custom of tending to theatrical business between January and June was well-established, and when he took a lease on the Little Haymarket for 1738 it started 1 January and ran twenty-one weeks—i.e. to around the end of May. He may have hoped to rent out the new theatre night by night during the summer

[77] For examples of such theatres from this period, see Richard Leacroft, *The Development of the English Playhouse* (London, 1973), Chapter 5. For convenient tables of theatre dimensions, see Edward A. Langhans, 'The Theatres', *The London Theatre World*, pp. 61–5.

[78] For details, see ch. 3, pp. 146–7, above.

and autumn. He probably hoped to operate his own company about 100 nights, and as a conservative basis for paying back investors, let us use that figure.

If investors of £100 were paid 2*s*. 6*d*. per acting day for 100 days in the spring season, they would recover their capital in eight years, with Fielding paying a total of £5 per night to his building investors. This would be a thoroughly manageable sum. If investors had been made nervous by Barnard's playhouse bill of 1735 and wanted a shorter pay-back time, Fielding could (for example) have offered to pay 4*s*. per night for five years (thereby repaying all capital) and 2*s*. per night thereafter for the full term of the agreement (probably at least forty years). This would have raised his daily charge for the building to £8 for the first five years, but from the figures for 1736, we realize that he could afford it.

We can feel confident that for about £2,500 Fielding could have built an attractive theatre seating at least 800 people. To offer a more varied repertory than he had presented in 1736—a necessity, since he could not count on a sixty-night smash hit every year—he would certainly have needed more actors and staff than the original Great Mogul's Company had required. A house carpenter, property-man, tailor, *et al*., would have been necessary. Allowing forty performers and twenty regular salaried staff at an average of 8*s*. per acting day would generate a daily salary total of £24. This may be generous. I am supposing that Fielding would try to acquire a few middle-rank actors, and that they might get as much as 15*s*. per day. If I am correct that Fielding intended to stick with a short season, he would not have been able to lure regulars away from theatres prepared to give them a salary from September to May. But if he intended to feature new and experimental drama, he would have less need of actors competitive in standard repertory with those in the patent houses.

Allowing £5 for the building, £24 for salaries, and £5 for 'incident charge' and new productions gives an estimated daily charge of £34 (as compared with above £50 at the patent theatres). Against this, what income might be expected? To be conservative, let us hypothesize that the new theatre would hold only 700 people, but that it divided them more advantageously than the Little Haymarket—say 200 in the boxes, 300 in the pit, and 200 in a single gallery. Filled to capacity at regular prices (4*s*., 2*s*. 6*d*., and 1*s*.), such a theatre would yield £87 10*s*.

Plainly, Fielding could not count on anything like full houses, especially over a season of 100 nights or longer.[79] But if he could average just 50 per cent of capacity, these figures show a projected gross around £44 and a profit of about £10 per night. Allowing twenty benefits leaves eighty nights, or a potential profit of £800, plus whatever benefits Fielding might allow himself. (He took three in the spring of 1737.) If he could rent the theatre occasionally to travelling companies, nonce troupes, amateurs, and musicians in the summer and autumn, an annual income in excess of £1,000 was entirely possible.

This hypothesis rests on a great many ifs. But five years earlier Giffard had been able to bring off a very similar scheme. Why should Fielding, easily the most popular living playwright, not hope to do as well? What Fielding actually planned, what assumptions he made, and what figures he used in his own projections, we will probably never discover. We do know that in February 1737 he was seriously pursuing a plan to build his own theatre, and I have tried to show that such a scheme was entirely feasible.[80]

Had the Licensing Act not supervened, Fielding would almost undoubtedly have built a theatre or remodelled the Little Haymarket and run a more permanent company of his own there in 1738 and beyond. In the spring of 1737 this was what he expected to do. Far from tiring of the theatre, or looking for greener pastures, he was embarked on an ambitious scheme to settle himself permanently as a proprietor and theatrical entrepreneur. In the mean time, however, he had the present season to worry about.

Company Operations and Repertory

For the new season Fielding significantly altered his *modus operandi* of 1736. The previous year the company had relied almost exclusively on *Pasquin*. This year Fielding tried to vary his offerings. Between 14 March and 23 May the troupe staged eleven different plays, six of

[79] Extant figures for Covent Garden show that the gross varied from a low of £27 to a high of £207 on non-benefit nights in 1732–33 (the inaugural season) and from £17 to £185 in 1735–36. The overall average (excluding benefits) was £77 in the earlier season, £70 in the later.

[80] Replying to Avery's discovery of the 2 Feb. 1737 notice, J. Paul de Castro denies that Fielding could have intended to build a theatre (*Notes and Queries*, 182 (1942), 346). His arguments are that Fielding was in no 'financial position' to do so, and that Fielding was 'probably liable under an existing lease' for the Little Haymarket. I have tried to show that the former is not true, and there is no evidence for the latter.

them mainpieces.[81] Of the mainpieces, two were revivals from 1736: *Pasquin* (three nights) and *Fatal Curiosity* (eleven nights). In other words, Fielding was running a company genuinely devoted to contemporary plays. Nothing of the sort had ever been tried in the modern history of the London theatre. The arch-conservative repertory policies at the patent theatres (emulated by Giffard at Goodman's Fields) made such an approach timely. Anyone who wanted variety and experimentation would have to seek it from Fielding's company. And given the difficulties of getting work staged elsewhere, Fielding would certainly have plenty of scripts to consider. Whether they would be works that interested him is another matter.

Fielding opened the 1737 season with *A Rehearsal of Kings*, a lost, anonymous work that has occasioned much confusion. It was puffed on 8 March: 'We hear that the Great Mogul has acceeded to the Treaty of the Hay-Market ... the Town will be entertain'd there Tomorrow ... with a new Performance call'd a Rehearsal of Kings: which will be immediately succeeded by a Dramatick Piece call'd the Historical Register, for the Year 1736, written by the Author of Pasquin. We hear this has given great Alarm to all the Pantomimical Houses in London. ...' The initial performance did not come off as planned. The *Daily Advertiser* of 10 March reported: 'Last Night the Representation of the Rehearsal of Kings was disappointed by some Persons taking clandestinely Possession of the Hay-Market Playhouse, who were about Eight o'Clock committed to Bridewell for the same. On this Account several hundred Persons were turn'd away. We are assur'd that the Publick may depend on the aforesaid Play's being acted, as writ, Tomorrow.' But on the 11th it was 'put off, by an unforeseen Accident, 'till Monday next'.[82] The illegal seizure of the house on the ninth may well have been the result of political opposition, but the play was performed without recorded protest or disruption on the 14th, 15th, and 17th. It seems to have failed, for after that no more is heard of it.

[81] Two further plays, announced but never actually performed, are discussed in Section III, below.

[82] Liesenfeld, p. 85, suggests that this 'Accident' was probably the Lord Chamberlain's order of 10 March 1737 (PRO LC 5/160, p. 318) directing the managers of Drury Lane, Covent Garden, Lincoln's Inn Fields, and the Little Haymarket 'not to suffer any more plays &c to be acted on Wednesdays and Frydays during the time of Lent'. The Little Haymarket had previously ignored the long-standing ban on performance on those days. The Lord Chamberlain's jurisdiction over non-patent theatres was questionable at best, but defiance would have been impolitic.

Most of what we know about *A Rehearsal of Kings* comes from a letter by Aaron Hill. Some time before 28 February Fielding had evidently sent him a copy and asked him to write a prologue and epilogue. Hill begged off, and his comments, missed by the editors of *The London Stage* and ignored by recent scholars, tell us a lot about both Fielding's company and the nature of the play.

I See clearly, by some names among your performers, that you are not in so much danger as I apprehended, on that quarter. But, I am afraid, you are in more, than you imagine, on another; and that is, from the choice of your subject, and allegorical *remoteness* of your satire.—What I mean is, that the necessity your prudence was under, to disguise your design with *caution*, has so perplexed it with *doubtfulness*, that I am fearful, in the hurry of action, some of the *most meaning* allusions, in your piece, may be mistaken for scenes, which want any meaning at all; while, on the other side, among the few, who can penetrate purpose, and unravel the *satire*, as fast as they hear it, you will find *some* persons malignantly disposed, upon a supposition, that royalty, in general, should never be the mark of contempt. . . .

From these apprehensions, I am compelled to depend on your good-nature for excuse, as to the Prologue and Epilogue: I have good reasons for declining every hazard, of being considered in a light this would very unseasonably shew me in. . . .

I am heartily sorry, I had not sooner an idea of your plan; and flatter myself, I might have had the good fortune of persuading you to change it, for some other, not only of less dangerous provocation, but more promising likelyhood, to fall in with the publick capacity. . . .

Upon the whole, if it were possible, in so short a time as is left you, to substitute any other of your pieces, in place of this *Rehearsal of Kings*, I am convinced, you would avoid a disappointment, and perhaps, a mortification. . . .[83]

Hill was a pompous ass, but he was a veteran playwright, a seasoned critic, and a knowledgeable observer of the theatrical scene. If he thought *A Rehearsal of Kings* both politically dangerous and likely to be incomprehensible to most of the audience, he probably knew what he was talking about. Fielding went ahead with the production, but since the play is lost, Hill's assessment cannot be verified.[84] From the exceptionally full newspaper bill, with its references to 'Macplunder-

[83] Hill, *Works*, I, 239–41. Reprinted with commentary by Jack Richard Brown, 'From Aaron Hill to Henry Fielding?' *Philological Quarterly*, 18 (1939), 85–8.

[84] The common assertion that it was a revision of an anonymous lost play of 1692 is, however, a canard. There was no such lost play. See Judith Milhous and Robert D. Hume, 'Lost English Plays, 1660–1700', *Harvard Library Bulletin*, 25 (1977), 5–33, no. 72.

kan, King of Roguomania' and others, we may certainly deduce political satire. The authorship is unknown. Hill implies, or seems to believe, that the piece was by Fielding. The puff of 8 March says it is by 'a Gentleman who never wrote for the Stage'. Since the same puff identifies Fielding as the author of *The Historical Register*, I am inclined to think that he did not write *A Rehearsal of Kings*.

The work's short run suggests that Hill's doubts about its comprehensibility were well-founded. After one night of fill-in with *Pasquin* on 19 March, Fielding revived Lillo's *Fatal Curiosity*, with *The Historical Register* premièring as afterpiece. *Eurydice Hiss'd* replaced Lillo's tragedy on 13 April (with *The Historical Register* becoming the mainpiece), and the political farces ran to the end of the month. On 3 May the company premièred *The Sailor's Opera* (anon., lost). We know that it was 'A new Ballad Opera'; that it was subtitled 'An Example of Justice to present and future Times'; that it was said to be 'Written in Honour of the Gentlemen of the Navy'; and that Charlotte Charke played a character called Kitty Cable. Whether it was a romp that fell flat or an ironic satire that failed, we will probably never know. The next night the company tried another new show, this one called *Fame* (plus four subtitles). This too is lost. A puff in the *Daily Advertiser* on 30 April implies that James Lacy was the author. From the puff and the long list of characters in the newspaper bill, we can make some deductions about this 'Satyrical, Allegorical, Political, Philosophical Farce'. 'Fustian turn'd Auctioneer' suggests hints taken from *Pasquin* and *The Historical Register*. 'The exemplary Zeal of a worthy Magistrate, who so strictly adheres to the very Letter of the Law, as to send a rich and honest Merchant, and Freeholder, to the House of Correction, as a sturdy Beggar' suggests reminiscence of the Harper case, together with some of the mockery against the law of which Fielding was so fond. *The Sailor's Opera* managed four performances, *Fame* just one. Of *The Lordly Husband* (anon., lost), presented 16 May, we know only that it was a farce of two acts and that it died its first night.

Most of the company's afterpieces are equally obscure and met similarly dismal ends. *Sir Peevy Pet* was offered the last night of *A Rehearsal of Kings*, and never again. *The Female Free Mason* (lost; possibly by William Hatchett) was a short farce added to the usual double bill on 25 April, probably as a vehicle for Hatchett's mistress, Eliza Haywood. The one new piece this season other than Fielding's own that survived and flourished was Henry Carey's delightful *The*

Dragon of Wantley (16 May). It enjoyed only three performances before the Little Haymarket was put out of business, but when it was picked up at Covent Garden the following October, it ran sixty-eight times during the season, and it was regularly revived for more than four decades. *The Dragon* is an exuberant operatic travesty with music by J. F. Lampe.[85] Handel himself is said to have admired the work, which had been refused at Drury Lane in 1735. Had Fielding's company been able to continue, *The Dragon* would have been another of its stunning successes.

The Little Haymarket repertory of 1737 was what gave Fielding his reputation as an anti-ministerial writer. Assessing it is difficult because so much of it is lost. *A Rehearsal of Kings*, *The Historical Register*, *Eurydice Hiss'd*, and *Fame* were clearly very political, and *The Sailor's Opera* appears to be at least somewhat so. A couple of these shows may have been withheld from print not because they were unsuccessful but because Fielding did not want the printed texts to make plain just how subversive they were. Fielding's reliance on topicality, innovation, and politics was virtually a matter of necessity; he could not compete with the patent houses on their own ground. Without impugning the sincerity of his new political outlook, we can admit that he capitalized brilliantly on it. Discounting Colley Cibber's personal animus, his shrewd account of this phase of Fielding's career is worth quoting.

> ... these so tolerated Companies gave Encouragement to a broken Wit to collect a fourth Company, who for some time acted Plays in the *Hay-Market* ... This enterprising Person ... had Sense enough to know that the best Plays with bad Actors would turn but to a very poor Account; and therefore found it necessary to give the Publick some Pieces of an extraordinary Kind ... that the greatest Dunce of an Actor could not spoil ... He knew, too, that as he was in haste to get Money, it would take up less time to be intrepidly abusive than decently entertaining; that to draw the Mob after him he must rake the Channel and pelt their Superiors.... (*Apology*, I, 286–7)

Fielding provided a genuine alternative in London entertainment, but one highly disagreeable to the ministry.

The failure rate at the Little Haymarket in 1737 is a sobering

[85] For an enthusiastic analysis, see Fiske, pp. 148–54. Fiske says that Rich produced the show because he 'found that [after the Licensing Act] the entire production ... could be had, fully rehearsed, for the asking' (150). I doubt this. The show could be staged by anyone who bought the published words and music, and I find no record of any of the Covent Garden performers having worked at the Little Haymarket in spring 1737.

reminder of how risky new plays can be, but one *Pasquin* or *Historical Register* or *Dragon of Wantley* could make up for a lot of flops, especially if they were staged on a minimal budget. Between 14 March and 23 May, Fielding's company gave forty-two performances, thirty-four of which included *The Historical Register* as either mainpiece or afterpiece. If it was not a triumph on the scale of *Pasquin*, it was clearly a great success; without it the season would probably have been unprofitable. Unlike the patent companies, Fielding could not coast comfortably for a month by putting on staple fare while rehearsing a new show. He might have mounted scratch productions of plays like *The Beaux Stratagem* and *All for Love*, but he never showed any disposition to do so. And without better actors, such productions could only have been woefully uncompetitive with those available at the other houses.

Despite Aaron Hill's grudging approval of the proposed cast of *A Rehearsal of Kings*, the performers Fielding advertised in the spring of 1737 do not seem to represent any advance over the previous season. Of eighteen actors named, only three are new: Ward, Eliza Haywood, and Mrs Lacy. Fielding's principals remained Charlotte Charke, John Roberts, Jones, and Miss Jones. He could hardly improve the group if he was offering support for only half a season each year.

Little can be said about finances in 1737. *The Historical Register* was very popular, but we have no evidence about how full the theatre was on its thirty-four nights, and nor can we tell how empty it may have been for some of the failures. That Fielding made a substantial profit seems certain, but I cannot find any way to estimate how much it was. The several occasions during the spring on which raised prices (5*s*., 3*s*., and 2*s*.) were charged suggest considerable success with the public.

Sixteen of the company's forty-two performances were benefits, three of them author-benefits for Fielding himself. The four benefits given to Lillo for eleven performances of *Fatal Curiosity* deserve special comment: by custom, the company owed Lillo *nothing* for the revival. James Lacy got a benefit (probably as author of *Fame*); Hatchett received one on 25 April (reasons unclear).[86] The anonymous author of *A Rehearsal of Kings* got its third night. Benefits were given to some principal actors (Roberts, Charke, Miss Jones), and the actor-treasurer Woodburn. A benefit for Eliza Haywood may have

[86] He may have been author of *The Female Free Mason*, but it was only a single 'scene'.

been just for acting or might indicate that she contributed one or more of the company's anonymous plays. A single charitable benefit was given 6 May. Payments to authors remain an unanswered question. Fielding was exceptionally generous in a couple of instances, but in others no benefit was advertised. Whether he paid the authors, and how much, we do not know.

The Historical Register and *Eurydice Hiss'd*

As in 1736, what made the season a success was new plays by Fielding himself. Once again, the afterpiece was a topical afterthought, and a happy one. Scholars usually dismiss the mainpiece politely as an almost plotless reprise of *Pasquin*, one whose heavy injection of partisan politics helped bring about the Licensing Act. There is a measure of truth in this, but it is not the whole story.

The Historical Register, For the Year 1736 extends the rehearsal technique Fielding had evolved in *Pasquin*, but it is a substantially different sort of work. Not only is it fiercely and openly hostile to Walpole, but it is built on different structural principles. Both make heavy use of reflexive commentary, but where *Pasquin* carefully preserves the pretence of a play within a play, *The Historical Register* does not. 'Trapwit's' *The Election* and 'Fustian's' *The Life and Death of Common-Sense* are (after a fashion) integral wholes, distinct from *Pasquin*. *The Historical Register* is both Fielding's play and Medley's interior play—and the author's name is an indication of 'his' work. Here Fielding abandons formal allegory for *satura* cum *potpourri*.[87] Like the annual survey from which the play takes its name (published since 1716), *The Historical Register* is basically a list, and one in which no connection is implied by juxtaposition. Modern critics have described the play as 'cabaret' and 'topical revue'. Fielding had not fully conceived the varied potentialities of 'That Was the Week that Was' or 'Monty Python', but he was getting there.

Fielding's principal targets are Cibber's odes (5);[88] taxation by the

[87] These terms are aptly applied by Morrissey in his introduction to *Tom Thumb* and *The Tragedy of Tragedies*, p. 1.

[88] All refs. are to the 48-page edn. of *The Historical Register* and *Eurydice Hiss'd* pub. J. Roberts (London, [1737]). Cross (III, 301) erroneously calls this 'The 2d edition, though not so named, with many alterations'. What he believed to be the 1st edn. (41 pages) turns out to be a piracy with a spurious 'J. Roberts' imprint, probably done in Edinburgh. The differences between the two are merely routine errors in a careless resetting. See William W. Appleton's Regents Restoration Drama Series edn. (Lincoln, Nebr., 1967), p. ix.

ministry (6–9);[89] society ladies' fascination with Farinelli (11–12); the priorities of high society, in which honesty, patriotism, and courage are unwanted, but interest at court is eagerly sought (14–20); Theophilus Cibber (20–2); Fleetwood's management of Drury Lane (24–5); Colley Cibber's revision of Shakespeare's *King John* (26–8); and the venality of opposition 'patriots' who are ready to abandon their principles for Walpole's gold (29–32).[90]

Fielding's handling of this *mélange* is simply brilliant. Unhampered by the constraints of plot and character development, he infuses each of the skits with genuine venom without ever becoming shrill or tedious. The felicitous touches are far too numerous to catalogue. Special mention may be made of the first politician (so 'deep' he never speaks), the appearance of the noted auctioneer Christopher Cock as 'Mr. Hen' (appropriately transsexed by Charlotte Charke), and 'Ground-Ivy's' (Colley Cibber's) sublime conviction that Shakespeare 'won't do' without a good deal of alteration and improvement by himself.[91] Many of the satiric targets are old favourites of Fielding's,

[89] Both overtly political scenes are, with ostentatious improbability, set in 'Corsica'. Dudden tells us that this was done 'with the object of avoiding trouble with the censor' (I, 199)—but at this time there was apparently no censor, and certainly no one vetted the scripts staged at unlicensed theatres.

[90] An exchange between Sowrwit and Medley implies that Fielding originally included a section mocking the 'two *Pollys*' row, but (as Medley says) cut it out because 'they were damn'd at my first Rehearsal' (28). This probably means that the first-night audience found the material stale or dull. In Nov. 1736 Fleetwood created an astonishing amount of fuss by proposing to replace the popular Kitty Clive with Theophilus Cibber's second wife, Susanna, as Polly in *The Beggar's Opera*. The 'Pollys' figure prominently in some 20 newspaper issues between 4 Nov. and 6 Jan. Giffard had already put the affair on stage at Lincoln's Inn Fields in *The Beggar's Pantomime: or, The Contending Colombines* (7 Dec.). It ran 29 times. Traditional actor rights as well as personalities were at issue. In her letter to the *London Daily Post, and General Advertiser* of 19 Nov. 1736, Clive cited 'a receiv'd Maxim in the Theatre, *That no Actor or Actress shall be depriv'd of a Part in which they have been well receiv'd, until they are render'd incapable of performing it either by Age or Sickness*'.

[91] In Feb. 1737 Cibber withdrew his alteration of *King John* from Drury Lane by walking off with the prompt copy after he realized at the end of rehearsals that the production could only be a fiasco. (See *An Apology For . . . T......... C....., Comedian*, pp. 82–3.) The work was not printed until it was performed at Covent Garden in 1745, but of course Fielding's actor friends at Drury Lane were able to tell him about the alterations. A performance of Shakespeare's original text at the Little Haymarket on 4 March (company auspices unknown) is clearly a swipe at Cibber. Thomas Davies states in his *Dramatic Miscellanies*, I, 4, that 'Fielding wrote a farce upon the subject [of Cibber's *King John*], which was played at the little theatre in the Haymarket, though I do not believe it is printed amongst his works.' No such play can now be identified in the Little Haymarket performance calendar for the spring of 1737.

but Medley's tolerant amusement at what he insists is merely fact deftly implies a less cheerful view of these subjects.

The highlight of the show is the marvellous auction in Act II. The crowd's response to 'A most curious Remnant of Political Honesty', 'Three Grains of Modesty', (etc.), amusingly insinuates points that Fielding tended to get preachy about. There are virtually no takers for anything but 'Interest at Court', but so greatly is that coveted that Lord Dapper (one of the 'spectators' watching the play) starts to bid for it (19). It goes for £1,000, and Fielding tops his point by having Banter sneer: 'I know a Shop where I can buy it for less' (i.e. from Walpole).

The somewhat random nature of its satire notwithstanding, *The Historical Register* was viewed (and is now remembered) as anti-ministerial propaganda. *Pasquin* had made a great deal of noise, but it was not seen as an offensively partisan document.[92] No one should doubt that *The Historical Register* is a biting attack on Walpole. It quickly generated the kind of partisan newspaper attack and defence so conspicuously absent in relation to *The Welsh Opera* and *Pasquin*.[93] If Broad Bottom policy were well served by a more balanced satire, why did Fielding, after seven years of relative caution, abruptly join the hue and cry after Walpole? Goldgar's explanation seems convincing. The opposition forces had recovered from the disappointment of the 1734 election, regrouped, and were barking fiercely by 1736 and 1737. Between the time of *Pasquin* and *The Historical Register*, the Prince of Wales had come into open opposition. A wit who proposed to amuse the town with topical satire could hardly ignore the political frenzy building against Walpole. Fielding's parliamentary friends probably egged him on; how personally committed he was to debunking Walpole is impossible to tell. Clever swipes at the minister sold tickets, and on present evidence there is no certainty that Fielding looked beyond that welcome fact.

The magnitude of the political difference between *Pasquin* and *The Historical Register* is evident in an angry ministerial denunciation of Fielding's new plays, published in the *Daily Gazetteer* on 7 May.[94] The

[92] Giffard produced it at Lincoln's Inn Fields, 24 Jan. 1737. It did not flourish there, but the production is evidence of its essential inoffensiveness to the ministry.

[93] See Goldgar, pp. 153–6.

[94] Signed 'An Adventurer in Politicks'; often ascribed to Lord Hervey. The heart of this essay is reprinted, together with Fielding's reply in *Common Sense* on 21 May, in Paulson and Lockwood, *Fielding: The Critical Heritage*, pp. 98–105.

anonymous author complains that Fielding's latest plays 'abuse ... Liberty of the Subject' in ways that '*might make a* RESTRAINT *necessary*'. In *Pasquin*, he says, 'the Author was general in his Satyr', but in *The Historical Register* and *Eurydice Hiss'd* he is offensively partisan, suggesting that '*all Government is but a Farce*'. Even Fielding's strokes against the opposition are turned against him. 'He has treated the Patriots no better than the Politicians: But this, instead of *extenuating* only *doubles* his Crime', for 'to turn *Patriotism*, the noblest of Characters, into a Jest . . . [is] equally blameable'. This is, he says, as bad as telling 'the *People*, that their *Religion* is a *Joke*. There are Things which ... ought to be Sacred; such are *Government* and *Religion*'. With some justice, the author inquires how Fielding's parliamentary friends will feel about such satire if they gain power.[95] Fielding replied with vigour just five days later in his 'Dedication to the Publick' of his new plays, and again in *Common Sense* on 21 May. He denies that he has called government a farce or that he has ridiculed patriotism, and insists loudly that freedom of the stage and freedom of the press ought to be held equally inviolable.

Whatever one's views on freedom of the stage, denying the acid factionalism of *The Historical Register* would be difficult. The bribes 'Quidam' gives the false patriots in Act III are not exactly a subtle comment on Walpole's *modus operandi*, and the bluntness of Fielding's views is only somewhat mitigated by the humour of Quidam's politics being linked to John Rich's picking the pockets of his customers by charging them extra for dancing (32). Whether Fielding wrote the piece in a spirit of outrage or merely with gleeful malice in the knowledge that it would make money makes little difference. The work is devastatingly nasty about Walpole, and no minister benefits from being made to look both craven and crooked.[96]

The addition of *Eurydice Hiss'd* on 13 April made Fielding's hostile intentions yet plainer.[97] The afterpiece is a dazzlingly skilful example of Fielding's superimposition of targets. Ostensibly ridiculing himself as 'Pillage' and the failure of *Eurydice* in February, he interweaves a

[95] On the evidence of *A Charge Delivered to the Grand Jury* (London, 1749), Fielding himself had little tolerance for dissent when writing as a ministerialist. His demands in that work for curbs on the licentiousness of stage and newspapers, and in particular for suppression of criticism of judges, suggest a considerable change of perspective since 1737.

[96] For the fullest political account of *The Historical Register*, see Cleary, pp. 96–102.

[97] For explication of the satire, see Woods, 'Notes on Three of Fielding's Plays', pp. 368–73; the Appleton edn.; and Cleary, pp. 102–6.

systematic set of allusions to Walpole, so that the 'farce' for which Pillage solicits and purchases supporters becomes a parliamentary bill. 'House' refers conveniently to both the theatre and the House of Commons. The poet's 'Levée' is a delicious burlesque of 'poetic' greatness, but also highly applicable to a certain great politician. 'Honestus' upholds fair judgement in the playhouse, but serves simultaneously as a handy mouthpiece for Broad Bottom principles and virtues.[98] No one can have been in much doubt about how to take all this. Having learned from the failure of *A Rehearsal of Kings*, Fielding was at pains to be clear. At the outset of *The Historical Register* one player says, 'I could wish, methinks, the Satire had been a little stronger, a little plainer', and another replies, 'I think it is plain enough' (2). Two pages later Sowrwit asks 'how is your Political connected with your Theatrical?' and Medley replies: 'O very easily—When my Politicks come to a Farce, they very naturally lead me to the Play-House, where, let me tell you, there are some Politicians too, where there is Lying, Flattering, Dissembling, Promising, Deceiving, and Undermining, as well as in any Court in Christendom.' When the Earl of Egmont attended the double bill on 18 April, he noted that *Eurydice Hiss'd* was 'an allegory on the loss of the Excise Bill. The whole was a satire on Sir Robert Walpole, and I observed that when any strong passages fell, the Prince [of Wales], who was there, clapped, especially when in favour of liberty.'[99] Little wonder the ministry was not amused.

To suggest that both parties engaged in some hanky-panky during elections was a far cry from exhibiting Walpole on stage as a scoundrel—and doing so three different ways in a single evening. With *Eurydice Hiss'd* Fielding escalated hostilities. When he had a politician say, 'Hang foreign Affairs, let us apply ourselves to Money' (8), or showed Quidam giving bribes, he definitely irked the ministry. But to judge by the article in the *Daily Gazetteer* of 7 May, the government found his equating Walpole with a failed farce-writer much more upsetting. *Eurydice Hiss'd* really is fiendishly clever, and Fielding elaborated the parallel with enthusiasm in his long dedication to the two plays. His solemn complaints about 'Mr. ------ . . . buying Actors at exorbitant Prices' makes no real sense when applied to Fleetwood (let alone Rich), but applies devastatingly to Walpole and Parliament. And

[98] 'Faith, Sir, my Voice shall never be corrupt. If I approve your Farce, I will applaud it; If not, I'll hiss it, tho' I hiss alone' (41).

[99] *The London Stage*, Part 3, II, 660.

the anecdote about the short-sighted gentleman named 'Bob' (who is tricked into protesting against a picture of an ass as a likeness of himself) does not pretend to be anything but an impudent swipe at Walpole. Never before had Fielding been so openly outrageous in anything he had staged or published. Brilliant and amusing it certainly was—but also highly offensive to the ministry.

III. THE LAST DAYS OF THE GREAT MOGUL'S COMPANY

Fielding's new farces were not the only plays that were annoying the government in the spring of 1737. Indeed, political plays of all stripes were getting produced. At Lincoln's Inn Fields Giffard tried the whole spectrum: a flaccid anti-opposition satire in John Hewitt's *A Tutor for the Beaus* (21 February); a virtual dramatization of Broad Bottom pamphlets in Francis Lynch's *The Independent Patriot* (12 February); and a dangerously outspoken 'parallel' play, William Havard's *King Charles the First* (1 March). Meanwhile Drury Lane mounted Robert Dodsley's *The King and the Miller of Mansfield* (29 January).[100] The Hewitt and Lynch plays survived just three nights apiece, but Havard's totalled twenty performances, and Dodsley's afterpiece ran seventeen straight nights and a total of thirty-five. Opposition propaganda was selling tickets at every theatre but Covent Garden, where John Rich prudently stuck to his usual fare.

King Charles the First is particularly striking because its 'majesty misled' theme leads to such dire consequences. Havard clearly implies that bad ministers can cause the downfall of kings. As published, the piece is at least as subversive as *The Fall of Mortimer*. In performance a good deal of detail reinforcing the parallels to George II and Walpole was cut,[101] but even so one can only wonder why the habitually cautious Giffard risked producing such a work. The 30th of January continued to be a fast-day for the martyrdom of Charles I (i.e. a time when theatres could not perform), and the suggestion that George II was doing things that might lead him to the block, however tactfully put, must have seemed seditious to many people. In his famous speech opposing the Licensing Act, the Earl of Chesterfield points to *King Charles the First* as a play that *should* have been

[100] For brief discussions, see Loftis, *Politics of Drama*, pp. 116–20; Cleary, pp. 95–6; Liesenfeld, pp. 80, 83.

[101] The cuts are indicated in the edn. of 1737.

suppressed.[102] *The King and the Miller of Mansfield* is far less radical, but in presenting a lecture on country ideology to an erring king, it verges on *lèse-majesté*, and its description of corruption at court is pretty blunt.[103] In the dedication to *The Historical Register*, Fielding links his play and Dodsley's as having been 'represented' as aiming at 'the Overthrow of the M----y'.[104] Not only Fielding but Fleetwood and Giffard seem to have lost all caution this spring.

Between the end of January and late May, approximately 100 performances of plays openly hostile to the ministry were staged at three of London's four theatres—an average of nearly one per night. Walpole probably felt that things were getting out of hand. But what could he do? He undoubtedly wanted to impose censorship, but attaching such a clause to Barnard's Bill in 1735 had made the bill's sponsors refuse to support it. Legislation to regulate and limit playhouses could probably be passed, though it would not silence offensive productions at Drury Lane or Covent Garden. But perhaps Walpole felt that half a prohibition was better than none.

If Fielding is right that Dodsley's play ruffled feathers at court, then the timing of the ministry's request on 14 February for leave to bring in a new bill against rogues and vagabonds is probably no coincidence. This bill reached its first reading on 9 March and then stalled, but it sent a nervous shudder through the theatre world.[105] The *Daily Post* of 29 March 1737 reports that 'The Actors of the several Theatres are in no small Pain about the present Act depending in the House of Commons call'd the Vagrant Act, for fear of being deem'd Vagabonds; and are therefore perpetually soliciting their Friends for a Clause in their Favour.' On the 25th a vigorous objection to regulation of the theatres was published in the *Daily Journal*'s 'Occasional Prompter'

[102] An imperfect version of the speech appeared in *Fog's Journal* on 2 July 1737. Different versions were published in the *Gentleman's Magazine* for July and the *London Magazine* for Aug. On the textual problems, see Liesenfeld, p. 232 n. 93.

[103] Some group produced *The King and the Miller of Mansfield* at the Little Haymarket on 2 March, testimony to its popularity, though it lasted only one night there. Cleary, p. 96, assumes that Fielding was responsible for this performance, and suggests that 'The Drury Lane management perhaps loaned it to tide him over' (i.e. until *A Rehearsal of Kings* was ready). But we have no proof that Fielding was involved (various groups were still using the Little Haymarket), and once published the play was in the public domain for any performers to use—hence no 'loan' was necessary.

[104] Fielding is inaccurate in saying that *The King and the Miller of Mansfield* is linked with his play in the *Daily Gazetteer* of 17 (i.e. 7) May. Martin Battestin points out to me that his reference is to a dialogue satire against Lyttelton in the *Daily Gazetteer* of 14 April, where the linkage is made.

[105] On this abortive bill, see Liesenfeld, pp. 81, 86.

series, a piece recently and plausibly attributed to Fielding.[106] Lockwood points out that 'any rogue-and-vagabond legislation always made the players jumpy', and this essay reflects their alarm.

The issue is possible reimposition of the patent monopoly: Fielding objects to 'Castration', but only in passing. The heart of the essay is his argument that a monopoly (or worse, a cartel) creates indifference to public opinion, and makes for discontented actors and a stodgy repertory. Fielding lambastes the old triumvirate management and pleads for toleration of the kind of theatre he was trying to run.

> ... any other Restraint whatever, than from the Laws now in being, would have prevented several Pieces, to which the Town have shewn great Favour, from ever appearing: Managers are always extremely cautious (while they flourish without it) of giving the least Offence to the higher Powers. This Caution has (to my Knowledge) struck out many beautiful and justifiable Strokes of Satire, from some Performances which have been, after Castration, exhibited. This Caution would, I am sure, intirely destroy the old Comedy, which seems at present greatly to flourish, in which we have an Author who is an acknowledged Proficient, and which may be of very signal Service to our Country; for Imposture has no greater Enemy than Theatrical Ridicule.

If Fielding wrote the article, it serves his own interests, but is not less true for that.

Why did Walpole allow this bill to die? Possibly he decided to approach the matter more circuitously by supporting the Universities of Cambridge and Oxford in their efforts to suppress theatrical performances in their vicinity—an issue which reached the floor of the House in March. Perhaps he thought that end of session would be more propitious than February. He may have realized that 'The Vision of the Golden Rump' (a satire published in *Common Sense* 19 and 26 March) could be used to support a demand for censorship if someone turned it into a play. We simply do not know. But the Licensing Act seems unlikely to have been a spur-of-the-moment inspiration on 20 May. The 'University' bill paved the way, and the *Daily Gazetteer* warning about the necessity of 'RESTRAINT' on 7 May looks very like a test of the political climate. The strong probability is that Walpole spent the spring grinding his teeth and laying plans that would not fail when he was finally ready to implement them.

[106] See Thomas Lockwood, 'A New Essay by Fielding', *Modern Philology*, 78 (1980), 48–58.

The Silencing of the Little Haymarket

As late as 12 May 1737 Fielding appears confident that he could proceed with his plans as entrepreneur. In his 'Dedication to the Publick' of *The Historical Register* he says:

> The very great Indulgence you have shewn my Performances at the little Theatre, these two last Years, have [*sic*] encouraged me to the Proposal of a Subscription for carrying on that Theatre, for beautifying and enlarging it, and procuring a better Company of Actors. If you think proper to subscribe to these Proposals, I assure you no Labour shall be spared, on my Side, to entertain you in a cheaper and better Manner than seems to be the Intention of any other. If Nature hath given me any Talents at ridiculing Vice and Imposture, I shall not be indolent, nor afraid of exerting them, while the Liberty of the Press and Stage subsists, that is to say, while we have any Liberty left among us.

Evidently he had decided to alter and improve the Little Haymarket rather than construct a new theatre from scratch. The reasons for his decision remain conjectural. His arrangements for a site may have fallen through; he may not have been pleased with plans or prices proposed by prospective builders; talk about new parliamentary regulation of 'rogues and vagabonds' may have alarmed potential investors. John Potter, anxious not to lose so regular a tenant, may have offered terms for the Little Haymarket too advantageous to refuse. Fielding's comment about 'while we have any Liberty left among us' I take as a dig at the *Daily Gazetteer* attacks of 14 April and 7 May. In short, we have every reason to believe that in mid-May 1737 Fielding fully expected to be in the 'scandal shop' business in 1738 and beyond.

On 20 May 1737 the House of Commons granted 'leave' to bring before it a bill 'to explain and amend' the vagrancy act of 12 Anne c. 23 'as relates to the common Players of Interludes'.[107] In all probability, Walpole had already drafted the relevant legislation, and the bill was duly presented for consideration on 24 May. This version—introduced by allies of the ministry, but without Walpole's direct participation—proposed to limit the number of playhouses, but not to impose censorship. Even before it was presented, this bill was ominously described in the *Daily Post* of 23 May:

[107] See Liesenfeld, ch. 6, esp. p. 123.

. . . a Bill is ordered into Parliament for suppressing the great Number of Play-Houses . . . so justly complained of, and for the future no Persons shall presume to Act any Play, &c. without first obtaining a Licence from the Lord Chamberlain of his Majesty's Houshold for the Time being, any Persons acting without such Licence to be deemed Vagrants and Punished as such, according to the Act of the 12th of Queen Anne.

Walpole needed to forge an alliance among members hostile to the theatre, both those who objected to the 'licentiousness' of the stage and those who simply wanted to suppress opposition satire. Not until the 24th or 25th did Walpole announce 'that he intended to move an additional clause to the bill that would empower the government to censor dramatic performances'.[108] The delay was deliberate: he had clearly planned to do so all along. By 28 May passage was considered inevitable. A letter of that date says simply: 'ye Bill will pass & no playhouse be allowed but in the Libertys of Westminster, & those to be licens'd & under the direction of the Lord Chamberlain.'[109]

Meanwhile, what of Fielding and his scandal shop? On 23 May the company gave what would be their final performance, *The Historical Register* and *Eurydice Hiss'd*. On Wednesday 25 May two new plays were advertised for the 30th:

Macheath turn'd Pyrate; or, Polly in India. An Opera. Very much taken, if not improv'd, from the famous Sequel of the late celebrated Mr. Gay. With a New Prologue proper to the Occasion. And after the Run of that, the Town will be entertain'd with a new Farce of two Acts, call'd *The King and Titi: or, The Medlars*. Taken from the History of Prince Titi. Originally written in French, and lately translated into English.

This is a very startling advertisement indeed. It says in so many words that Fielding will stage Gay's *Polly*, banned in 1729 amidst great controversy. Gay had made nearly £1,200 when he published it, but no company had ever risked performing the piece. To advertise *Polly* was to issue a direct challenge to Walpole: could he again block production? The second piece is lost, but its purport is plain. As Liesenfeld explains, *The King and Titi* was based on Hyacinthe Cordonnier de Saint-Hyacinthe's *Histoire du Prince Titi*, published in Paris in 1735, a work suggesting that the King and Queen would disinherit their eldest son (the Prince of Wales) in favour of a younger son (the Duke of

[108] Ibid., p. 129.
[109] Cited ibid., p. 140.

Cumberland).[110] Lockwood remarks that 'by the common understanding of the day' the piece 'might as well have been entitled *The Humours of King George and his Troublesome Son Frederick*'.[111]

To advertise such works daringly escalated Fielding's political risk. Perhaps he planned these productions before he realized what danger his theatre was in. Alternatively, we may wonder if he decided on the 20th that only desperate measures remained to him and hence threw caution to the winds. Public resentment over the banning of *Polly* had run high,[112] and Fielding may have hoped that its performance would provoke Walpole into retaliation of a sort that would give Parliament pause.

If Fielding hoped to create another *cause célèbre*, his scheme failed. Apparently no performances took place. Indeed, after the advertisements of 25 May there is total silence from and about the Little Haymarket. Virtually all scholars have assumed that, in Emmett Avery's words, Fielding 'simply closed the theater'.[113] But Fielding was neither frightened into silence nor resigned to the inevitable. We have strong evidence that Walpole did not wait for the passage of the Licensing Act to put Fielding out of business, but that instead he persuaded John Potter to prevent any further performances. The Licensing Act did not become law until 21 June, and did not take effect until the 24th. Walpole evidently did not relish the prospect of Fielding's spending a month kicking up all the fuss he could at the Little Haymarket while the town flocked there to rejoice in the scandal.

Our evidence is a letter from John Potter to Lord Chamberlain Grafton of 7 January 1737[/8] and a bill of 13 June 1737 that he resubmitted on 24 February 1737[/8].[114]

[110] Fielding's friend James Ralph reportedly had a manuscript related to this work among his papers at the time of his death, and he may well have been the adapter of the advertised farce. See ibid., p. 136, and John B. Shipley, 'James Ralph, Prince Titi, and the Black Box of Frederick, Prince of Wales', *Bulletin of the New York Public Library*, 71 (1967), 143–57.

[111] Thomas Lockwood, 'Fielding and the Licensing Act', forthcoming in *Huntington Library Quarterly*. I am grateful to Professor Lockwood for sending me an advance copy of this important article.

[112] It was mentioned by the *Gentleman's Magazine* in Dec. 1735 as one of the reasons Barnard would not accept Walpole's censorship provision in the playhouse bill that year.

[113] Avery, 'Fielding's Last Season', p. 291.

[114] Both items are preserved in Folger MS T.b. 3, a transcription by J. Payne Collier (inserted in a copy of Algernon Sidney's *Discourses concerning Government*, used as a scrapbook, between pp. 150 and 151). Despite the Collier connection, I see no reason to

To his Grace the Duke of Grafton. The representation of John Potter, owner of the new Theatre in the Haymarket.

May it Please your Grace

as my Inclination Lead me to my duty to obtain leave to waite on you and also to aply to the Right Honble Sir Robt. Walpole In Order to prevent what was Intended to Be Represented In my theatre in may last it was your Graces pleasure to declare I should meet with a Reward for such dutifull Behavior, and I have Rec'd the promise of Sir Robt walpole to the same purport with this addition soe soon as your Grace and Sir Robt should taulk on that head I should with the Rest of mankind find due Incurragement to bear an honnest mind. I therefore Begg Leave to address my self to your Grace that you would Be pleased to Remember me when you shall see sir Robt and I att the same time begg your Grace to beleive me faithfully attached to the utmost of my Power against all scandall & defamation. I am with all due defference your Graces most devoted Obedient and most humble servant

7 Janry 1737[/8] John Potter

We may deduce that in May 1737 Potter waited on Grafton and Walpole to inform them that something scandalous and defamatory was about to be produced at the Little Haymarket (i.e. *Macheath turn'd Pyrate* and *The King and Titi*?) and that they assured him that if he could 'prevent what was Intended to Be Represented' in his theatre, he would 'meet with a Reward for such dutifull Behavior'.

The proof that Potter did as he was bid is in the account of 'Loss by my theatre' he evidently submitted on 13 June 1737 and resubmitted in February 1738. There is no address or salutation.

24 Feb. 1737

Inclosed is the acct of my theatre youle please to Remember I Left a Coppy of my Representation with you on monday Last which I hope youle put in your Pockett on Sunday when you goe to the Duke of Graftons mr heidegger hath spoke to his Grace I am sir very desirous to have his Grace and Sir Robert walpole Informed of my Real Intention not to offend which I flatter my selfe youle doe me Justice In. I Recommend my selfe to your Good offices and am sir your most Obedient humble servt.

John Potter

doubt the authenticity of these documents. The letter was published by J. Paul de Castro in his reply to Avery's 'Proposals for a New London Theatre in 1737', where de Castro states that 'the original ... was in the possession of the late Percy Fitzgerald'. Nothing in the documents rings false; only a specialist would find them of interest; and Collier never seems to have used them.

13th June 1737	Loss by my theatre	
To one day Pullin		
To one day davie	seven days in all	
To one day Roberts	there were. Some	
To one day hatchet	agreed & the money	29.08.0
To one day Kaywood [Haywood?]	Returned all four	
To one day dapper	Guineas Each day	
To one day mathisone		

To taking down the scenes & decorations so that the theatre was Renderd Incapable of haveing any Play or other performance, and mens time & Carts To fill the same with deale & timber Bricks and Lime Charge of moveing those things	12.12.0
To money to Return mrs Coopper on her Contract	52.10.0
To money to Be paid By mrs Coopper and I suppose Mr fielding (he haveing Begun a subscription) for twenty one weeks from the first day of January next.	212.02.0
	306.12.0

This I submitt wholly to your own Liking

John Potter

In crudely eloquent words, this document tells us that Potter did not simply forbid Fielding to use the theatre, but ensured that it 'was Renderd Incapable of haveing any Play or other performance' by taking down the scenery and stacking the building high 'with deale & timber Bricks and Lime'. Potter plainly had no confidence that his orders would be obeyed, and he made certain that the building could not be seized and used in defiance of him. Fielding's company may well have held a short-term lease still in effect that entitled them to use the premises.

Other parts of the account rendered are also extremely interesting. Pullin, Davie[s], Roberts, Hatchett, and Mrs Haywood were all current performers with Fielding's company. Each of them appears to have paid four guineas for use of the theatre for 'one day', either for scheduled benefits or perhaps as part of a summer company. Whether the four guineas was the total fee (payable in advance) or merely a down-payment would be nice to know. No 'Dapper' appears in our records of London theatre personnel, but Dapper is a character played by Mr Ward in *The Historical Register*, and members of Fielding's company sometimes advertised character names instead of their own for benefits. 'Mathisone' I cannot identify. He or she may, of course, be unconnected with Fielding's troupe. Fielding may have had an exclusive contract for the use of the theatre after 14 March 1737, but it is unlikely to have extended much past the end of May.

The final two entries in the list of losses are fascinating but cryptic. A Mrs Cooper had evidently paid £52 10*s*. for an unspecified number of nights' use of the theatre. She was probably the Elizabeth Cooper whose play *The Nobleman* had been performed in May 1736 at James Ralph's urging.[115] Her connection with the company remains a mystery. Was she an investor in Fielding's company? Was she serving as business manager? The £52 10*s*. payment might concern a summer venture of her own, but the association of Cooper and Fielding in the next entry suggests her involvement in the regular company.[116] The information that Fielding had 'Begun a subscription' for 'twenty one weeks' from 1 January 1738 is new and important. Since Potter is calculating prospective loss—the money had not yet been paid—we may deduce that £212 2*s*. was the total price agreed for the use of the theatre for twenty-one weeks. Subtracting Sundays and dates lost in Lent, Fielding might have expected to give about a hundred performances, making the cost of the house just over £2 per night. Obviously this was an extremely attractive deal. The term 'subscription' might refer to investment in the company, to season tickets (imitating the opera companies), or to special ticket arrangements of the sort Giffard had tried at Lincoln's Inn Fields.[117]

The dutiful Mr Potter seems unlikely to have collected even his out-of-pocket expenses from Walpole or Grafton, but his bill explains very satisfactorily why the Little Haymarket fell so suddenly silent. It does not, however, tell us why the newspapers contain no protest about the episode. Why, we must ask, was the aggrieved Mr Fielding not trumpeting his wrongs in every opposition newspaper? This question carries us into some larger puzzles about Fielding's response—or lack of it—to the Licensing Act.

[115] She was also the author of *The Rival Widows*, which ran six nights at Covent Garden in Feb. 1735. I would guess that this is the same Mrs Cooper who performed occasionally with fringe companies between 1722 and 1734.

[116] Judith Milhous suggests to me the possibility that Mrs Cooper was renting the fruit (i.e. refreshments) concession at the Little Haymarket.

[117] In the *London Daily Post, and General Advertiser* of 13 November 1736 Giffard offered cut prices on blocks of 20 tickets paid for in advance: boxes £2 10*s*.; pit £1 10*s*.; gallery £1. One ticket per week to be valid (except at benefits); tickets could be transferred privately, but not advertised for sale or sold at the door. On 22 Nov. Giffard amended the scheme to allow use of two tickets per week and explained that 'those mark'd for any preceding Week will be taken during the Season'.

Fielding and the Licensing Act

Despite Pulteney's opposition in the House of Commons and Chesterfield's famous speech in the Lords, the Licensing Act sailed through Parliament without significant resistance.[118] The amendment incorporating Walpole's censorship provision passed in the Commons by 185 to sixty-three, and the bill as a whole was approved by voice vote. The final margin in the Lords was thirty-seven to five.[119] The details of the bill's introduction, amendment, and passage have been exhaustively presented and analysed by Liesenfeld, and I see no reason to cover the ground again.[120] My concern here is with Fielding in relation to the act.

The bill contains two central provisions.[121]

(1) Any person involved in performing plays for money, except by authority of a Royal patent or a licence from the Lord Chamberlain 'shall be deemed to be a Rogue and a Vagabond' and subject to applicable 'penalties and punishments'.

(2) A 'true Copy' of all plays, entertainments, prologues, and epilogues must be submitted to the Lord Chamberlain two weeks before intended performance for his approval. Any company presenting material not so approved is subject to a fine of £50 and loss of its authority to perform.

The first provision put Giffard and Fielding out of business. The second effectively removed political and social controversy from the British stage.[122]

Was the Licensing Act aimed specifically at Fielding? The ministry was clearly angered by *The Historical Register* and *Eurydice Hiss'd*.

[118] So quickly did Walpole move the bill through Parliament that virtually no public opposition was organized until passage was assured. *Common Sense* attacked the bill on 4 June. The *Craftsman* ran pieces against it on 28 May and 4 June (the latter tentatively ascribed to Fielding by Cleary, pp. 114–15), and *ex post facto* complaints on 18 and 25 June. The government put out a concentrated barrage in the *Daily Gazetteer*, with major items appearing on 4, 6, 8, 9, and 10 June. The proprietors of Goodman's Fields petitioned against the bill (PRO SP 36/25, fol. 256) and so did the lessees of Drury Lane (both petitions are printed by Liesenfeld, pp. 189–90), but there was nothing like the outcry generated by the Barnard bill in 1735.

[119] Liesenfeld, pp. 139, 141, 150.

[120] Liesenfeld's book so thoroughly supplants all previous studies of the subject that I see no reason even to cite them.

[121] The full text of the Licensing Act is printed by Liesenfeld, pp. 191–3.

[122] On the practical effects of licensing plays, see Conolly, *The Censorship of English Drama, 1737–1824*.

Indeed an anonymous writer in the *Daily Gazetteer* of 4 June says that 'the Government had no Thought' of introducing censorship until Fielding '*pav'd* the Way for the Subversion of the Stage, by introducing on it Matters quite foreign to its true Object'. The cliché in twentieth-century criticism is that Fielding's plays provoked the Licensing Act. This notion remains current despite a number of cautionary statements from modern authorities, but even the most cursory consideration shows that the idea is ridiculous. Walpole introduced his censorship provision in spring 1735, *before* Fielding had ever staged an obviously partisan play. Support for Barnard's bill demonstrates the degree to which a significant part of the public was hostile to the theatre *per se*. And the censorship imposed by the Licensing Act would not have survived many decades, let alone more than two centuries, if the act had been merely a device to silence Fielding. As Calhoun Winton has observed, throughout the eighteenth and nineteenth centuries, 'most segments of British society with anything approaching political or social influence believed in dramatic censorship'.[123] 'Walpole's act' was not specifically aimed at Fielding (though Walpole was doubtless happy to suppress a pest)—and the censorship it imposed reflected the will of the public.

The calamitous effects of the Licensing Act on British drama follow from the limitation to patent theatres, not from censorship. Political plays became virtually impossible, but the drama turned stodgy not because of censorship, or sentimentalism, or bourgeois audiences, but because without competition the theatre managers saw no reason to risk money on new plays, and certainly not on experimental ones. Fielding had to leave the theatre in 1737 not because he could no longer write political satires but because Drury Lane and Covent Garden reverted to the monopolistic ways of the mid-1720s. They had been heading that way as early as 1735, and the Licensing Act allowed them to settle comfortably into a non-competitive rut. Fielding could have written more afterpieces for Kitty Clive, but he could not have any hope of earning from Drury Lane and Covent Garden the £300 per annum to which he was accustomed. As in the 1720s, earning a living as a professional playwright became impossible, and it was to remain impossible for twenty years.

One nagging question about the passage of the Licensing Act concerns *The Golden Rump* and whether Fielding had anything to do

[123] Calhoun Winton, 'Dramatic Censorship', *The London Theatre World*, p. 286.

with it. Anecdotal evidence tells us that the obscene farce was sent to Giffard, who carried it to Walpole, who used it to horrify the House of Commons into accepting his censorship amendment.[124] As early as 1740, the knowledgeable author of 'Theophilus Cibber's' *Apology* says that the piece was written 'by a certain great Man's own Direction', with 'as much Scurrility and Treason larded in it as possible', and that '*Giffard* had a private Hint how to act in this Affair, and was promis'd great Things'—including a '*separate Licence*, or an Equivalent' (which Walpole then failed to deliver).[125] Some confirmatory evidence for part of this allegation is a letter from Giffard (evidently to Walpole): ''Tis with the greatest Difficulty, I have prevaild with my self to entertain a Thought of receiving any thing for the Stage, wch might carry in it the remotest Construction against any part of the Conduct of the present happy Administration ... I do a Violence to my Inclination, in being oblig'd to receive a Premium, for what my Principle disclaims, & on that Score shou'd reject, were I not bound by Fatal Necessity.'[126] How far in cahoots Giffard and Walpole may have been we do not know. To me, the letter seems to say that Giffard's financial problems at Lincoln's Inn Fields force him to ask for a reward for suppressing a play hostile to the administration. This may be disingenuous. If the play was *The Golden Rump*, we cannot suppose that Giffard would have dreamt of producing it, any more than a 1670s manager would have thought of staging *Sodom*. A play that so outraged Parliament was not a play that a sane manager would think of putting on. Whether *The Golden Rump* was a plant by Walpole, or a scurrilous joke that Giffard carried to Walpole for his own advantage, we may never know.

But did Fielding have anything to do with it? *The Golden Rump* is attributed to him in *An Historical View of the ... Political Writers in Great Britain* (1740) and later by Horace Walpole.[127] The nearly unanimous denials by Fielding scholars that he could have been the author have generally been made on the sentimental and unsatisfactory ground that he would not have written such a piece.[128] Thomas Lockwood bluntly reminds us that we have no reason to doubt either that

[124] See particularly *The Town and Country Magazine* (Oct. 1787), pp. 467–8.

[125] *An Apology For ... T......... C....., Comedian*, pp. 93–4.

[126] Cambridge Univ. Library, Cholmondeley (Houghton) MS Corr. 3253. Printed by Liesenfeld, p. 188.

[127] For discussion, see Liesenfeld, pp. 132–3.

[128] John Loftis, for example, doubts that Fielding would 'have written such a coarsely vulgar piece' (*Politics of Drama*, p. 141).

Fielding was capable of writing such a thing or that he would have been willing to use it 'to bargain with Walpole'.[129] True, but unless we suppose that Walpole commissioned Fielding to write it, or that Fielding wrote it to attempt to blackmail Walpole, I have difficulty seeing why Fielding would have bothered to write such a piece. Granting that he could have done so, I doubt that he did. For the work to be attributed to him is no surprise: Fielding was much the most conspicuous and best known of the dramatists who were hounding Walpole in 1737. And just as every anonymous dirty poem of the 1670s was attributed to the Earl of Rochester, so *The Golden Rump* was readily associated with Fielding's not-very-savoury name.[130]

A much more interesting and significant puzzle about Fielding and the Licensing Act is his rather astonishing public silence about it. He could certainly have filled the London papers with the tale of Potter's *coup de théâtre*. He could have published pamphlets full of libertarian justifications for Aristophanic drama. He could have written a 'patriot' play to be suppressed by the censor and then published at great profit—as Henry Brooke was to do with *Gustavus Vasa* in 1739. But such protests as he vented were restricted to discreetly anonymous periodical essays, some of them well after the fact.[131]

The biographers evade the question with complacent praise for Fielding's maturity and good citizenship. 'Fielding, be it said to his credit, submitted quietly to the law.' 'He accepted his fate . . . with stoical resignation. He did not raise an outcry, or pose in public as a martyr to Government persecution.'[132] Many critics are glad to see Fielding leave drama for the novel, and take his silence about the Licensing Act as tacit evidence of his foresight. But in 1737 Fielding was England's most successful living playwright; he had just enjoyed two phenomenally successful seasons as impresario; and we know that he was busy with plans for improving his theatre and strengthening his company. The Licensing Act deprived Fielding of his livelihood. We might expect a loud protest or two, and we might certainly imagine that Fielding would make what money he could from the situation. But he did nothing of the sort. Why not?

[129] Thomas Lockwood, 'Fielding and the Licensing Act'.

[130] Victor's ref. to the time when 'the late Justice *F-----g* . . . was in the dishonest Employment of an Incendiary Writer' (I, 50) seems indicative of public opinion.

[131] For attribution of some relevant pieces in the *Craftsman* to Fielding (in particular, the essay of 28 May 1737), see the forthcoming book by Battestin and Farringdon.

[132] Cross, I, 233; Dudden, I, 211.

The more one thinks about the problem, the more puzzling Fielding's silence is. Perhaps he was as dignified, manly, and uncomplaining as the school of Cross and Dudden would have him—but the picture does not accord well with the fiery young man who had been a storm-centre in the London theatre. Repulsive though traditional Fielding scholars may find the idea, the most probable explanation of Fielding's passivity and silence is that Walpole bought him off. This theory has been skilfully advanced by Thomas Lockwood, and I refer the reader to his exposition of it.[133]

Fielding's silent acquiescence in the ruin of his chosen career is explained by such a hypothesis, but what actual evidence do we have for it? Lockwood points to an odd and persistent pattern of references in which Fielding alludes to Walpole and himself, 'each time glancing repeatedly, not to say compulsively, at the themes of bribing, and being bribed, into silence'. In an anonymous letter to *Common Sense* of 13 May 1738, for example, he refers to 'A certain ludicrous Poet' who wrote *The Historical Register* and whose 'Muse hath been silent ever since', and then mentions 'a Coffee House Politician' who 'would Bribe Persons to hold their Tongue'.[134] The implication is clear. In the *Champion* of 11 December 1739 he wrote a harshly ironic encomium on the Licensing Act.[135] In the issue of the 13th he recounts a 'dream': 'I came within the Reach of the huge Man, who gave me such a Squeeze by the Hand, that it put an End to my Dream, and instead of those flowry Landskips which I painted in the Beginning of my Letter, I found myself three Pair of Stairs in the *Inner-Temple*'.[136] Squeezing the hand is the term for bribery in *The Election*.[137] Fielding could hardly find a clearer way to say that his theatrical 'dream' was ended by Walpole (a fat man), who gave him the money he needed to pursue his legal studies. How Fielding lived for two years without visible means of support has always bothered scholars. Perhaps he had saved money from his successes in 1736 and 1737, or had held on to part of his wife's inheritance of 1735, but, as Lockwood observes, Fielding was a spendthrift accustomed to a substantial income.

[133] Lockwood, 'Fielding and the Licensing Act'.

[134] See M. C. with R. R. Battestin, 'A Fielding Discovery, with Some Remarks on the Canon', *Studies in Bibliography*, 33 (1980), 131–43. The attribution is from handwriting and seems very solid indeed.

[135] For discussion, see George R. Levine, 'Henry Fielding's "Defense" of the Stage Licensing Act', *English Language Notes*, 2 (1965), 193–6.

[136] McCrea was, I believe, the first scholar to see the implications of this passage (pp. 79–80).

[137] *Pasquin*, p. 7.

If Fielding was indeed bought off—and the probability seems high—we can only guess at the terms. They presumably included silence in June 1737 and his promise to stop writing plays. No 'conversion' or 'betrayal' was involved. Fielding had always been a Whig, and after the passage of the Licensing Act, he could be of no further use to his Broad Bottom friends as a theatrical writer. On the other side, Walpole would merely have been carrying out long-standing policy: he was accustomed to purchasing silence.[138]

Fielding had every reason to accept such an offer. The Licensing Act put him out of business as impresario, and he probably understood very well that his future as a playwright was bleak at best. Whether he was weary of writing plays or devastated by his enforced departure from the theatre we may never know. Fielding was hot-tempered and thin-skinned, but he was very much a pragmatist. He had to begin a new career at the age of thirty, and he would have been a fool not to make a profitable fuss unless he was well paid for his silence. The probability seems high that he salvaged what he could by striking a bargain with Walpole.

IV. FIELDING AND THE THEATRE

The Licensing Act abruptly terminated Fielding's promising career as a theatrical entrepreneur, and the monopoly it created ended any possibility of his supporting himself as a playwright for the patent theatres. A surprising number of critics have regarded this turn of events with complacency, content that Fielding should be rid of his theatrical entanglements and free to get on with *Tom Jones*.[139] But the catastrophic effects of the Licensing Act upon the British theatre are hardly a reasonable trade for the fiction of any one novelist. The stultifying effects of the patent monopoly choked the London theatre well past its official end in 1843, and censorship by the Lord Chamberlain continued until 1968. The damage to drama and theatre is incalculable.

[138] See Thomas Davies, *The Characters of George the First, Queen Caroline, Sir Robert Walpole* . . . (London, 1777), p. 22.

[139] Dudden (I, 233) holds that 'we have reason to be grateful for the Licensing Act', and even Hunter (whose book remains the best general study of Fielding yet written) says that 'Fielding's separation from the theater was a forced one, but the expulsion was fortunate, freeing him from a relationship and commitment that had always been in some sense against the grain' (p. 69).

Even if we concern ourselves solely with Fielding, the Licensing Act cannot be considered a happy accident. It certainly did not 'free' him to write fiction. Rather, it deprived him of his livelihood and forced him to turn to the law. And if Fielding could write *Shamela*, *Jonathan Wild*, *Joseph Andrews*, *Tom Jones*, and *Amelia* while carrying on a career in the law, he could have written them while running a playhouse. Critics primarily interested in fiction have inclined to the comfortable theory that Fielding's ten years in the theatre were a false start, luckily truncated by Walpole's influence.[140] How 'fortunate' Fielding felt is questionable, especially considering that he was never again able to support himself as a man of letters. He paid dearly in his personal circumstances for the 'freedom' to write *Tom Jones*.[141]

This book has traced Fielding's career in the theatre season by season as he lived it, attempting to recreate the conditions that affected him. As Paul Hunter rightly says, Fielding always worked within 'the chains of circumstance', and I believe that only by investigating the particulars of the milieu in which he worked can we hope to understand his aims, achievements, and limitations. The presentation of fact has been my primary object, and a 'summary' seems to me neither feasible nor desirable. But by way of conclusion I should like to address two interrelated questions. Does Fielding's theatrical career have a clear pattern or direction? Was he developing as a playwright?

Because Fielding wrote several different sorts of plays and had them produced in various theatres, his early career has seemed chaotic and undirected, especially to people who have found the plays irregular and the milieu unfamiliar. Brian McCrea's elaborate theory that political and personal 'uncertainty' appears in 'vacillation'

[140] Even those critics who have realized the high degree of continuity in themes and techniques between Fielding's plays and his novels have argued that dramatic form inhibited Fielding's need to interject himself as narrator/commentator. See, e.g., the fine essay by C. J. Rawson, 'Some considerations on Authorial Intrusion and Dialogue in Fielding's novels and plays', *Durham University Journal*, NS 32 (1971), 32–44. I would argue, contrariwise, that in 1736 and 1737 Fielding was discovering a form of 'dramatick satire' that gave him the flexibility he needed. The degree of continuity in Fielding's work is usually underestimated. The most thorough demonstration of it remains Sheridan Warner Baker, jun., 'Setting, Character, and Situation in the Plays and Novels of Henry Fielding' (diss.; Berkeley, 1950).

[141] Pat Rogers (pp. 97–8) makes the excellent point that Fielding's turning to the law was anything but a 'foregone conclusion' in 1737. He had spent most of his life rebelling against his mother's family's legal tradition, and 'most of the references to the law' in the plays are 'opprobrious'. I agree with Rogers that if Fielding had thought he could support his family as an opposition journalist, 'he would probably have preferred that'.

between different genres and theatres is an attempt to make sense of evidence he finds bewildering.[142] Comprehension of the early career has been impeded by long-standing confusion over the place of politics in Fielding's early career. Only in the last ten years—since Goldgar's book—have we realized that until 1736 politics was merely incidental in Fielding's plays.[143] The Fielding who could call Walpole 'one of the best of men and of ministers' in 1754 was neither ironic nor traitor to his early principles.[144] Fielding's attacks on Walpole in *The Historical Register* and *Jonathan Wild* represent a temporary mid-career phase, not a settled position abandoned or betrayed.

I have tried to demonstrate that Fielding's 'shifts' of theatre were entirely beyond his control and have nothing to do with politics. Fielding was a freelance writer who peddled his scripts where he could in the midst of rapidly changing conditions. Drury Lane, for example, had radically different managements in the winters of 1732, 1733, 1734, and 1735, and to speak of Fielding's relations with 'Drury Lane' is misleading unless one understands which management he was dealing with and what its circumstances were at the time.

Fielding's career in the theatre has a clear and simple structure. (1) He started as a gentleman amateur in 1728. (2) When earning a living in the theatre became possible around 1729, Fielding promptly returned to London to try his luck. In two years of intensive practice he progressed from clumsy apprentice to assured professional. (3) In 1732, with competition forcing the patent theatres to mount new plays, Fielding became Drury Lane's most conspicuous, prolific, and successful writer. He probably imagined that this would be a permanent state of affairs, but the demise of the triumvirate management quickly ended this phase of his career. (4) In 1733 and 1734 the theatre world underwent radical upheavals, and Fielding soon found himself without a venue for his plays. (5) Fielding's solution was to turn impresario in 1736, and by 1737 he was busy with plans to extend his activities as entrepreneur.[145]

[142] McCrea, ch. 3.

[143] As Lockwood comments in 'Fielding and the Licensing Act', we are still trying to come to terms with the realization 'that Fielding, despite his long-lived reputation as an opposition wit who tormented Walpole upon the stage for years, in truth was a young writer who from the first had adopted or been willing to adopt a Walpolean interest, according to the custom and convenience of patronage'.

[144] *Journal of a Voyage to Lisbon*, Henley edn., XVI, 248.

[145] Fielding became very friendly with Garrick, and Cross suggests that but for the Licensing Act 'Garrick would have won his spurs' on 'Fielding's stage rather than

Any assessment of Fielding's theatrical career must start with the realization that he was enormously and conspicuously successful. He had a few failures and rough times, but no other English playwright of the eighteenth century was so dominant in his own time, so frequently successful, or so well paid for his efforts. To speak of 'Fielding's Undistinguished Career as a Dramatist' is extremely misleading. Whatever one's critical assessment of his plays, his career in the theatre can only be called 'vastly successful'. If Fielding had been 'uncomfortable' in the theatre, he would probably have departed quietly in 1735 after the shattering failure of *The Universal Gallant*. He certainly became disgusted with the managers at the patent theatres, but the delight with which he ran his company at the Little Haymarket is evident in his innovative repertory policy and imaginative advertising. Irritation with managers should not be mistaken for weariness with the theatre.

Like his theatrical career as a whole, Fielding's writing of plays has seemed more chaotic than it actually was. To make sense of his development as a writer one must pay attention to dates of composition (as well as dates of performance) while refusing to impose inappropriate categories on the plays. Traditional generic categories simply do not work for Fielding. Critics have usually distinguished 'regular comedies' (five-act mainpieces), 'farces', 'ballad operas', and 'dramatick satires'. These categories blur important distinctions. Fielding's social satire mainpieces (*The Modern Husband* and *The Universal Gallant*) must be distinguished from his 'traditional' comedies (all of them prentice work); burlesques must not be lumped together with 'farces'; and 'ballad opera' is not a separable entity, since Fielding uses the technique in a mainpiece like *Don Quixote*, an afterpiece like *The Lottery*, and a burlesque like *The Welsh Opera*. Without trying to make fine distinctions, we can usefully view Fielding's plays, taken in chronological order, in relation to five generic groupings: traditional comedy, serious satire, 'entertainment', burlesque, and topical satire. (See Table 4.)

Fielding began by writing traditional five-act comedies—*Love in Several Masques*, *The Wedding-Day*, *The Temple Beau*, and *Rape upon*

Giffard's,' and that 'Fielding and Garrick, working together, would have given the British theatre a fame unequalled since the days of Shakespeare' (I, 235). Fanciful speculation, no doubt. But in the 1740s James Lacy, one of Fielding's actors at the Little Haymarket, became manager at Drury Lane, and then co-patentee with Garrick. One can easily imagine Fielding becoming Garrick's first partner, at Drury Lane or elsewhere.

TABLE 4: Fielding's Plays by Type and Date of Composition

	Traditional Comedy	Serious Satire	Entertainment	Burlesque	Topical Satire	
1728	*Love in Several Masques*					1728
	Don Quixote in England[a]					
1729	*The Wedding-Day*[b]					1729
1730	*The Temple Beau*				*The Author's Farce*	1730
				Tom Thumb		
	Rape upon Rape					
		The Modern Husband[c]				
1731			*The Letter-Writers*			1731
				Tragedy of Tragedies		
				The Welsh Opera		
				Grub-Street Opera[d]		
1732			*The Lottery*			1732
			The Old Debauchees			
				Covent-Garden Tragedy		
			The Mock Doctor			
1733		*The Miser*				1733
		The Universal Gallant[e]		*Deborah*[f]		
1734			*Intriguing Chambermaid*			1734
1735			*Old Man taught Wisdom*			1735
		The Good-Natur'd Man[g]				
1736					*Pasquin*	1736
				Tumble-Down Dick		
1737					*Eurydice*	1737
					Historical Register	
					Eurydice Hiss'd	

[a] Staged in 1734.
[b] Staged in 1743.
[c] Staged in 1732.
[d] Not performed.
[e] Staged in 1735.
[f] Lost.
[g] Date of composition conjectural; staged in 1778.

Rape. All of them were written by 1730, when Fielding was just 23 years old—as was the original version of *The Modern Husband*. He never again wrote a play of that type. Indeed, with the exception of his ambitious but ill-fated ventures into Juvenalian social satire, he virtually abandoned the five-act form at this time. Of the twenty-one plays he was to write in the next seven years, only three were to be five-act mainpieces: *The Universal Gallant*, *The Miser*, and *The Good-Natur'd Man* (unproduced). What Fielding really wanted to write was harsh social satire, but even there 'undistinguished' is probably too kind a verdict. The blunt truth is that Fielding had no talent for constructing five-act mainpieces. The only one to become a stock piece was *The Miser*, which leans heavily on Molière for plot and character.

What brought Fielding his initial success was burlesque. *The Author's Farce* verges on the topical satire form he was to develop in 1736 and 1737, though without a political component. In this play and *Tom Thumb* Fielding discovered his real talent. His plots tend to be mechanical (and often ill-controlled), his characters shallow and formulaic—but as a contriver of incongruous imitation and travesty he has no equal in British drama. *The Welsh Opera* (and its unstaged revision, *The Grub-Street Opera*), *The Covent-Garden Tragedy*, *Tumble-Down Dick*, and *Eurydice* are savagely funny and effective debunkings.

The works that became staples in the eighteenth-century repertory fall into a category I would call entertainments. *The Lottery*, *The Mock Doctor*, *The Intriguing Chambermaid*, and *An Old Man taught Wisdom* are generally called farces, but all of them have a tart flavour and a judgemental view of their characters that relates them to the burlesques and differentiates them from 'farces' by Fielding's contemporaries. All are unabashedly commercial work, but Fielding was not simply grinding out imitative pot-boilers. He learned to provide popular entertainment, but without losing his own viewpoint. All of these 'entertainments' after *The Letter-Writers* were written as vehicles for Kitty Clive. In *Eurydice* we see Fielding trying to meld entertainment, burlesque, and social/topical satire. Its failure notwithstanding, the work has the kind of imagination and ambition too rarely found in eighteenth-century afterpieces. Fielding was attempting to vitalize and toughen a form that sagged into triviality after the Licensing Act.

In 1736 with *Pasquin* Fielding found a better way to use his talents—topical satire. *Pasquin*, *The Historical Register*, and *Eurydice Hiss'd* differ radically in technique, but all three represent a major departure from anything Fielding had done before. They are related to his burlesques, but they bring seriousness and depth to a form whose potentialities he had never fully realized.

The key dates in his development are 1730 and 1736. At the age of twenty-three Fielding discovered his natural bent as a dramatist, and at twenty-nine he hit on a formula that freed him from the exigencies of conventional plots. All signs in the last five plays suggest that he had made a significant advance in the creation of a unique form suited to his decidedly individual talents. Back in 1730 he had verged on this discovery in Act III of *The Author's Farce*, but he was hampered by plot and format conventions. The 'plotlessness' of *The Historical Register* is no accident: Fielding was moving towards topical cabaret.

Had there been no Licensing Act, we may presume that Fielding would have gone ahead with his plans for a company and ultimately a theatre of his own. Drury Lane would probably have continued to specialize in classic repertory with a heavy bias towards pre-1708 plays, and Covent Garden would have done much the same, with more emphasis on music and pantomime. Goodman's Fields or Lincoln's Inn Fields would have continued in the Giffard style, offering a conservative repertory with an eighteenth-century emphasis. London had plenty of room for a fringe venture dedicated to contemporary and experimental scripts.

In 1737 Fielding was just thirty years old, and he had needed nearly a decade to free himself from conventional dramatic structures and false ambitions. His early inclinations were at odds with his talent. He had yearned to be a Juvenalian scourge, and only gradually did he fully accept that his talent was for burlesque and travesty. His forte was not indignant preachment but mockery. What Samuel Foote did in the 1750s and 1760s Fielding could have done in the 1740s, and done better. His reference to himself in 1737 as 'an Author who is an acknowledged Proficient' in the 'old Comedy' says in so many words that he had started to think of himself as an 'English Aristophanes'. Murphy reports Fielding's belief that 'he left off writing for the stage, when he ought to have begun'.[146] One can easily imagine that in 1740 he would have written not only *Shamela* but his own version of Foote's *Piety in Pattens: or The Handsome Housemaid* (1773)—and gone on from there.

Fielding's abilities as a traditional dramatist—as one of Cibber's 'singing birds'—were extremely limited, but his career was cut off just

[146] Murphy, I, 26.

when he was finding his Aristophanic voice. Without regretting his later career in fiction and journalism, we may certainly lament his demise as a mocking-bird. Uneven as the plays are, several of them are truly brilliant. Despite their raucous high spirits and 'irregularity', the plays are tough, surprisingly serious, and uniformly moral in their design. Indeed, as his ponderous social satires show, Fielding tended to be excessively sour and didactic: he needed the leaven of burlesque to be an effective satirist. Despite all their high jinks, the plays are never merely frivolous. Nor can one fairly say that 'Fielding wasted his impressive literary gifts' in his plays,[147] for, as Pat Rogers rightly says, Fielding 'made the theatre count in national life as it has rarely done, before or since'.[148]

Fielding started his career as a dramatist with ambitions he lacked the talent to fulfil. He set out to become—as it were—a Royal Academy painter and wound up a brilliant political cartoonist. This is failure or misdirection only by a very narrow definition of success. Had Fielding been able to continue in the theatre, we can only guess what he would have written and what his theatre would have become. The stodgy history of the mid-eighteenth-century British theatre is a sad fact, but it was made inevitable only by the Licensing Act. Perhaps Fielding would have remained a solitary voice or dwindled into mediocrity—but we have to wonder what he would have contrived to do with a career that he carried on for ten years with passion and success. He was flourishing as an impresario, and he had found the flexible form he needed to exercise his satiric talents. Fielding's subsequent success as a novelist is indisputable, but in 1737 the arc of his theatrical career was upward, and by all indications a distinguished career in the theatre lay ahead of him.

[147] McCrea, p. 76.
[148] Rogers, p. 86.

APPENDIX I

Giffard's Proposal for the Second Goodman's Fields Theatre

What follows is the complete text of Giffard's offering of stock to investors in order to finance construction of the second Goodman's Fields theatre in 1732. Copy-text is Guildhall Broadside 7.57. For the terms actually arranged with investors, see pp. 146–7, above.

Proposals offered by *Henry Giffard*, of the Parish of *White-chappel* in the County of *Middlesex*, Gent. for the erecting a *Theatre* or *Playhouse*, by Subscription, in or near *Goodman's-Fields*, in the said Parish of *White-chappel*, and County of *Middlesex*, aforesaid.

Imprimis. The said *Henry Giffard* proposes, with all convenient Speed imaginable, to obtain a Lease for a Term of 41 Years, at least, of a Piece of Ground, in or near *Goodman's-Fields*, aforesaid; whereon to erect and build, or cause to be erected and built, by an experienced Architect, a Structure or Edifice, proper and convenient for a *Theatre* or *Playhouse*, in a Theatrical Manner, and to illustrate the same with proper Paintings and Decorations, and provide Scenes and other Necessaries, and to engage and retain fit, proper, and expert Actors and Actresses, Dancers, Singers and Musicians, who, every Evening, during the usual Seasons of acting (*Sundays* and other Days improper for acting excepted) shall act therein Comedies, Tragedies, Interludes, or some other proper and usual Diversions of the Stage.

Item. The said *Henry Giffard*, for the better enabling him to begin and compleat the said Undertaking, proposes to raise the Sum of 1500*l*. by way of Subscription, the same to be proportioned into 25 Shares, at 60*l*. each Share, and the several Sums of Money which shall be subscribed, to be deposited in the Hands of a Banker, or in the Bank of *England*, on or before the first Day of *May* 1732, and the Moneys so subscribed and deposited, shall be drawn out and apply'd, in the Manner herein after express'd.

Item. That so soon as the said Subscription shall be compleated, the said *Henry Giffard* proposes to article with an experienced Architect or Builder, for the erecting and building the said intended *Theatre* or *Playhouse*, in a Theatrical Manner, according to a Plan thereof to be approved of by the said Subscribers or the Majority of them, with proper Covenants that the same shall be compleatly built and finished by a certain Time therein to be limited, with the like Approbation of the said Subscribers or a Majority of them.

Item. That for every 60*l*. so subscribed, as aforesaid, such Subscribers thereof shall be intitled to have and receive from the said Henry Giffard, the

Sum of one Shilling for every Night of acting, and shall have the Liberty of seeing the Play, *Gratis*, every Night, and to sit in the Boxes, Pit or Gallery, as he, she, or they, shall think fit; and if such Person is possessed of two or more Shares, he or she shall be intitled to see the Play, *Gratis*, every Night in the Manner as aforesaid.[1]

Item. That during the Time the said intended *Theatre* or *Playhouse* shall be building, for the Satisfaction of the Subscribers, and other Parties concerned, it is proposed, That no Part of the Money shall be drawn out of the *Bank*, or out of the Hands to whom the same shall be intrusted, but by the Consent of seven or more of the Subscribers, who shall sign an Order for that purpose, and who shall likewise be privy to the distributing thereof to the Person or Persons, who shall be employed in building the said *Theatre*; and that the remainder of the said 1500*l*. after the said *Theatre* shall be erected, shall be employed, and go towards providing Scenes and Cloaths for the Actors and Actresses, and other necessary Expences, with the like Approbation of seven or more of the said Subscribers.

Item. That the said *Henry Giffard* proposes, for the better securing the Payment of the said one Shilling for every Evening of acting, for every 60*l*. Share, which shall be paid once a Week, if required, by the said *Henry Giffard*, to make a legal Conveyance of the said *Theatre* and Premises, with their Appurtenances so far as relates to the said 1500*l*. Subscription Money, to any two or more Persons, who shall be approved of by a Majority of the Subscribers in Trust, for the Purposes aforesaid. Which said Assignment shall be executed with all convenient Speed after the obtaining the said Lease, and in the mean time, the equitable Right of the said Lease and Premises shall be deem'd to exist in the said Subscribers, as a Security for the said Sum of 1500*l*.

Item. That in case the said whole Sum of 1500*l*. shall not be subscribed for, on, or before the first Day of *May* 1732, all Persons who shall have subscribed to these Proposals, shall be discharged from paying their Subscription Money.

We whose Hands and Seals are hereunto subscribed and set, have perused and approved the above-written Proposals, and do hereby for ourselves, severally and respectively, promise and agree that we will respectively, on, or before the said First Day of May *now next ensuing, on the Conditions and Agreements, and under the Provisoe above-mentioned, advance and pay into the Bank of* England, *or to a Banker, the several Sums of Money against our Names respectively by us set down, as Witness our Hands and Seals this* [*blank*] *Day of* [blank] Anno Dom. 1731.

N.B. The Days of Acting will at least be a Hundred and Sixty, for each Year, but more frequently a Hundred and Eighty.

[1] This passage was probably meant to say that the possessor of two shares would be entitled to two free passes every night, and so forth.

APPENDIX II

The Good-Natur'd Man (*The Fathers*, pub. 1778)

What we know of this play comes from Fielding's comments about it in the preface to the *Miscellanies*, the 'Advertisement' to the first edition (published in 1778), Garrick's correspondence, and scattered newspaper stories about the discovery of the manuscript and its production at Drury Lane in 1778.[1] Fielding reports that he promised the play to Garrick in 1743, but found it 'on the Reading, to be less completely finished than I thought its Plan deserved' and that he had allowed himself 'too little Time for the perfecting it' and hence substituted *The Wedding-Day*.[2] I have already explained my reasons for hypothesizing that the play was written in the summer or autumn of 1735 (see Chapter 5, pp. 200–1, above). Since Garrick identified 'Harry Fielding's Comedy' before it was performed and published in 1778, we have good reason to believe that the work is genuine.[3]

Analysis of the play is complicated by our inability to determine what Fielding wrote in 1735 (?), what he added in 1743, and what may have been added (or cut) by Garrick and Sheridan in 1778. The basic design of the play, however, fits tidily into Fielding's ill-starred career as a would-be writer of social satire mainpieces in the mid-1730s. I would guess that Fielding recognized, however reluctantly, the sourness and lack of action in *The Universal Gallant*, and determined to write a livelier play with some positive characters, seeking a formula more appealing to the town.

As was his habit, Fielding constructed the play around character contrasts. Mr Boncour (a man of excessively good nature) is set against his blunt brother, Sir George, and opposed to Old Valence, a dissembling schemer. A fourth father-figure is introduced in Sir Gregory Kennel of Dirty Park, like Squire Badger in *Don Quixote in England* a preliminary sketch towards Squire Western. As Cross observes (III, 103), Fielding takes some hints from Terence's *The Brothers*—and also, I suspect, from Shadwell's adaptation of it, *The Squire of Alsatia* (1688). The play quite explicitly poses a question: how should fathers bring up their children? Boncour is trusting and generous (his

[1] For a convenient list, see Cross, III, 108.

[2] *Miscellanies*, vol. I, ed. Miller, p. 6.

[3] On the discovery of the manuscript and its production at Drury Lane, see Cross, III, 99–109. I have virtually nothing to add to his account save a correction of Cross's optimistic estimate that 'Mrs. Fielding should have realized two or three hundred pounds' from the play—echoed by Dudden, II, 1068. The receipts reported in *The London Stage*, Part 5, I, 218–21, show that three benefits produced a total profit of £100 19*s*. 6*d*. The net on the third benefit was only £3 0*s*. 6*d*.

brother says too much so); Valence preaches a doctrine of 'severity'; Sir Gregory brings up his heir as a replica of himself—a hard-drinking fox-hunter without an idea in his head. Fielding's conclusion in favour of 'rational education' (109) is predictable.[4]

The plot is very creaky indeed. Sir George's pretence that Boncour has lost all his money shows Old Valence in his true character, and the behaviour of Valence's son and daughter convinces the young Boncours that their affections have been ill-bestowed. But Valence and his son are simplistic villains, easily baffled, and the other characters seem underdeveloped. Boncour does learn that he must assert himself more—but Fielding chooses to demonstrate this by having him stand up to his obnoxious wife, and unfortunately this relationship is so minimally presented that it does not integrate properly with the rest of the play. Fielding flaunts his defiance of the 'constant rule, that comedies should end in a marriage', but the ending is both flat and heavily didactic.

The Good-Natur'd Man is of interest more for its philosophy than for its dramatic merits. Cross characterizes it justly as 'a homily by a very earnest preacher'. The play can usefully be read in conjunction with Fielding's poem 'Of Good-Nature' and his 'An Essay on the Knowledge of the Characters of Men' in the *Miscellanies*.[5] Boncour is Fielding's practical illustration of a good man learning the scepticism and prudence he will need to survive in a world full of scoundrels and hypocrites. Boncour is not a perfect character, but as a genuinely good man he comes fairly close to being so. In this play we see Fielding trying to combine satire with exemplary comedy as conceived by Steele, and hence the idea behind the comedy is an interesting one, unsatisfactory execution notwithstanding.

[4] Citations are to the Cadell edn. of 1778.

[5] For an interesting application of this essay to all of Fielding's 'regular' comedies, see Jack D. Durant, 'The "Art of Thriving" in Fielding's Comedies', *A Provision of Human Nature*, ed. Donald Kay (University, Ala., 1977), pp. 25–35.

APPENDIX III

Miss Lucy in Town (1742)

On 6 May 1742 Fielding's last piece for the legitimate theatre received its première at Drury Lane. *Miss Lucy in Town* is a sequel to his popular *An Old Man taught Wisdom*. Shortly after Lucy's marriage to Thomas, the sensible footman, he brings her to town to see the sights. They take lodgings by mistake in Mrs Haycock's bordello. The madam promptly offers this tasty piece to some of her regular customers, including the Jewish stockbroker Zorobabel, Lord Bawble (one of the directors of the opera; probably a hit at Lord Middlesex), Mr Ballad (an English singer), and Signor Cantileno (an Italian opera singer played by Beard). The silly girl is quite prepared to abandon her husband in favour of keeping with Lord Bawble, but her virtue is preserved by the timely arrival of her husband and her father.

As usual in concocting such an entertainment, Fielding devised it as a vehicle for Kitty Clive. Like *Eurydice*, *Miss Lucy* is an attack on London society mores and also on opera. The confrontation between the singers vying for Miss Lucy's services is nicely handled in a three-way song. Horace Walpole wrote to his friend Horace Mann that 'Mrs Clive mimics the Muscovita [Lord Middlesex' mistress] admirably, and Beard Amorevoli intolerably'.[1] This kind of personation was to become characteristic of Fielding's successor Samuel Foote.

Great confusion has surrounded the stage history of this play. Because of the personation and a hostile pamphlet called *A Letter to a Noble Lord . . . occasioned by . . . a Farce call'd Miss Lucy in Town*[2] the compiler of the playlist attached to *Scanderbeg* (1747) got the idea that the play was banned by the Lord Chamberlain.[3] This tale is repeated as fact by all later authorities, including Cross (I, 370), *The London Stage*, and Arnott and Robinson, but, as Woods has shown, it is entirely without foundation.[4]

Of Fielding's connection with the sequel we know two facts. On 13 April 1742 Fielding sold the copyright to Andrew Millar for £10 10*s*. as part of a package deal for *Joseph Andrews* and his *Vindication* of the Dowager Duchess of Marlborough.[5] And in the preface to *Miscellanies* the next year Fielding

[1] Cited in *The London Stage*, Part 3, II, 991.

[2] London, 1742. Arnott and Robinson, no. 3897.

[3] The pamphlet actually complains that the farce *should* have been banned.

[4] Charles B. Woods, 'The "Miss Lucy" Plays of Fielding and Garrick', *Philological Quarterly*, 41 (1962), 294–310.

[5] MS in the Forster Collection, Victoria and Albert. Reported by Cross, I, 316. Millar duly published the farce in the summer of 1742.

includes among works he had published since June 1741 '*Miss Lucy in Town*, (in which I had a very small Share)'.[6] The farce was published anonymously, and no author is named in the newspaper bills. Since Garrick used Lucy and her husband in the first version of his *Lethe* (15 April 1740), and he and Fielding were friendly, Charles Woods offers the plausible but unprovable hypothesis that he was Fielding's collaborator. H. K. Miller questions this on the grounds that Fielding owned the copyright, but we do not know what arrangements were made between the putative authors. Garrick might, for example, have been allowed the proceeds of the unidentified author's benefit on 19 May 1742. If so, Garrick was unlucky, for the total take that night was only £40—i.e. less than house charges.

Miss Lucy in Town had six performances in May 1742 and another dozen the following autumn.[7] Fielding's last venture in the legitimate theatre came in February 1743 when Drury Lane mounted *The Wedding-Day* (written around 1729). Not even Garrick as Millamour could reconcile the audience to it. Fielding says glumly in the preface to *Miscellanies* that 'tho' it was acted six Nights, I received not 50*l*. from the House for it'.[8] Fielding's only known return to the theatre was as proprietor of a puppet show in 1748—something hinted at by Murphy, long denied by stuffy scholars, and finally proved only twenty years ago.[9]

[6] *Miscellanies*, vol. I, ed. Miller, p. 15.

[7] It was revived for a couple of nights in 1770 under the title *The Country Madcap in London*.

[8] *Miscellanies*, vol. I, ed. Miller, p. 7.

[9] See Martin C. Battestin, 'Fielding and "Master Punch" in Panton Street', *Philological Quarterly*, 45 (1966), 191–208.

APPENDIX IV

Fielding on Tragedy: The Puff for *Fatal Curiosity*

On 25 May 1736 the *Daily Advertiser* printed a lengthy letter to the editor (unsigned) commenting on the state of tragedy and commending a new play about to open at the Little Haymarket theatre. I think we can be virtually certain that Fielding was the author of this missive—a piece of advance publicity for his friend George Lillo's *Fatal Curiosity*, which opened on the 27th.[1] The complete text follows.

To the Author, *&c.*

SIR,

In an Age when Tragedy is thought so much out of Fashion, that the great establish'd Theatres dare hardly venture to attempt it, an Author may probably seem bold who hazards his Reputation with a Set of young Actors on a Stage hitherto in its Infancy; where he is sure, besides the Judgment, to encounter the Prejudice of the Town; and has not only the Chance of not being liked, but of not being heard.

But as to the ill Success of Tragedy in general, I shall not attribute it entirely to the Audience; I cannot persuade myself that we are sunk into such a State of Levity and Childhood, as to be utterly incapable of any serious Attention; or are so entirely devoted to Farce and Puppet Shew, as to abandon what one of the greatest Criticks who ever liv'd has call'd the noblest Work of Human Understanding.

I am afraid the Truth is, our Poets have left off Writing, rather than our Spectators loving Tragedy. The Modern Writers seem to me to have quite mistaken the Path: They do not fail so much from want of Genius as of Judgment; they embellish their Diction with their utmost Art, and concern themselves little about their Fable: In short, While they are industrious to please the Fancy, they forget (what should be their first Care) to warm the Heart.

Give me leave, Sir, to recommend to you, and by you to the Town, a Tragedy, written in a different Manner, where the Fable is contriv'd with great Art, and the Incidents such as much affect the Heart of every one who is not void of Humanity. A tender Sensation is, I think, in one of a Humane Temper, the most pleasing that can be rais'd; and I will venture to affirm, no such Person will fail of enjoying it who will be present on Thursday next at the Hay-Market Theatre; where, without the bombast Stile of Kings and Heroes,

[1] This letter was independently found and assigned to Fielding by Martin Battestin, who has very kindly confirmed my attribution.

he will see a Scene in common Life, which really happen'd in King James I's Time; and is accompany'd with the most natural, dreadful and tender Circumstances, and affording the finest Moral that can be invented by the Mind of Man.

As to the Performers, I shall only say, if the Town will once more wave their Prejudice against a young Company, I believe they will not repent it; and I am deceiv'd, if Mr. Roberts and Mrs. Charke do not convince them, that if they are not equal to some of their Predecessors, they are, at least, so to any of their Cotemporaries on the Stage.

I shall only add, that this comes not from the Author of the Tragedy, and is no more than what a Love to Truth and real Merit has extorted. I am, &c.

Unless the writer was blatantly untruthful, Lillo did not write this puff. The obvious candidate for authorship is Fielding, who managed the company and had seen the play to the stage. The only plausible alternative associated with the Little Haymarket this season is James Ralph, and neither the style nor the sentiments accord well with his known views on tragedy. The comments on humane temper and warming the heart have the ring of Fielding. Thomas Davies tells us that Fielding 'warmly recommended the play to his friends and to the public' (p. 208 n. 24, above). This letter I take as his recommendation to the public.

On Friday, 28 May, the day after the première, the *Daily Advertiser* ran a follow-up item:

Last Night the new Tragedy call'd Guilt its own Punishment, or Fatal Curiosity, was acted at the New Theatre in the Hay-Market, with the greatest Applause that has been shewn to any Tragedy for many Years. The Scenes of Distress were so artfully work'd up, and so well perform'd, that there scarce remain'd a dry Eye among the Spectators at the Representation; and during the Scene preceding the Catastrophe, an attentive Silence possess'd the whole House, more expressive of an universal Approbation than the loudest Applauses, which were given to the many noble Sentiments that every where abound in this excellent Performance, which must meet with Encouragement in an Age that does not want both Sense and Humanity.

The probability is again that Fielding was responsible for this notice.[2] These two items seem to bear out Davies's account of Fielding's generous efforts on Lillo's behalf, and they make a significant addition to what we know of his views on theory of tragedy and audience response in the theatre.

[2] How literally we should take the report of success is hard to say, especially when we remember the account of the première of *The Covent-Garden Tragedy* that the *Daily Post* had to retract (see pp. 129–30, above).

Index

Major discussions of Fielding's plays are indicated by **bold face**.